Descartes' Dualism
Mechanism
Affect on Psych.

Descartes

CRITICAL AND INTERPRETIVE

ESSAYS

DESCARTES

Critical
and Interpretive
Essays

EDITED BY
Michael Hooker

THE JOHNS HOPKINS UNIVERSITY PRESS
BALTIMORE AND LONDON

The Johns Hopkins University Press, Baltimore, Maryland 21218
The Johns Hopkins Press Ltd., London

Library of Congress Catalog Card Number 78-8419
ISBN 0-8018-2111-8   ISBN 0-8018-2122-3 (pbk.)
Library of Congress Cataloging in Publication data will be found
on the last printed page of this book.

Contents

Preface   vii

List of Abbreviations   x

The Geometrical Presentation of Descartes's A Priori Proof
WILLIS DONEY   1

Descartes on the Consistency of Reason   HARRY G. FRANKFURT   26

Certainty and Cartesian Method   JEFFREY TLUMAK   40

A Discourse on Descartes's Method   JAAKKO HINTIKKA   74

Doubt, Reason, and Cartesian Therapy   MIKE MARLIES   89

Science and Certainty in Descartes   DANIEL GARBER   114

Limitations of the Mechanical Model in the Cartesian Conception
of the Organism   GENEVIÈVE RODIS-LEWIS   152

Descartes's Denial of Mind-Body Identity   MICHAEL HOOKER   171

Descartes's "Synthetic" Treatment of the Real Distinction between
Mind and Body   ALAN DONAGAN   186

Cartesian Dualism   MARGARET D. WILSON   197

Descartes's Correspondence with Elizabeth: Conceiving Both the
Union and Distinction of Mind and Body   RUTH MATTERN   212

Dualism in Descartes: The Logical Ground   FRED SOMMERS   223

Can I Know That I Am Not Dreaming?   DAVID BLUMENFELD AND
JEAN BEER BLUMENFELD   234

Descartes's Dream Argument   GEORGE NAKHNIKIAN   256

The Representational Character of Ideas and the Problem of the
External World   ARTHUR DANTO   287

Some Recent Work on Descartes: A Bibliography   WILLIS DONEY   299

List of Contributors   313

Index   315

Preface

JUST OVER a decade ago Willis Doney published *Descartes: A Collection of Critical Essays*, and in the ensuing years Doney's collection has become the standard secondary reference work for Descartes studies. Though Doney's anthology contains many of the most important essays on Descartes written prior to 1965, Descartes has been subjected to intense scholarly attention in the last decade, and it is time to make clear both the direction and the scope of that work. None of the works in this collection has previously been printed; each is in its own right a new contribution to Descartes scholarship; and taken together the chapters serve both as a secondary reference for instruction at the graduate and advanced undergraduate levels, and represent currently popular topics in Descartes studies.

A view of the last decade of scholarly attention to Descartes shows an interesting convergence. Ten years ago there was a fairly wide array of topics that excited the interest of Cartesian scholars, and chief among those were doubt, the *cogito,* arguments for the existence of God, the Cartesian circle, and dualism. Work on all but the last of those topics has tended to converge to the point where it is now difficult to talk about one without including a fairly substantial treatment of the others, and in every case what is said about the one will affect what one can say about the others. The convergence has been toward concentration on Descartes's overall method and purpose in the *Meditations,* and it can be seen in a number of the essays gathered here, especially those of Frankfurt, Tlumak, Hintikka, Marlies, and Garber. The most general and most perplexing issue that emerges from these discussions concerns the question whether Descartes was attempting to use reason to defend the use of reason, and if so whether that can be done and how. This issue should be of interest to present-day epistemologists and metaphysicians as well as to historians of seventeenth-century philosophy.

Another issue of considerable interest to contemporary philosophers concerns the nature of persons and the mind-body problem. In light of this interest it is not surprising that the last five years have seen a number of philosophers examining the origin of dualism in Descartes. Of special interest is the question how Descartes sought to establish and defend dualism, and that problem is discussed here by Hooker, Donagan, Wilson, Mattern, and Sommers.

Cartesian method and philosophy of mind are brought together in discussions of the dream argument by Nakhnikian and the Blumenfelds, and in Danto's discussion of Descartes's doctrine of ideas. The relationship between Descartes's philosophy and his science is growing in scholarly interest and concern, and that topic is discussed here by Garber and Rodis-Lewis. The ontological argument is perennially vexing both to historians of philosophy and to contemporary philosophers, and in his discussion of the argument Doney addresses matters of interest to both groups.

I want to acknowledge with gratitude the support of the authors represented here, and I am especially appreciative that Professor Doney has provided an updating of the very useful bibliography in his anthology.

Descartes

CRITICAL AND INTERPRETIVE
ESSAYS

LIST OF ABBREVIATIONS

AG   Descartes, René. *Philosophical Writings*. A selection, translated and edited by Elizabeth Anscombe and Peter Thomas Geach. London: Nelson, 1954.

AT   ————. *Oeuvres de Descartes*, edited by Charles Adam and Paul Tannery. 12 vols. Paris: Cerf, 1897–1910; reprinted, with new appendices, Paris: Vrin, 1964————.

CB   ————. *Descartes' Conversation with Burman*, translated and edited by John Cottingham. Oxford: Clarendon Press, 1976.

HR   ————. *The Philosophical Works of Descartes*, translated by Elizabeth S. Haldane and G. R. T. Ross. Cambridge: Cambridge University Press, 1911–12; reprinted, with corrections, 1931; reprinted New York: Dover, 1955.

K   ————. *Philosophical Letters*, translated and edited by Anthony Kenny. Oxford: Clarendon Press, 1970.

References to these writings of Descartes will appear in parentheses in the text.

The Geometrical Presentation of Descartes's A Priori Proof

WILLIS DONEY

IN THE GEOMETRICAL exposition of his philosophy at the end of the "Replies to Objections II," Descartes presents one of his proofs of God's existence, the proof which he says is "from the essence or nature" of God and which is sometimes called his "a priori" or "ontological" proof, in the following way. There is first an enunciation of the proposition to be proved, that is, Proposition I: "God's existence is known from a mere consideration of his nature." There follows what he later refers to as a "syllogism" ostensibly serving to demonstrate this proposition. The first or major premise of the syllogism is: "To say that something is contained in the nature or concept of some thing is the same as to say that it is true of that thing" (AT 7:120; HR 2:22).[1] The citation given for this premise comes from the definitions, postulates, and axioms stated immediately before: it is Definition IX; and the reference provides a reason for thinking that Descartes intended this premise to be taken to be, or to be true by virtue of, a definition. The second or minor premise is "Necessary existence is contained in the concept of God." The supporting reference here is Axiom X. It is suggested that this premise is unarguable not, in this case, because it is true by definition but because it is (or is in fact part of) an axiom.[2] The conclusion is then stated: "Therefore, it is true to say of God that necessary existence is in him, or that he exists." To this curious bit of reasoning, Descartes adds the following short and cryptic comment: "And this is the syllogism of which I made use above in replying to the sixth objection [namely, in his reply to the objection numbered "Sixth" in the "Second Set of Objections"]; and its conclusion can be self-evident to

1

those who are free of prejudices, as was said in the fifth postulate; but, because it is not easy to attain such perspicacity, we seek to establish it in other ways." In the Adam and Tannery edition, the enunciation of the proposition, the "syllogism" that serves as the demonstration, and the appended comment occupy just sixteen lines.

Descartes presents his famous proof here with breathtaking speed and in a form that is certainly stark and forbidding. We find a "conclusion" which, he says, can be obvious in its own right but which he derives here from two premises that are apparently supposed to be in need of no support and to be unarguable and indubitable. Some additional information is supplied in the supporting references, namely, Definition IX, Axiom X, and Postulate V. But the passage remains obscure and puzzling, and this is not just because of its brevity and the not very helpful form in which Descartes elected here to express himself. In this paper I have directed myself to this problem, and I distinguish three sources of puzzlement and grounds for critical concern regarding Descartes's statement of his proof here. (1) An initial impression of the passage is that the argument stated here bears very little if any resemblance to what Descartes says when he states his renowned proof in the *loci classici*, that is, in the Fourth Part of the *Discourse* and in Meditation V. In the first section of the paper, I have isolated and commented on four differences. In each case, it can be argued that the difference is merely apparent or superficial. The cumulative effect of these attempted explanations, however, is an uneasy feeling that some very real and important difference or differences are being explained away. (2) I then showed that Descartes is committed to the view that, appearances to the contrary, the "proof" here is identical with, or is closely related to, the proof stated in Meditation V. From what he says here, conjoined with certain statements made earlier in the "Replies to Objections," it clearly follows that this is indeed that very proof. Yet in the paragraphs prefacing the geometrical exposition, Descartes's statements about the relation of the arguments to be presented and the arguments in the body of the *Meditations* are equivocal; and it is not made clear whether what we are presented with here are supposed to be the same arguments (or, more accurately, some of the same arguments) in a stylistically different guise, or whether what is announced in these paragraphs is a different set of arguments, though of a kind that are in a certain way derived from, and in some way logically related to, the arguments set forth earlier. (3) Finally, I have argued that, on a plausible interpretation of one premise of the argument here, this argument simply cannot be identical with, or "basically" or "essentially" the same as, the proof in Meditation V. Moreover, there appears to be no satisfactory way in which the arguments in the two places can be supposed to be related. I can make these points, I believe, without saying what exactly the argument in Meditation V is. Elsewhere, I have pointed out that this is a task which is not so easily accomplished.[3] I leave the reader with a problem, namely, why, at this stage in his thinking, Descartes presents an argument that is so strikingly different from what he said before and, furthermore, that seems to be a mere appearance, or sham, of a proof of God's existence.

I

There are four features of the argument in the geometrical presentation which contribute to the impression that it can hardly be the same as, nor related in any obvious way to, the argument to which it is supposed to correspond in the *Discourse* and the *Meditations*.

(a) Perhaps the most salient difference can be attributed to the absence of any reference to God's perfection or to an idea of God, as a (or the) perfect or supremely perfect being. In the *Discourse*, part IV "l'idée que i'auois d'vn Estre parfait" is followed several lines farther on by "Dieu, qui est cet Estre parfait" (AT 6:36; HR 1:104). In Meditation V, the progression from a descriptive phrase to a name is reversed. *Deus* is used in the first sentence of the passage, and *ens summe perfectum* is introduced in the second sentence by way of the appositive expression *ejus ideam, nempe entis summe perfecti*, which can be read, "This idea [of God], that is, of a supremely perfect being" (AT 7:65; HR 1:180). In the geometrical exposition, the adjective *perfectus* and the phrase "ens summe perfectum" are not to be found; nor, as in some other places, is there any ostensible equivalent of, or surrogate for, such expressions.[4] In the second premise and in the conclusion, we find simply the term "Deus" (with a capital D), no equivalent or possible substitute given or apparently implied. We also do not find the proposition associated with the expression of such a conception of God, namely, "Existence is a perfection." This proposition is not in fact stated in the *Discourse* either, but it seems to be clearly implied there.[5] It is stated in Meditation V, though its entrance is rather curious. At first it is implied by certain parenthetical remarks (AT 7:66, 11. 12–14, and 67, 11. 8–10; HR 1:181, 11. 18–20, and 181, 1. 41–182, 11. 1–2); it is then stated in the formulation of a possible objection (AT 7:67, 11. 14–15; HR 1:182, 1. 6); and finally it is stated outright and sanctioned by Descartes in his answer to that objection (AT 7:67, 11. 26–27; HR 1:182, 11. 19–20). In the geometrical exposition, "necessary existence" is asserted in the second premise to be contained in the concept of God; and, in the conclusion, necessary existence is affirmed to be "in him." In neither place is it asserted or implied that existence (or "necessary existence") is a *perfection*. Because of these omissions, it seems impossible to identify the argument here with arguments that certain commentators have extracted from Meditation V. It is a very far cry indeed from what Jonathan Barnes takes to be "the ontological argument" in Descartes.[6] According to Barnes, that argument is: "(1) Necessarily, a God has all perfections; (2) Existence is a perfection; Therefore: (3) God exists." Nor can the argument be identified with an argument which is similar to the one Barnes finds in Meditation V, and which is expressly put in syllogistic form by Martial Gueroult: "*Majeure*: Dieu a, par définition, nécessairement toutes les perfections; *Mineure*: l'existence est une perfection; *Conclusion*: Dieu a nécessairement la perfection d'exister."[7] According to Gueroult, this argument is clearly implied (among other things) in the attempted proof of God's existence in Meditation V; and it is manifestly not the "syllogism" of the "Replies to Objections," as Gueroult is indeed concerned to point out. Nor is that argument identifiable with a rather different syllogism which, in a popular account of the proof in Meditation V, has been taken to be the "crux" of Descartes's ontological argument: "All supremely perfect beings exist . . . ; God is a supremely perfect being . . . ; ∴ God exists."[8] In the geometrical syllogism, Descartes neither expresses nor asserts a notion of God as a perfect or supremely perfect being.

(b) A second factor contributing to the markedly different appearance of this passage is the omission of any reference to an operation or state of mind by which someone pursuing this line of inquiry, i.e., an a priori proof of God's existence, can come to know of God's existence. In the corresponding passages in the *Discourse* and the *Meditations*, Descartes does refer to such a state; and, in these passages, it appears that mention of this way of coming to know of God's existence is an important step in, and an integral part of, his statement of the proof. In the *Discourse*, he refers to a rule stated earlier regarding what we "evidently conceive" (AT 6:36; HR 1:103). This is presumably the first of the rules of method in part II, the elaboration of which contains the resolution "to include nothing more in my judgments than *what was so clearly and so distinctly present to my mind* that I should have no occasion for placing it in doubt" (AT 6:18; HR 1:92; my emphasis). In Meditation V, the topic of God's existence is introduced by a rhetorical question: "But now, if just because I can draw an idea of some thing from my thought, it follows that *whatever I clearly and distinctly perceive* to pertain to that thing really does pertain to it, can there not also be derived from this [*nunquid inde haberi etiam potest*] an argument proving the existence of God?" (AT 7:65; HR 1:180; my emphasis.) In this question, Descartes entertains the principle that, if an idea of a certain thing can be drawn from thought, whatever can be clearly and distinctly perceived to pertain to that thing does pertain to it; and he clearly implies here that, in a sense that is not indeed made clear in the passage, this principle involving the notion of clear and distinct perception "underlies" the proof that is about to be stated and that that proof is in some way "derived" from it. In the geometrical exposition, there is no mention of either "evident conception" or "clear and distinct perception"; and, once again, what seems to be an important feature of the proof as it is stated earlier vanishes. That the reference to a certain operation or state of mind by which a person comes to know of God's existence has been taken to be an integral part of the proof in Meditation V is evident in Henri Gouhier's valiant, if not altogether successful, attempt to give a succinct, one-sentence summary of that proof: *"Dieu est l'Être parfait; par conséquent, toutes les perfections sont dans son essence; or l'existence est une perfection; on ne peut donc pas penser clairement et distinctement l'idée de Dieu sans voir l'existence nécessairement incluse dans son essence."*[9]

(c) In the *Discourse* and the *Meditations*, Descartes compares his proof with demonstrations in geometry; and, in Meditation V, he makes explicit a basis for the comparison and a reason which he has for drawing it:

When I imagine a triangle, although there may nowhere in the world be such a figure outside my thought, or ever have been, there is nevertheless in this figure a certain determinate nature, form, or essence, which is immutable and eternal, which I have not invented, and which in no wise depends on my mind, as appears from the fact that diverse properties of that triangle can be demonstrated, viz. that its three angles are equal to two right angles, that the greatest side is subtended by the greatest angle, and the like, which now, whether I wish it or do not wish it, I recognize very clearly as pertaining to it, although I never thought of the matter at all when I imagined a triangle for the first time, and which therefore cannot be said to have been invented by me. [HR 7:64; HR 1:180]

There is, he points out, a certain similarity between ideas of geometrical figures e.g., of the triangle, and the idea of God. In both there is a detectable sort of objectivity: both are recalcitrant to manipulation or change on our part, and both are deductively fertile in the sense that they can yield unimagined and unforeseen consequences. We are not, he notes, free to assert of a triangle whatever we will; and so, too, of God. Moreover, by consideration of the ideas of a triangle and of God, we can make discoveries and ascertain truths of which we were not aware when we first thought of a triangle or of God.

In Meditation V, he marks these characteristics of these ideas—characteristics distinguishing them from ideas of other sorts—in several ways. Contrasting ideas in geometry both with ideas that are "made by us" and with ideas that "come through the senses," he alludes to a distinction made in Meditation III (AT 7:37–38; HR 1:160) and implies that these ideas are neither factitious nor adventitious but innate. He does not, in fact, use the word *innatus* in Meditation V; instead, with regard to geometrical figures, he says we have ideas exhibiting "true and immutable natures." In similar fashion, regarding the idea of God, he makes the point farther on that it, too, is an "image of a true and immutable nature" (AT 7:68; HR 1:182). When he also says of the idea of God in this passage that it is "true," he invokes yet another distinction made earlier in Meditation III between truth and falsity in ideas (AT 7:43–44; HR 1:164–65). According to that doctrine, true ideas are ideas "of things" and false ideas are ideas "not of things" or perhaps "of non-things" (*ideae . . . non rerum*); and, by "true ideas," he does not mean, either in Meditation III or here, ideas of actually existing things. It appears, therefore, that he is making the same distinction as before only in different terms; that is, to say that an idea is true in this sense or is "of a thing" is the same as to say that it is of, or exhibits, a "true and immutable nature." Earlier in Meditation V, he indicates that he also thinks that ideas of geometrical figures are true in this sense, for he contends there that they are not "mere nothing" but "ideas of things" (AT 7:65; HR 1:180). Descartes's concern to make this point, which he goes about doing in various ways, indicates that he thinks it of importance to his proof in Meditation V. Yet in the geometrical exposition, this point is not expressly made. In the first premise, he uses the locution "nature or concept of a thing," but does not specify that the nature in question be true and immutable; indeed, the term *natura* disappears in the second premise, and we have there only the Thomistic and seemingly more "psychological" or "subjective" *conceptus*. This is, I believe, surprising; for, earlier, in the "Objections I," Descartes is presented with a powerful objection (Caterus's "existent-lion" objection), and, in his reply, he places very considerable weight on the distinction which he indicates he had made in Meditation V between ideas exhibiting true and immutable natures and what is made by us.[10] Moreover, in the predecessor and ostensible prototype of the geometrical syllogism in "Replies to Objections I," Descartes carefully qualifies "natura" in this way.[11] In the geometrical syllogism, it is true that he uses "res" in stating the first premise; but he does not indicate that he is using the term in a technical sense, such as is given it in Meditation III, and, if that is indeed his intention, it is certainly not made clear. The failure to call attention to a distinction emphasized earlier seems to me to be a point of some significance.

(d) There is an addition to be noted in the geometrical exposition as well as the three omissions mentioned thus far. In the second premise, it is "necessary existence" that is said to be contained in the concept of God. Earlier in the "Replies to Objections," Descartes distinguishes this kind of existence, i.e., "necessary existence," from "possible existence."[12] The view expressed there is that, though existence is contained in the idea of every (distinctly conceivable) thing, possible existence is contained in some ideas, while necessary existence is contained exclusively in the idea or concept of God. When Descartes asserts in the second premise that necessary existence is contained in the concept of God, it seems clear that he is invoking and making use of the distinction developed earlier in the first and also the second "Replies." The distinction has no ancestor or counterpart in the statements of the proof in the *Discourse* and Meditation V. In the *Discourse*, it is existence simpliciter that is said to be contained in the idea of a perfect being (AT 6:36; HR 1:104); and, in Meditation V, "actual existence" (*existat actu*) is asserted to pertain to a certain nature (AT 7:65; HR 1:180–81).[13] In both places, there is a distinction between two kinds or types of existence: in the *Discourse* between "being in the world" and "being supposed"; and, in the *Meditations*, between "existing outside my thought" or "outside me," on the one hand, and "existing in me," on the other.[14] Neither of these is the distinction that Descartes has in mind when he introduces the expressions "necessary existence" and "possible existence" in the first and second "Replies." It is an understatement to say that much has been made of the latter distinction, as in the discussions generated by Charles Hartshorne and Norman Malcolm.[15]

In reverse order, I shall briefly set forth reasons that can be adduced for minimizing or discounting these differences. (d) It can be argued that, by "necessary existence," Descartes means simply "actual existence at all times" and that, when he uses this expression in the geometrical syllogism, he is just stating in other words, or in a more definite and precise way, what he intended to say before. Evidence for such a stand can be found in the change made in the second edition of the *Meditations* where, in the sentence cited earlier, "actually exists" is replaced by "exists forever."[16] Also, the vagaries and apparent inconsistency of Descartes's qualifications and lack of qualification of "exists" and "existence" can be duly noted and taken to indicate that not too much importance should be attached to what appear to be mere changes in wording. (c) With regard to the distinction between ideas which are "true," or are "of things" or "of true and immutable natures," on the one hand, and "factitious" ideas, on the other, it can be pointed out that, in Postulate IV preceding the proof in the geometrical exposition, the idea of God is expressly compared with the idea of a triangle, and

it can be argued that the distinction which is made explicitly in Meditation V is implicit in this postulate and that what is at first part of
the statement of the proof is transposed here, perhaps because of the
"formal" style of presentation, to the apparatus of definitions, postulates, and axioms stated prior to the proofs themselves. It can also be
noted that, in the geometrical syllogism itself, Descartes does make use
of the term "res" in the expression "nature or concept of some thing."[17]
(b) The omission of reference to a certain act or state of mind by which
a person is supposed to come to know of God's existence, namely, "evident conception" or "clear and distinct perception," can also be
attributed to the mode of exposition adopted here. In the *Discourse*
and in the body of the *Meditations*, Descartes is writing autobiographi-
cally or quasi-autobiographically in the first person; and, presenting
his views in this way, he finds it relevant and important to say how he
personally came to know of God's existence a priori and, by implication, how any person can in similar fashion come to know of God's
existence. In the geometrical exposition, on the contrary, his clearly
stated intention is to provide a more formal and, as it were, deper-
sonalized statement of his arguments, employing—in terms which he
uses in the paragraphs prefacing this exposition—"synthesis" rather
than "analysis."[18] As a result of this change in style or method, the way
in which the proof was, or can be, discovered is no longer relevant or
important, and so reference to it is omitted in the statement of the
proof proper. The point might also be made that "clear and distinct
perception" is in fact mentioned in Postulate VI and that, perhaps
once again, the manner of presentation dictates that what was formerly
stated in the course of the proof should be excised from it and trans-
ferred to its appropriate place, that is, in a postulate in the intro-
ductory apparatus.[19]

(a) The first and most striking difference remains to be accounted
for. With regard to expressions like "supremely perfect being," it can
be argued that, since Descartes regards them as synonyms of the term
"God"—synonyms that can be freely substituted in any context—, an
immediate and obvious consequence of this view is that, for him, these
expressions cannot be irreplaceable in, or essential to, any argument;
and it can be suggested that their use in the loci classici is heuristic or
pedagogical. It can also be pointed out that, in the Definitions, Postulates, and Axioms, Descartes makes his conception of God as perfect or
supremely perfect explicit; and it can be argued that, in the geometrical
syllogism itself, there is indirect or implicit reference to such a conception of the deity. In Definition VIII, "God" is defined as "substance
which we understand *to be supremely perfect* and in which we conceive nothing at all involving some defect or limitation of *perfection*"

(AT 7:162; HR 2:53; my emphasis). Postulate V, which is invoked in the comment, begins: "I require my reader to dwell long and much in contemplation of the nature of the *supremely perfect being*" (AT 7:163; HR 2:55; my emphasis). And Axiom X, which is cited in support of the minor premise, makes explicit reference to the concept of a supremely perfect being:

X. In the idea or concept of every thing, existence is contained, since we can conceive of nothing except under the notion of existing, that is, possible or contingent existence is contained in the concept of a limited thing, but necessary and perfect [existence] in the *concept of a supremely perfect being*. [AT 7:166; HR 2:57; emphasis added][20]

Since both Axiom X and Postulate V are cited in the geometrical exposition and since both refer explicitly to the nature or concept of a supremely perfect being, a conclusion that can be drawn is that the notion of God as a supremely perfect being is in this way implied in the geometrical statement of the proof, and that the argument there cannot be fully or adequately stated unless this notion is included in some way or other in the statement of the proof. (It would, of course, be inconsistent to draw this conclusion while also attempting to make the first point against the importance of [a]). But when one considers (a) collectively with (b), (c), and (d), it seems that, although each attempt to account for an individual apparent difference has some credibility, a rather great deal of explanation is required to assimilate the argument in the geometrical exposition to the proof stated in Meditation V.

II

There is perfectly clear evidence that, according to Descartes, the argument in the geometrical exposition is related in a very intimate way to the proof in Meditation V. In fact, it can be shown to follow from what he says that the argument is not just closely related to, but is indeed the same as, the proof in Meditation V. This follows from what he says in three places in the first and second "Replies." (a) In the geometrical presentation, he says in the appended comment, "And this is the syllogism of which I made use above in replying to the sixth objection . . ." Here Descartes refers to his reply to objection no. 6 in the "Objections II." The objector there claims to find a fallacy in a syllogism which Descartes constructs in "Replies I";[21] and in "Replies II," Descartes charges his objector with misconstruing that syllogism. To correct the misunderstanding, he attempts to restate the syllogism. (b) "Replies II," no. 6, begins:

At the point where you criticize the conclusion of a syllogism constructed by me, you yourselves seem to make a blunder in the form of the argument. In order to derive the conclusion you desire, you should have worded the major premise thus: *that which we clearly understand to belong to the nature of any thing can truthfully be asserted to belong to its nature*; and consequently nothing but an unprofitable tautology will be contained in it. But my major premise was as follows—*that which we clearly understand to belong to the nature of any thing can truly be affirmed of that thing. . . .* My minor premise was *yet existence does belong to the nature of God.* Whence it is evident that the conclusion must be drawn as I drew it: *hence it can be truly affirmed of God that He exists*; but not as you wish: *hence we can truthfully affirm that existence belongs to the nature of God.* [AT 7:149–50; HR 2:45]

It is evident that, in this paragraph, Descartes is attempting to restate in a clear and exact way, the syllogism in "Replies I" in view of an objection allegedly based on a misunderstanding of that syllogism. From what he is attempting to do here, it clearly follows that this syllogism is supposed to be identical with the syllogism stated earlier in "Replies I"; and, by virtue of the transitivity of the relation of identity, it follows from what he says here in conjunction with what he says in the comment in the geometrical exposition that the argument there is identical with the syllogism in "Replies I."

When we turn to "Objections I," we find that Caterus likens Descartes's argument in Meditation V to an argument criticized by Aquinas, i.e., Aquinas's version of Anselm's argument in *Proslogion* II.[22] In reply, Descartes denies that the argument imputed to him is in fact the argument stated in Meditation V; and, to correct Caterus's supposed misinterpretation, he attempts to say what that argument, viz, the argument in Meditation V, is. (c) To this end, he constructs the syllogism referred to in "Replies II":

My argument was such—that which we clearly and distinctly understand to belong to the true and immutable nature of anything, its essence, or form, can be truly affirmed of that thing; but, after we have with sufficient accuracy investigated the nature of God, we clearly and distinctly understand that to exist belongs to his true and immutable nature; therefore, we can with truth affirm of God that he exists. [AT 7:115–16; HR 2:19][23]

Here Descartes asserts or clearly implies that the argument in this passage *is* his proof in Meditation V. By reasoning of the form that, if $D = C$ and $C = B$ and $B = A$, then $D = A$, it follows that the argument in the geometrical exposition is identical with the argument in Meditation V.

It is a well-known fact in the history of philosophy that what follows from what a person thinks or says and what that person in fact thinks or says are not necessarily or invariably the same, no matter how esteemed and renowned for logical acumen that person may be, and there is reason to believe that, with regard to the relation of the argument in the geometrical exposition and the argument in Meditation V, Descartes is guilty of an inconsistency of this sort. It clearly follows from what he says in the three places quoted from the first and second "Replies" that the argument stated earlier in Meditation V and the argument stated later in the geometrical presentation are one and the same, yet certain other remarks in the first and second "Replies" can be taken to mean that, although the argument stated later is related in a very special and intimate way to the argument stated earlier, it is not, or is not exactly, the same argument. These remarks are not, unfortunately, as clear as we might like, but they do show that Descartes is at least inclined to recognize and acknowledge a difference, though the nature of this difference is not clearly and unambiguously described, and he seems indecisive on the question whether the arguments are or are not, in fact, the same.

In "Replies I," after stating an argument for God's existence which is ostensibly an a priori argument and yet which seems to echo nothing at all in Meditation V, Descartes writes, "All this is manifest to one who considers the matter attentively, and it differs from what I have already written only in the method of explanation adopted, which I have intentionally altered in order to suit a diversity of intelligences" (AT 7:119–20; HR 2:22).[24] It would not be carping at this point to ask Descartes whether a difference *in modo explicationis* is supposed to be a genuine or significant difference in argumentation or not. Does he mean to say, that is, that the argument just offered is in reality the same as the argument in the fifth Meditation, though couched in different terms? Or does he mean to say, rather, that it is not exactly the same argument but one that is closely related to, or is similar in some way to, the argument in that Meditation? Given the lack of any clear criterion for sameness or difference in argumentation, the question is itself unclear; but, in the sentence quoted, Descartes seems to be trading on this obscurity. His remark does clearly show two things. First, he is himself aware of a difference between what he has just said and what is said in Meditation V; and, second, he is aware that an attentive reader may also be aware of a difference. Indeed, the remark appears to be gauged to forestall a question or allay a doubt as to whether he may not have embarked on an entirely new line of reasoning. It is perhaps worth noting, at this point, a not uncommon tendency in Descartes to gloss over changes and genuine differences of view by maintaining that something is "basically" ("fundamentally," "essentially") the same as what was said before. Descartes's remark appears to be evasive in precisely this way, whether deliberately so or not.

In the paragraphs immediately preceding the geometrical exposition (AT 7:155–59; HR 2:48–51), he makes a number of remarks about the arguments he is about to state and compares them with what is said in the body of the *Meditations*. Again, however, he does not make his thinking on this matter as clear and unequivocal as we might like. At first he draws a distinction in the "geometrical mode of writing" between "order" and "method" of proof (*ordinem . . . & rationem demonstrandi*—AT 7:155; HR 2:48). After a short discussion of "order," he turns to "method" and makes a further distinction with respect to method between "analysis" and "synthesis," giving brief accounts of both (AT 7:155–56; HR 2:48–49)—accounts, I might add, that can hardly have been intended to enlighten many of his readers. Following these bare characterizations of analysis and synthesis is the assertion that both can be used in metaphysics as well as in geometry. Concerning analysis, he observes, "I have used in my Meditations only analysis, which is the best and truest method of teaching" (AT 7:156; HR 2:49); and he announces that, in what follows, he will employ synthesis, issuing a prefatory warning to the reader that synthesis cannot be so readily deployed in the case of metaphysical issues as it is in matters geometrical. So far in the discussion, the overall impression we gain is that here, as in a similar passage in the *Regulae*, i.e., in Rule IV (AT 10:373–78; HR 1:11–13), Descartes is talking about distinguishable kinds or methods of reasoning and about sorts of arguments that are different, though related in a not clearly explained way. Moreover, from what he says in roughly the first half of these prefatory comments (AT 7, to 157; HR 2, to 49), it seems clearly to follow that the argument in the geometrical exposition supporting Proposition I, i.e. his "a priori" argument, is an argument in accordance with the method of synthesis and that, since the arguments in the body of the *Meditations* are supposed to follow the method of analysis, this "synthetic" argument is not the same as, though it is related in some close way to, the argument corresponding to it in Meditation V, which is "analytic."

Midway in the course of the discussion, however, there appears to be a shift from the topic of method of reasoning to that of style of writing. In the penultimate paragraph, for instance, the discussion appears not to be about *rationes demonstrandi* but about *modi scribendi*. Referring to the six Meditations themselves, he observes, "I rightly require singular attention on the part of my readers and have especially selected the mode of writing [*scribendi modum*] which I thought would best secure it and which, I am convinced, will bring my readers more profit than they would acquire if I had used the synthetic mode of writing [*ex modo scribendi synthetico*], one which would have made them appear to have learned more than they really had" (AT 7:158–59; HR 2:51). The term *stilus* replaces *modus* in the next paragraph. "Consequently," Descartes writes, "I append here something in the synthetic style (*synthetico stilo*) that may, I hope, be somewhat to my readers' profit." In these sentences, the difference between what is to come and what came before is represented as a difference in mode or style of writing; and that difference seems to consist, as he says earlier on, in "employing a long series of definitions, postulates, axioms, theorems and problems, so that, if one of the conclusions that follow is denied, it may at once be shown to be contained in what has gone before" (AT 7:156; HR 2:49). The view suggested here is that, although the arguments to be stated will be stated in a rather different way, they are for all that the same old arguments to be trotted out once again. And indeed, apart from some compression and formalization, the a posteriori arguments for God's existence in the geometrical exposition seem to be the same arguments that we find in Meditation III.[25] Further evidence that Descartes took the difference to be stylistic is a sentence earlier on in which he is expressly discussing philosophical style. Pointing out the difficulty of apprehending "first notions" in metaphysics, he says, "This is why my writing took the form of Meditations rather than that of Philosophical Disputations or the theorems and problems of a geometer" (AT 7:117; HR 2:50). Contrasting here three possible forms that his writing might have taken, he tells us why one of them—presumably, what he elsewhere calls "analysis"—is most suited to the end he had in mind. That Descartes became dissatisfied with his confusing and confused discussion of the use of analysis and synthesis in metaphysics is indicated by the fact that the latter part of the discussion is omitted in the French translation, which ends rather abruptly with this addition: "Mais neantmoins, pour témoigner combien ie défere à vostre conseil, ie tacheray icy d'imiter la synthese des Geometres, & y feray vn abregé des principales raisons dont i'ay vsé pour démontrer l'existence de Dieu, & la distinction qui est entre l'esprit et le corps humain: ce qui ne seruira peutestre pas peu pour soulager l'attention des Lectures" (AT 9:123). How nice it would be if we could ask Descartes just what he means here by "vn abregé"!

In the not particularly illuminating literature on Descartes's distinction between analysis and synthesis, the shift which I detect in this section of "Replies II" from a discussion of method to a discussion of style has not, so far as I know, been remarked. In the statements about analysis and synthesis in mathematics earlier in the discussion, there is no such ambivalence, nor is there an equation of synthesis with such an apparatus as in Euclid's *Geometry*.[26] The view expressed there seems to be as Wolfson puts it: "Whichever kind of demonstration of the geometrical method is used, the synthetic or analytic, there is no indication in anything Descartes says that it has to be written in the form which Euclid employs in his *Elements*."[27] The same is unhappily not the case when we scrutinize his remarks about analysis and synthesis in philosophy. These leave us with two possibilities: the "synthetic" arguments are indeed in reality the same as their "analytic" predecessors; or they are not the same but closely related to the arguments in the body of the *Meditations*, i.e., related as "synthetic" arguments are to their "analytic" counterparts, whatever that may be taken to mean.[28] On either of the two possibilities, there is a special problem in the case of Descartes's ontological argument. As I pointed out in the first section, the statement of the proof in the geometrical exposition seems to differ so markedly from the statement of the proof in Meditation V that it is difficult to see how they might be thought to be, if not indeed the same, even similar or closely related in some way.

III

In this section of the paper, I shall raise a problem about the interpretation of the first premise of the geometrical syllogism and attempt to establish two points. (a) Contrary to the view to which Descartes is committed, it can be shown that, on a plausible reading of this premise, the argument of which it is a premise cannot possibly be the same as the proof intended in Meditation V. Moreover, (b) it appears that no satisfactory account can be given of the way in which the arguments in the two places are supposed to be related.

(a) The first premise contains the locution "Idem est dicere . . . ac dicere," and there are various possible ways of understanding this locution. The premise is, in full: "Idem est dicere aliquid in rei alicujus natura sive conceptu contineri, ac dicere idipsum de ea re esse verum." To allow for the various possibilities of interpretation, it can be translated, as in fact it was translated: "To say that something is contained in the nature or concept of some thing is the same as to say that it is true of that thing." Three interpretations can be distinguished. (1) Descartes can be taken to mean that to say that something is contained in the nature or concept of a thing and to say that this is true of that thing are to say precisely the same thing (i.e., "make the same assertion," "express the same proposition"), though of course different words appear in the sentences which are used to say this. On this interpretation, "a is contained in the nature or concept of r" and "a is true of r" are synonymous. (2) He can be taken to mean that to say that a is contained in the nature or concept of r is "logically equivalent" to saying that *a* is true of *r*. In another terminology, "*a* is contained in the nature or concept of *r*" and "*a* is true of *r*" are not synonymous; rather, they are, or are expressions of, two propositions which are "logically equivalent." Finally, (3) when Descartes uses the locution "To say that so-and-so is the same as to say that such-and-such," he can be taken to mean something which I believe we, too, when we are not speaking as philosophers, sometimes mean when we speak in this way; namely, that, for all practical purposes or so far as we are concerned, saying that so-and-so comes down to ("amounts to the same as," "is tantamount to") saying that such-and-such, when this is taken to commit us only to the conditional proposition that, *if* so-and-so, *then* such-and-such. According to this interpretation of the first premise, what Descartes is in fact asserting, whatever it is that he may seem to be asserting or to be implying, is that, if *a* is contained in the nature or concept of *r*, then *a* is true of *r*. Alternatively, his actual assertion on this interpretation can be put in the form of a kind of *a*-proposition: "Whatever is contained in the nature or concept of some thing is true of that thing."[29]

For our purposes, the important difference is between (1) and (2), on the one hand, and (3), on the other. To the best of my knowledge, Descartes—for better or for worse—nowhere clearly distinguishes the use of two synonymous sentences to say the same thing, or express the same proposition, and the use of two sentences to express distinct but logically equivalent propositions. Consequently, both of these possibilities can be included or conflated in what I have called "a plausible reading of the first premise." I will call it henceforth the first interpretation. This can be contrasted with (3), i.e., the reading of the premise as a hypothetical proposition or, alternatively, as a kind of *a*-proposition —a reading, which I shall now refer to as the second interpretation. The first interpretation is, I believe, prima facie plausible; and, if we look more closely at the texts, it appears to be at least as plausible as the second interpretation. It seems, for instance, to fit the French translation, which is: "Dire que quelque attribut est contenu dans la nature ou dans le concept d'vne chose, c'est le mesme que de dire que cét attribut est vay de cette chose, & qu'on peut assurer qu'il est en elle" (AT 9:129). The translation at this point is expanded from the Latin in accordance with Definition IX, viz., the support cited for the first premise: "Cum quid dicimus in alicujus rei natura, sive conceptu, contineri, idem est ac si diceremus id de ea re verum esse, sive de ipsa posse affirmari" (AT 7:162; HR 2:53). The statement of Definition IX, in French as well as in the Latin, is compatible with the first interpretation.[30] Still, the form of expression *Cum . . . dicimus . . . , idem est ac si diceremus . . .* (and its equivalent in the French translation) can be taken to suggest and support the second interpretation. On textual grounds, however, I believe we are moved here in two directions. On the one side, Definition IX is after all stated as a definition; and it is possible to regard it as a kind of contextual definition explaining the locution "being contained in the nature or concept of some thing."[31] Accordingly, "a is contained in the nature or concept of r" is to be taken to mean the same as (or perhaps to be logically equivalent to) either "a is true of r" or "a can be affirmed of r." On the other side, it can be pointed out that, though Descartes undoubtedly calls this a definition, he is none too rigorous in other respects in making use of the geometrical apparatus and its associated nomenclature. Also, he calls the argument of which this is a premise a "syllogism," and this can be taken to indicate that the first premise is in reality intended to be a kind of a proposition doing duty in a "subsumptive" syllogism of sorts.[32] This suggestion seems to be corroborated by the ways in which Descartes states the first premises in the ancestors and ostensible prototypes of this argument in the first and second "Replies." In "Replies I," the first premise is: "Quod clare & distincte intelligimus pertinere ad alicujus rei veram & immutabilem naturam, sive essentiam, sive formam, id potest de ea re cum veritate affirmari" (AT 7:115; HR 2:19). The corresponding premise in "Replies II" is: "Quod clare intelligimus pertinere ad alicujus rei naturam, id potest de ea re cum veritate affirmari" (AT 7:150; HR 2:45).[33] In both places, the first premise seems to be a kind of a-proposition. But this is by no means conclusive evidence for treating the first premise of the geometrical syllogism in similar fashion: for, in view of certain other changes made in the first and second "Replies," it is not safe to assume that what comes later, i.e. what comes after he deals with some rather powerful criticism, is just the same as what comes before.[34] Finally, in support of the second interpretation, there are two nontextual objections to the first interpretation which are rather obvious and can seem to be strong and indeed decisive. Before treating these objections, however, I believe it can be concluded that, on textual grounds alone, the first interpretation is plausible and seems to be as plausible as its rival. I also want to point out some perplexing consequences that can be derived from this reading.

If we take the first premise in the way I have suggested, it can be shown to follow that the argument of which it is a premise is "nondemonstrative" in a certain sense of that term that will be indicated. It can also be established that, granted the assumption that Meditation V contains an argument for God's existence that is not nondemonstrative in the sense indicated, the geometrical syllogism cannot be identical with that argument. The introduction of the term "nondemonstrative" perhaps needs some justification as well as explanation. In the assessment of arguments, it is, I believe, evident that we need some term or terms in addition to such commonly used terms as "valid" and "invalid," "sound" and "unsound"; for an argument which is, for instance, rejected as *petitio principii* can very well be a valid and a sound argument in the senses of these terms commonly accepted among philosophers. Again, as a proof of the proposition that Nixon was president of the United States, we should certainly want to condemn or reject or fault in some way the argument—"Nixon was president of the United States; therefore, Nixon was president of the United States"—, though the argument is valid and sound in the commonly accepted logical and philosophical senses of these terms.[35] Some term or terms of opprobrium, such as "question-begging," *petitio,* or "nondemonstrative," are required if we are to say some of the things about arguments that we want to say. It is a notorious fact that accounts of what terms like these mean, for instance, in discussions of "informal fallacies," are not very clear or helpful. I shall not, therefore, attempt to say what is, or is commonly, meant by the term I have selected, namely, "nondemonstrative"; but rather I shall stipulate what I shall mean by it here. In my sense of the term, an argument is nondemonstrative if, and only if, a premise of the argument is the same as, or is the logical equivalent of, the conclusion. A number of questions can be raised about this admittedly not very precise and exact definition. What, for instance, is to count as *a* premise of an argument? What, also, is to count as "the *same as*"? Do we want to have on hand a pejorative term that could be used to fault all immediate inferences? Also, do we want a term such that invalid or unsound arguments can be said to be "demonstrative" or at least not "nondemonstrative"? This is not the place to pursue these questions, interesting though some of them may be, since, fortunately for me, the points I want to make about Descartes's geometrical proof can be made independently of tackling these questions. The only admission I require of the reader is that a nondemonstrative argument in my sense of the term cannot be identical with an argument that is not nondemonstrative.

On the suggested first interpretation of the first premise, it follows from this premise that the second premise and the conclusion of the argument are either the same proposition expressed in different ways or are logically equivalent propositions. The second premise was, "Necessary existence is contained in the concept of God"; and the conclusion, "Therefore, it is true to say of God that necessary existence is in him, or that he exists." Some niceties of wording aside, it clearly follows from the first premise interpreted in the way suggested that the second premise and the conclusion are the same proposition or logically equivalent propositions; and the first point I want to make can now be made, namely, that the geometrical syllogism on this interpretation is nondemonstrative in the sense explained. My second point is that, on the assumption that Meditation V contains an argument that is not nondemonstrative in this sense, the geometrical syllogism so interpreted cannot be identical with that argument, whatever that argument may be taken to be. It is, I want to add, reasonably clear, if not obvious, that Meditation V is *intended* to contain such an argument. In the "Synopsis" of the *Meditations*, for example, Descartes says, regarding Meditation V, that "the existence of God is demonstrated [*demonstratur*] by a new proof [*nova ... ratione*]" (AT 7:15; HR 1:142); and he clearly implies here that this Meditation (like the third) contains an argument that is not nondemonstrative in my sense of that term. Moreover, even if we were inclined to look with some favor on the thesis proposed by Gueroult that the proof in Meditation V is not intended to be "independent" or "self-sufficient," we could nonetheless consistently maintain, as Gueroult does, that Meditation V does contain an argument for God's existence that is not nondemonstrative in my sense of that term.[36] Whether in fact it does is a question I shall not attempt to answer here; for that question presupposes an answer to a question which, as I noted earlier, is most difficult, namely, what precisely the argument in Meditation V is.[37]

Against the suggested interpretation of the first premise, the first of the two very tempting nontextual objections to which I alluded consists in an attempt, as it were, to turn the tables on what I have just said by arguing that, if this interpretation yields these consequences, it is apparent by reductio ad absurdum that it cannot be the correct interpretation. In reply to this objection, the two consequences distinguished earlier need to be considered separately, and their ostensible unlikelihood or absurdity examined. With regard to the consequence that the argument in the geometrical presentation cannot be identical with the intended proof in Meditation V, this conclusion does not seem to me to be absurd or even unlikely. There is, as I mentioned earlier, an abundance of evidence that, in the first and second "Replies," Descartes reasons in a way that has no parallel or counterpart in Meditation V; and so it is not unlikely that, when at the end of "Replies II" he attempts to state his proof *more geometrico*, the argument should not be the same as the line of reasoning in Meditation V. As for the nondemonstrative character of the argument on this interpretation, this would be a strong objection if it were clear that, in this passage, Descartes intends and is attempting to state an argument which is not nondemonstrative in my sense. For two reasons, this is not clear. It is not clear because of the lack of clarity, discussed earlier, that surrounds his discussion of analysis and synthesis in metaphysics. If we take him to mean a distinction of two methods of argumentation, it may be, for all we are told about what "synthesis" in metaphysics comprises, that some formal "synthetic" arguments are by the nature of the case nondemonstrative. And, for all we know, this nondemonstrative argument may be the "synthetic" analog of an "analytic" argument or arguments in Meditation V or earlier in the first and second "Replies." The more important reason for saying that he does not clearly intend to state in this passage an argument which is not nondemonstrative is independent evidence that, at this stage in his thinking, he was inclined to regard his famous "proof" as consisting in an intuition rather than in a deduction or demonstration.[38] Perhaps the strongest evidence is Postulate V, in which Descartes gives as analogs of "God exists," not demonstrable mathematical propositions like "The sum of the angles of a triangle equals two right angles," but propositions that seem "simpler," in some sense, and self-evident:

Fifthly, I require my readers to dwell long and much in contemplation of the nature of a supremely perfect being. Among other things, they must reflect that while possible existence indeed attaches to the ideas of all natures, in the case of the idea of God, that existence is not possible only but wholly necessary. For from this alone and without any train of reasoning [absque ullo discursu] they will learn that God exists, *and it will be not less self-evident to them than the fact that the number two is even and the number three odd, and similar truths.* For there are certain truths evident to some people, without proof, that can be made intelligible to others only by a train of reasoning [*non nisi per discursum*]. [AT 7:163–64; HR 2:55; emphasis added][39]

In the French translation, *non nisi per discursum* becomes *que par vn long discours & raisonnement* (AT 9:127); and this suggests that those who come to know of God's existence by an argument come to know of it, not by an a priori argument, but by a "long train of reasoning" as in the posteriori proof or proofs in Meditation III. The comment appended to the geometrical syllogism is ambiguous: it is not made clear there whether those who fail to find "God exists" self-evident can come to know it only by the reasoning that follows, i.e., the a posteriori proofs, or by the reasoning that precedes as well, i.e., the geometrical syllogism.[40]

The second and perhaps more immediate and compelling objection is that, on this reading of the first premise, a view is attributed to Descartes which is so exceedingly odd that it is, if not utterly impossible, at least most unlikely that he should have held it. It can be pointed out that, if by an "analytic proposition" is meant, roughly, a proposition in which the predicate is contained in the concept of the subject, it seems to be asserted in, or to follow from, the first premise interpreted in this way not simply that all analytic propositions are true but also that all true propositions are analytic; and it can be objected that the latter view, i.e., that all true propositions are analytic, is, pace Leibniz, so bizarre or perverse that it would certainly not have been acceptable to Descartes. In conjunction with this objection, it can also be said (if anything more need be said) that Descartes does distinguish "contingent" propositions, such as "The dog is running," and "eternal truths"; and he describes the former in such a way, i.e., as having factual content, as to indicate that he by no means regards them as "analytic."[41] In reply to this objection, several points need to be made. First, as the premise is stated, no use is made of a term like "proposition" or "true proposition" or "truth." Descartes speaks of what is "true of a thing" (*de ea re . . . verum*) and, in Definition IX, of what "can be affirmed of it" (*de ipsa posse affirmari*). Secondly, as was noted earlier, he sometimes uses the term "res" in a technical sense: only those nonfactitious things having "true and immutable natures," such as "the triangle" or *res extensa* or God, are genuine "res." Thirdly, it is not clear whether Descartes is using the term "res" here in this technical sense. The use of "conceptus" and the lack of qualification of "natura" is some evidence that he is not. But, fourthly, if it is not clear that he is not using "res" in a technical sense, it is not clear that the class of what is "true of a thing" is intended to be coextensive with the class of true propositions, and it is not clear that Descartes is asserting that all true propositions (as opposed to those about genuine "res") are analytic. Finally, it is not implausible or perverse to assert that all true propositions about "res" in Descartes's technical sense, e.g., about "the triangle," are necessary or analytic truths such that the predicate is contained in the concept of the subject. Therefore, this objection, which appears at first to be overwhelming, is not so forceful as it might at first seem. By showing that the second interpretation is not the only sensible or viable interpretation, I hope to have shown at least that the first interpretation is not implausible and indeed that it is plausible. I also want to disclaim in the same breath any attempt to say that, in this passage, Descartes is *clear* about what he intends to say. On the contrary, I think he is not.

(b) In "Replies I," Descartes, observing that the minor premise of the syllogism stated there is apt to cause difficulty, argues in its support;[42] and his procedure there suggests a way in which the proof in Meditation V (as well as the ensuing argument in "Replies I") might be thought to be related to the geometrical syllogism.[43] The relation suggested is that of a subsidiary argument used to prove the truth of the minor premise (viz., that necessary existence is contained in the concept of God) to the main argument, i.e. the geometrical syllogism itself, of which this is a premise. If the first interpretation is given to the major premise and the argument is deemed nondemonstrative in the sense I indicated, this suggestion appears to be nonsense; for, given that the minor premise and the conclusion are the same proposition or logically equivalent propositions, whatever would prove the minor premise would eo ipso prove the conclusion, and vice versa, and it is difficult to see how ostensibly a subsidiary argument could in such a case be a subsidiary argument and not an independent, full-fledged proof of God's existence.[44] In the first and second "Replies," however, suggestions are made as to how the major premises in the respective syllogisms stated in these places are to be interpreted; and, if we give the second interpretation to the major premise of the geometrical syllogism, the suggestions in the first and second "Replies"—suggestions which are strikingly different—can be used to provide variants of that interpretation.

In Replies I, Descartes maintains that "the major premise cannot be denied because it was previously conceded that *whatever we clearly and distinctly perceive is true*" (AT 7:116; HR 2:19); and he suggests that the function of the major premise is to license an inference from what is clearly and distinctly perceived to what is true and that the inference involved in the syllogism is from a clear and distinct perception with respect to God to a truth about God, namely, that he exists. The suggestion in "Replies II" is quite different (AT 7:149–50; HR 2:45). There, to correct an alleged misapprehension, he insists that his first premise is not, "That which we clearly understand to belong to the nature of any thing can truthfully be asserted to belong to its nature"— which he says is a "useless tautology"—but rather, "That which we clearly understand to belong to the nature of any thing can be truly affirmed of that thing." He implies that the latter proposition, i.e. his own first premise, is not a "useless tautology" and that its function, or part of its function, is to license an inference from the nature of a thing to the thing in question itself. The suggestion here is that the inference involved in the syllogism in "Replies II," or one aspect of it, is a nontrivial inference from a perception of the *nature* of God to a truth about God himself. Applying this suggestion to the geometrical syllogism, we get a first premise licensing an inference from the nature or concept of a thing to the thing itself; and, on the suggested interpretation, the inference in particular is a nontrivial inference from the nature or concept of God to God himself.

Neither of these suggestions provides a satisfactory interpretation of Descartes's intention in this passage, however. We can reject the first suggestion, namely, that the inference intended is from what is clearly and distinctly perceived to what is true, on the ground that, in the geometrical syllogism, there is no mention of clear and distinct perception nor of any comparable act or state of mind. The second suggestion is more plausible; but it, too, does not provide a satisfactory interpretation of the passage. If Descartes had clearly intended his syllogism to be understood in this way, i.e. as having a nontautological first premise and as involving a nontrivial inference from the nature or concept of God to God himself, it is unlikely that he would have worded the first premise as he does and that he would have assigned it the status of being, or being true by virtue of, a definition. As the first premise is worded, it seems to comprise the denial of a step, or of a step of any significance, from the second premise to the conclusion. Along the lines suggested in the first and second "Replies," it seems, therefore, that no satisfactory account can be given of how the proof in Meditation V is supposed to be related to the puzzling argument that we find at the end of "Replies II."

NOTES

Some ideas in this paper were developed while I was at the Institute for Advanced Study in Princeton. I am very grateful to the Institute for the year that I spent there. Part of my support was provided by the National Endowment for the Humanities under Grant H5426. I also want to express my gratitude for this. An earlier version of the paper was read at a conference at Rockefeller University in June 1976. I received helpful comments and criticisms from Harry Frankfurt, Michael Hooker, Ruth Mattern, Robert Sleigh, and Margaret Wilson.

1. I have altered the HR translation in places.

2. About the axioms in his geometrical exposition, Descartes warns us, however: "Quanquam sane pleraque ex iis potuissent melius explicari, & instar Theorematum potius quam Axiomatum proponi debuissent, si accuratior esse voluissem" (AT 7: 164; HR 2:55).

3. In a paper "Descartes's A Priori Proof in the Fifth Meditation," versions of which I have read but which I have not published.

4. For instance, *ens primum & summum* in the course of the statement of the proof in Meditation V (AT 7:67; HR 1:182).

5. Perhaps "clearly implied" is an overstatement. It seems to me to be implied by the short statement of the proof (AT 6:36; HR 1:104), taken in conjunction with the discussion of divine perfections in the paragraph that precedes.

6. Jonathan Barnes, *The Ontological Argument* (London: Macmillan, 1972), p. 16.

7. Martial Gueroult, *Descartes selon l'ordre des raisons* (Paris: Aubier, 1953), 1: 349–50.

8. George Nakhnikian, *An Introduction to Philosophy* (New York: Knopf, 1967), pp. 219–20.

9. Henri Gouhier, *La Pensée métaphysique de Descartes* (Paris: Vrin, 1962), p. 143. My emphasis.

10. Caterus's objection is at AT 7:99–100; HR 2:7–8; Descartes's reply begins when he attempts to defend the minor premise of his syllogistically formulated proof at AT 7:116, 1.8; HR 2:19–21.

11. "Quod clare & distincte intelligimus pertinere ad alicujus rei veram & immutabilem naturam, sive essentiam, sive formam, id potest de ea re cum veritate affirmari; sed postquam satis accurate investigavimus quid sit Deus, clare & distincte intelligimus ad ejus veram & immutabilem naturam pertinere ut existat." (AT 7:115–16; HR 2:19).

12. The first attempt to make this distinction is the passage in the "Replies I" in which Descartes attempts to defend the minor premise of his syllogistically formulated proof: "est distinguendum inter existentiam possibilem & necessariam, notandumque in eorum quidem omnium, quae clare & distincte intelliguntur, conceptu sive idea existentiam possibilem contineri, sed nullibi necessariam, nisi in sola idea Dei" (AT 7:116; HR 2:20). In "Replies I," Descartes commits himself to the view that possible existence as well as necessary existence is contained in the idea of God. It is not at all clear that this is the view adopted in "Replies II." In the geometrical exposition, cf. Postulate V (AT 7:163; HR 2:55) and Axiom X (AT 7:166; HR 2: 57). The view expressed in Axiom X seems to be that necessary existence but *not* possible existence is contained in the idea of God. HR misses the ambiguity with regard to this point in Postulate V.

13. In the second edition of the *Meditations*, "ut existat actu" becomes "ut semper existat"; and, in the French translation, the two expressions are conflated in "vne actuelle & externelle existence" (AT 9:52).

14. Just before his very short statement of the proof in the *Discourse*, he observes, regarding "a triangle": "ie voyois bien que, supposant vn triangle, il falloit que ses trois angles fussent esgaux a deux droits; mais ie ne voyois rien pour cela qui m'assurast qu'il y eust au monde aucun triangle" (AT 6:36; HR 1:103–4). In Meditation V, he says, again about a triangle: "cum, exempli causa, triangulum imaginor, etsi fortasse talis figura nullibi gentium extra cogitationem meam existat"; and, earlier in the discussion, he says: "invenio apud me innumeras ideas quarundam rerum, quae, etiam si extra me fortasse nullibi existant" (AT 7:64; HR 1:180–81).

15. Cf. C. Hartshorne, *The Logic of Perfection* (La Salle, Ill.: Open Court, 1962), p. 48, and N. Malcolm, "Anselm's Ontological Arguments," *The Philosophical Review* 69 (1960):50–51.

16. See n. 13. In "Replies I," immediately after distinguishing "possible existence" and "necessary existence," Descartes gives an account of the two which can be taken as evidence that, by "necessary existence," he means simply "actual existence at all times": "Qui enim ad hanc diversitatem quae est inter ideam Dei & reliquas omnes diligenter attendent, non dubito quin sint percepturi, etiamsi caeteras quidem res nunquam intelligamus nisi tanquam existentes, non tamen inde sequi illas existere, sed tantummodo posse existere, quia non intelligimus necesse esse ut actualis existentia cum aliis ipsarum proprietatibus conjuncta sit; ex hoc autem quod intelligamus existentiam actualem necessario & semper cum reliquis Dei attributis esse conjunctam, sequi omnio Deum existere" (AT 7:116–17; HR 2:20).

17. The first premise is: "Idem est dicere aliquid in rei alicujus naturae sive conceptu contineri, ac dicere idipsum de ea re esse verum" (AT 7:166; HR 2:57). *Chose* is used for "res" in the French translation (AT 9:129). In the passage in Meditation III in which the truth and falsehood of ideas are distinguished, the words in the translation are *quelques choses réelles* and *quelque chose* (AT 9:34–35).

18. This distinction, which is discussed in the second section of the paper is in AT 7:155–59; HR 2:48–51.

19. Postulate VI begins, "Ut, perpendendo exempla omnia clarae & distinctae perceptionis, itemque obscurae & confusae" AT 7:164; HR 2:55). See also Postulate VII. A very great deal of Descartes's "procedure" in the body of the *Meditations* is assigned to, and located in, the Postulates.

20. It is worth noting that Descartes passes from "ens summe perfectum" in Axiom X to "Deus" in the second premise of the geometrical syllogism without invoking Definition VIII. This is an instance both of the lack of rigor in the geometrical presentation and of Descartes's tendency to treat the terms as synonyms which can be substituted ad libitum.

21. "Sexto, ubi respondes Theologo, videris aberrare in conclusione, quam ita proponis: 'Quod clare & distincte intelligimus pertinere ad alicujus rei veram & immutabilem naturam, &c., id de ea re cum veritate affirmari potest; sed (postquam satis accurate investigavimus quid sit Deus) clare & distincte intelligimus ad ejus naturam pertinere ut existat.' Oporteret concludere: 'ergo (postquam satis accurate

investigavimus quid sit Deus) cum veritate possumus affirmare ad naturam Dei pertinere ut existat'" (AT 7:127; HR 2:28).

22. Caterus suggests that the arguments are the same (AT 7:98–99; HR 2:6–7). It seems to me that he detects a not insignificant likeness between a part of what Descartes says in Meditation V and the argument criticized by Aquinas, though I do not mean to suggest that Descartes took this argument from Anselm or indeed from Aquinas.

23. The quotation begins, "Meum autem argumentum fuit tale"; and then Descartes states the syllogism. It can be objected that, at the beginning, Descartes maintains, not that his argument in Meditation V is "as follows," but that it is "of the following sort." I am unmoved by this objection. Having just rejected an argument as his in Meditation V, he clearly implies here, if he does not assert, that the argument that follows *is* his argument in Meditation V. A more plausible point that can be argued is that, in this passage, Descartes is trying to be evasive.

24. The new argument is an argument based on the attribute of omnipotence (AT 7:118, 1.29–119, 1.26; HR 2:21–22). The novelty of the argument is concealed in HR, where "enti summe potenti" is rendered "a being of the highest perfection."

25. More precisely, the first a posteriori argument in the geometrical exposition, viz. the "Demonstration" of Proposition II, seems to be a highly compressed version of the main argument for God's existence in Meditation III. The second a posteriori argument in the geometrical exposition, i.e. the "Demonstration" of Proposition III, is a less highly compressed version of a second a posteriori argument in Meditation III.

26. When Descartes first contrasts synthesis with analysis, his account appears to be in two parts, the second of which begins: "utiturque longa definitionum, petitionum, axiomatum, theoratum, & problematum serie" (AT 7:156; HR 2:49). In what comes before and what comes after, however, it is made clear that synthesis in mathematics does not invariably or necessarily involve the use of definitions, postulates, etc. Descartes adds here, "Hac sola Geometrae veteres in scriptis suis uti solebant" (AT 7:156; HR 2:49; my emphasis).

27. Harry A. Wolfson, *The Philosophy of Spinoza* (Cambridge: Harvard, 1948), p. 48. It does not seem to me that this is clearly Descartes's view with regard to "synthesis" in philosophy, however.

28. I know of no helpful account of Descartes's conceptions of analysis and synthesis in philosophy. This may very well be because his views on this subject were inchoate and confused.

29. That is, in a form similar to that of the first premises of the ancestors of the geometrical syllogism in the first and second "Replies."

30. "Quand nous disons que quelque attribut est contenu dans la nature ou dans le concept d'vne chose, c'est de mesme que si nous disions que cet attribut est vray de cette chose, & qu'on peut assurer qu'il est en elle" (AT 9:125).

31. To do so, we must not be swayed by the seemingly decisive nontextual reasons discussed farther on.

32. That is, in the form of "reasoning from generals to particulars."

33. Descartes adds in explanation: "Hoc est, si esse animal pertinet ad naturam hominis, potest affirmari hominem esse animal; si habere tres angulos aequales duobus rectis pertinet ad naturam trianguli, potest affirmari triangulum habere tres angulos aequales duobus rectis; si existere pertinet ad naturam Dei, potest affirmari Deum existere, &c."

34. See, for instance, the argument from the attribute of omnipotence referred to in n. 24.

35. It might be maintained that this "argument" is neither valid nor invalid, sound nor unsound, on the ground that it makes no sense or is a pseudo-argument.

36. The syllogism which Gueroult constructs and which is quoted on p. 4 is not nondemonstrative in my sense of that term.

37. There are, as I argue elsewhere, at least two strong candidates.

38. Cf. Henri Gouhier, *La Pensée metaphysique de Descartes*, p. 161, and Martial Gueroult, *Descartes selon l'ordre des raisons*, pp. 350–51.

39. The view which I take Descartes to express in Meditation V is that "God exists" can either be intuited or be deduced; whereas the view toward which he seems to be inclined in the geometrical presentation is that "God exists" can only be intuited and cannot be deduced, i.e. deduced from "the essence or nature" of God or "a priori."

40. "Atque hic est syllogismus, de quo jam supra ad objectionem sextam; ejusque conclusio per se nota esse potest iis qui a praejudiciis sunt liberi, ut dictum est postulato quinto; sed quia non facile est ad tantam perspicacitatem pervenire, aliis modis idem quaeremus (AT 7:167; HR 2:57). *Aliis modis* can be taken in two ways.

41. "Conversation with Burman," AT 7:167.

42. "Sola minor restat, in qua fateor esse difficultatem non parvam" (AT 7:116; HR 2:19). Descartes then distinguishes two sources of the difficulty and attempts to remove them.

43. The ensuing arguments in "Replies I" are presented as arguments in support of the minor premise.

44. An assumption that might be questioned here is that, if p and q are "logically equivalent," then any argument that is a proof of p is also a proof of q, and conversely. It is tempting to suppose that, if p is proved, then an additional argument is required to prove q; namely, (1) p iff q; (2) p; Therefore, (3) q. Though such an argument can be formulated—as I have just done—it would be misleading to call the argument (in the circumstances described) a "proof" of q.

Descartes on the
Consistency of Reason

HARRY G. FRANKFURT

IN ONE OF THE most central and familiar lines of argument of the *Meditations*, Descartes professes to perceive the following propositions clearly and distinctly: an omnipotent and benevolent deity exists; the existence of this deity entails that men cannot be subject to irretrievable deception, as they would be if they could ever have clear and distinct perceptions of what is false; whatever we perceive clearly and distinctly must, accordingly, be true. The apparent aim of the argument these propositions comprise is to establish that clear and distinct perception is unimpeachably reliable—that whatever we perceive clearly and distinctly is true.

How could Descartes have hoped to make any progress whatever in the direction of this goal, by means of an argument whose steps, as he himself acknowledges, are justified by nothing other than clear and distinct perception itself? The movement of his thought here seems egregiously circular. From an initial assumption that clear and distinct perceptions *are* reliable, which alone appears to enable him to regard each step of the argument as legitimate, Descartes proceeds to the final conclusion that it is justifiable to rely on such perceptions. It is no wonder that this piece of reasoning has puzzled and frustrated so many of his readers. It gives the strong impression of being utterly worthless, since the acceptability of its conclusion seems to be taken for granted throughout its construction.

Circular arguments are not formally fallacious. On the contrary, they are necessarily valid. Circularity in argument, after all, is essentially a matter of deriving a proposition from itself; and one is always entitled to do that. The troublesome question with respect to Descartes's argument is not whether it can be valid, but how it can have any point. Repeating at the end of a train of reasoning something which was assumed at its start is not a formal error in logic, but it appears to be quite a gross error in strategy. To say the least, it can hardly amount to a very productive demonstration of anything that needs to be proved.

Why does Descartes's argument arouse so much interest? No doubt part of the explanation is provided by considerations of charity, reinforced by the piety one tends to feel toward a great ancestor. The argument is at first glance a very bad one; yet Descartes is manifestly a very good philosopher. It is natural, and perhaps only decent, to wonder if the argument may not somehow turn out to be, if not altogether sound and fruitful, at least a little better than it looks.

Not that we ought to be incredulous at finding a flaw in the reasoning of one of the giants of our intellectual tradition. In fact this is very much to be expected. So far as I know, at any rate, there is not one really cogent and definitive argument of any consequence in the entire history of philosophy.[1] The best philosophers—that is, the most interesting and stimulating ones—have generally preferred to devote their energies to more important things than polishing away every trace of uncertainty or equivocation in the arguments they have contrived as vehicles for their insights. The contemporary mania in certain circles for absolute rigor and perfect clarity, regardless of any specific need, succeeds on the whole just in making philosophy a bore. Still, mistakes as blatant as the one Descartes appears to have made are not so common even among the greatest thinkers. The evidence of disorder in his thought understandably constitutes, for his interpreters, a provocative challenge.

This may not suffice to persuade those without a special interest in Descartes to take his argument seriously. Surely only a dedicated antiquarian could interest himself, they may feel, in reasoning which is concerned with such quaint concepts as "clear and distinct perception" and "divine benevolence." The former smacks too much of notions like "self-evidence" and "intuition," which are now regarded by sophisticates as thoroughly discredited. As for the latter, there are natural qualms not only as to whether the idea of God can be permitted to play an essential role in philosophy. It has always been a question, even while Descartes was alive, whether what he says about God gives an authentic account of his own convictions. Despite his explicit professions of Roman Catholicism, and substantial evidence of his piety, Descartes's theological views have always aroused the darkest suspicions.[2] He has been mistrusted on this score, in fact, by practically everyone. The Catholics accused him of being a Protestant, the Protestants thought he was an atheist, and the atheists have tended to speculate that he was a hypocrite. It is not only the viability and pertinence of his problematic argument, then, which are uncertain. Descartes's very sincerity in promulgating it is under a cloud.

Considering just what is at stake in Descartes's concern with clear and distinct perception will help to identify more fully the source of the fascination his argument evokes. In brief, an attempt to establish the infallibility of clear and distinct perception as a guide to truth amounts to a defense of the authority of human reason. This is because clear and distinct perception conveys, to whatever propositions we clearly and distinctly perceive, the most impeccable credentials reason can provide. Moreover, since there is no appeal from reason to any superior natural source of knowledge, we can possess no natural basis for correcting a belief in what we have clearly and distinctly perceived. We can do no better in the formation of our judgments, accordingly, than to rely upon such perceptions. They constitute the best testimony of our highest faculty. If we will not or cannot be satisfied by that, then we must give up hoping to satisfy ourselves at all. By the same token, any error into which we might be led by clear and distinct perception would be altogether ineradicable and beyond redemption by reason.

What is it, exactly, for a person to perceive something clearly and distinctly? It consists in his recognizing that the evidence he has for some proposition, or his basis in experience for accepting the proposition, is logically definitive and complete. He perceives clearly and distinctly that p when he sees that his evidence or basis for accepting p is conclusive, in the sense that it is consistent and that no body of evidence which would warrant rejecting or doubting p is logically compatible with the evidence or basis he already has. Given the evidence or basis for p that he already has, in other words, he need not fear that the addition to it of further evidence will require him to change his mind.

A person who attentively grasps the rigorous connection of the premises and the conclusion of a valid argument, for example, perceives clearly and distinctly that the conclusion must be true if the premises are true. He apprehends that there is no gap between the evidence affirmed by the premises and the conclusion for which the premises cite evidence, into which opposing considerations might enter. Sensory experience itself may provide, as reason may recognize, a similarly complete and conclusive basis for a belief. Someone who feels a pain may perceive clearly and distinctly that he feels a pain; that is, he may understand that his feeling provides him with a conclusive basis for accepting the proposition that he has that feeling.

Every experience, indeed, provides a conclusive basis for the acceptance of *some* proposition; for every experience, there is some proposition that fits it perfectly—a proposition that captures the experience without asserting more than it warrants, and thus without leaving anything uncertainly awaiting confirmation by further experience. It is not only necessary truths like those of logic and mathematics, then, which can be perceived clearly and distinctly. Logically contingent propositions may also be objects of clear and distinct perception.

Descartes is sometimes thought to have advocated a kind of lunatic apriorism, according to which a person might spin all of philosophy and all of science out of his own head without ever needing to turn to perceptual data. This was by no means Descartes's view. He does, to be sure, deny that sense perception is in itself an adequate source of certainty. We cannot attain certainty even about perceptual matters, he insists, if we rely exclusively upon the senses. But he does not go on to maintain that we do not need the senses at all. Although genuine knowledge can be acquired only with the use of reason, not all of it is to be acquired by the use of reason alone. Clear and distinct perception, which consists in recognizing that a proposition and the basis for accepting it are perfectly matched, requires logical analysis and rational insight. Our acquaintance with the basis for accepting the proposition in question may well have its origin, however, in sensory experience.

In arguing for the reliability of clear and distinct perception, Descartes is attempting to establish the reliability of reason itself—that is, of our perceptions of logical relationships. How does this task come to present itself as one which needs to be undertaken? Exactly what question about reason does Descartes think must be asked, and in what way does he believe he can reasonably go about trying to answer it? The mere formulation of questions like these reveals how natural it is that Descartes's argument should have, at the very least, an appearance of circularity. Anyone who sets out to defend reason faces what seems to be an unavoidable and disastrous dilemma. How is he to escape having his defense turn out to be either circular or gratuitous? On the one hand, he may try to develop rationally compelling arguments in behalf of reason. But in that case he will certainly be told—as Descartes has been told by innumerable critics—that his procedure begs the very question he has set out to answer. On the other hand, he may offer in support of reason considerations of some nonrational sort, whose effect is in one way or another independent of their demonstrative value. In that case he may not need to worry about being charged with circularity, but he will find that few philosophers are interested in listening to him. What he says will rightly be dismissed by everyone who is committed to rationality.

Despite this, however, it is difficult to believe that we must be altogether silent when a question is raised about the credentials of reason.
Surely there is *something* worthwhile to say concerning whether reason
merits our trust? There must be *something* reason can offer in its own
behalf, without being guilty of plain violations of the conditions of
substantive argument. Descartes's treatment of these matters is philosophically intriguing, because it purports to cope with a serious
question about the legitimacy of reason. One wonders just what question this can be, and what useful response to it could possibly be made.

Let us consider Anthony Kenny's proposal concerning what question
about reason Descartes thought it both necessary to ask and possible to
answer.[3] Kenny calls attention to the fact that it may be sensible for a
person to entertain a general doubt concerning his own beliefs, without
questioning any of those beliefs in particular. We have all discovered,
at one time or another, that opinions we have been holding are incorrect; and it is likely that some of our present opinions are also false. It
is reasonable to acknowledge this, Kenny suggests, even though doing
so involves a certain inconsistency—the inconsistency of believing p
and q and r (our current opinions) while at the same time believing
that either p is false or q is false or r is false. Now Kenny claims that
Descartes's doubt about reason is similar to this doubt—he calls it
"omega doubt"—which a person may have concerning his own beliefs.
Descartes does not, that is to say, mistrust any particular clear and distinct perception. What he questions is only the general proposition
that everything perceived clearly and distinctly is true. In Kenny's
judgment, this distinction illuminates the problem with which Descartes is contending, and makes it clear that the argument by which
Descartes purports to solve the problem is not circular.

Before proceeding to evaluate Kenny's interpretation, it is important
to understand what Descartes takes to be the relation between perceiving a proposition clearly and distinctly and assenting to it. Descartes
maintains that when our perception of a proposition is clear and distinct, we have no choice but to give the proposition our assent. He
insists not merely that we *should* not, but that we *cannot* doubt what
we are actually perceiving clearly and distinctly. It may well be possible for us to doubt the very same thing at another time, when we are
not having a clear and distinct perception of it. But while we are in the
midst of perceiving it clearly and distinctly, we simply cannot withhold
our assent. Doubt and belief, as Descartes conceives them, are functions
of the will; and the will is irresistibly constrained when the perceptions of reason are clear and distinct. When reason is fully satisfied, in
other words, assent follows necessarily.[4]

Kenny proposes to construe Descartes's procedure in the problematic argument as follows. Descartes perceives each of its premises clearly and distinctly, and hence he believes each of them to be true. These beliefs are entirely accounted for by the irresistibility of what is clearly and distinctly perceived. Descartes cannot help believing the premises of the argument, in virtue of his perceptions; and his believing the premises does not depend in any way upon his assuming the argument's conclusion that whatever is perceived clearly and distinctly is true. He can reach that conclusion, accordingly, by means of an argument in which its truth is not assumed. Thus, Kenny says,

it is . . . clear why there is no circle in Descartes's argument. The clear and distinct perceptions used in the proof of God's existence are perceptions of particular propositions. . . . The veracity of God is used to establish not any particular clear and distinct perception, but the general proposition that whatever I clearly and distinctly perceive is true.[5]

The point of this interpretation is that the acceptance of the premises of Descartes's argument does not require legitimation by knowledge that the argument's conclusion is true. Assent to the premises is assured by their being clearly and distinctly perceived. It requires no epistemological warrant at all, since clear and distinct perception carries assent with it in any case.

For my own part, I cannot see in what way this interpretation can help to resolve the problem of circularity. If Descartes is to establish the unimpeachable truth of his conclusion, as Kenny supposes he intends to do, he must provide premises for it whose truth is reliably guaranteed; and it must be possible for him, if he is to avoid begging the question, to provide this guarantee for the premises without relying upon the assumption that the conclusion is true. What Kenny's approach can explain, however, is only how Descartes might come, without assuming the truth of his argument's conclusion, to believe that each of its premises is true. The question of whether the premises are true—and hence, of whether they establish that the conclusion is true—will then remain, even though it cannot be raised while the premises are being clearly and distinctly perceived. The answer to this question will depend, moreover, upon whether what leads Descartes to believe the premises is a reliable guide to truth. But what leads Descartes to believe the premises of his argument is, of course, just that he perceives them clearly and distinctly. And whether the fact that he thus perceives them entails that they are true, plainly depends upon nothing else than whether the conclusion of the argument is true or false. How, then, does the argument as Kenny understands it avoid circularity?

It is Kenny's claim that Descartes never doubts the truth of particular clearly and distinctly perceived propositions. Now Descartes does believe that there are certain propositions which can never be doubted, because they cannot be considered at all without being perceived clearly and distinctly and hence without assent to them being constrained.[6] The very fact that he especially considers propositions of this kind, however, makes it clear that he thinks *some* propositions are of a different kind. A person can doubt the latter even after he has perceived them clearly and distinctly, whenever the evidence that supports the clear and distinct perception of them is absent from his mind. Then he may remember perceiving p clearly and distinctly, and at the same time wonder whether p is true. Doubts can be raised, accordingly, about the value of particular clear and distinct perceptions; though not, to be sure, while the perceptions are actually occurring.

Such doubts do not concern whether there is as much evidence for the proposition in question as reason demands. To remember that the proposition was once perceived clearly and distinctly is precisely to remember that there is logically conclusive evidence for it. What the doubt concerns is whether logically conclusive evidence is compatible with the falsity of the proposition supported by that evidence. It is not a doubt concerning whether the reasons for believing something are as solid as they might be. It concerns whether reasons of even the most solid kind possible are good enough. In other words, it is a doubt about reason itself. Descartes's question is this: what basis is there for accepting what we clearly and distinctly perceive *besides* the irresistible conviction which having a clear and distinct perception arouses? I shall explain this question further later on.

Descartes cannot help believing the premises of his argument while he clearly and distinctly perceives them. But when he is not in the midst of clear and distinct perception of those premises, and therefore not irresistibly constrained to believe them, he may well wonder whether they are true or whether his having once perceived them clearly and distinctly is in fact compatible with their falsity. When he looks back over his argument, he can say no more than that certain premises, of whose truth he was at one time entirely convinced, lead to the conclusion that anything with the sort of warrant those premises had at that time is true. But whether the premises are actually true, and whether the conclusion to which they lead is consequently true, are still quite open questions. Open, that is, unless we assume that the sort of warrant the premises had—namely, that of being clearly and distinctly perceived—means that they must be true. If we assume this, however, we beg the question.

In my opinion, it is hopeless to approach Descartes's argument with the presumption that its point is to provide a demonstration that its conclusion is true. This presumption has, I concede, a very high initial plausibility. But if we start with it, we are bound to discover both that the argument is patently circular and that its circularity is fatal to its purpose. Now what other way of construing the argument is there? If Descartes's aim is not the normal one of demonstrating that his conclusion is true, what can his aim be? I suggest that his primary aim is to display the connection between the premises of his argument and its conclusion. The argument is not designed to demonstrate that its conclusion is true, in other words, but to show that a correct exercise of reason leads us to it.

The argument terminates in the clear and distinct perception that whatever is clearly and distinctly perceived is true; and Descartes reaches this perception by means of other clear and distinct perceptions, which comprise the argument's earlier steps. That reason leads in this way to the principle that what reason endorses is true, is something Descartes can establish without claiming either that the conclusion of his argument is true or that its premises are true. What is necessary is only that he should clearly and distinctly perceive the premises, and that he should also perceive clearly and distinctly that the conclusion follows from them. There is plainly no circularity in such a procedure. It remains to make clear, however, what point it can have.

In this connection, it is pertinent to recall that before Descartes undertakes to evaluate the evidence of reason—that is, before formulating and attempting to validate the principle that whatever is perceived clearly and distinctly is true—he conducts, in Meditation I, an exhaustive critique of the evidence that the senses provide. The general outcome of his investigation into the reliability of sense perception is, of course, that the evidence of the senses is not good enough. Now it is both extremely natural and entirely reasonable to suppose that, having reached this outcome with respect to sensory evidence, the question Descartes then thinks it essential to ask about reason is the *same* question he has just finished asking and answering about the senses. As he turns from a consideration of the one kind of evidence to a consideration of the other, he can hardly avoid wondering whether the latter is capable of passing the test the former has failed. It is a compelling supposition, then, that the doubts Descartes will try to allay concerning reason must be analogous to the doubts he has been unable to allay concerning the senses.

Descartes's skeptical conclusion concerning the senses is based essentially upon the following consideration. Even if someone has the best sort of evidence the senses can provide for a belief, it is still possible that the senses will subsequently provide him with equally good evidence against the belief. However strong his sensory evidence for a proposition may be, Descartes finds, it is possible that he may acquire additional sensory evidence of opposite import. Anyone who relies merely upon his senses, then, runs the risk that they will betray him. For it is always possible that, having provided him with evidence of their best sort in favor of some belief, they will subsequently provide him with equally good evidence against it.

In other words, Descartes's fear about the senses is that their best testimony may be inconsistent. And if the senses do provide a person with conflicting testimony of what is, by their own measurement, equal weight—some during a dream, for example, and some while the person is awake—he will not be able *by using his senses* to decide which of this evidence to accept and which to reject. The senses cannot yield certainty, in short, because they are capable of permitting conflicts of evidence which they cannot themselves resolve.

When Descartes undertakes to evaluate the testimony of clear and distinct perception, he *must* consider the risk of being similarly betrayed by reason. The question he is committed to asking about reason is, in other words, whether it is possible that one clear and distinct perception should contradict another in the way that one sensory perception may contradict another. The best evidence reason provides cannot be good enough if beliefs based upon it may be contradicted by evidence which is equally good, anymore than beliefs based solely upon sensory considerations are acceptable once it is recognized that they may be contradicted by beliefs with equally strong sensory support. Descartes has concluded that having the best evidence the senses alone can provide—that is, evidence acquired under conditions that seem to the senses to be ideal for accurate perception—is not good enough. When he considers the value of reason, he needs to know whether *its* best evidence leaves open the possibility of encountering the same sort of dilemma to which he has found that a reliance on sensory evidence may lead.

Once we understand that it was this question about reason which Descartes was led to ask, we can also understand more exactly what value he supposed his answer to it would possess. The problem he faced was to rebut the skeptical contention that reliance upon reason may give rise to inconsistencies which reason cannot resolve, in the same way that reliance upon the senses may lead to inconsistencies which cannot be resolved by sensory testimony. Now the skeptic's position concerning this matter is, according to Descartes, tantamount to the claim that human reason is not the product of a benevolent deity. Remember that in Descartes's view we cannot *help* believing what we are perceiving clearly and distinctly. If our clear and distinct perceptions should conflict, therefore, we would find that reason had betrayed us, by constraining us to give our assent to one proposition and then to give it to another proposition inconsistent with the first. Thus reason would lead us unavoidably into contradiction, from which we could escape only by abandoning the use of reason altogether. For we have no other faculty superior to reason, which we might invoke in an effort to resolve a conflict generated by reason itself.

This would imply a corruption in our nature so deep and so hopeless that it cannot be intended by a benevolent creator. The assumption that we are creatures of a benevolent creator is compatible with the fact that we are flawed, and hence that we are susceptible to doubt and to error. But it could not be God's intention that we be condemned to incompatible beliefs without any recourse short of giving up the use of reason, as we would be if the results of reason's best work might be inconsistent. Only on the assumption that reason has some origin other than in God, then, is there a basis for fearing that the set of clear and distinct perceptions is incoherent.

But is this assumption reasonable? Is it really conceivable, in other words, that we are not creatures of a deity who is both omnipotent and benevolent? Is the supposition that we have a different origin than that a logically coherent one? It is only if this supposition is indeed coherent that the position of the skeptic is viable—that is, only if it is reasonable to suppose that we might have originated through the malicious work of a demon, or by chance, or from a blind succession of causes. Otherwise the skeptic is committed to a self-contradictory proposition, and his claim against reason is therefore one which it is not reasonable to credit.

Descartes's strategy is to show that the assumption required by the position of the skeptic is in fact not a reasonable one at all. In effect, the skeptic's argument must have the form of a reductio ad absurdum: if we rely upon reason we are led to the conclusion that reason is, or may be, unworthy of reliance. The skeptic has no alternative to this mode of argument; the only plausible line he can take is, after all, that his skeptical conclusion is one for which there are good reasons. What Descartes undertakes is to rebut this reductio by showing that reason does not, as the skeptic maintains, lead us to conclude that the circumstances of our origin are compatible with the radical deceitfulness of reason. Rather, he attempts to show, it leads us to the conclusion that God exists. Since we perceive clearly and distinctly that we are products of benevolent omnipotence, he claims, the opposite supposition—upon the coherence of which the skeptic's case depends—is logically inconceivable. It cannot be reasonable, therefore, to entertain fundamental doubts concerning reason.

The value to Descartes of his proof that God exists is not that it establishes as a fact that there is a benevolent and omnipotent being to whom we owe our existence and our nature. Descartes could not purport to demonstrate that this is a fact without begging the question of whether the premises of his argument are true. But he does not need to suppose that the premises of his argument for God's existence are true, in order to achieve the aim to which the argument is devoted. He needs only to make the point that he clearly and distinctly perceives both the premises and that the proposition that God exists follows from them. This is sufficient, because it means that if a person relies upon reason he is led to a conclusion which excludes the possibility that there is a demon (or that human existence is a product of chance, or whatever). The point of the argument is, in other words, that skepticism about reason is not reasonable; for reason leads to a judgment incompatible with the assumption upon which skepticism depends. The outcome of a reliance upon reason is the discovery of a reason for being confident that the best reasons—those provided by clear and distinct perception—will not conflict with one another. The reductio of which the skeptic warned does not materialize. What develops is, on the contrary, a conclusion which entails that the position of the skeptic involves a contradiction.

There is, however, a further question. Given that reason is reliable, in the sense that it does not betray itself by providing reasons for doubting its own reliability, is the testimony of reason a sufficient proof against what may be called "absolute" error? Even though reasons of the best kind provide a certainty with which no other reasons of that kind will interfere, is it not possible that we may achieve this certainty concerning something which is in fact false? A set of propositions may be consistent, after all, without any of them being true. Is it proper to conclude from the fact that judgments based upon clear and distinct perception form a consistent set, then, not only that it is safe for us to accept such judgments without fearing that we will later have to doubt them, but also that they are in the fullest sense true?

Descartes's argument appears to do nothing to show that what is perceived clearly and distinctly corresponds with reality. Even if it succeeds in establishing that propositions which are clearly and distinctly perceived cohere with each other, in other words, it seems to leave open the possibility that none of those propositions is true. And yet Descartes does claim to establish, of course, that what is clearly and distinctly perceived is true.

At one time I believed it appropriate to deal with this difficulty by ascribing to Descartes a coherence theory of truth. If he did conceive truth in terms of coherence, then the problem disappears: showing that what is clearly and distinctly perceived satisfies the condition of coherence is, in that case, the same as showing that it is true. I now think, however, that it was a mistake on my part to suggest that Descartes entertained a coherence conception of truth. The fact is that there is no textual evidence to support that suggestion; on the contrary, whenever Descartes gives an explicit account of truth he explains it unequivocally as correspondence with reality. It might still be possible to claim that Descartes is committed to conceiving truth in terms of coherence, even if he does not appreciate that he is. Even this claim now strikes me as unwarranted, however, since it may be that there are other ways—philosophically as plausible as a coherence theory of truth—of coping with the problem at issue.

Descartes was deeply preoccupied with certainty—with finding beliefs he could trust without qualification or reserve. He was above all concerned to determine what it was reasonable for him to regard as altogether unshakeable and permanent—that is, immune to any legitimate fear that he would someday discover it necessary to recant his adherence to it. It is unclear in what way, if at all, he worked through the relation between this ambition and the desire for truth. My present view of the matter is that he may never have thought through the implications of his defense of reason sufficiently to become fully aware of the question about truth to which it leads, and that he actually provides no clear or readily visible answer to that question.

There are plain indications, however, that Descartes was aware of the possibility that what satisfies the demand for certainty may not satisfy the conditions of truth. In his "Reply to Objections II" he says:

What is it to us if someone should feign that the very thing of whose truth we are so firmly persuaded appears false to the eyes of God or of the Angels and that hence, speaking absolutely, it is false? Why should we concern ourselves with this absolute falsity, since we by no means believe in it or even have the least suspicion of it? For we are supposing a belief or a conviction so strong that nothing can remove it, and this conviction is in every respect the same as perfect certitude. [AT 7:145; HR 2:41]

In this passage, Descartes explicitly acknowledges the possibility that what is certain may not be true "speaking absolutely," and he makes it clear that certainty takes priority over absolute truth in his conception of the goals of inquiry.

It is sometimes suggested that Descartes does not really concede the possibility that there is a discrepancy between the certain and the absolutely true. The fact that someone might "feign" that such a discrepancy exists, it is argued, in no way implies that such a discrepancy is possible; rather, Descartes's use of the word "feign" indicates that he takes what he is describing to be only a pretense. But Descartes's response to whoever is doing the feigning is not to argue or to assert that this person is proposing something inconceivable or known not to be the case. Descartes responds, not by denying the genuineness of the possibility "feigned," but by denying its pertinence to his interests. This shows that in his view the possession of certainty and the possession of absolute truth are not the same. The first suffices for his purposes, he insists, regardless of the presence or absence of the second.

Descartes may appear here to be denying what he is elsewhere at pains to assert, concerning the implications of God's benevolence. For if we have been created in such a way that what we find certain is absolutely false, then it may seem that our Creator is after all deceptive. But this is incorrect. Assuming that we recognize the limitations of our faculties, what we are condemned to by the possibility that absolute truth and certainty may diverge is not error, but only a certain sort of ignorance. Now to be sure, condemning someone to ignorance may do him serious injury. For us knowingly to suffer the ignorance in question here, however, is not incompatible with divine benevolence. Descartes's view is that God may have created us in such a way that we must in certain respects remain inescapably in the dark. To keep someone in the dark is to harm him, however, only if he cannot get along in the dark. Since our darkness is compatible with our possession of perfect certitude, which ensures that we need never stumble, it involves no harm to us.

Suppose that Descartes does show without circularity that reason leads to the conclusion that God exists and that whatever is perceived clearly and distinctly is true. How do we know that reason does not also lead to the conclusions that there is no God, that instead there is an omnipotent demon, and that what is clearly and distinctly perceived may well be false? That is, how do we know that reason does not lead in contrary directions? If it did, of course, that would mean that reason is hopelessly unreliable and inconsistent. But since it is precisely the reliability and consistency of reason that is at issue, it would seem that the opposite cannot be taken for granted. This suggests that Descartes's reasoning is ultimately circular after all. For it appears that his argument that what is perceived clearly and distinctly is true, while not circular in itself, serves its purpose only on the question-begging assumption that it is not possible to develop an equally good argument leading to a conclusion which contradicts the conclusion Descartes purports to derive.

It is useful to recognize, in this connection, that a difficulty very much like this one can be raised with equal point about any effort to demonstrate consistency. When we discover a proof that a certain logical calculus is consistent, how do we know that it is not also possible to find a proof that the calculus is inconsistent? Our knowledge of the existence of the first proof does not justify denying the possibility that the second exists, unless we assume that our inquiry cannot lead to contradictory results.

The precise value and import of consistency proofs, particularly in an unlimited context such as the one in which Descartes operates, are difficult to specify exactly. It might perhaps be desirable, instead of construing his argument as an attempt to prove the consistency of reason, to understand Descartes as attempting just to establish that there is no reasonable ground for doubting that reason is consistent. The skeptic might then persist in maintaining that a reductio ad absurdum of the supposition that reason is reliable can be found, whatever Descartes's success in showing that it is not found along the route followed in the *Meditations*. Unless the sceptic actually produces the destructive argument with which he threatens reason, however, his threat remains an idle or capricious one. There is no reason to credit it or to find it disturbing. As long as the skeptic provides no good reason for his mistrust of reason, it is reasonable to ignore him. Descartes can reasonably continue to rely upon reason, which he has shown to confirm its own reliability, since no reason for fearing that reason might also betray itself remains.

NOTES

1. This is no more than a rather provocative formulation of the familiar observation that philosophical theories are never conclusively demonstrated, and that philosophy is not a cumulative discipline. One may well wonder why philosophers continue to seek to prove their doctrines, since historical precedent suggests overwhelmingly that they will fail. On the other hand, argument plainly does have an integral role in philosophy. If its role is not probative, what is it?

2. For some of this evidence, see H. Gouhier, *La pensée réligieuse de Descartes* (Paris, 1972), pp. 11–12.

3. Anthony Kenny, "The Cartesian Circle and the Eternal Truths," *Journal of Philosophy* 67 (1970):685–700.

4. "Our mind is of such a nature," Descartes says, "that it cannot refuse to assent to what it apprehends clearly" (letter to Regius, 24 May 1640; AT 3:64; see also *Principles* I. 43). Descartes does not elaborate or attempt to justify this claim, and I do not propose to explore its basis here. I will say, however, that I find it plausible. It is at any rate no less plausible than the similar doctrine, whose plausibility is perhaps more readily apparent, that a person cannot simultaneously assent to incompatible propositions *while* fully aware of and attending to their incompatibility.

5. Kenny, "Cartesian Circle," p. 690.

6. Cf. AT 7:146; HR 2:42. Kenny mistakenly believes that propositions like "2 + 3 = 5" belong to this class. No such proposition appears in any of Descartes's lists of examples, and Descartes makes it clear in the First Meditation that simple arithmetic propositions can be doubted.

Certainty

and Cartesian Method

JEFFREY TLUMAK

IN THIS PAPER I try to determine the nature and role of certainty in
Cartesian method, and their implications for interpreting key passages of the *Meditations*. Consolidating, developing, and sometimes re-
forming valuable work by others, I offer a picture of Descartes's method
and its application which strives to relate his central psychological,
evidentiary, and semantic notions in a textually and philosophically
satisfying way. Descartes's descriptions of his epistemological procedure
are rendered internally consistent, mutually consistent, and consistent
with his practice, which is exhibited as neither circular nor implausibly
dogmatic. To this end, pivotal, yet strikingly controversial theses I plan
to defend are (1) that certainty is always at least partially an evidentiary notion, and never a purely psychological or purely semantic
one; (2) that only one of the diverse notions employed by commentators
—a suitably defined irrevisability condition—is a plausible candidate
for metaphysical certainty; (3) that metaphysical certainty and "compelled assent" are distinct, but intimately related in undetected ways;
(4) that metaphysical or contemplative doubtmakers, though described
as "powerful and maturely considered," need not have respectable
epistemic status; (5) that Descartes nongratuitously thinks that some
propositions are autonomously metaphysically certain, independent
of divine guarantee; and (6) that if Descartes's probative procedure
were exhausted by his eliminative method of doubt, then no rule of
truth could be established, but that he does intend scrupulous use of
his method to establish truth, and so has a richer conception of "analytic" method. Finally, my account of this conception aims to be sensitive to Descartes's atomistic theory of time, "vertical" theory of
causality, voluntaristic theory of divine omnipotence, representational

theory of external consciousness, and nonrepresentational theory of internal consciousness as that applies both to thoughts (mental acts) and to ideas (mental contents). The gist and relevant consequences of these theories surface as the project unfolds.

I

The first stage of the project is to clarify, test, and where it is revealing, to interrelate various suggested analyses of metaphysical certainty.[1] As guidance, I elicit a set of six adequacy conditions from Descartes. Such conditions represent general demands on the explication of certainty, and are not intended to be jointly exhaustive. Consequently, we should not be tempted to propose the conjunction of adequacy conditions as the explication itself.

The first condition states that certainty is not a manifest, intrinsic property of propositions, but is a relation between a person or persons, a proposition or set of propositions, and a time or set of times. Descartes insists on this point in several places in his reply to Bourdin's objections (the seventh set), in which he complains that his critic "treats doubtfulness and certainty not as relations of our thought to objects, but as properties of the objects and as inhering in them eternally. The consequence is that nothing we have once learned to be doubtful can ever be rendered certain" (HR 2:276–77). Another consequence is that a given proposition is (or is not) certain for anyone who entertains it, regardless of his evidence (HR 2:282). Very many arguments in Descartes rightly depend upon treating certainty as a relation of the sort described.[2]

The second condition of adequacy states that a person may at a time be certain about a logically contingent proposition. Certainties need not be logically necessary truths. As Descartes argues, the logically contingent propositions, "I think"—where that includes "I am persuaded" and "I am deceived" (HR 1:150), "I believe that I am breathing" (K 52), "I seem to see" and "I seem to walk" (HR 1:222), and generally all subjective reports of the occurrence of mental states (HR 1:157, 2:207)—and "I exist" (HR 1:7), are certainties for me whenever I pronounce them or mentally conceive them (HR 1:150).

On the evidence of Descartes's statement that "I am, I exist, is necessarily true each time that I pronounce it, or that I mentally conceive it," it may be urged that "I exist" is a logically necessary truth for Descartes.[3] The familiar response is that the necessity-operator is intended to govern the connection between "I conceive that I exist" and "I exist," not "I exist" directly. But such a response, whatever its exegetical merits in the present case, cannot allay the core of the worry,

since on so many other occasions Descartes ascribes necessity to instances of the kinds of nonconditional propositions we would classify
as logically contingent, such as "it seems to me that I see light, that I
hear noise and that I feel heat" (HR 1:153), and perhaps "I am not
more than a thing which thinks" (HR 1:152).

A direct way to meet the threat to the second adequacy condition
is to show that logical necessity is not the operative notion in the problematic passages. One strategy which suggests itself appeals to Descartes's theological voluntarism. Adopting the view that there is no distinction between divine understanding and will (HR 1:228), Descartes
rejected the view that eternal truths, truths about essences, depend on
God's understanding but not His will. So eternal truths must either
depend on Gods' will, or be independent of Him entirely. But independent eternal truths would be a limitation on divine power. Since
God is infinitely powerful, eternal truths must depend on His will;
God created the eternal truths (K 13–14, 15, 236–37, 240–41; HR
2:250–51). Essences and existents are ontologically contingent creatures
alike. Now if God were bound to create what he did, the set of eternal
truths he created could not have been otherwise. But although God
willed truths about essences to be necessary, He did not necessarily so
will, since He is free (K 15, 151; cf. CB 50).[4] The alleged upshot is
that Descartes's notion of necessity is far weaker than popular contemporary notions of logical necessity—weaker than modal system S4,
and so S5—since for him, what is necessarily true might have been false.

This strategy seems unacceptable for several reasons. First, the falsity
of the axiom definitive of S4, that what is necessarily true is necessarily
necessary, follows from the fact that God nonnecessarily created what is
necessary, only if "necessity" as it applies to divine decree is equivalent
to "necessity" as it applies to propositional products of divine decree,
that is, only if divine free activity amounts merely to logically contingent activity. But the point of voluntarism is that they are not
equivalent. The way the voluntarist proceeds to falsify an axiom such
as that all possibilities are necessarily possible is by distinguishing
(incomprehensible) possibility in the absolute sense from (conceivable
to us) possibility as ordained by God, and then reading iterated
modality claims so that an operator prefixed directly to a proposition
signifies ordained possibility (conceivability), while an operator once
removed signifies absolute possibility. Only then would affirming the
axiom be tantamount to denying God's absolute omnipotence.

Second, a coherent voluntarist must insist that God's nature does
not rule out the truth of even the strongest modal system; otherwise he
is committed to denying that God could have made a given set of
propositions, those constituting the strongest modal system, true.

Third, even if Descartes does repudiate S4 (and S5), "necessity" as used in the problematic passages might still express a logical notion of sufficient strength to sustain the attack on the second adequacy condition. Still, for example, necessary truths would follow from anything, and still we would refuse to admit that propositions such as "I seem to see a light" follow from anything.

Fourth, and more generally, unless Descartes, waxing Spinozist, is prepared to obliterate the logico-metaphysical distinction between the necessary and the contingent altogether, or, waxing Frankfurtian, intends to disregard the metaphysical modalities in favor of the epistemic ones, he must have some metaphysical account of the difference between eternal and noneternal truths. Yet one suspects that, on any plausible alternative, it is a mistake to include propositions such as "I seem to see a light" in the former class, as signalled by their shared, honorific title of "necessity."

All this strongly suggests that in the present contexts necessity is not a logical or metaphysical notion, but an epistemic one. Forthcoming discussion of how precisely various modal locutions are to be construed will systematically support and broaden this conclusion. For now, note that Descartes *says* in the Preface to the *Meditations* that the modal talk in question is epistemic (HR 1:137–38; and see 2:133n, and K 52).

The third condition of adequacy states the converse of the second: necessary truths need not be certainties. Otherwise, Descartes could not have been, and the atheist geometer could not remain, uncertain about the truths of mathematics (HR 2:39); and each person, regardless of his evidence and skills at proof, would be equally certain of all the necessary truths he entertained, no matter how complex.

Metaphysical certainty is a standard-setting concept of epistemic appraisal. The term "certain" may have purely descriptive force in some contexts, but it has normative force in the context of the Cartesian problem. Descartes's recurrent characterizations of metaphysical certainties as immune to invalidation by reasons (HR 1:150), without grounds for suspicion (HR 2:266), and so on, indicate this.

Hence, neither purely behavioral nor purely psychological or introspective analyses of metaphysical certainty are viable. To say that someone is certain about a proposition just in case he is indisposed to inquire whether that proposition is true, or just in case he is indisposed to seek out or consider further information that bears on that proposition, or just in case he takes no precautions against the possibility that the proposition is false, or just in case he is (compellingly) free from doubt about the proposition, is to give an account of certainty unsuited to our epistemic purposes. Aside from the internal difficulties of these views—the person's indispositions may be the result of apathy, his unwariness and (compelled) freedom from doubt the result of ignorance (or pathology), and so on—they violate the fourth condition. Such behavioral dispositions or psychological states may be a causal consequence of certainty, but they are not to be identified with it.

No satisfactory analysis of certainty should directly imply that all certainties must be inferentially justifiable. The possibility that there are propositions which are certain for a person at a time, even though there is no available premise-set containing other propositions which are certain and essential to their derivation, should not be ruled out prima facie. Descartes held that intuition and deduction were the only two routes to knowledge with certainty, and that deduction is based on self-evident intuition (HR 1:7–8). And it may be that admission of self-justifying or "intuitive" certainties is required to avoid the dilemma that all justification is either viciously regressive or circular. But even if not, the fifth condition should be retained so as to avoid begging preeminent questions of interpretation.

The final guiding desideratum is that some species of knowledge do not require metaphysical certainty. Everyday empirical knowledge, or perhaps better, what in ordinary practice passes for true knowledge, does not require metaphysical certainty, but only "moral" certainty. Morally certain opinions are highly probable, far more reasonable to accept than reject (HR 1:148; 2:315). But Descartes frequently distinguishes the requirements of the search for truth and the practical activities of life, where the moral mode of knowing suffices for the regulation of life, but falls short of the metaphysical mode of knowing (HR 1:104, 301; 2:206, 266, 278; K 50, 110). And even higher grade, non-practical knowledge, such as mathematical knowledge, may lack metaphysical certainty (if it is "unsystematic" and "unenduring"— notions to be discussed). Descartes grants the atheist geometer knowledge of mathematical theorems, but denies that such knowledge constitutes "true science"; since it can be rendered dubious, it is not "immutable and certain" (HR 2:39, 245). Again, Descartes suggests that (at earlier stages of the meditative process at least) metaphysical proofs are more certain than mathematical ones (CB 79; HR 1:135).[5]

I propose the foregoing six conditions as criteria of adequacy for the explication of Cartesian, metaphysical certainty. No satisfactory account of metaphysical certainty entails that it is a manifest, intrinsic property of propositions, that all certainties are logically necessary, that all necessities are certainties, that ascriptions of certainty lack all force of epistemic appraisal, that all certainties must be inferentially justifiable, or that all species of knowledge require certainty.

Various interpretations of metaphysical certainty have been employed by Descartes's commentators and others interested in Cartesian epistemology. Nearly all are variations on one of three themes: that certainties are indefeasibly justified beliefs; that certainties are optimally justified beliefs; or that certainties are beliefs which cannot be mistaken. I shall call these "irrevisability," "maximal warrant," and "unmistakability" analyses, respectively. Most versions of irrevisability and maximal warrant make certainty an evidentiary notion that does not entail truth; but some add a truth-guaranteeing clause to the account. A variant on unmistakability is truth-entailing if "cannot" is construed logically; otherwise, as I shall argue, it reduces to an irrevisability analysis.

The philosophical motivation for irrevisability has been well impressed on us by Harry Frankfurt.[6] The skeptical gambit is to induce doubt by driving a logical wedge between a belief and its supportive evidence. Fully reliable beliefs, immune to skeptical attack, have logically conclusive evidence-bases. So long as such evidence-bases are retained there is no possibility that additional evidence will make abandonment of belief reasonable. Such beliefs cannot be overthrown or defeated by enrichment of evidence; they are "unshakably solid and permanent." There can be no reason to doubt such beliefs; they are indubitable or certain.

The textual support for certainty as irrevisability is massive. The sorts of phrase-selection which bespeak irrevisability are by now well rehearsed (HR 1:92, 101, 144, 314–15; 2:39, 41–42, 245, as a sampling). And how an irrevisability interpretation helps clarify Descartes's method, with due appreciation to other Cartesian doctrines, will be developed shortly.

To test irrevisability against the six adequacy conditions, a working formulation is necessary. The basic idea is that a proposition h is irrevisable for a person S at a time t if and only if S is justified in believing h at t, and it is impossible that any additional considerations at any later t' would warrant S's retraction of h, that is, warrant S's withholding h or believing not-h at t'. That neither conditions 1 nor 3–6 are violated seems uncontroversial. But spurred by the belief that no synthetic proposition is immune to revision, it may be objected that the account violates adequacy condition 2, that certainties need not be necessities, as follows.[7] If h is contingently true, it is possibly false. But if h is possibly false, it is possible that a later, expanded evidence-base fails to justify h—namely, an evidence-base which includes not-h (since every set e of evidential propositions, when conjoined with not-h, fails to justify h). Therefore, only necessary truths could be certainties on the irrevisability account.

Although initially persuasive, this objection is misguided. As discussion of adequacy condition 1 made clear for the upper limiting case of certainty, the making-evident or confirmation relation is not a purely formal relation between propositions on the model of truth-functions. "p confirms q" does not simply state a certain relation between p and q; another term of this relation is the epistemic situation of those who aim at assessing the rational credibility of q. To ask whether p confirms q is roughly to ask of a person whose epistemic situation is assumed to include a group of certain standard rules of inference, whether the addition of the belief that p to his other beliefs tends to rationally persuade him to adopt the belief that q. But mere repetition is not rational persuasion; that is why we reject question-begging support. So no proposition can confirm itself or make itself evident—which is not to say that no proposition is directly or non-inferentially evident. So the relevant confirmation relation is irreflexive. But p disconfirms q if and only if p confirms not-q, to the same degree. Substituting not-p for q here, we get the result that p disconfirms not-p if and only if p confirms p, to the same degree. Given the irreflexivity of the confirmation relation, this last equivalence shows that appeal to the negation of a proposition in order to disconfirm that proposition is illicit.

To foreclose a source of future misunderstanding, let us explicitly incorporate this proviso in the definition of "irrevisability." We want to say that exactly when a person's justification is preserved through all possible, permissible enrichment, is the proposition so justified a certainty for the person at the time:

(I) h is irrevisable for S at t if and only if (i) on the basis of some (possibly empty) set of evidential propositions, e, S is justified in believing h at t; and (ii) there is no t' and possible e' such that t' is later than t, e is a subset of e', and e' fails to justify S in believing h at t', where not-h is not a member of e'.

When we talk of a belief's rational constancy through all possible, permissible enrichment, do we mean to demand that the belief withstand the challenge of *every* potential defeater (except its negation)? This question, as to how we understand "possible" in the phrase "possible e'," is the key question of the nature of metaphysical doubtmakers. The more liberal our attitude toward doubtmakers, the more stringent our account of irrevisability, and the heavier our epistemological burden.

Fred Feldman has recently argued that only moral or practical possibilities—propositions whose negations are not practical certainties or propositions whose negations lack the ordinary sort of justification which gives us the "epistemic right" to believe them—can serve as metaphysical doubtmakers.[8] Using this thesis, he provides a reconstruction of Descartes's main argument which escapes all hint of circularity. Early in the *Meditations*, the existence of a deceptive God was practically possible for Descartes, and this possibility cast metaphysical doubt on various practical, but not metaphysical, certainties, including all otherwise untainted clear and distinct perceptions. The proposition that God exists and is no deceiver is then made a practical certainty by proof using only clearly and distinctly perceived, practical certainties. The deceptive-God hypothesis is then no longer practically possible, and so it can no longer cast metaphysical doubt on clear and distinct perceptions; and since it was assumed to be the only residual metaphysical doubtmaker, all practically certain, clear and distinct perceptions become upgraded to metaphysical certainties, including the premises of the God-proof, and so (given that the proof has been gone through) its conclusion. Thus we secure the divine guarantee that all which we clearly and distinctly perceive is true, avoiding circularity.

This attractive strategy for rectifying Descartes's reputed circle rests on the thesis that only practical possibilities are legitimate doubtmakers. That reasons for doubt must be "very powerful and maturely considered" (HR 1:147–48; 2:266), that doubt must be based on "clear and assured reasonings" (HR 1:99), and that the concluding paragraphs of Meditation V suggest so, are offered as textual support. But these passages seem misconstrued, and nearly everything that Descartes says and does in this matter indicates that the class of doubtmakers is not restricted to practical possibilities.

First, Descartes typically describes his policy as that of withholding judgment on anything "as to which I could imagine the *least* ground of doubt" (HR 1:101, 219), so as to achieve the metaphysical certainty which "all the *most extravagant* suppositions brought forward by the skeptics were incapable of shaking" (HR 1:101, my emphases). Second, after identifying "powerful and maturely considered" or "valid and well-considered" (HR 2:277) reasons for metaphysical doubt with "the *very least ground(s)* of suspicion," he explains that doubtmakers may themselves be doubtful, and only temporarily useful to induce doubt, but that they are valid so long as they are not eliminated. His reasons for doubting everything he entertained in Meditation I were valid because, since he perceived nothing clearly there, those reasons were not discredited. A reason is valid until proven invalid. And to say such reasons are "very powerful" is simply to say they are "very effective for their purpose." This sentiment is expressed in his description to Burman of the demon's function: "The author is here making us as doubtful as he can and casting us into as many doubts as possible. This is why he raises not only the customary difficulties of the Sceptics but every difficulty that can possibly be raised; the aim is in this way to demolish completely every single doubt" (CB 2). To marshal mere practical possibilities is not to wield very powerful doubtmakers.

Third, after again noting his practice to withhold in each matter if there is *"anything* which could make it subject to suspicion or doubt" (HR 1:99), he favorably compares his procedure to that of the skeptics in that his is positively designed to eliminate unreliable grounds so as to replace them with solid foundations, and his rigorously elicits the implications of the sorts of doubts about which the skeptics merely speculate. To examine doubtful opinions by clear and assured reasonings is not to base doubtful opinions on clear and assured reasons. Nor would a mere practical possibility be a clear and assured reason anyhow. Fourth, I do not see how the review of now discarded doubtmakers at the end of Meditation V reveals anything about their erstwhile epistemic status, except that they were not clearly and distinctly perceived.

Fifth, and more important than any of the verbal evidence, is the fact that none of the doubtmakers used seriously by Descartes are practical possibilities for him. That his senses are generally trustworthy is a practical certainty for Descartes (HR 2:206); hence, a general doubt about the reliability of the senses is a practical impossibility. Similarly, Descartes is morally certain that he is awake, and that a benevolent God exists, at the beginning of his meditations.

So the potential defeaters of a candidate, irrevisable belief need not be practical possibilities. Nor, however, need they be logical possibilities. The existence of a supremely powerful, deceitful demon is logically impossible (CB 3, 10; K 219), but until one clearly recognizes this impossibility, the demon hypothesis is a serious doubtmaker (CB 11).[9] Descartes follows the order of "recognized" possibilities and necessities, not the true logical order (HR 1:137–38). This is part of what he means when he says he uses the analytic, not synthetic method, following the order of discovery, not syllogism (HR 2:48–49, 127; K 197; CB 17). Let us say that p is epistemically possible for S at t just in case S lacks *conclusive* reasons for believing not-p at t. We may then say that epistemic possibilities need not be logically possible, and that it is epistemic possibility (in this weak sense) that defines the set of potential doubtmakers at any given stage of our meditations. Hence, irrevisable belief is justified belief which cannot be rationally overthrown by any subsequent epistemic possibilities, excluding the negation of the belief, so long as original justification is preserved.

Irrevisability as just defined does not guarantee truth. Anthony Kenny, however, does seem to endorse a truth-entailing variant when he says, "It is not enough, for Cartesian certainty, that I should here and now unhesitatingly make a true judgment on the best possible grounds. It is necessary also that I should be in such a position that I will never hereafter have reason to withdraw the judgment."[10] Along with adding this semantic feature, Kenny seems prepared to treat the indefeasibility requirement in even stricter fashion than I have done above. In response to the criticism that he has foisted on Descartes the unrealistic goal of achieving an immutable state of mind—unrealistic because even after a successful God-proof, later forgetfulness or loss of faith opens the door to recurring doubt—Kenny admits that the goal appears unrealistic, but thinks it is Descartes's goal nevertheless.[11] In countenancing objections from forgetfulness, one allows impoverishment as well as enrichment of a belief's original evidence-base. But the resulting, stronger irrevisability condition would seem epistemologically less interesting. For example, whereas it is plausible to argue that sense-datum reports satisfy my irrevisability condition, this stronger condition clearly rules them out as certainties. On the other hand, Descartes repeatedly insists that, once the existence of a good God, who is the source of all truth, is acknowledged, we are certain of the conclusion of a proof we correctly remember having clearly and distinctly perceived, even though we cannot reproduce its premises. I shelve further consideration of this interesting conflict until I develop the resources to resolve it, returning to my survey of interpretations of metaphysical certainty.

Kenny's phrase, "on the best possible grounds," suggests that he may also require that certainties be maximally warranted. The notion of maximal warrant may be explicated in various nonequivalent ways, depending on the classes of comparison to which one appeals.[12] That is, various definitions of "maximal warrant" can be formulated by changing the range of the three variables of persons, propositions, and example, we might say that S is maximally warranted in believing h at times, which must be included in virtue of adequacy condition 1. For t if and only if (1) h has at least as much warrant for S at t as h ever has for anyone who asserts it; or somewhat stronger, (2) it is inconceivable that h would have more warrant for someone asserting it than it has for S at t; or, still stronger, (3) it is inconceivable that any proposition would have more warrant for anyone than h has for S at t.

Versions (1) and (2) are too weak. They are satisfied if h has no (conceivable) warrant for anyone at any time. On the other hand, (3) may seem too strong, leading immediately to the result that almost nothing is certain. And why saddle a private meditator with an account of certainty which requires interpersonal comparisons? Perhaps we should replace talk of the best justified propositions anyone can have with talk of the best justified propositions an individual can have. This would capture Feldman's characterization that a proposition is a metaphysical certainty for a person if "he is justified in believing it, and could not be more justified in believing anything than he is in believing it."[13]

I suspect that the distinction between (3) and its solipsistic revision effectively collapses, since, as his summary dismissal of the madman hypothesis exemplifies, Descartes procedurally assumes that he is in principle no better nor worse equipped than others to undertake the search for indubitable knowledge. But to delineate most vividly the logical relations between competing proposals, I shall conduct forthcoming arguments in terms of (3); none would be affected by replacing (3) with its revision. And to facilitate such argument, (3) is more explicitly formulated as follows:

(M) h is maximally warranted for S at t if and only if S is warranted in believing h at t, and it is inconceivable that there is an h', a t' (where there are no restrictions on the choice of t'), an S' (which may or may not be restricted to S) and an e', such that e' confers greater warrant on h' for S' at t' than h has for S at t.

Descartes's repeated use of phrases such as "best evidence" and "most manifest" (HR 1:158), "grounded on the highest evidence" (HR 1:170), "I do not think the human mind is capable of knowing anything with more evidence" (HR 1:172), "apprehended with the greatest evidence" (HR 1:184), and "surest knowledge" (HR 2:206) suggest a maximal warrant interpretation of metaphysical certainty. And (M) fulfills all adequacy criteria. So unless it turns out to be too strict, ruling out indubitable knowledge of the superstructure of Descartes's reconstructed science, (M) seems a worthy contender.

Some commentators, such as Alexander and Morris, construe certainties as propositions about which one "cannot be mistaken" or "cannot be deceived"; Bernard Williams expressly has Descartes seeking "beliefs whose truth is in some way guaranteed by the fact that they are believed."[14] Focus on Descartes's widespread use of error-precluding notions, and his efforts to discover beliefs whose acceptability resists even the possibility of demonic deception, might tempt one to adopt such an interpretation. After all, it may be reasoned, doubt is possible if error is possible. But error is false belief. So error is possible whenever belief does not entail truth. Hence, since a certain proposition is one about which the possibility of error is excluded, a proposition is certain only if believing it logically implies its truth.

Analyzing metaphysical certainty as logical unmistakability seems untenable. First, the analysis lets in too much. Since all necessary truths satisfy the unmistakability condition (U)—necessary truths are entailed by anything—adequacy condition 3, above, that not all necessities need be certainties, implies that (U) is not a sufficient condition of certainty. And since all entailments are necessary, given the rule that if $\ulcorner p \urcorner$ is a certainty, and $\ulcorner p$ entails $q \urcorner$ is a certainty, then $\ulcorner q \urcorner$ is a certainty, we are forced to admit that all the logical consequences of a contingent certainty for a person at a time are also certain for him at that time.

Second, the analysis lets in too little. Belief is not a truth-entailing propositional attitude. So it would seem as if, when p is contingent, believing p would entail p's truth only if p itself asserts the occurrence of belief, or the truth of something implied by the occurrence of belief (such as thinking or existing). If so, the analysis excludes indefinitely many logically contingent certainties such as "I seem to see a light."[15]

One may rejoin that these are at best objections to the philosophical adequacy of (U), not to its attribution to Descartes. It is anachronistic to appeal to a "paradox" of strict implication here. And since Descartes thinks that a logically contingent, foundational proposition need not have farreaching and intricate deductive consequences—as when he says "one should not require the first principle to be such that all other propositions can be reduced to it and proved by it. It is enough if it is useful for the discovery of many, and if there is no other proposition on which it depends, and none which is easier to discover" (K 197)—perhaps it is not paradoxical for him to say we are certain of all its entailments. Owing to its simplicity, our apprehension of it is not only clear but distinct as well. And after all, Descartes does not *deduce* very much from the cogito or cogito-type propositions, whether taken as either existential claims or implication claims. And as regards the second objection, Descartes does maintain that our identifications of all our mental acts and their representative contents are logically infallible.

I shall not assess the merits of this rejoinder. My real concern at this juncture is to complete the development of those conceptual resources which will be systematically applied to interpret what Descartes does, and what he says he does. To this end, I want to show that when viewed abstractly, and not in the context of other Cartesian doctrines, irrevisability, maximal warrant, and unmistakability are logically distinct notions.[16]

If h is irrevisable for S at t, no further tests on h could yield results which would warrant S's retraction of h. Now such irretractability would be guaranteed if new evidence for h will never become available for S, since the current adequate evidence is exhaustive or complete, or also if no other proposition could ever be better justified for anyone than h is for S at t, since the evidential warrant for h is maximal. But although both exhaustively and maximally warranted propositions guarantee irrevisability, irrevisable propositions need be neither exhaustively nor maximally warranted; it is enough that their evidence-bases suffice to rule out the possibility of subsequent overthrow.

Specifically, that maximal warrant entails but is not entailed by irrevisability may be shown as follows. Suppose that h is maximally warranted. Then there is no conceivable e', h', S' and t' such that e' provides better justification of h' for S' at t' than the justification that S has for h at t. The proposition not-h is distinct from the proposition h. If h were revisable, if h could be warrantedly disbelieved or withheld by S in light of future evidence, then the evidence for not-h would be stronger than or equal to the evidence for h. But then h would not be maximally warranted. Hence, revisability entails lack of maximal warrant. Hence, maximal warrant entails irrevisability.

But irrevisability does not entail maximal warrant. For suppose that no evidence over and above that which supports h for S at t could conceivably overturn h. Even if this required that h have maximally good evidence (of the relevant sort of evidence) bearing on *it*—and the preceding paragraph suggests that this need not be true—other propositions of other kinds, for which other kinds of evidence are relevant, could conceivably have still more impressive credentials. Constant rational acceptance of h is compatible with greener pastures in an entirely different ball park.

Unmistakability does not entail irrevisability. All necessary truths are unmistakable. Some necessary truths are revisable. One can readily imagine a persuasive argument coming along warranting suspension of judgment on a necessary truth. Therefore, some revisable truths are unmistakable, so that unmistakability does not entail irrevisability.

One might insist, "But of course revisability entails mistakability. How could any future evidence generate warrant for withholding or believing the negation of a proposition whose truth is entailed by the fact that it is believed?" This objection confuses the obtaining of the entailment between belief and truth and the knowledge that the entailment obtains. For as long as one knew that the belief guaranteed its truth, presumably one could not reasonably disbelieve that proposition. But such knowledge is not implied by the unmistakability condition.

One might try to establish the converse, that irrevisability entails unmistakability, as follows: Suppose the entailment does not hold. Then three conditions must hold: (1) S believes that h at t, (2) h is false, and (3) S cannot warrantedly believe not-h or withhold h. But (2) and (3) are inconsistent. Therefore, irrevisability entails unmistakability.

The argument rests on the assumption that for any proposition what-

soever, it is possible warrantedly to withhold it if it is false, and possible warrantedly to believe it if it is true. But this assumption falsely
rules out the possibility of unconfirmable truths. Generalizing, since
truth conditions, justification conditions, and belief conditions are not
invariably correlated, one may say that irrevisability (a concept of privileged evidentiary status) does not entail unmistakability (a concept
of privileged doxastic status). For again, suppose mistakability, that
is, the possibility of false belief. Revisability does not follow, since just
because you *can* be mistaken, it does not follow that you can be warranted in thinking so or withholding on the matter. And the same sorts
of considerations show that maximal warrant does not entail unmistakability.

If unmistakability entailed maximal warrant, then it would entail
irrevisability; since the latter entailment has been shown to fail, the
former fails as well. Just because you cannot be mistaken about
something, it does not follow that you must be unshakably warranted
in thinking that you cannot. (Imagine a patient, who reports to his
psychoanalyst that he is believing something, being rationally persuaded by the analyst's bogus observation that he is refusing to commit
himself, and not really believing at all.) And if you are not unshakably
warranted, you are not maximally warranted.

Further, all necessary truths are unmistakable. Some necessary truths
are such that their warrant is weaker than the warrant for some other
proposition. Even the fact that some necessary truths are better justified than others suffices to show this. Therefore, some propositions that
are not maximally warranted are unmistakable. Therefore, unmistakability does not entail maximal warrent.

In sum, maximal warrant guarantees irrevisability, but no other
entailment relations hold between the three main analyses of certainty,
each of which enjoys prima facie textual support. Of the three, perhaps
unmistakability fares least well, largely because it lacks an evidentiary
component relativizing certainty to persons in epistemic situations. I
now turn to show how, by applying this somewhat abstract conceptual
apparatus, and combining it with a few other Cartesian doctrines, we
can explain Descartes method in a way which exonerates him from
charges of circularity, inconsistency, and dogmatism.

II

The traditional charge against Descartes's procedure is that, since he
purports to establish reliably the existence of a benevolent God by
appeal to clear and distinct perceptions, and then deduces the reliability of clear and distinct perceptions from the existence of a benevolent

God, he assumes the reliability of clear and distinct perceptions to justify the reliability of such perceptions; and this is a circular, that is, roundabout, question-begging procedure, formally valid, but probatively useless.[17] Further, if Descartes describes his procedure as showing that meticulous use of our most trustworthy faculty not only can, but must receive divine guarantee, so that certain theological knowledge is a prerequisite for all certified belief, and also successfully proving the relevant theological knowledge, he is contradicting himself, professing to prove something by steps insufficient to provide proof. Given that Descartes does argue for this theological knowledge—that God, who is the cause of all and only positive reality, exists—this contradiction can be avoided only by denying that all certified belief requires divine guarantee. Yet Descartes apparently affirms, not denies, this dependency. So in the search for indubitable knowledge, Descartes seems to argue in a circle; and in the search for the correct philosophical account of indubitable knowledge, he seems to hold inconsistent views.

The basic strategies for defending Descartes seem to be determined by three main variables: one's view of his psychology or theory of mental activity; one's interpretation of metaphysical certainty and its relation to truth; and one's interpretation of "compelled assent" (*persuasio*) and its relation to metaphysical and moral certainty. The one datum in connection with the third variable is Descartes's unwavering contention that he cannot refrain from believing whatever he clearly and distinctly perceives, so long as he clearly and distinctly perceives it (HR 1:176, 183; K 73, 149; CB 6, as a sampling). Fixing the meaning and role of this pivotal contention is central to discovering the structure of Cartesian method.

Assuming that everything before the God-proof (except perhaps the cogito) is metaphysically dubious, noting that there is plenty of clear and distinct perception prior to establishing the God-conclusion, and not distinguishing clear and distinct perception, natural light perception, and intuition, Feldman holds that clarity and distinctness do not by themselves guarantee metaphysical certainty.[18] Not distinguishing, however, practical certainty from some intermediate notion such as compelled assent (which might lead one to wonder about the relation between compelled assent and metaphysical certainty), he holds that clear and distinct perceptions are (merely) practically certain. To convert practical to metaphysical certainties, he is then obliged to hold that only practical possibilities may be doubtmakers; this we saw to be mistaken. In general, it would seem that any "bootstraps" strategy such as Feldman's must hold that the kind of certainty characteristic of clear and distinct perception—call it X-certainty—is weaker than metaphysical certainty, and that doubtmakers can only be X-possibilities. But if my argument that doubtmakers need only be weak epistemic possibilities is correct, and if metaphysical certainty is immunity to revision by epistemic possibilities (irrevisability), then it follows that the premises of the God-proof must be metaphysically certain. But then, of course, there is no "bootstrapping" at all. A bootstrap strategy rejects the idea that if the premises of the God-proof are metaphysically dubious, so is the conclusion, if circularity is to be avoided. It allows that a single faculty may be vindicated by its own use. The twist is that "self-validation" is easier than we thought, since potential threats to validity are severely restricted. Hence, such a strategy is defensible only if the restriction on potential defeaters is justifiable. Feldman's restriction seems unjustifiable, and so his version of the present strategy seems indefensible.

It is somewhat puzzling that Feldman did not distinguish practical certainty and compelled assent, since several of the true things he says call for such a distinction. Ascriptions of practical certainty imply nothing about the psychological state of a person. Clear and distinct perception does.[19] So the kind of certainty which characterizes clear and distinct perception must not be (merely) practical certainty. And no special insight or talent is needed to gain practical certainty. But Descartes thinks that disciplines studying the simple and universal, lacking existential import, are epistemically better off than those studying composite, existing things (HR 1:147), and that they proceed by the special method of clear and distinct perception. And the atheist geometer's mathematical knowledge is more than practically certain; it is more certain than his knowledge-claims based on sensory evidence. Yet Descartes insists that it is not metaphysically certain. The moral is that it is compelled assent, not practical certainty, whose relations to metaphysical certainty should be examined.

Frankfurt treats intuition, clear and distinct perception, natural-light perception, and reason interchangeably, and views the Cartesian project as one of self-validation, using reason to show that it is irrational to deny the existence of a nondeceiving God, and so irrational to doubt the reliability of reason.[20] The project is not question-begging because the possibility that scrupulous use of reason will generate a reductio ad absurdum is left open. (Yet Frankfurt admits that the ultimate consistency of reason is assumed, since a clear and distinct proof of a good God is assumed to rule out a clear and distinct proof of the opposite conclusion (*Demons*, pp. 177–78).) But to certify reason is not to show that its proper use leads to truth, and in the end, Frankfurt embraces the conclusion that science and revelation pursue noncompeting goals; the former seeks irrevisable opinion (certainty), the latter provides knowledge of absolute truth (ibid., pp. 184–85).

Whatever the flaws in Frankfurt's rendition of Descartes's enterprise, an entirely just insight here is that an eliminative method of doubt, a method which strives to isolate privileged propositions or rules of evidence by rationally destroying all their detractors, cannot show the proposition or rule of evidence to be true, but only irrational to deny. This is a lesson not appreciated by Doney and Gewirth, if I understand their arguments rightly.[21] Gewirth argues (pp. 682–83): "God is a deceiver" supports the denial of the clarity rule only insofar as "God is a deceiver" is clearly and distinctly perceived. "God is a deceiver" is not clearly and distinctly perceived, but its negation is. So there is no support for the denial of the clarity rule. Therefore, the clarity rule is true. Gewirth's use of the *modus tollens* form is illicit. He needs the premise that the clarity rule is false only if "God is a deceiver" is clearly and distinctly perceived, but he only has the premise that the consequent is the only reason for believing that the clarity rule is false. The moral is that evidentiary certainties cannot conclusively destroy semantic doubt. If truth is to be established, it must already be secured at the level of premises. A rational belief in a nondeceiving God cannot convert rational belief into knowably true belief; a knowably true belief in God is needed. To say that all warrant may demand acceptance of a false proposition is just to deny that it must be possible to warrantedly withhold the false, as we did in section I.

Identifying clear and distinct perception with intuition, and noting that intuition guarantees metaphysical certainty, even independently of God, (early) Doney and A. K. Stout conclude that all clear and distinct perceptions are autonomously metaphysically certain; this they tend to equate with the knowledge that all (present) clear and distinct perceptions are true.[22] Since the unmistakable testimony of clear and distinct perception is demon-resistant, the target of hyperbolic doubt is sought elsewhere, in the need to validate the accuracy of memory (under certain conditions). On this strategy, no single faculty is being vindicated by its own use. Although substantially discredited, this interpretation has the merit of properly stressing Descartes's preoccupation with retrospective judgment. The nature of this preoccupation was misunderstood.

Kenny, agreeing that no single mental function can be vindicated by its own use, reads Descartes as using particular intuitions to prove the general proposition that all clear and distinct perceptions are true, which proposition dispels doubts about intuitions generically described and retrospectively induced by the second-order, general reason that one may be created by a deceitful God.[23] Intuitions are logically and psychologically the best way to establish the truth of a proposition, and do not need divine certification. But after the intuition occurs, general doubts about it, under oblique and roundabout descriptions which avoid advertence to its content, may arise. To preclude rational mind-changing about what is once intuited, the clarity rule is established via God. This last feature, the appeal to God to remove the last obstacle to the permanent acceptability of self-evident intuition, strikes me as showing especial sensitivity to Descartes's aims, as I shall soon argue.

Lynn Rose, John Morris, and Peter Schouls rest their interpretations on the claim that clear and distinct perception, natural-light perception, intuition, and reason are not all the same.[24] Schouls notes that reason consists of intuition and deduction, distinguishes intuition of simples and of composites (which are the products of continuous and uninterrupted deductions), and argues that self-certifying simple intuition is used to validate knowledge of what is complex. Rose and Morris treat natural-light perception as a self-certifying species of clear and distinct perception, and for Morris at least, as a faculty of recognizing truth. These strategies relieve the appearance of circularity by arguing that the clear and distinct premises of the God-proof are not of the same sort as those whose reliability depend on God, but are better, autonomous certainties. The key here is to explain fully why the premises are special, how they are demon-resistant, and how, if such is the goal, they are truth-guaranteeing.

A final strategy, suggested by Jaakko Hintikka's process-product model for establishing the indubitability of the cogito, would be to treat compelled assent as a strictly psychological state induced, ceteris paribus, by clear and distinct perception, a mental process. One might then argue that the casual efficacy of clear and distinct perception is neutralized by and only by general worries about whether my entire psychological mechanism is perverted, but that the God-proof forces assent to the God-conclusion, which causally dispels mechanism-anxieties, thereby causally resulting in steadfast irresistable assent to all I clearly and distinctly perceive.[25] There is no circular inference here because there is no two-way inference at all. The clarity rule is not deduced from the God-conclusion; instead, after God is acknowledged, devoted acceptance of the clear and distinct is forced.

A psychological assurance of the clarity rule does nothing to establish its truth. Fanatic acceptance of exclusively false propositions is possible. And one explanation of this misguided fanaticism might be the existence of a demon, who could easily cause the scenario described above. This makes attribution of the strategy to Descartes implausible. Further, the account violates adequacy condition 4. The moral is that compelled assent is not a purely psychological notion.

I have sketched six defenses of Cartesian method which differ largely

as a function of differing interpretations of the roles of key psychological and evidentiary notions, trying to draw morals in each case.
Given all this diversity, the first remarkable thing to appreciate is that
Descartes's own descriptions of the structure of his argument are uni-
formly consistent. The accounts he provided to Regius in 1640 (K 73–
74), even before confrontation with the charge of circularity, to Burman
(CB 1, 6, 81), in the last recorded discussion of the issue, and to the
second-set objectors, Arnauld, and Clerselier in between (HR 2:38–39,
41–43, 115, 130–31) are entirely mutually supportive, and square with
the crucial passages of Meditations III and V (HR 1:158–59, 183–85),
as well as Principle I, 13 (HR 1:224). A consolidated presentation of
these passages goes as follows.

Axioms are used to prove the existence of God. Their truth is self-
evident when, and just as long as, they are clearly and distinctly attended to. The prejudiced, prephilosophical man does not pay attention to them, but as soon as one focuses one's attention on them, considering them abstractly, one cannot doubt them. A person knows he is
not being deceived with regard to them even without knowing that
God exists; even if the demon hypothesis is simultaneously contemplated. Why? Because the mind cannot help assenting to (cannot deny,
cannot doubt, is constrained to admit, is unable to refrain from believing) what it clearly and distinctly perceives. Whatever proofs one
uses, in the end it is only clear and distinct perception which *entirely*
persuades.

So long as I apply my mind to the clear demonstration of a conclusion based on self-evident axioms, it is not possible for me not to
believe it. But as soon as I discontinue attending to the proof, though I
correctly recall having clearly and distinctly comprehended it, I may
come to doubt the truth of the conclusion, just in case I lack the
knowledge that all and only truth has its origin in God, who exists.
Why? Because then I can persuasively entertain the possibility that
by nature I go wrong (am deceived) even in matters which (seem)
are most evident. Since I cannot pay attention to all clear and distinct
perceptions at once, this exaggerated, and in its own right groundless
doubt can frequently intrude. But if a conclusion (theorem) can *at any
time* be doubted—even if there is some currently unexplored reason
which might someday lead us to doubt it—it was *never* scientific knowledge (perfect knowledge, true and immutable science, scientia) in the
first place, but only conviction (compelled assent, persuasio). Science
is conviction based on an unshakable argument, not revisable by future
considerations.

So scientia requires knowledge of God, and the proof from self-certifying axioms of such theological knowledge, which must be clearly

and distinctly perceived in a single, focused attention (intuited, or grasped in its entirety), thereafter guarantees that its conclusion, and all other conclusions correctly recalled as clearly based on clear and distinct premises—whether those premises are recalled or not—are scientia. Full proofs need no longer be reproduced to remove the exaggerated, retrospective doubt about such conclusions. This is so because knowledge of God guarantees me the general rule that *everything* clearly and (very) distinctly perceived is true, which eliminates the residual doubt that perhaps I go wrong even in matters which (seem) are most evident.

I entreat the reader to reexamine all the key passages and observe that the argument's structure is always described as above. Most especially, as concerns the charges of circularity and inconsistency, notice how feeble is the evidence for the claim that knowledge of axioms and first truths depends on knowledge of God. For example, not only does the whole line of argument at the end of Meditation V conform to the outline above, but even the often cited, isolated claim that "the certainty of all other things depends on it (knowledge of God) so absolutely, that without this knowledge it is impossible ever to know anything perfectly," does not conflict with it, since the theological knowledge is said to be required for *perfecte sciri* (AT 7:69), which is repeatedly explicated as *veram & certam scientiam* (AT 7:69), which is enduring, systematic knowledge, not fragmentary, axiomatic knowledge or isolated knowledge of first principles. And in summing up at the end of this meditation, Descartes does not say that "the certainty of all knowledge depends alone on the knowledge of the true God" (HR 1:185), but that *scientiae certitudinem & veritatem* (AT 7:71) depends on (but not only on, since proper method is needed too) knowing God. And that sentence goes on to say that before knowing God, I could not have "perfecte sciri." Even the dialecticians distinguish knowledge of first principles from science (!), and only science is claimed to depend on knowing God; first principles are known per se (HR 2:38).

The same holds for other reputed sources of inconsistency. In Principle XIII Descartes explicitly says that the certainty of conclusions not presently clearly and distinctly perceived is what depends on acquaintance with the creator (HR 1:224), and the passage as a whole echoes the consolidated outline. And at Principle XXX he says that after knowledge of God delivers us from the supreme doubt, the "truths of mathematics should now be above suspicion, for they are the clearest" (HR 1:231). Mathematics is the paradigm of systematic knowledge. And the *theorems* of mathematics are the clearest propositions subject to supreme doubt; surely they are no more clear than the axioms.

The only passage of which I am aware in which phrases such as "scientia" or "perfecte sciri" are not used with respect to a divine dependency claim is the apparently dialectical one early in Meditation III (HR 1:158–59; AT 8:35–36). But even here, unless one insists on reading "I am so persuaded of their truth" (compelled assent) as a psychological claim, and not one of momentary indubitability, Descartes says (by example) that first truths and theorems simple enough to clearly and distinctly perceive are demon-resistant when attended to. And this squares with the opening of that paragraph which states that the only reason for thinking clearly and distinctly perceived, simple mathematical propositions dubious *after* I perceived them was that perhaps I am by nature deceived even in things which seemed to me most manifest.

These are the most credible references to support the view that everything is dubious without knowledge of God, and they come to very little. The passages from "Replies to Objections," private letters, and the conversation with Burman contradict the view in clear-cut ways. Our outline accurately depicts Descartes's intentions; but we must portray and explain it more fully.

When an axiom is clearly and distinctly perceived, it is indubitable; it is demon-resistant, and one knows one is not being deceived with respect to it (pace Frankfurt, with a forthcoming defense). But an axiom is not, as a rule, clearly and distinctly perceived whenever it is entertained.[26] One must focus on it abstractly. To achieve this ability, one must be disabused of prejudices, especially reliance on the senses. This is accomplished by the therapeutic method of doubt set forth in Meditation I: that part of analytic method designed not to establish truth, but to prepare the mind for recognition of truth (HR 2:127, 315). The method of doubt prescribes withholding judgment on everything one is free to reject; if acceptance is optional, do not accept. Since one is *compelled* to assent to clearly perceived axioms, they cannot be withheld or disbelieved, and so are, contemporaneously with their clear apprehension, indubitable. When one attentively and abstractly considers *modus ponens*, for example, one "sees" it is true, and even demonic considerations cannot then dissuade. One is unable to pay heed to the imaginings of one who pretends that what is clearly recognized to be true may appear false to God or an angel (HR 2:41–42).

As regards the momentary certainty of immediate recognition, clear and distinct theorems are on a par with clear and distinct axioms. But axioms are epistemically better off than theorems in that they can be clearly perceived in isolation from other propositions, and there is no gap between occurrent and retrospective assessments of their evidentiary status, so long as we contemplate them with advertence to their content. Axioms are self-evident, or "carry their evidence always with them." But to perceive a theorem clearly and distinctly, you must produce a clear and distinct proof of it; that is why only simple mathematical propositions are instanced as objects of clear and distinct perception of conclusions from axioms.

But when a theorem is correctly recalled to have a presently unrecalled clear and distinct proof (and of course if the existence of such a proof is not even recalled), it is not indubitable, because *now* the theorem is not clearly and distinctly perceived—one is not compelled to believe it in the face of anything—and is made dubious by the epistemic possibility that even the best evidence is inadequate or misleading. Such a doubtmaker questions the consistency and correctness of our entire evidentiary framework, questions whether its meticulous use can lead to discovery of the truth, and is in this sense a second-order doubt. No propositions other than this framework doubt, which is epistemologically equivalent to the imperfect origins (demon) hypothesis, can cast doubt on retrospective clear and distinct judgments. Recognized as clear and distinct, they are realized to provide the best sort of evidence available through natural faculties, and conjoining other *internal* evidence with that fact can never persuade one to withhold. The will cannot refrain from assenting to the recognizably maximally trustworthy and uncorrectable testimony of the understanding; so any suspicion must be retrospective, without reattention to the clear evidence, and external.

Our goal is to secure metaphysical certainty in the sciences, by basing them on firm metaphysical foundations. Scientia requires a vast array of interconnected, fully reliable propositions, since it purports to know the world as a single, ordered, and continuous system, universally and predictably applicable to all future events. Since one cannot simultaneously attend to all clear and distinct perceptions, and so must rely on conclusions of past demonstrations as science grows, such a system is subject to the framework doubt. But then such a system is not really science, which is unshakable or irrevisable compelled assent. Unfaltering assent cannot be won through one's own attentive resources; to dispel the framework doubt some external, systematic guarantee is required.[27] For when I recall the conclusion of a past demonstration and contemplate the threat of framework frailty, I cannot fall back on the original, at-the-time certainty-inducing evidence, since by hypothesis it is presently irretrievable. So the only way of discrediting the single, outstanding, general doubtmaker is by appealing to the general proposition which is its epistemic negation, that everything clearly and distinctly perceived is true in the manner in which I perceive it. But this general proposition can only be derived, and can intuitively be derived, from the knowledge that an absolutely perfect and infinite Being exists. Once such a derivation is effected, everything ever clearly and distinctly perceived becomes fully irrevisable, perfectly certain. Science can now be achieved.

So the only difference between compelled assent and the metaphysical certainty which characterizes scientia is temporal. Compelled assent is as evidentially privileged as metaphysical certainty restricted to the attentive moment. Compelled assent has both an evidential and psychological component, and the former is the normatively causal basis for the latter. In its evidential aspect, to say that I cannot help believing p is to say that now, given the current, recognized state of things, it is inconceivable that p is false. But, I have argued, in the context of the analytic method of discovery, inconceivability is epistemic impossibility. So to say that I cannot help believing p is to say that now, given the current, recognized state of things, it is epistemically impossible for me that p is false. But this is to say that as things recognizably stand now, I have conclusive reason for believing that p is true. No additional, presently accessible consideration could warrant my believing not-p or withholding p.

In general, however, a certainty of the moment does not guarantee the rational constancy definitive of full irrevisability.[28] This is a consequence of Descartes's theories of time, causality, and omnipotence. Time is discrete; each moment of time is independent of every other (HR 1:168; 2:14; K 222). And so a thing which endures through independent, successive moments may at any moment cease to exist (K 232); its present existence does not entail even its immediately subsequent existence (HR 1:227). So continued persistence requires no less a cause than that needed to produce the thing in the first place (HR 2:56). Conservation or sustenance is recreation at each moment. And so an efficient cause cannot merely be temporally prior to its effect; it must be simultaneous with it—existing at the same independent moment of time— also (HR 2:14). So contingent beings, creatures, have a present causal dependency on their creator, which exists per se (HR 2:16), by its own inexhaustible power (HR 2:14). But the infinitely powerful creator is the cause of abstract essences as well as concrete existents (recall the discussion of voluntarism).

The meditator comes to perceive all this clearly and distinctly. Appreciating the creator-sustainer's role and power, it is understood that his nature must be known before the everlasting reliability of a belief can be inferred from its certainty of the moment. That is, since the moments of the history of a persistent are connected by an infinitely powerful external source, fully confident judgment about a span of that history requires knowledge of that source. So to prove by clear and distinct method, without appeal to divine guarantee, that $2 + 3 = 5$, is to prove only that, given the way things are at the time of proof, two and three taken together make no more nor less than five.[29] But numbers are created, contingent essences, and, merely on the basis of clear and distinct perception, one has no epistemic right to infer from their present relations any facts about their future relations. Without knowledge of a nondeceiving, immutable God as their source, it is epistemically possible that presently recognized necessary implications can change. One needs divine guarantee that two and three together *always* form five (HR 1:147).

There seems to be a methodological difficulty here. In general, the present certainty of compelled assent does not entail full irrevisability. But the theological propositions which must be known to defeat the framework doubt are *theorems* just like mathematical conclusions. Yet suppose I use a mathematical conclusion as a lemma for further derivation. As I progress with the derivation, can I not come to doubt the lemma retrospectively, undermining the reliability of its implications? Why not the same for the conclusion that God exists? Why is it not momentarily certain only?

To answer this is to understand why acknowledgment of God is the turning point in the meditative search for permanent knowledge. For to prove that an infinitely perfect being exists *now*, is ipso facto to prove that such a being exists eternally. God is not a changeable, created essence. Necessary and immutable existence is part of God's essence (HR 1:182–83), so if He exists at a moment, He exists eternally. When one clearly and distinctly proves that God exists, that theorem is immediately converted from a momentary certainty to a fully irrevisable one—from persuasio to scientia (K 73). Since God can exist by His own inexhaustible power, He is essentially always existent (HR 2:14). If one understands this, one sees that in the unique case of the God-conclusion, "the truth of what I perceive now holds" is equivalent to "the truth of what I perceive always holds"; no future consideration could overthrow it. That God exists is the first metaphysically certain theorem. And it (strictly, an intuitable implication of it) is used to upgrade to metaphysical certainties all other theorems which constitute persuasio by ruling out the only outstanding epistemic possibility which casts metaphysical doubt on those theorems, the second-order, framework doubt. The recognition of God prevents clear and distinct perceptions from losing their compelling lustre, retrospectively viewed; one's present inability to reproduce their original evidence does not constitute impoverishment of such evidence. The full reliability of past demonstrations needed for the unfrustrated growth of systematic knowledge is thus secured.

To stress the centrality of God's role is not, however, to assert its epistemological primacy. That honor remains with simple intuitions, and we can now understand the reason. Simple intuitions are a special subset of clear and distinct perceptions, namely those that can be grasped fully all at once, and not successively (HR 1:33). These can be divided into three further subsets, the members of which are conceptual, propositional, and existential. Like all objects, they depend ontologically on God. But if they are conceptual entities, they are not explicitly, in the order of recognition, conceptually dependent on anything else. These are the simple notions expressing simple natures (HR 1:40–42; K 113–14; and see my note 1). If they are propositional entities, they express necessary relations obtaining at a moment. These are either immediate implications between particular items, such as "if I think, then I exist," or generalizations immediately recognized on the basis of a particular implication, such as "everything which thinks, exists." These are to be construed as "each time I think, I exist" (HR 1:150, 151–52), and "whenever anything thinks, it exists." The generalization, an innate principle knowable by the natural light, is known implicitly first—it is logically prior—but is brought to explicit awareness via knowledge of the particular, and so is posterior in the (epistemic) order of discovery (CB 4). The particular implications are called "first principles" (HR 2:38), while the generalizations are called "axioms" or "common notions" (HR 1:41, 224; 2:55; CB 1). Finally, if the entities are existential, they are the immediate *objects* of consciousness, thoughts. Thoughts, mental acts, are to be distinguished from ideas, the immediate contents of consciousness, or representations (HR 2:52). Ideas belong to the first subset of intuitions, and necessary connections between them belong to the particular subspecies of the second subset. Whereas there are necessary connections between ideas, there can be no necessary connections between thoughts, given the atomic nature of time.

So there is no more basic or cogent way to prove something than by using simple, intuitive premises. They are formulated in terms of ideas which can be understood by everyone without definition. Some are first and easiest to discover by a careful, unprejudiced investigator, and these facilitate the discovery of the rest. Not only are they, individually, utterly demon-resistant, but they are simple enough to be attentively focused as a set, thereby excluding intrusion of retrospective doubt while proof in terms of them is being conducted. And if retrospectively doubting p requires recalling p in terms of its propositional content, since they express facts of the moment, simple intuitions are perhaps even always immune to retrospective doubt, vacuously since strictly nonrepeatable. (For example, if the sentences "I am thinking" and "I exist" never express the same proposition on two occasions of utterance, and if they never express the same proposition as those expressible by use of the sentences "I was thinking" and "I existed," then the propositions expressed by "I am thinking" and "I exist" are vacuously irrevisable. For God, compelled assent immediately collapsed into irrevisability; for simple intuitions, perhaps irrevisability immediately collapses into compelled assent.)[30]

As regards truth, in canvassing basic strategies earlier, I argued that if known truth, and not just evidential certainty, was to be established anywhere in the Cartesian system, it would have to be secured at the level of premises. But how could simple intuitions be truth-guaranteeing? That Descartes thinks some are seems unproblematic. "[T]here can exist in us no thought of which, at the very moment that it is present in us, we are not conscious" (HR 2:115; also 105 and other more familiar passages). But our consciousness of our thoughts (but not of our selves) is immediate, not representational. Our knowledge of our thoughts is, for Descartes, *de re* knowledge by acquaintance. That mental states occur in us is something we can directly know to be true. So the third, existential class of intuitions are truth-entailing because reality-presenting. What about ideas? "[I]f we consider them only in themselves and do not relate them to anything else beyond themselves, they cannot properly speaking be false"; the idea is the idea it is even when representationally false, and we can know what idea it is (HR 1:159). We do not represent representatives; representations are presented to us. But if conceptual entities comprising the first class of simples are given, then perhaps immediately perceived connections between such entities, first principles, are known by acquaintance. And if the axioms are thought *in* the first principles (CB 4), they too may enjoy immediately recognizable truth.[31] Such might be the tack that a defender of Descartes's project as the search for *truth* would take.[32]

Finally, notice that, although I failed to adjudicate decisively between competing accounts of metaphysical certainty, I have been operating with an irrevisability account—sometimes in a truth-entailing way, sometimes not. And shelving the desirability of including a truth condition, recall that a proposition is irrevisable for a person at a time if and only if he is then justified in believing it, and his justification is immune to rational overthrow by any epistemic possibility from then on; belief in irrevisable propositions is conclusively justified. At the same time, when I outlined Descartes's argument, I followed him in freely shifting from one description of certainty to another. Yet, in the abstract, the accounts suggested by the various descriptions were provably distinct.

The fact is, that if we apply the systematically supported trend toward construing most pre-God modality talk epistemically, and remain sensitive to some basic Cartesian doctrine, unmistakability and maximal warrant are equivalent to irrevisability. For then to say that I cannot be mistaken about p at t is just to say that it is epistemically impossible for me at t that I believe p falsely. But recall that p is epistemically possible for S at t just in case S lacks conclusive reasons for believing not-p at t. So I cannot be mistaken about p at t just in case it is false that I lack, that is, true that I have, conclusive reasons for believing not-p—instantiating, just in case I have conclusive reasons for believing I do not believe p falsely. But given the natural assumption that what is at stake for Descartes is not the occurrence of belief, as opposed to some other mental state, but only *what* I believe, this says that I have conclusive reasons for believing p is true, which is irrevisability. So when "cannot" is understood epistemically, unmistakability is equivalent to irrevisability.

What about maximal warrant? Suppose that, after the existence of a benevolent God has been established, I clearly and very distinctly, but not fully distinctly, and so not "adequately," perceive that p. Then a more distinct perception of p is yet possible. Nevertheless, I may have a sufficient basis for p rationally to resist all legitimate challenges to its credibility (HR 2:97). If we say that the more distinct perception provides more warrant, then maximal warrant is distinct from, and superior to, irrevisability. But if the best evidence is conclusive evidence, if anything more is justificatorily valueless overkill, then maximal warrant is equivalent to irrevisability. If rationally appreciated, one good argument is as good as ten; enough is enough.

The issue boils down to whether or not warrant is a quantitative notion for Descartes. If it is, then since conclusive warrant need not be exhaustive warrant, more warrant than conclusive warrant is possible. In other words, if it is, maximal warrant would have to be exhaustive warrant, which could only be the result of "adequate" perception. Now adequate perception is possible—though it cannot be known by the perceiver to be possessed (HR 2:97, CB 14)—but it is not necessary for metaphysical knowledge. Clear and very distinct perception, the product of methodical use of my most trustworthy and naturally uncorrectable faculty, suffices (post-God) for metaphysical knowledge. Hence, if warrant is not a quantitative notion, so that forever sufficient evidence constitutes full metaphysical certainty, then maximal warrant is equivalent to irrevisability. If a quantitative rendition of warrant were adopted, there would be very few metaphysical certainties indeed, and nothing could be known to be a metaphysical certainty. At least the first of these consequences is un-Cartesian. Hence, maximal warrant is equivalent to irrevisability.

Metaphysical certainty is irrevisability; compelled assent is momentary irrevisability. Revisers need only be epistemic possibilities. Follow this outline of Descartes's argument with continuous, uninterrupted attention, and you will see that Cartesian method is neither circular nor inconsistent:

(1) If I clearly and (very) distinctly perceive p at t, then I am compelled to assent to p at t.

(2) If I am compelled to assent to p at t, then p is indubitable for me at t.

$\overline{(3)}$ If I clearly and distinctly perceive an axiom at t, then that axiom is indubitable (demon-resistant) for me at t. (1,2)

(4) If I focus my attention on an axiom, I clearly and distinctly perceive it. (Doubt therapy disabuses reliance on the sensory and allows such focused consideration.)

$\overline{(5)}$ If I focus my attention on an axiom, it is then indubitable for me. (3,4)

(6) If I clearly and distinctly perceive a theorem at t, then that theorem is indubitable for me at t. (1,2)

(7) I clearly and distinctly perceive a theorem at t if and only if I provide a continuous and uninterrupted clear and distinct proof for that theorem at t.

(8) I can know *that* a theorem has been clearly and distinctly perceived without now clearly and distinctly perceiving it.

(9) When I do not clearly and distinctly perceive a theorem, even if I remember having clearly and distinctly perceived it, that theorem is dubious if and only if it is an epistemic possibility for me that even the best evidence is not a reliable guide to truth.

(10) Scientia requires the indubitability of past demonstrations—I cannot attend to every lemma as the system of knowledge grows (scientia is not isolated, axiomatic certainties).

$\overline{(11)}$ Scientia requires removal of the (second-order) epistemic possibility that even the best evidence—that of clear and distinct perception—is misleading or inadequate. (9,10) (This possibility is epistemologically equivalent to the possibility of inferior ("demonic") origins.)

(12) At t, I provide a continuous and uninterrupted, clear and distinct proof for the theorem that God, an infinitely perfect substance (eternal, immutable, omniscient, omnipotent, and creator of all things [if any] which are outside me), exists.

$\overline{(13)}$ At t, that God exists at t is indubitable for me. (6,7,12)

(14) If God exists at t, then God eternally and immutably exists. (12)

$\overline{(15)}$ At t, that God eternally and immutably exists is indubitable, that

is, fully irrevisable for me. (13, 14; there is an immediate con-
version from "the truth of what I perceive now holds" to "the
truth of what I perceive always holds.")

(16) I go on to indubitably prove that given that God is not a deceiver, and is the cause of all positive reality, since all clear and
distinct perceptions are positively real, they must be true.

(17) If it is indubitable that all clear and distinct perceptions are
true, then it is epistemically impossible that the best evidence
(the evidence of clear and distinct perception) is not a reliable
guide to truth.

(18) It is epistemically impossible that the best evidence is inadequate
or misleading. (16,17)

(19) Once clearly and distinctly deduced, all theorems are indubitable
so long as there is correct record of the deduction. (9,18)

(20) By the method of clear and distinct perception, born of the
method of doubt, perfect knowledge (scientia) may be achieved.

This line of argument is neither circular nor inconsistent. And it is
dogmatic only if a radical epistemological solipsism of the moment
is dogmatic. The threat to the strategy is the claim that the deduction
from axioms to the clarity rule cannot be continuously attended to—
it is too long—and so the theorem that God exists becomes dubious
when its further implications are being elicited. I think Descartes's
response would be that until you clearly and distinctly realize the implications of God's existence, the final epistemically possible doubtmaker is not ruled out, and that is why you have to meditate seriously
and repeatedly before you succeed (HR 1:135, 139). Achieving indubitable knowledge of the truth requires strenuous application of the
mind. "But all things excellent are as difficult as they are rare."[33]

NOTES

I thank Scott Shuger for helpful discussions on many of the topics of this paper.
My primary source of Latin expertise is Debora Shuger.

1. Some may balk at the attempt, citing Descartes's claim that certainty is among
the simple notions, not subject to definition (HR 1:222). Leonard Miller goes so far
as to urge that we cannot attribute any property to a simple, since a thing with a
property is composite (see his "Descartes, Mathematics, and God," *The Philosophical
Review* 66 [1957]:451–65). I think such resistance rests on a misunderstanding. First,
simples are nominally definable (K 65–66). What Descartes repudiates is real definition of something's nature by the Aristotelian method of genus and specific difference (HR 1:324; K 66), which he rejects for all notions, including complex ones
such as "man" (HR 1:150). He replaces this method by one which explains things
in terms of the properties expressed by simple notions—simple natures—and their
interrelations (HR 1:40–43). So simple notions are interconnected.

Second, it is always a mistake to define a simple in terms of a complex, or define a simple of one class in terms of a simple of another class (K 138). Some simples express transcendental properties, applicable to substances of all categories, some express ubiquitous physical properties, and some express mental properties (HR 1: 41). The attempt to use a notion of one class to explain the essence of something expressed by a notion of another class inevitably leads to error. This does not entail that no, nontrivial, essential connections between simple natures of a single class hold. In fact, third, there are essential connections between simples, such as figure and extension (HR 1:42). And there are very powerful indications that simple notions can stand in analytic relations. Minimally, privative and negative terms are expressly included among simples (HR 1:42), and surely the relation between a notion and its negation is analytic. And the fact that thought is itself a simple does not require that modes of thought be sui generis (K 138). On the contrary, Descartes says that knowledge and doubt, for example, are analytically incompatible (HR 2:276).

It may be complained that these examples exhibit only a trivial, nominal sort of (partial) interdefinability, and so do not reveal genuine complexity in the concepts involved. But even if simples lack conceptual complexity, so that composites are ultimately generated out of synthetic relations of necessity and incompatibility— since at least one term of an analytic relation must be complex—it is indisputable that they stand in necessary connections. And we still give an account by displaying these connections, as the synthetic postulates of a science may implicitly or contextually define the fundamental notions of that science. Descartes says that simples are necessarily connected "when one is so implied in the concept of another in a confused sort of way that we cannot conceive either distinctly, if our thought assigns to them separateness from each other" (HR 1:42). Whether such talk relates simples analytically or synthetically, it does not seem to ban the clarificatory effort I aim to make.

At bottom, Descartes's point is merely the conceptual analyst's point that, before we systematically interconnect basic ideas, we have an independent understanding of those ideas; this is what he suggests to Mersenne (K 65). No simple is conceptually dependent on anything else; each can be understood alone. But its being understandable apart from its relations does not imply that necessary connections cannot obtain between it and others. Descartes's attitude toward mental simples is the same as Locke's toward simple ideas of reflection (*An Essay Concerning Human Understanding*, II, ch. 6). Each simple is conceptually independent because each can be understood by direct introspection (HR 1:325). Simplicity is more a phenomenological notion than an analytic one.

Finally, Miller's claim that simples must be propertyless since all propertied things are composite is radically ambiguous. If "property" is being used in Descartes's sense, then only substances have properties (and all substances have at least one property—their essence or principal attribute) (HR 1:240; 2:53, K 257). And in the sense of "simple" appropriate to substances, a simple substance, a mind, can have various properties. If an entity has a property just in case something is true of it, then simple ideas do have properties—for example, the property of having objective or representative reality—but it would be bizarre to regard this as a detraction on simplicity. A nonpropertied idea would then be a vacuous one, but a vacuous idea could not play the role intended for simples, which are fundamental concepts in terms of which scientific description and explanation is conducted.

2. Condition (1) is not meant to preclude that the *objects* of clear and distinct perception have notable characteristics, there to be discovered. Commentators such as Merrill Ring ("Descartes' Intentions," *Canadian Journal of Philosophy* 3 (1973): 27–49; see esp. p. 46) and Mike Marlies ("Doubt, Reason and Cartesian Therapy," ch. 5, below), who view Cartesian method as a therapeutic process of removing prejudicial debris so as to uncover the innate knowledge that was waiting to shine forth, seem to construe certainty as a property of propositions. So long as it is a dispositional property, whose discovery is relativized to person and time, this will count as satisfaction of adequacy condition (1).

3. For example, Robert Alexander, in "The Problem of Metaphysical Doubt and its Removal," in R. J. Butler, ed. *Cartesian Studies* (Oxford: Basil Blackwell, 1972), pp. 106–22, especially 107–9, holds this view, and in fact the more general view that all certainties are logical necessities.

4. For CB, marginal no., not book page no., is provided.

5. Note that the truth of the converse of condition 6, that metaphysical certainty implies knowledge of some sort, must not be imposed as an adequacy condition. If knowledge entails truth for Descartes, the converse condition would imply that certainty entails truth, which would beg the question against commentators such as Harry Frankfurt. See his *Demons, Dreamers, and Madmen* (Indianapolis: Bobbs-Merrill, 1970), or his "Descartes' Validation of Reason," *American Philosophical Quarterly* 2 (1965):149–56.

6. Frankfurt, *Demons*, especially ch. 3 and 12; and his "Philosophical Certainty," *The Philosophical Review* 71 (1962):303–27. Other notable epistemologists, such as Nelson Goodman in "Sense and Certainty," *The Philosophical Review* 61 (1952):161, treat certainty this way.

Many contemporary epistemologists, to expel the wedge between evidence and truth imposed by Russell-Gettier type of counterexamples to justified true-belief analyses of knowledge, have similarly traveled the road to indefeasibility. It has been suggested that knowledge requires justification which would be preserved even if new, justified true beliefs were acquired, or stronger, even if (for the sake of argument) some additional truth were assumed. Although these indefeasibility conditions are weaker than Cartesian irrevisability, it can be shown that they nevertheless render the account of ordinary empirical knowledge unreasonably stringent. This is argued in an unpublished manuscript, "The Epistemic Role of Certainty, Extendability, and Indefeasibility," jointly authored by Scott Shuger and myself.

7. For example, Israel Scheffler, in *Science and Subjectivity* (Indianapolis: Bobbs-Merrill, 1967), pp. 115–16, holds that everything synthetic is revisable. The proposed objection is lodged by Marshall Swain against a suggested analysis of knowledge in his "Epistemic Defeasibility," *American Philosophical Quarterly* 11 (1974):16.

8. Fred Feldman, "Epistemic Appraisal and the Cartesian Circle," *Philosophical Studies* 27 (1975):37–55. See sect. 1 for the development of the thesis, and sect. 2 for the reconstruction based on it.

9. The interpretation of the demon hypothesis is controversial. Some regard the demon as (a) epistemologically equivalent to a deceiving God, and consequently as omnipotent; some as (b) an extremely powerful and cunning malign spirit, but not omnipotent; some as (c) equivalent to the supposition of nondivine origins, origins from chance, evolution, or an imperfect creator; and some as (d) just a heuristic device to disabuse prejudice. The benevolent-God conclusion would be the contrary of the demon hypothesis on (a), would be its contradictory on (c), and would stand in no straightforward, logical relations to the hypothesis on (b) and (d). Two data seem to be that (1) proof of the existence of a nondeceiving God removes hyperbolic, demonic doubt, and (2) the recognized certainty of the cogito does not. It might be argued that (1) counts against (b), since omnipotent benevolence is compatible with the existence of nonomnipotent malevolence—witness theological explanations of evil in terms of the devil; and that (2) counts against (a), since the indubitability of the cogito shows that wholly systematic deception cannot succeed. I think the demon is treated as an imperfect-origins hypothesis, not only because of its neater logical relation to the benevolent-God conclusion, but because in both the French and Latin editions (vol. 9 and 7 of AT), Descartes typically presents the hyperbolic doubt in terms of his constitutional tendency to *fool himself* in matters which seem most evident, and not in terms of externally induced error. But of course on interpretation (c) the hyperbolic doubtmaker does not seem logically impossible. Appearances notwithstanding, Descartes does argue that it is impossible (HR 1:167–70), although not explicitly so. And recall that for the voluntarist Descartes, logical possibility is ordained, not absolute possibility.

10. Anthony Kenny, *Descartes: A Study of His Philosophy* (New York: Random House, 1968), p. 192.

11. The criticism appears in Fred Feldman and Arnold Levison, "Anthony Kenny and the Cartesian Circle," *Journal of the History of Philosophy* 9 (1971):495–96, with Kenny's response on pp. 497–98.

12. The rest of this paragraph summarizes pp. 9–12 of Roderick Firth's excellent article, "The Anatomy of Certainty," *The Philosophical Review* 76 (1967):3–27.

13. "Epistemic Appraisal and the Cartesian Circle," p. 43. Although Feldman characterizes metaphysical certainty this way, he seems to operate with a brand of irrevisability—indefeasibility by practical possibilities—as, for example, his principle (9) suggests, pp. 45–46. Bertrand Russell gives a maximal warrant analysis of certainty in *Human Knowledge: Its Scope and Limits* (New York: Simon and Schuster, 1948), p. 396, and suggests a closely related minimal dubitability account in *An Outline of Philosophy* (New York: Meridian, 1960), ch. 16.

14. Williams's quotation is from the 'Rene Descartes' entry in Paul Edwards, ed., *The Encyclopedia of Philosophy* (New York: Macmillan & The Free Press, 1967), 2:346. Alexander's article is cited in n. 4. John Morris's treatment of certainty is indicated in his "Descartes' Natural Light," *Journal of the History of Philosophy* 11 (1973):169–87. See H. A. Prichard's account of the relation between certainty and unmistakability in Descartes in his "Descartes's *Meditations*," in Willis Doney, ed., *Descartes: A Collection of Critical Essays* (Garden City, 1967), pp. 140–68. And see the excerpt from A. J. Ayer's *The Problem of Knowledge* reprinted in ibid., pp. 80–87, for one of several variations on the unmistakability theme: p's truth is entailed by the fact that p is doubted. But this is surely not a necessary condition for certainty, since most subjective reports, such as "I seem to see a light," fail to satisfy it.

15. It may be urged that Williams identified certainties with "beliefs whose truth *is in some way guaranteed* by the fact that they are believed"; perhaps he had in mind the sort of performatory or pragmatic guarantee involved in some discussions of self-affirming or self-verifying beliefs. Roughly, a proposition is "self-verifying" in this sense if it is verified by some inescapable aspect of its assertion. But for reasons given in n. 14, this cannot be a necessary condition of certainty.

16. I omit needlessly complicating discussion of some influential commentators here. For example, Edwin B. Allaire, in "The Circle of Ideas and the Circularity of the *Meditations*," *Dialogue* 2 (1966):131–53, argues not only that "true" is ambiguously used by Descartes to mean both "represents" and "indubitable," but that there is no univocal account of indubitability either. As regards conditional propositions, he counts them certain if and only if their negations are inconceivable (alternatively for Allaire, do not express an idea), which he equates with the proposition's being analytic. This is dubious, and if simples are analytically indefinable, wrong. But what is interesting for our present concerns is that inconceivability is treated logically, not epistemically. Also, I am not confident that I understand Alan Gewirth's view ("The Cartesian Circle," *The Philosophical Review* 50 (1941):368–95; and "The Cartesian Circle Reconsidered," *The Journal of Philosophy* 67 (1970):668–85) well enough to discuss it. He sometimes says that metaphysical certainty *is* truth ("Cartesian Circle," p. 378), rather than that it merely guarantees truth. Even if metaphysical doubt is a semantic doubt, it seems implausible to construe metaphysical certainty as truth. Such an account would violate nearly every adequacy condition I proposed. Gewirth's actual argument treats metaphysical certainty as guaranteeing truth, and not as identical with it. What truth-entailing account he has in mind, I cannot discover.

17. I shall not discuss another, alleged, "smaller" circle, in which the clarity rule is derived from the cogito, whereas the truth of the cogito is derived from the rule. It seems to me that neither derivation is made by Descartes. When he first discovers the clarity rule by reflecting on the certainty of the cogito, he says that it seems (*videor*) as if he is already in a position to establish it as universally applicable (HR 1:158; AT 7:35). But he immediately challenges this induction on the basis of

one instance, and argues that the general rule requires divine certification (HR 1: 158–59; AT 7:35–36). And there is no indication that the cogito is derived by appeal to indubitability-conferring characteristics. It is recognized as the first proposition immune to, because required by, attempts at systematic doubt, or any meditative process.

18. Feldman, "Epistemic Appraisal and the Cartesian Circle," esp. pp. 40–41.

19. The view that a clear and distinct understanding produces an irresistable inclination of the will (to judge accordingly) (HR 1:176; K 149) does not seem implausible to me. It is at least a normative truth that if one fully recognizes necessary connections, including simple entailments, one is induced to affirm the necessity. Can any normal person deny that if p and q are true, then p is true?

20. Demons, especially ch. 15, and "Descartes' Validation of Reason." Frankfurt also identifies clear and distinct perception, intuition and reason in his "Memory and the Cartesian Circle," The Philosophical Review 71 (1962):504–11; see pp. 504–5.

21. Willis Doney, "Descartes' Conception of Perfect Knowledge," Journal of the History of Philosophy 8 (1970):387–403. Gewirth, "The Cartesian Circle Reconsidered."

22. Willis Doney, "The Cartesian Circle," Journal of the History of Ideas 16 (1955):324–38; A. K. Stout, 'The Basis of Knowledge in Descartes," in Doney, Descartes, pp. 169–91.

23. Kenny, Descartes, ch. 8, and "The Cartesian Circle and the Eternal Truths," The Journal of Philosophy 67 (1970):685–700; see pp. 687–90.

24. Lynn E. Rose, "The Cartesian Circle"; "Reply to Mr. Kretzmann," Philosophy and Phenomenological Research 26 (1965):80–89, 93. Peter Schouls, "Descartes and the Autonomy of Reason," Journal of the History of Philosophy 10 (1972):307–22; Morris, "Descartes' Natural Light."

25. To say this strategy is suggested by Hintikka's in "Cogito, Ergo Sum: Inference or Performance?" (see Doney, Descartes, pp. 108–39, e.g. p. 122) is more to report what caused me to devise it than to claim formal analogy. After this paper was written, but before it went to press, Ronald Rubin's "Descartes' Validation of Clear and Distinct Apprehension," The Philosophical Review 86 (1977):197–208, appeared, proposing much the same strategy.

26. Some axioms may be exceptions to this rule. Descartes in one place suggests that we cannot help believing some axioms whenever we directly think about them (HR 2:42). But if compelled assent is, prior to knowing God, produced by present clear and distinct perception only, then these axioms must be clearly and distinctly perceived whenever directly thought about. If there are such exceptions, presumably they are not the axioms needed for the God-proof. Otherwise, therapeutic doubt would be superfluous.

27. Compare Hume and Berkeley on continued and uninterrupted existence. See Hume, A Treatise of Human Nature, bk. I, pt. 4, sect. 2. For Berkeley, the theme recurs in both The Principles of Human Knowledge, and Three Dialogues Between Hylas and Philonous.

28. The distinction between momentary certainty and full irrevisability is, I think, the same as that drawn by another Cartesian meditator, Husserl, between "absolute certainty" and "apodictic evidence," in section 6 of the "First Meditation" of his Cartesian Meditations. Absolute certainty excludes every doubt, but does not entail excluding the conceivability that what is evident could subsequently become doubtful. Apodictic evidence does have that exclusionary entailment.

29. If one holds that compelled assent and irrevisability differ only in their rational constancy, then if irrevisability is truth-guaranteeing, compelled assent is also. This gives rise to a substantial difficulty. How can mathematical judgments, based on present clear and distinct perception, guarantee even momentary truth, when the objects of such judgments, mathematical entities, are mind-independent objects of indirect representation, and all indirect representative knowledge requires divine guarantee, by hypothesis not yet available? It is representative knowledge that requires divine guarantee, so that treating numbers as created essences, nonexistent things which have essences, etc., instead of as somehow dependent on corporeal

nature, fails to alleviate the difficulty. (For a concise summary of the main interpretations, and defenses of the realist interpretation of Descartes's philosophy of mathematics, see Gewirth, "The Cartesian Circle Reconsidered," and Kenny, "The Cartesian Circle and the Eternal Truths.") The evidence for realism is considerable, and needs to be explained by an interpreter who cites passages such as Principle I. 57, in which Descartes says that "number and all universals are simply modes of thought" (HR 1:242), as proof of Descartes's conceptualism. The point is that one seems committed to conceptualism in holding that simple mathematical propositions can be clearly and distinctly perceived, that the momentary authority of intuition is no better than that of present clear and distinct perception, and that intuition guarantees momentary truth. Then you just treat essence-talk adverbially, and claim that one can recognize how the mind structures things by clearly and distinctly attending to it, but note that perhaps the most careful application of this recognitional procedure will give different testimony about the relations between ideas at different times. Since such vicissitudes would undermine the coherent connectability of scientific results, the appeal to God as creator of a trustworthy mind would be required for scientia.

Why should Descartes be a realist? Mathematical ideas are not adventitious, and so we do not need essences with causal or explanatory efficacy; Descartes rejects scientific explanation in terms of substantial forms anyway. Mathematical ideas are innate (K 104). Now, of course, not all innate ideas are just ways of thinking, signifying nothing outside themselves, since the idea of God is innate. But obviously this is not a telling case, since God is the cause of *all* positive reality. And it is not as if the mathematical entities stand in utterly independent, eternal relations; they are ontologically contingent creatures (voluntarism), just as our minds are. Given voluntarism, what essential epistemological role does the mind-independence of numbers play?

30. Note that my stress on the momentary force of compelled assent, prior to the proof that a nondeceiving God exists and is no deceiver in Meditations III and IV, implies that in Meditation II, the thinker, if he is not just identified with his thoughts, is a substance as substratum, not a substance as continuant. The natural-light principle that an attribute requires a substance treats substance as substratum, which is how "substance" is, typically, officially defined (HR 2:53). "Substance" is sometimes defined as "independent existent," or "created substance" as "existent needing no other thing in order to exist except God" (HR 1:239, 240), but never as "continuant." A persisting self is not yet indubitable in Meditation II.

31. Morris, in "Descartes' Natural Light," provocatively traces the passive, receptive, recognitional manner in which natural-light apprehension occurs.

32. One might try to explain the special semantic status of axioms (and so those used in the God-proof) as follows. All possibility and necessity concerning created essences is conditional on God's ordination, but what is incompatible or required by His uncreated essence is absolutely impossible or necessary. (This restricted voluntarism is ascribed to Descartes by Martial Gueroult, *Decartes selon l'ordre des raisons* (Paris: Aubier, 1953), 2:26–29, as cited by Harry G. Frankfurt in "Descartes on the Creation of the Eternal Truths," *The Philosophical Review* 86 (1977):36–57. Frankfurt rejects the restriction.) Axioms, unlike the truths of mathematics, the laws of motion, and the truths of morality, are absolutely necessary. For example, though particular causal laws depend on God's will, the mechanism of efficient causation does not; God could not make His will causally inefficacious. Similarly, it is absolutely necessary that what is done is done, and cannot be undone. God cannot retrieve a supremely willed past state of the universe (CB 50). It would be a violation of immutability and omnipotence if the past were changed. Even if all this is true, however, a *pre*-God meditator (see n. 30) cannot be metaphysically certain of it. To take account of this, it might be argued that any system, whether it is divine or demonic, requires the truth of the axioms; they are presuppositions of any framework whatsoever.

33. The final sentence of Spinoza's *Ethics*.

A Discourse

on Descartes's Method

JAAKKO HINTIKKA

DESCARTES BELIEVED that ancient mathematicians had suppressed their chief method of discovery "with a certain pernicious craftiness, just as we know many inventors have suppressed their discoveries, being very much afraid that to publish this method . . . would make it seem worthless" (*Regulae*: HR 1:12; AT 10:376). But was this self-confessed secretive man any more candid himself? The actual rules listed in the second part of the *Discourse* are but pale shadows of the *Regulae*, which Descartes never completed and which were never published during his lifetime. But even from the *Regulae*, the import of Descartes's method is not immediately clear or distinct. What *is* Descartes's method, which was so dramatically revealed to him in his famous dream and which he valued so highly? What does it amount to in his actual scientific or philosophical work?

In this paper I shall argue for a familiar and apparently unexciting answer to this question about Descartes's own method: I shall suggest that it can be profitably considered as a variant of the method of analysis which was used in Greek mathematics and whose discovery was ascribed by some sources to Plato. There does not seem to be anything surprising or novel in this suggestion. Indeed, it turns out that it is largely just this analytical method that Descartes accused (as we saw) the Greek mathematicians of having hidden. (This is shown by Descartes's "Reply to Objections II," in HR 2:49.) The epithet "analytic" commonly associated with Descartes's own geometry referred originally to his use and systematization of the Greek method of analysis rather than to the use of "analytic" tools in any of the several modern senses of the word, e.g., by reference to "higher" analysis, by reference to "analytic," i.e., algebraic and equational methods, or by reference to "analytic" functions. Descartes himself acknowledged that in *Meditations on the First Philosophy* he had used "only analysis, which is the best and truest method of teaching" (HR 2:49). In his replies to objections (to the *Meditations*) as well as in these objections themselves, Descartes and his adversaries several times refer as a matter of course to his "analysis." (See HR 2:234, 256–57, 324, 352.)

Moreover, Descartes's reliance on the method of analysis seems to be only a special case of a much more widespread use of this method by all the leading philosopher-scientists of the early modern period. Galileo's method has often been described as consisting of "resolution and composition," and in the famous Query 23/31 in the second English edition of his *Opticks*, Newton emphatically formulates his own method by reference to apparently the same method:

As in Mathematicks, so in Natural Philosophy, the Investigation of difficult Things by the Method of Analysis, ought ever to precede the Method of Composition. This Analysis consists in Making Experiments and Observations, and drawing general Conclusions from them by Induction, and admitting no Objections against the Conclusions, but such as are taken from Experiments, or other certain Truths. For Hypotheses are not to be regarded in experimental Philosophy. . . . By this way of Analysis we may proceed from Compounds to Ingredients, and from Motions to Forces producing them; and in general, from Effects to their Causes. . . . This is the Method of Analysis: And the Synthesis consists in assuming the Causes discover'd, and establish'd as Principles, and by them explaining the Phaenomena proceeding from them, and proving the Explanations.

We shall have occasion to return to this Newtonian statement later. It is clear that Newton thinks of his own work in the *Opticks* and in his investigations into other difficult things as having proceeded by the method of analysis.

In view of all this direct and indirect evidence, why has this diagnosis of Descartes's method as a variant of the old method of analysis been so frequently rejected or at least underemphasized recently? The basic reason seems to be that the nature of the method of analysis as it was preached and practiced by Greek mathematicians has not been understood clearly enough. Among other things, the difficulties that there are in the practice of the method and in attempts to describe it in precise philosophical and logical terms have not been appreciated sufficiently keenly. As a consequence, the difference between the geometrical method of analysis and certain other techniques which have been given similar labels has not been kept in mind by philosophers and historians, nor have they been able to master the perplexing multiplicity of different directions into which the old geometrical method was developed in the early modern period. As a consequence, the recognition of the analytic character of Descartes's method has not served to illuminate his thought in the way it could do. An extreme example of the desperation to which scholars have been driven by these failures is perhaps Gerd Buchdahl's attempt to distinquish several allegedly entirely different senses of "analysis" in Descartes.[1]

Yet one can easily sympathize with the frustration of many scholars and philosophers with the simple identification of Descartes's method with the analytic one. For it is not always the clear, positive aspects of the legendary Greek method that help us to understand Descartes's methodological struggles, but often rather the ambiguities and difficulties with which this method was inflicted.

What do we actually know of the Greek method? Not very much, yet enough to disprove the paranoid theory of intentional secrecy on the part of the Greeks held by Descartes and his contemporaries. The only extensive, explicit description of the method is found in Pappus. It goes as follows:

Now analysis is the way from what is sought—as if it were admitted—through its concomitants, in their order, to something admitted in synthesis. For in analysis we suppose that which is sought to be already done, and we inquire from what it results, and again what is the antecedent of the latter, until we on our backward way light upon something already known and being first in order. . . . In synthesis, on the other hand, we suppose that which was reached last in analysis to be already done, and arranging in their natural order as consequents the former antecedents and linking them one with another, we in the end arrive at the construction of the thing sought. And this we call synthesis."[2]

Pappus goes on to distinguish two kinds of analysis, theoretical and problematical. In the former, we search for a proof of a theorem, in the latter for a construction to solve a problem. He then characterizes briefly these two kinds of analysis.

What are the interpretational difficulties connected with this description of the method of analysis and synthesis? How was this method developed so as to yield the methods of Descartes and Newton? I have previously discussed, with Unto Remes, the interpretation of the ancient method. Here I can only summarize some of the main points, trying to relate them to Descartes.[3]

(1) It may appear that Pappus is describing a kind of hypothetico-deductive method in mathematical heuristics. According to this construal of method, one assumes in following it the desired theorem (or assumes the desired construction to have already been accomplished) and studies step by step the logical consequences of this assumption. However, the only consistent (or almost consistent) interpretation of

Pappus's statement is to take him to say that analysis consists in looking for premises from which the desired result can be deduced.[4]

This fact is far from obvious, however, and in many later discussions there is considerable confusion on this point. Nor is Pappus himself completely free from confusion, as his statement concerning the different possible outcomes of theoretical and problematical analysis shows. If analysis consists in looking for suitable premises, eventually reaching an established truth suffices to prove the desired result. If analysis consists of a sequence of inferences, reaching an impossibility disproves it. Both of these cannot hold, however, contrary to what Pappus seems to say, unless analysis consists of a series of equivalences. But this can be excluded by collateral evidence. And even in the best of circumstances, the convertibility of all the steps of analysis can only be established afterwards in the synthesis.

This uncertainty concerning the direction of analysis in Pappus reappears in many later descriptions and applications of the method of analysis.

(2) A further complication is that Pappus's logical and philosophical description of analysis agrees neither with his own mathematical practice nor with Greek mathematical practice in general. In that practice, a geometer assumed the conjunction of earlier theorems, an instantiated form of the antecedent of the general implication that a geometrical theorem is, and a correspondingly instantiated conclusion of the implication, and examined the joint consequences of these three.

Then there is, of course, no certainty that the process can be inverted or otherwise transformed into a proof of the desired theorem. This explains an important part of Pappus's description as well as the corresponding feature of ancient mathematicians' practice, namely, the fact that in ancient mathematics analysis was typically followed by a synthesis, that is, an ordinary deductive proof of the theorem. Indeed, we perhaps ought to speak of the method of analysis and synthesis rather than just of the method of analysis. Descartes himself registers in the passing the fact that in geometry synthesis finds a place after analysis.

Descartes apparently thinks of analysis as consisting of deductive inferences. This is strongly suggested by a comparison of Descartes's description of his *Meditations* as proceeding analytically with his statement in the *Regulae* (HR 1:43; AT 10:421–22) that the connection expressed in "I exist, therefore God exists" is a necessary one, and likewise for "I think, therefore I have a mind distinct from the body." He also indicates, in the same place, that the converse implications do not hold. Hence, the steps of analysis cannot be merely converted in order to obtain the synthesis, according to Descartes.

It is especially tempting to view Descartes's procedure in the *Meditations* as analysis in the light of the widespread view (which we have seen formulated by Newton) that in an analysis one moves "from effects to their causes." Descartes proceeds from the certainty of his existence as uncovered in the cogito insight to the idea that his essence is thinking. How and why? Highly interesting light is thrown on this step by Descartes's identification of the essence of any one thing with a kind of efficient cause of its being, albeit in an extended sense of the word (HR 2:110). (A little later, HR 2:112, Descartes runs together the formal cause of a thing and its essential nature.) This squares particularly well with my "performative" interpretation of the cogito, according to which Descartes in his insight as it were produces the grounds of his certainty of his own existence by an act of thinking.[5]

Likewise, Descartes argues in the *Meditations* from our ideas of God and perfection to the first cause of all these ideas, that is, to God's existence.

I do think that this idea of analysis as consisting of logical inferences is part and parcel of what Descartes means by saying that in the *Meditations* he employed analysis. However, at the same time we can see that Descartes was far from being clear about the logic of his own method. When he presented a sketch of his arguments transformed into a synthetic (deductive) form (HR 2:52–59), the direction of his main lines of thought is the same as in the original *Meditations,* and not the inverse of the latter, as we were led to expect. For instance, God's existence is again proved from "the mere fact that the idea of God exists in us." Hence, Descartes's ideas of the relation between analysis and synthesis are obviously very unclear. He can scarcely hold that synthesis is obtainable by reversing the direction of the several steps of analysis, as Pappus asserted. It is not surprising that this uncertainty concerning the direction of analysis as compared with the direction of logical inference should surface in Descartes, as it happens, in the form of the famous problem of the so-called "Cartesian Circle."

Furthermore, Descartes's description of his procedure in the empirical sciences is at variance with his method in his metaphysical meditations. For in the former the starting points, the effects, are said to be "deduced" from their causes (HR 1:129), thus reversing the direction of Descartes's alleged logical implications as compared with the *Meditations.* A little earlier, Descartes also speaks of causes and effects as being "reciprocally demonstrated," thus affirming the kind of convertibility he denied in the *Regulae* in philosophical (and theological) contexts. Nor are these remarks casual comments *en passant.* They are a part of Descartes's defense against allegations of arguing in a circle.

All told, Descartes can scarcely escape an indictment on charges of confusion as far as the direction of analysis is concerned.

(3) A mere reversal of the order of one's steps when one moves from analysis to synthesis will not work anyway in the simple-minded way Pappus seems to think. The reason for this lies in the need of what are often called auxiliary constructions in geometrical analysis. In order to prove a geometrical theorem, it does not usually suffice to operate with those geometrical objects which are depicted in the figure illustrating the theorem. New geometric objects will have to be "constructed," that is, introduced to the argument, if it is to succeed. Elsewhere I have shown that the reliance on such auxiliary individuals can be thought of as the main nontrivial ingredient not only in geometrical proofs but in deductive arguments in general.[6] As Leibniz aptly put it, the "greatest art" in geometry frequently consists in finding the best constructions. A deductive theory is undecidable precisely when these generalized "auxiliary constructions" are recursively unpredictable.

It follows that in an analysis these auxiliary constructions must be thought of as having been carried out before the rest of the argument, for otherwise we could not find the desired proof by means of the analysis. But by the same token the constructions cannot be carried out last in the corresponding synthesis. Hence, more must be involved in synthesis than merely traversing in the opposite order the same steps as were taken in the preceding analysis.

Concerning this point there was no clarity among the pre-Cartesian theorists of the analytic method. Descartes likewise pays little attention to the problem. In Greek geometrical practice, the initial analysis proper ("analysis" in the narrower sense of the word) was followed by a "resolution" in which the feasibility of the requisite auxiliary constructions was established.[7]

(4) Clearly we have not yet found the main link between the classical method of analysis and Descartes's method. In order to see this connection, we have to ask what is probably the single most important question concerning the ancient geometrical analysis. This is the question: What is geometrical analysis analysis *of*? What is it that is being analyzed, i.e, taken apart, in this process? Pappus's text might suggest that what is being anatomized is the deductive leap from "the given," presumably axioms and earlier theorems, to the theorem to be proved (and analogously in the case of problems instead of theorems). This is a mistaken view, and it would in effect assimilate the geometrical method of analysis to other kinds of analysis, notably to the Aristotelian idea of reducing syllogistic arguments to a number of minimal steps of inference. This is the sense of analysis which has given Aristotle's *Prior* and *Posterior Analytics* their name. Most of the medieval dis-

cussion of resolution and composition belongs to this Aristotelian tradition rather than to the geometric one. Hence, it is misleading to see anticipations of the analytic method of the early modern scientists in medieval or renaissance references to resolution and composition. Several scholars as impressive as Ernst Cassirer and John H. Randall have, for instance, claimed to find anticipations of Galileo's method of resolution and composition in Giacomo Zabarella and other Paduan Aristotelians. In reality, however, the Paduan ideas of resolution and composition were rooted in the Aristotelian tradition and hence basically foreign to Galileo's use of geometrical analysis as a paradigm of scientific method in general.[8] This is one of the many places where we must separate the (in the last analysis) Aristotelian questions of the direction of the scientific procedure and of the analysis of syllogisms into finer ones from questions concerning the (in the last analysis) geometrical questions of the interdependencies of the ingredients of a physical or mathematical configuration.

(5) An illuminating answer to the question of what is analyzed in analysis is obtained from a study of the actual practice of ancient Greek mathematicians in applying the method of analysis. As I helped to show before, what was being analyzed in the Greek method was essentially a geometrical configuration illustrated by a figure.[9] The several steps of analysis were steps from a geometrical object to another one, or perhaps from a number of objects to a number of others. Likewise, the beginning and the end of an analysis, that is to say, "the given" and "what is sought" (cf. the quote from Pappus above), were typically (in the former case, well-nigh exclusively) geometrical *objects* (possibly with a determined position, determined orientation, or otherwise determined characteristics), not geometrical *truths*. Steps from a geometrical object to another were mediated by their interdependence within the framework of the rest of the configuration. By studying such interdependencies, an analyst was almost literally "analyzing" the configuration ("figure") in question in the commonsense meaning of taking it apart.

Incidentally, we can now see an intuitive reason why auxiliary constructions are typically indispensable in geometrical analysis. Their vital role is made understandable by the idea of analysis as a series of steps from one geometrical object to another. Auxiliary constructs are unavoidable intermediate links in these chains of dependencies that are ultimately hoped to connect the unknown with the known.

This idea of analysis as an analysis of configuration, not proofs, is the most important aspect of the old method that Descartes and his contemporaries were generalizing and developing further. As was indicated, in analyzing a geometrical figure in the appropriate sense, the main questions pertain to the interrelations of the different geometrical objects in the figure. In the practice of ancient Greek geometers like Euclid, these interrelations are typically (but not exclusively) simple equivalences between the different lines and angles in the figure. With a greater use of algebraic methods by Descartes's immediate predecessors, these interdependencies gradually grew more flexible, till in Descartes's analytical geometry any polynomial dependency could be represented geometrically. In his geometry, in fact, Descartes strongly emphasized this algebraic representability of a wide variety of different kinds of geometrical interdependencies.

It is the same liberated idea of geometrical analysis as turning on a wide variety of algebraic dependencies between different geometrical magnitudes that easily led to generalizations of the ancient method of analysis. In the same way as a geometrical analyst studied the different algebraically expressible dependencies between the several parts of a geometrical figure, in the same way a physicist or other natural scientist studied the mathematically expressible dependencies between the different factors of a physical configuration, for instance forces, masses, and motions. Hence, a natural scientist who examined these interdependencies could also be thought of as practicing analysis. This is precisely what we saw Newton describing in the passage quoted above. The generalization is not restricted to him, but appears also in several of his predecessors, contemporaries, and followers. It is my thesis that Descartes's method can be viewed as a result of this sort of extension of the method of analysis from geometrical configurations to all complexes of interdependent elements.

Of course, there is a difference between the two cases in that the actual physical dependencies can only be ascertained by experimentation and observation while the geometrical dependencies are consequences of our explicit assumptions concerning geometrical objects. But this difference was not perceived as being fundamental. In the same way as a physicist uncovers functional relationships experimentally by varying certain factors in an experimental setup, so a geometer could be thought of as varying certain parts of his configuration, viz. his figure, in his mind. The general geometrization of the world undoubtedly also contributed to the force of this analogy.

I would go so far as to think of this generalized conception of analysis as analysis of configurations, not of proofs, as a highly interesting and highly topical methodological model, even today. Most philosophers of science have overlooked it, no one has analysed it satisfactorily, and yet in some disciplines, especially in theoretical linguistics, it could provide a highly salutary correction to current methodological excesses.

It is a more flexible paradigm than those fashionable ones which rely on straightforward generalization ("inductive generalization") from data. Instead of such a simple schema:

observations of particular date →

inductive leap to a general law

Newton's double (or triple) method requires a more sophisticated schema:

"analysis" of a complex phenomenon into ingredients →

experimental or observational discovery of dependencies between different ingredients →

inductive generalization of these dependencies to all similar cases →

deductive application of the generalization to other cases.

The last, synthetic step can often be thought of as assembling a new, more complex situation from the same kind of interacting ingredients as were included in the original experimental situation.

In the tradition of analysis, Descartes belongs in an important respect together with Pappus and Newton rather than with Aristotle or Grosseteste. This respect is the very idea on which we have just been commenting, viz. the conception of analysis as an analysis of configurations rather than of proofs, in other words, analysis as a systematic study of functional dependencies between known and unknown factors. It is worth registering Descartes's way of expressing himself on this point. He did not have at his disposal any general concept of function (functional dependence). Hence, he had to resort to speaking of "comparisons." His point is nonetheless clear. Descartes, in fact, goes as far as to say that "absolutely every item of knowledge which [one] does not acquire through the simple and pure intuition of a single object in isolation is obtained through the comparison of two or more with each other." (*Regulae*, AT 10:440.)

Thus we can now perceive the most important respect in which Descartes's characteristic mode of philosophical argumentation can be said to turn on the analytical method. Take, for instance, the famous strategy of radical doubt. Is there anything more to this strategy of asking whether anything (call it x) retains its certainty in the teeth of total doubt than in the method of an algebraist who takes an equation one side of which contains an unknown quantity x and who then manipulates the equation in such a way that only the unknown remains on that side as, e.g., in the transition from $(x + a)^2 = \sqrt{b}$, to $x = b - a$ through an application of the same "elimination operation" $\sqrt{z} - a$ to both sides of the original equation? In order to see my point, consider the characteristic strategy that underlies typical Cartesian arguments from the doubt that prompted Descartes's famous cogito insight to his determination of what the essence of a piece of wax is by considering what stays constant when it is subjected to various manipulations. In such typical arguments, Descartes is studying the interdependencies of different factors in an ontological or epistemological situation by letting certain factors vary systematically. (In some cases, e.g., in the case of the doubt, the variation is pushed by him to the limit, to an extreme case.)

The same diagnosis of Descartes's method can be expressed by saying that the three allegedly different types of analysis which Gerd Buchdahl has distinguished in Descartes are in reality one and the same method, and that the peculiar flavor of Descartes's method consists precisely in this identification.

The three types of analysis Buchdahl separates from each other are the following:

(i) Analysis as a technique of operating algebraically with unknowns, in the hope of finding equations that contain them, and then solving these equations for the unknowns.

(ii) Analysis as a literal or metaphoric "taking apart" of an actual physical or geometrical complex of phenomena.

(iii) The Pappian hypothetico-deductive procedure of "assuming what is to be proved as though it were known."

Of these, the algebraic technique (i) can be thought of, as we already saw, as a mere further technical development of the Pappian idea (iii). Actually, a little more than this is involved in the identification of types (i) and (iii) of analysis. This additional element is the insight mentioned earlier that, in the proof that we are looking for in an analysis of type (iii), we need certain auxiliary constructions without which the proof cannot be carried out. Conversely, when these auxiliary constructions have been found, the proof is obvious. Hence, the problem one is faced with in a "theoretical" analysis of the kind (iii) is basically the same as in a "problematical" analysis of the type (i), viz. finding (and constructing) the magnitudes needed for the solution of the problem in question, whether it is the problem of proving a proposed theorem or something else.

All this is intrinsic in the logic of the situation. Ancient mathematicians seem to have been dimly aware of the same features of the conceptual situation, at least in their working practice. What is especially relevant here, a recognition of this link between analysis of kind (i) and of kind (iii) is part and parcel of Descartes's methodology. Not only does he speak of his geometry of lines needed for the solution of any given problem. In this *Regulae*, he makes it crystal clear that according to his view *every* problem can be construed as a search for certain "unknowns," and more specifically construed on the algebraic model (i).

This explains the identification of (i) and (iii). As far as the identification of (ii) with the other kinds of analysis is concerned, it was explained above how already in Greek mathematicians like Pappus the actual course of analysis is better described as an analysis of figures or configurations than as an analysis of deductive connections. Thus, Buchdahl overlooks precisely those ideas which connect the allegedly different kinds of analysis with each other in Descartes.

This way of looking at Descartes's method deserves further documentation and further explanation. Descartes's main statement of his method of geometry is as follows:

If, then, we wish to solve any problem, we first suppose the solution to be already effected, and give names to all the lines that seem needful for its construction—to those that are unknown as well as to those that are known. Then, making no distinction between known and unknown lines, we must unravel the difficulty in any way that shows most naturally the relations between these lines, until we find it possible to express a single quantity in two ways. This will constitute an equation. . . . We must find as many such equations as there are supposed to be unknown lines. [*La Geometrie*, AT 6:372]

Then Descartes goes on to describe the ways of solving sets of equations. He has already earlier correlated the algebraic operations needed in the solution of equations with certain geometrical operations. Hence, the algebraic solution of an equation will yield a construction of the desired line.

Here we can see how Descartes's method is related to Pappus's. The basic idea is precisely the same. Both start from the assumption that the problem has already been solved. This involves the assumption that the unknowns are at hand, that they can be symbolized ("named"), and treated as if they were known. What has happened between Pappus and Descartes is that algebraic methods have been introduced to systematize the whole procedure. One of the crucial steps here is the systematic use of symbols for the unknowns. Once they have been introduced, the main cash value of the Pappian injunction to deal with "what is sought as if it were admitted" is to feel free to apply to them all the same algebraic operations that can be applied to symbols for known quantities. (In this way, the Pappian injunction became very much like an invitation to apply algebra to geometry.) The stepwise search backwards for connections with the given in Pappus becomes in Descartes a search of suitable equations to connect the unknowns with the known lines. The actual solution of an equation or a set of equations will correspond to the synthesis in Pappus.

From this algebrization of Pappus's procedure several differences

between Descartes and the Greeks ensue. One of them is a partly acci-
dental shift of interest from the problem of finding the right auxiliary
constructions to the problem of solving the resulting equations. In
the quoted passage, Descartes in effect brushes aside the whole problem of auxiliary constructions by speaking casually of "all the lines
that seem needful for its construction."

It is of some interest to see what the counterpart of Descartes's glib
assumption in his geometry is in the realm of physical science. The geometrical assumption that all auxiliary individuals have been introduced
corresponds to the assumption that all the relevant factors in (say) a
physical configuration have been taken into account. It is hard not to
see traces of Descartes's bad methodological conscience on this score in
his frequent expressions of concern about the "completeness" of our
"enumerations" or about making sure that "nothing has been left out"
(see, e.g., *Regulae*, Rule VII).

Another thing that we can now see is that Descartes has freed himself
of the old preoccupation with the direction of analysis. Since we need
several different equations to solve a problem with more than one unknown, we have to connect the unknowns and the given in several
different ways.

So much for Descartes's method in geometry. A number of Descartes's general methodological ideas likewise become clearer when we
realize that he is thinking in terms of a network of functional dependencies between the known and the unknown, not in terms of a linear
sequence of inferences. That this geometrical procedure was really
Descartes's general methodological paradigm is perhaps best shown
by a comparison with his *Regulae*. In explaining what a perfectly
understood problem is like, Descartes writes:

First, in any problem it is necessary that something is unknown, for otherwise
it would be pointless to search for it; second, this unknown must be designated in some manner, for otherwise we would not be led to the discovery of
that thing rather than any other; and third, it cannot be so designated except
in terms of something else which is already known. [AT 10:430]

Moreover, Descartes adds:

"All this is also true of imperfectly understood problems." What is
characteristic of imperfectly understood problems is that in them the
given does not yet determine the unknowns. Descartes's program includes showing "how all imperfect problems can be reduced to perfect
ones" (*Regulae*, AT 10:431).

Likewise, in Rule XII of the *Regulae*, Descartes writes: "Lastly, we
must make use of every assistance of the intellect . . . also for correctly
comparing what is being sought with what is known, . . . and for find-

ing those things which ought to be compared with each other. . . .
This rule comprehends everything which has been said before" (cf. also
the passage in *Regulae*, partly quoted above [AT 10:440]). Thus Descartes's whole method turns on connecting the unknowns with the
known via functional dependencies.

Of course, the algebrization of geometry which we find in Descartes
does not change completely the problems involved in the generalizations of the method of analysis. Rightly understood, the original Greek
method already turned on establishing connections between the known
and the unknown geometrical objects. Perhaps the most characteristic
feature of Descartes's method is the way he thinks of the dependencies
to be established. In his general methodological practice, he follows
the mathematical paradigm and thinks of the basic interrelations as
being intuitively perceived, from which it follows that our search for
them has the nature of conceptual clarification which prepares the
ground for the operations of intuition. Much of the *Regulae* is devoted
to explaining how this is to be accomplished. In this respect, Descartes
remained rather similar to Aristotle, to whom the basic premises of a
science are likewise seen intuitively and are likewise partially conceptual.

Another aspect of this comparison may also be helpful. Descartes's
preoccupation in geometry with equations and their solution carries
over to his general methodology. Even in his general philosophical
methodology, his attitude is that of a mathematician who is setting up
equations and solving them. This attitude is one of the factors which
lend a strong flavor of logical or conceptual analysis to Descartes's
method, as used both in philosophy and in science.

It is this conceptual (a priori) character of Cartesian science and not
his characteristic variant of the idea of analysis that creates the simi-
larities between Descartes and Aristotle.

This characteristic feature of Cartesian analysis as a kind of *conceptual* analysis would deserve further comments, as it is not always
easy to pinpoint by reference to explicit pronouncements. One of the
more easily discernible manifestations of this characteristic is Descartes's adherence to the so-called "principle of plenitude." I have
briefly considered the role of this principle as a symptom of the
Aristotelian idea of scientific truths as conceptual truths in two earlier
papers.[10]

The conceptual-analysis character of Cartesian analysis betrays an
especially sharp contrast between Descartes and Newton. For according
to Newton we find the basic dependencies which can often be expressed equationally by *experimental* analysis. When a geometer notes

a dependence between the different ingredients of a geometrical figure, we can perhaps metaphorically think of him as varying (perhaps "in his thinking") the different ingredients so as to see how the others change accordingly. In contrast, Newton thinks that in typical cases of experimental analysis the dependencies are established by an actual variation of some of the relevant parameters. Newton's analysis, unlike Descartes's, thus "consists in making Experiments and Observations, and in drawing general conclusions from them by Induction."

It is not impossible that this contrast between Newton and Descartes is connected with Newton's idea that geometry itself is founded on mechanical practice (see Newton's preface to the first edition of the *Principia*.) This enabled him to consider any old analysis carried out in his mechanics to be completely on all fours with geometrical analysis. What is even more important, it made it possible for Newton to consider any use of geometrical intuition as a mere tacit appeal to our mechanical experience. Whichever of these differences between Descartes and Newton is in the last analysis the basic one, the contrast could scarcely be sharper.

The conceptual character of Descartes's method also helps to lend it a wide scope far beyond the purview of Newton's experimental analysis. It was thus instrumental in enabling Descartes to think that he had in his possession a single method, as fully applicable in his metaphysical meditations as in the methodological exercises that were appended to the *Discourse*. We do not appreciate Descartes's characteristic way of thinking until we realize that in his philosophical system, too, he is studying certain functional dependencies. For instance, in his metaphysical *Meditations* Descartes is thus studying (according to his own lights) certain interdependencies of different ingredients of our ontology. Using intuitively clear connections between those factors he hoped to argue backwards to the metaphysical structure of the world and to its determinants, including God's existence.

It is Descartes's use of his analytic method (in the sense of a procedure that focuses on the study of functional dependencies) in his philosophy that makes his philosophical thought so novel and so modern. It is at the same time what makes Descartes's philosophy hard to understand and to reconstruct if one relies only on propositional methods, for instance, methods that turn on relations of logical consequence between propositions. Perhaps we can thus have a glimpse of one of the reasons why Descartes has exerted the fascination on subsequent philosophers that he has done, and also why the usual logico-deductive methods have contributed relatively little to our understanding of his characteristic way of thinking and arguing.

NOTES

1. Gerd Buchdahl, *Metaphysics and the Philosophy of Science* (Oxford: Blackwell, 1969), pp. 118–41.

2. Pappus, *Pappi Alexandrini Collectionis Quae Supersunt I-III*, ed. Fr. Hultsch (Berlin: Weideman, 1876–77), 2:634.

3. Jaakko Hintikka and Unto Remes, *The Method of Analysis* (Dordrecht: D. Reidel, 1974), and "Ancient Geometrical Analysis and Modern Logic," in Robert S. Cohen et al., eds., *Essays in Memory of Imre Lakatos* (Dordrecht: D. Reidel, 1975), pp. 253–76.

4. Hintikka and Remes, *The Method of Analysis*, ch. 2.

5. Jaakko Hintikka, *"Cogito, Ergo Sum:* Inference or Performance?" *Philosophical Review* 71 (1962):3–32.

6. Jaakko Hintikka, *Logic, Language-Games and Information* (Oxford: Clarendon, 1973).

7. Hintikka and Remes, *The Method of Analysis*, ch. 6.

8. This is convincingly shown by Nicholas Jardine, "Galileo's Road to Truth and the Demonstrative Regress," *Studies in the History and Philosophy of Science,* 7 (1976):277–318.

9. Hintikka and Remes, *The Method of Analysis*, chs. 4 and 7.

10. Jaakko Hintikka, "Leibniz on Plenitude, Relations, and the 'Reign of Law'," in Harry G. Frankfurt, ed., *Leibniz* (Garden City, N.Y.: Doubleday, 1972), and "Gaps in the Great Chain of Being," *Proceedings and Addresses of the APA* 49 (1976):22–38.

Doubt, Reason,
and Cartesian Therapy

MIKE MARLIES

I

CENTRAL TO ANY study of Descartes is the method which he employs in the *Meditations* and related works. In this paper, I argue for a somewhat different understanding of this method than has, to my knowledge, been offered elsewhere. In particular, I stress that the method is intended as a discursive therapy, meant, on the one hand, to destroy "prejudice"—an habitual preoccupation with corporeal matters, which impairs a man's reason—and, on the other hand, to emend the reason so impaired.[1]

In its main outlines, my interpretation of Cartesian method conforms to that of Harry Frankfurt.[2] But I differ from Frankfurt in two important respects. First, Frankfurt and most other interpreters believe that Cartesian method incorporates a broad-ranging doubt *ab initio*, that is, prior to the discovery of skeptical arguments in support of such doubt. If such ab initio doubt were really part of the method, the Cartesian enterprise, I argue against Frankfurt, would be plunged into insuperable difficulties. However, in my judgment, Cartesian texts do not show definitely that Descartes wanted to adopt ab initio doubt (one could argue the reverse), and emphasizing the therapeutic nature of his method makes it seem unlikely that he did.

My second important difference with Frankfurt involves the doubting of reason in the *Meditations*. Since Frankfurt credits Descartes with ab initio doubt, and wants, at the same time, to represent Cartesian method as plausible and coherent, he argues that the power of reason is exempted from ab initio doubt, and, indeed, is not doubted even in the light of the skeptical arguments in Meditations I and II. Frankfurt tries to show that the exemption of reason from ab initio doubt is neither question-begging nor otherwise objectionable; and that the doubts of the first two Meditations are directed at things other than reason. By this means, he hopes to save Descartes from the difficult problems that seem to arise if reason is put into doubt in the first Meditation. I argue, first, that Frankfurt's arguments in defense of the exemption of reason from ab initio doubt do not work; second, that, for therapeutic reasons, the faculty of reason has to be—and is— brought into doubt (but not ab initio doubt) in Meditation I; and third, that it is owing to a misunderstanding—shared by both Frankfurt and the critics of Descartes about whom he is worried—that the doubting of reason in Meditation I is thought to mean shipwreck for the Cartesian search after truth.

I begin with discussion of prejudice, which we must understand more than superficially if we are to see how Cartesian therapy is supposed to work; this discussion includes, as a useful part, some important points about reason and other faculties. I then turn to the issue of ab initio doubt, and try to show that it is neither defensible nor Cartesian. Finally, I review the Meditations, from the first through the early part of the third, showing, by example, the progress of Cartesian therapy. In the course of this, I try to clarify the "methodological rule," as I call it, which directs the skeptical arguments of the early Meditations, and about which I disagree with Anthony Kenny. I also claim that the discrediting of faculties, like sense and reason, is more difficult on the Cartesian method than is usually supposed. I compare the attempt to discredit sense, which is successful, with the attempt to discredit reason, which is not. Both attempts may be seen to proceed in two stages. I try to show that the attempt to discredit reason in Meditation I is, in a very important respect, comparable to the *first* stage in the attempt to discredit sense. I try to show likewise that the second, unsuccessful, stage in the attempt to discredit reason (the one which is usually discussed), not given until Meditation III (I try to say why it cannot be given until then), is comparable to the second, successful, stage in the attempt to discredit sense. All of these points conform well with, though not all are strictly required by, my interpretation of the Cartesian method as therapy.

II

The *Search after Truth* is a dialogue between Polyander, "a man endowed with ordinary mental gifts" who has never philosophized, Eudoxus, a man of enlightenment who is an idealization of the mature Descartes, and Epistemon, a scholar, "well acquainted with all that can be learnt in the Schools" (*Search*: HR 1:307).[3] In the prologue to this work (of which no complete text is extant), Descartes wrote that a man:

requires to have good natural endowments or else instruction from a wise man, both in order to rid himself of false doctrines with which his mind is filled, and for building the first foundations of a solid knowledge, and discovering all the means by which he may carry his knowledge to the highest point to which it can possibly attain. [HR 1:305]

Descartes evidently thought that his own enlightenment was the result of "good natural endowments"; but, having become one of the wise, he was willing to instruct others. The instruction he uses is discursive, but is intended to be therapeutic rather than expository.

The target of Cartesian therapy is the "state of prejudice," a morbid condition of thought into which, according to Descartes, it is natural for a man to fall. To understand the therapy, we need to understand this condition and its etiology. The following paragraphs summarize Descartes's account.[4]

We are all born, Descartes evidently thinks, with the faculties of sense, memory, imagination, and reason; but while sense operates at full strength from the first, our reason, while we are infants, is rudimentary and weak.

Indeed, in infancy, reason operates only when "stimulated [*impulsi*] by sense": confronted with an array of sensations, such as those of pleasure and pain, hunger and thirst, heat and cold, color, taste, texture, and smell, we are able to apprehend, by reason, "a matter which is extended in length, breadth, and depth, the various parts of which have various figures and motions, and give rise to the sensations we have of colors, smells, pains, etc." (*Principles* II. 1: *HR* 1:254). But, because reason operates, at first, only in intimate conjunction with sense, and because our sensations, being very clear and lively, utterly captivate our attention, we fail to notice that it is not by sense alone, but by reason applied to sensory stimuli, that the idea of extended matter is brought to mind. As a result, we overestimate the power of sense, and mistakenly include magnitude, figure, and motion with heat, cold, color, texture, and the like as perceptions of this one faculty; and discerning, therefore, no difference in kind between attributes of the former and latter sorts, we come to regard both as equally intrinsic to extended matter. Consequently, the lively ideas—supposedly presented by sense—which we frame of corporeal objects (objects, that is, which are at once extended, figured, etc., *and* colored, textured, etc.) seem to us not only very clear, but distinct (containing nothing extraneous or unnecessary). Actually, these ideas are confused, since color, texture, etc., are not in fact qualities of extended matter.

Now, by nature, we are wont to affirm, or place confidence in, ideas to the extent that they seem clear and distinct. And affirming our (evidently quite clear and distinct) "sensory" ideas of and about corporeal objects amounts to judging that there are objects beyond our thought which cause, and exactly resemble, these ideas. This is because "magnitudes, figures, movements, and the like," which are amalgamated into such lively ideas of corporeal things, are exhibited "as things or the modes of things existing, or at least capable of existing, outside thought" (*Principles* I. 71: HR 1:250); and nature "teaches" or inclines us to believe that whatever is thus exhibited actually derives from things outside of ourselves. Indeed, since it is as characteristics of corporeal things—bodies—that we conceive magnitude, figure, and motion, nature teaches us first and foremost that there are objects beyond thought which cause our apparently clear and distinct ideas of bodies. Further, as Descartes says (describing his own case): "having no knowledge of those objects excepting the knowledge which the ideas themselves gave me, nothing was more likely to occur to my mind than that the objects were similar to the ideas that were caused" (*Meditations*: HR 1:188). In addition, we find that the lively ideas which "sense" brings to mind are not subject to control by our wills, and this reinforces our conviction that these ideas arise from things other than ourselves.

Our infant minds thus construe "sense" not merely as a faculty of thought, but as a faculty by which, without the mediation of any other faculty, we come to ideas which command our fullest confidence—to knowledge, in a word. Moreover, this knowledge is evidently a knowledge of things—in particular, corporeal things—existing beyond our thought.

Is any faculty other than "sense" regarded by the infant mind as a source of knowledge? Reason may be quickly dismissed; for, as noted before, the apprehensions of reason, since they occur in infancy only in conjunction with attention-grabbing sensory stimuli, are never recognized for what they are, but are mistaken for perceptions of sense. An infant is therefore totally unaware of his reason, and so cannot regard it as a knowing faculty.

Neither the memory, which recollects ideas formerly brought to mind by some other faculty, nor the imagination, which constructs ideas out of ideas given in the memory, presents ideas which seem as clear or distinct as those brought to mind by "sense." Because of this, and the fact that the operations of memory and imagination are evidently subject to our wills, we are not taught by nature to affirm these ideas— not, at least, on their merits as products of the memory or the imagination. We are not, that is, inclined to judge that the cause of such ideas is anything beyond ourselves, even though they be ideas of corporeal things, exhibiting an aspect of "externality." It is true with regard to the memory that it may recollect something as a former perception of sense, and therefore as something known; but we do not suppose that we came to this knowledge by means of memory. In such cases, we suppose only that we recall, by the memory, something known by means of sense.

Further exploration of the memory and the imagination yields another important fact about the thoughts of infancy. Memory, it may first be noted, brings nothing original to mind; indeed, to identify an idea as a presentation of memory is to regard it as a recollection from previous thought. Now, unlike the memory, the imagination does present us with ideas which are, in a certain sense, original: it combines, in new ways, ideas which it finds in the memory, thus creating "images" (as Descartes calls them) which, as wholes, have never previously been brought before the mind. But since the imagination does not, evidently, create the "pieces" out of which it constructs images; and since, in infancy: (1) "sense" presents only ideas of or about corporeal things, (2) reason presents nothing but what is assimilated to "sense," and (3) memory presents nothing original; it transpires that, in infancy at least, nothing is brought to mind by the imagination except ideas of or about corporeal things. And this result applies as well to the memory, which recollects only what is "sensed" or imagined.

These, in sum, are the modes of thinking and judging that characterize infancy: (1) finding ourselves in apparent possession of a faculty of "sense," which presents ideas—seemingly quite clear and distinct—of corporeal things; (2) affirming these ideas, which amounts to judging that they arise from, and resemble, real, extramental things; (3) accepting "sense," therefore, to be a faculty of knowledge, the knowledge being, moreover, of things beyond our thought; and (4) since we discover in ourselves no ideas save those concerning corporeal things, coming to accept such things as the only things that can be known of or even conceived. According to Descartes, there is much to be deplored in this infantile outlook; but because there is nothing to correct them in youth, these modes of thought and judgment acquire, through continued use, the force of habits, habits which become, before very long, so deeply entrenched that, unless we are saved by philosophy, they dominate us all through life.

A man who is dominated by such habits—who is, in effect, persuaded that "sense" is a power of knowledge, that corporeal things and their qualities are known through it, and are the only things which are known, or which can be conceived—is a man in the "state of prejudice." Of course, such a man is unaware that his is a prejudiced state; by his lights, he believes just what is plainly evident. He little suspects that he is so firmly bound to mistakes made in infancy that he would be unable even to understand (since he would inevitably *mis*understand) the real truth of things, were this described or explained to him by any ordinary means. To see why this is so, we must look at how prejudice affects a man's reason; for it is through this power—and only through it—that a man can, according to Descartes, arrive at truth.

Now, as a man grows from infancy into adulthood, his reason likewise develops, and is able to make itself felt as the rudimentary reason of infancy was not. But if his reason develops within the constraints imposed by the powerful habits which constitute prejudice, it is in consequence impaired: Descartes's terms are "corrupted," "impure," and "incomplete." Such impaired reason is reason subjugated to "sense"—used, that is, only in application to ideas of corporeal things already present to "sense," memory, or, most commonly, the imagination—and which, correlatively, cannot bring to fruition its own unique power to present matters of pure understanding to the mind.

The prejudiced man grown beyond infancy can and does recognize certain of his ideas as presentations of reason as opposed to "sense," memory, or imagination. He finds that by the self-conscious application of reason, he can evidently see that the idea of one thing or quality can be drawn (or "inferred"), in certain instances, from the idea of another; this yields a "demonstration" (itself an idea[5]) that the first thing or quality is a part or feature of the second. In the light of the inferences upon which they rest, some of these demonstrations, although they do not seem as clear and distinct to the man of prejudice as the ideas given by "sense," appear sufficiently so that he is wont to affirm them; thus, he acknowledges that reason provides knowledge in at least some cases. Even so, he does not suppose that reason discovers that anything exists beyond his thoughts; he will regard a demonstration of reason as being about such things just in case it happens to concern things whose extramental existence he has determined independently through "sense."

Let us notice that, in the prejudiced, the ideas out of which demonstrations of reason are framed, and thus the demonstrations themselves, concern corporal things or their qualities—for let a prejudiced man try to conceive a thing, and habit will force him to bring to mind an idea of something corporeal. Likewise, the inferential process of drawing one idea from another does not, in the prejudiced, proceed by unencumbered rational insight; indeed, it could not, for the ideas of corporeal things to which this insight would presumably be applied are, as we saw earlier, confused, and thus antagonistic to reason in its purity. The corrupted reasoning of the prejudiced amounts to a sort of calculation applied to ideas of corporeal things (typically, those given in the imagination): thus, in arithmetical inferences, it may amount essentially to counting; in geometrical inferences, to manipulating and examining mental diagrams; and in logical inferences ("dialectic"), to the application of formulaic rules to patterns of words (for an example, see *Regulae* X). This is all very different from the exercise of pure rational insight. A counterpart to the perversion of reasoning brought about by a forced concern with corporeal matters is the prejudiced man's inability to get a true grasp of the most fundamental principles of right reason. As Descartes remarked to Burman:

with regard to common principles and axioms, such as, *It is impossible for the same thing to be and not to be*, men of the senses, as we all are prior to philosophizing [*ante* philosophium], do not consider or heed . . . except in a confused way; never truly by themselves [*vero in abstracto*], and apart from matter and particulars. [AT 5:146]

III

Although he never guesses it, the prejudiced man lives in a state of epistemological disaster. Nothing he thinks is in fact clear and distinct; nothing he affirms is true. Of course, there is much that *seems* very clear and distinct to him, but that is quite a different matter. "It is the wise alone," says Descartes, "who know how to distinguish rightly between what is so perceived, and what merely seems or appears to be clear and distinct" ("Replies to Objections VII"; HR 2:267). As we saw, the prejudiced man can bring to mind only ideas of or about corporeal things, ideas which, although sometimes very clear and lively, are confused, and which therefore could not possibly be true, according to Descartes.

The faculties upon which the prejudiced man relies for knowledge are "sense" and reason, and of the two he places far more faith in "sense." But in fact "sense" produces only convincing confusion. It is, we saw, no true faculty, but rather an amalgam of sense and reason, neither of which is rightly appreciated for what it is. Sense *proper* is a faculty of "feelings"—ideas which, although they may be caused by things that exist, are not perceptions of existent things (corporeal or otherwise); indeed, they are not perceptions *of* anything at all. Sensations represent nothing, and resemble nothing but one another; they are mere modes of thought.

Reason, the other faculty upon which the man of prejudice relies, would indeed lead him to truth, if only he were able to use it uncorrupted, and with full vitality. But, says Descartes, uncorrupted reason concerns itself only with purely intelligible—never with corporeal—things. Only of and about purely intelligible things is it possible to have ideas which are clear and distinct to the fullest degree, and which represent actual knowledge. Now prejudice is, precisely, an obstacle to conceiving any purely intelligible thing—pure thinking substance, for example; or God, as a perfect being, of whom no image can be formed; or even extended (but *nonsensible*) matter. Thus, a prejudiced man cannot make use of uncorrupted reason—"Reason," as I shall sometimes call it in the sequel—indeed, he cannot even conceive of it. What he recognizes as reason is the corrupt power described in section II, above, which I will, for convenience, commence to call "reasoning." And reasoning, like "sense," can bring no truly clear and distinct idea before the mind. Both reasoning and Reason are, indeed, manifestations of reason,[6] a faculty of which all men are possessed. But to be possessed of a faculty, and to be able to make proper use of it are two different things, and until a man is loosed from the grip of prejudice, he is bound by habit to reasoning and is devoid of the use, and even of any notion, of Reason. The ability to use Reason—"the Natural Light which is in our souls"—is what characterizes enlightenment. Once a man can use his reason unencumbered, confusion is dispelled, and truly clear and distinct ideas—ideas of and about purely intelligible things—can be brought to mind. Then and only then, Descartes believes, does a man achieve genuine knowledge.

Now Cartesian method is, as Descartes explains in many places, intended as a means to overcome prejudice and gain enlightenment. I find it helpful to call the method "therapeutic" because what is implied is that a change is to be worked in the prejudiced man, at whom the method is directed. And this change is much more than a change of opinion—it is a change in his abilities to use his powers of thought, and most especially, a change in the condition of his reason: the repair and invigoration of what prejudice has impaired and enervated.[7] But this, in turn, requires working changes in powerful habits of thought; therefore, we can expect the Cartesian method to be the sort of method more appropriate to changing habits than opinions.

It is hopeless, for instance, to try to teach the truth to a prejudiced man by simply telling him about it, or even by arguing for it. For although the "primary notions of metaphysics," purely intelligible notions, such as that of thinking substance, are, in their own nature, as understandable as anything can be, a man of prejudice will misunderstand them, because habit will make him think that he has no notion of them unless he can imagine (that is, form an image of) them. So, Descartes tells us, when the prejudiced man tries to conceive of mind, he thinks of it either as a power of the body (*Principles* 1.12), or as an attribute of a confusedly conceived "unity" compounded of body and mind ("Replies to Objections VI": HR 2:257), or some such. The difficulty of the prejudiced in knowing the nature of their souls, Descartes emphasizes, is that: "they are so accustomed to consider nothing except by imagining it, which is a mode of thought specially adapted to material objects, that all that is not capable of being imagined appears to them not to be intelligible at all" (*Discourse,* part IV: HR 1:104). And since such people cannot understand the notions of which we might wish to persuade them, no argument will avail. Cartesian therapy is a way of bringing a prejudiced man into a condition where he can grasp ideas which are intelligible-but-not-imaginable, and to accomplish this requires extraordinary means. It is these *means*—the Cartesian method —and not any *doctrine* that Descartes saw as his unique contribution to philosophy. "[A]lthough many have already maintained that, in order to understand the facts of metaphysics, the mind must be abstracted from the senses," he told the second objectors, "no one hitherto, so far as I know, has shown how this is to be done":

The true, and in my judgment, the only way to do this is found in my Second Meditation, but such is its nature that it is not enough to have once seen how it goes; much time and many repetitions are required if we would, by forming the contrary habit of distinguishing intellectual from corporeal matters . . . obliterate the life-long custom of confounding them. [HR 2:31–32]

It should be clear from preceding considerations that Cartesian therapy must actually have a twofold thrust. In the first place, it must break down and remove the habitual attachment of thought to corporeal matters in which prejudice consists. This part of the therapy, though vital, is purely negative; the therapy cannot rest there, or its result would be skepticism. It must, in the second place, force the exercise of uncorrupted reason, and set the mind on its way down the path of truth. A man's reason, newly liberated from its attachment to corporeal things, is still weak and shaky; Cartesian therapy nurses it along by giving it, at first, what it can most easily digest. As Eudoxus says to Polyander in the *Search after Truth*:

We can, . . . Polyander, while we are busy destroying the ["edifice" of prejudice] . . . at the same time form the foundations which may serve our purpose, and prepare the best and most solid materials that are necessary in order to succeed in our task; provided that you are . . . willing to examine with me which of all the truths men can know, are those that are the most certain and easy of knowledge. [HR 1:313]

If Cartesian therapy is to be conducted as described above, it must, at each stage, present only what is comprehensible and convincing to the subject. Such works as the *Meditations* begin, therefore, by adopting the prejudiced point of view, and then proceed by stages to force the prejudiced man—if he reads and studies attentively—to abandon prejudice and acquire enlightenment. As students of such works, we must, when we try to understand what Descartes is doing at this or that point, remain constantly aware of the supposed condition of the subject of the therapy, else we cannot fail to import grave misunderstandings.

IV

The *Meditations* are addressed to Everyman, a man like Polyander. The autobiographical Descartes—the "I" of the *Meditations* (to distinguish him from Descartes-as-author, I shall hereafter call him "René")—who is not enlightened, but has evidently progressed some way in skeptical meditations, begins Meditation I like this:

Some years ago now, I discerned how many fallible things [*falsa*] I had, from an early age, taken for veracious ones [*pro veris admiserim*], and how doubtful was every thing that I had thereafter built upon them; and that, consequently, once in life, everything had to be turned completely upside-down [*funditus evertenda*] and begun anew from first foundations, if ever I wished to establish something firm and lasting in the sciences. But the work seemed vast, and I awaited an age that was sufficiently mature that none more suitable for undertaking my training [*disciplinis*] would follow. Wherefore I lingered so long that I should indeed be blameworthy were I to use up in deliberation such time as remains for action. Accordingly, I have today opportunely freed my mind from all cares; I have found myself quiet leisure; I retire alone; I shall at last have time for the earnest and general upset of my opinions. [HR 1:144; AT 7:17–18]

This "general upset," René explains in the succeeding paragraph, will not require a review of each of his opinions; for his opinions, he says, all depend upon certain "principles." By "principles," as Frankfurt points out, "Descartes is not thinking of a set of logically ultimate axioms from which his opinions can be deduced." Rather, René has in mind (and here my view differs from Frankfurt's) faculties—sense and reason, for instance—by which ideas are brought to mind.[8] If these principles are shown to be fallible, he says, "whatever has been built up upon them will collapse of itself," (HR 1:145) and he straightaway resolves to attack them.

It is widely supposed that René is, in these paragraphs, either arguing for, or declaring the methodological necessity of, a comprehensive "doubt," ab initio—prior, that is, to the continuation of the investigation. This doubt is most often thought to include both a suspension of judgment about matters formerly believed, and a suspension of trust in principles in which faith was formerly placed. Hume, for example, evidently understood Cartesian method in this way; "There is a species of skepticism," Hume says in his *Enquiry*:

antecedent to all study and philosophy, which is much inculcated by Descartes and others, as a sovereign preservative against error and precipitate judgment. It recommends an universal doubt, not only of all our former opinions and principles, but also of our very faculties, of whose veracity, say they, we must assure ourselves.[9]

Borrowing Hume's terms, we can call the kind of doubt (or suspension of belief) introduced *prior* to skeptical arguments "antecedent doubt," and that introduced *in consequence of* such arguments, "consequent doubt."[10] Since what is typically attributed to Descartes is what I will call *general* antecedent doubt—antecedent doubt which is either *universal*, or universal save for circumscribed exceptions[11]—I will mean general antecedent doubt when I speak of "antecedent doubt" in the sequel. Consequent doubt will not be assumed to be general.

The view that antecedent doubt is a fixture of Cartesian methodology has not diminished. Among recent writers in English, Kenny and Frankfurt, for example, seem to agree that the rule is: suspend judgment first, meditate afterwards. Moreover, they agree that René is *arguing* for this rule in the paragraph from Meditation I translated above.

Kenny, whose treatment of the matter is brief, does not rehearse the distinction between fallible principles and doubtful opinions mentioned above. He thinks that René is asserting "that we grow up uncritically accepting many beliefs which may be false" (which Kenny is ready to grant), and arguing enthememematically from that assertion to the conclusion that we must at once suspend judgment about all of our beliefs. One of the missing premises is that none of a person's beliefs can be certain unless all are certain; "Descartes's argument presupposes this," says Kenny, "but he offers no proof of it." Kenny finds the "presupposed premiss," and consequently the whole argument, suspect, declaring further that "A universal doubt is neither necessary nor rational."[12]

Frankfurt treats the same matter in more detail. His considered view seems to be that:

the *first step* [it is clear that Frankfurt means this quite literally] in . . . [Descartes's] attempt to establish something "solid and permanent in the sciences" is to be no less radical a measure than the "general overthrow of my opinions." Since he has observed that a number of his most fundamental beliefs are false, he decides that all his opinions must be "thoroughly overthrown . . . and begun anew from first foundations."[13]

This quotation from Frankfurt shows that (as mentioned earlier) he, like Kenny, sees Descartes as *arguing* for antecedent doubt:

[Descartes] needs, to be sure, a reason to justify the decision to "overthrow," i.e. suspend judgment on, all his opinions. But the reason he needs is provided quite satisfactorily by his observation in the opening sentence . . . that his opinions lack a secure foundation.[14]

It is hard to see why Frankfurt approves of this argument that he takes to be Descartes's. For an obvious question would seem to be, "What reason could René have, *prior to taking up the skeptical arguments given later in the Meditation,* for thinking that his opinions lack a secure foundation?" Not only is Frankfurt sanguine about this supposedly Cartesian argument, he is far from disapproving of antecedent doubt. He argues that "This kind of general suspension of assent is a normal and appropriate step in any inquiry that purports to be systematically rational. . . . Far from being heroic, it is simply routine."[15]

Because Frankfurt's study of Descartes is scrupulous, he wonders about the considerable textual evidence indicating that Descartes's methodology requires not antecedent but *consequent* doubt, that is, an extensive suspension of judgment *in the light of* the skeptical arguments of Meditation I. Frankfurt also worries about an evident procedural inconsistency: if (as Frankfurt thinks) Descartes's "argument" in the first paragraph of Meditation I is sufficient to justify the "general overthrow" of one's opinions, for what *additional* purpose would the skeptical arguments that follow be required? Frankfurt finds the answer to this last question in a letter to Clerselier, where Descartes remarks that "whatever resolution one has made to deny or affirm nothing, one easily forgets it if he has not impressed it firmly on his memory."[16] This is why the additional arguments are needed: not to create doubt, but to reinforce it.

Still, Frankfurt labels "quite unequivocal and decisive" Descartes's claim (in the same letter to Clerselier) that "one needs some reason for doubting before determining to do so, which is why I propounded in my First Meditation the main reasons for doubting" (HR 2:126). These "reasons" are given in the skeptical arguments in which the bulk of the Meditation consists. In Frankfurt's view, then, Descartes both affirms and denies the methodological necessity of antecedent doubt. Frankfurt consequently judges that "Descartes's account . . . is not entirely coherent. . . . He tends to confuse the first and second phases of his program, and at times he speaks incorrectly [!] as though the skeptical arguments precede the overthrow of his beliefs."[17]

V

But even if one approves of antecedent doubt, as Frankfurt does, he must recognize the difficulties of maintaining it, especially given Descartes's objective: the refounding of our knowledge. Hume remarked that "the Cartesian doubt . . . were it ever possible to be attained by any human creature (as it plainly is not) would be incurable; and no reasoning could ever bring us to a state of assurance on any subject," since, he says, we are "diffident" of any "faculties" by which we might do so.[18] Others have echoed this sentiment in our own time. Thus, Kenny argues that antecedent doubt makes even the skeptical arguments of Meditation I impossible:

Descartes' own execution of his plan falls far short of "doubting whatever can be doubted." If he believed that the senses have sometimes deceived him and that mathematicians have made mistakes, then it seems that he must be trusting both to his memory and to the subsequent experience or checking calculation that revealed the errors in question. . . . He must [also] continue to accept the principle that contradictories cannot both be true.[19]

The last point is especially crucial. If Descartes thinks, for whatever reason, that antecedent doubt is called for—and if, in particular, as Hume and Frankfurt point out, this doubt applies in a thoroughgoing way to the *principles* upon which all of his knowledge is based—how can such doubt, as Frankfurt would have it, be "a normal and appropriate step in any inquiry that purports to be systematically rational"? For have we not—in holding all of our "principles" suspect—already denied ourselves the use of reason, which is, after all, one of these principles? And, if we exempt reason, have we not, in a fundamental way, begged the question? After all, no grounds are initially given by René for forbearing to think that it is reason itself which has infected the superstructure of our opinions. And, even if we feigned (to wax Cartesian) that René has some undisclosed grounds on which to exempt reason, why should Everyman be willing to follow along without knowing what these grounds are?

Now Frankfurt wrestles, on Descartes's behalf, with this knotty problem. "The key to the solution," he maintains, ". . . lies in appreciating the problem with which Descartes intends his inquiry to deal":

His aim . . . is to determine whether or not there are *reasonable grounds* for doubting his former opinions, and . . . how a reasonable man can find a foundation for the sciences. The authority of reason is . . . built into the very conception of his enterprise.[20]

It is not at all evident, though, that Descartes's program to provide firm foundations for the sciences calls for antecedent doubt; nor is it clear how this program could be carried out at all, or at least without crippling inconsistency, in the face of such doubt.

But Frankfurt has a further argument:

The fact that [Descartes's] inquiry cannot proceed unless he commits himself to reason does not decisively undermine his resolution to avoid all prejudice. For his commitment to reason is of a kind that does not involve making an assumption that is gratuitously exempted from examination.

Descartes' procedure permits him to acknowledge . . . that his enterprise may end in failure. . . . If he should not succeed, his failure would reveal that the confidence in reason with which he begins is unjustified.

Descartes' assumption that reason is entitled to authority has the status of a working hypothesis. . . . Viewed in this light, it begs no questions; it does not contravene his resolution to empty his mind.[21]

Now this argument on behalf of reason is *so* plausible that it argues against antecedent doubt. Strictly speaking, of course, Frankfurt is wrong: if reason is exempted from initial suspicion, then it *does* contravene Descartes's supposed resolution to "empty his mind." If Frankfurt's argument succeeds, it shows that it is methodologically unimpeachable to contravene the resolution in this way and assume the veracity of reason as a working hypothesis—until grounds appear for giving it up. But the same might just as well be argued in favor of any other principle. Why doubt the veracity of the senses *antecedently*— that is, prior to finding grounds for distrusting them? If we are willing to do so for reason, why not also admit the authority of the senses as a working hypothesis (until something goes wrong)? What does seem to beg the question is the drawing of an antecedent distinction among reason, the senses, and other principles (if any), which allows one an entry where the others are denied. Surely that is not methodologically unimpeachable.

VI

How would René or Everyman—men in the state of prejudice— receive Frankfurt's argument in favor of accepting reason "as a working hypothesis" exempted from antecedent doubt? Cartesian procedure, we said, must, if it is to be effective, at all times appear plausible to its intended audience.

Now antecedent doubt, Frankfurt says, is a workable device if we exempt reason from it; so, according to Frankfurt, we are to ask Everyman, just after we shake hands, so to speak, (1) to doubt virtually everything, but (2) to exempt reason from the doubt.

For the sake of discussion, let us assume for the moment that

Everyman is amenable to antecedent doubt; that he is willing, without the pressure of skeptical arguments, to suspend judgment on his former beliefs and suspend his trust in formerly accepted principles. Now we say to him, "Wait a minute! We have just noticed that our enterprise collapses unless you except reason from this doubt; would you, please, therefore do so?" Will Everyman find this an attractive request?

Let us note, as Frankfurt does not, that if you broach this question to Everyman, he will think that you are talking about *reasoning*, which is what he understands reason to be. And, although he places a certain amount of faith in this principle, he will ask, as Polyander is made to ask in the *Search after Truth*: "Is there anyone who can doubt that sensible things . . . are much more certain than others?" (HR 1:313). But if *this* is what one believes—that what is most evident is given in sense—he will certainly balk at suspending his faith in sense while giving a favored place to reason.

Now let us go back to the assumption we recently granted for the sake of discussion: that Everyman would be amenable to antecedent doubt. This is a strange assumption indeed if we keep the man of prejudice in mind. He is no philosopher, willing to entertain as serious possibility the most abstruse sort of supposition or posture. He is a "down-to-earth" man who believes that nothing is more evident than the everyday corporeal world that he knows through "sense"; he is Everyman. On what whim would he adopt antecedent doubt? Well, say Frankfurt and Kenny, perhaps it is not quite on a *whim*; René, after all, has upon occasion discovered false beliefs in himself—and, indeed, who has not? This, they say, makes the need for antecedent doubt appear plausible to him. But if so, he is a most curious fellow. For when he suggests to himself, shortly afterwards, that the senses are untrustworthy because they sometimes deceive, he immediately answers himself back that a general distrust of the senses is unreasonable since he can distinguish between deceptions of sense and cases in which sense does not deceive. Is he, then, supposed to find it plausible to doubt *everything* on the grounds that *some* things are dubious?

Finally, I shall ask, "How would antecedent doubt serve the therapeutic purposes of Cartesian method? In what way could it help to break the force of the habits which impair reason and keep it weak?" Given what we know about the state of prejudice, what would seem to be called for in the first instance is to break the hold that "sense" and its objects have on a prejudiced man's thought. It is this after all, that enslaves reason, a principle which would really be—if we could free it from its bonds—worthy of his confidence. To break this hold, whose tremendous power Descartes repeatedly emphasizes, it would seem necessary first of all to *single out* "sense" and find a way to discredit it—a

way that would seem persuasive to a man of prejudice. And since his
faith resides first and foremost in "sense," we have somehow to get
sense to defeat itself. Having once managed to do this, the man of
prejudice would be left with his reason, still bound, however, by habit
to applying itself to *images*. What we would like to do next is to break
this residual habit in its turn. By forcing a crisis in which reason, too,
will evidently be discredited unless it forsakes images for ideas of
purely intelligible things, we can perhaps accomplish our purpose.
Thus would the habits of prejudice be broken, and reason emended.

Therapy, therefore, evidently demands a selective and ordered procedure; not a procedure which commences with wholesale, unselective
doubt. Antecedent doubt would pit the will against the powerful habits
of prejudice, and the will could hold sway in such a battle for a short
time at most. Moreover, subsequent to the struggle, habits which constitute prejudice would remain unaffected. Thus, antecedent doubt is
therapeutically pointless. The force of Cartesian therapy comes from
the skeptical arguments which pit bad habits of mind against one
another or against themselves—a purpose which would little be served
by *suspending* them. This, I believe, is precisely what is accomplished
by the skeptical arguments of the *Meditations*. A therapeutic interpretation explains not only why such arguments are needed, but even the
order in which they are presented.

In the *Search After Truth*, Eudoxus says that a man

should set himself once for all to remove from his imagination all the in-
exact ideas which have hitherto succeeded in engraving themselves upon it,
and seriously begin to form new ones, applying thereto all the strength of
his intelligence. [HR 1:312]

"That would be an excellent remedy," Epistemon agrees,

if we could easily employ it; but you [Eudoxus] are not ignorant that the
opinions first received by our imagination remain so deeply imprinted there,
that our will alone, if it did not employ the aid of certain strong reasons,
could not arrive at effacing them. [HR 1:312–13]

"It is certain of these reasons that I hope to teach you," replies
Eudoxus, and thereupon enters upon skeptical arguments almost
identical to those of the *Meditations*.

I have argued, as have many before me, that antecedent doubt is a
troublesome affair. I have further argued that it is useless for—even
antagonistic to—Descartes's purposes. It is time we left off thinking that
it is any part of Cartesian method.

VII

In this section, and the three that follow, I sketch, very selectively, an account of the progress of Cartesian doubt through the stages represented in Meditations I–III. I tolerate some deliberate oversimplifications, my aim being to reinforce points already made, to bring out some important further details of Descartes's method, and to show further how understanding of the method is promoted by keeping its therapeutic purpose in mind.

Let us begin at the beginning. While others, as we have seen, make much more of it, I find only these two points of methodological interest in the opening paragraph of Meditation I: the somewhat understated declaration committing the whole enterprise to the search for "something firm and lasting in the sciences," and the resolution, seen as deriving from that commitment, to devote time to "the earnest and general upset" of opinions formerly held. Frankfurt sees this last resolution as "an unequivocal commitment," on René's part, "to overthrow [antecedently, Frankfurt means] all his opinions," but I cannot agree. There *is*, surely, a commitment on René's part to *try* to doubt his opinions in general, but no indication that this is to be attempted *in advance* of skeptical arguments, and no promise that the attempt to doubt will *succeed*.

Perhaps even more important than the initial paragraph of the Meditation is the second paragraph, where René says:

reason already persuades me that assent must be withheld no less scrupulously from things that are not entirely certain and indubitable than from things that are plainly false. For the rejection of all my opinions, therefore, it will be enough if I discover in each one of them some reason for doubting. And they need not be gone over one by one for that purpose. . . . when the foundations have been undermined, whatever has been built up upon them will collapse of itself. Hence, I shall immediately attack the very principles upon which everything I once believed depended. [HR 1:148; Frankfurt, *Demons*, p. 10]

Here, there are several things of interest to us.

(1) The search for "something firm and lasting in the sciences" is equated to a search for something "entirely certain and indubitable." This equation has farreaching consequences, but it is not argued for in the *Meditations*. If one insists that antecedent doubt is a part of the Cartesian procedure, large problems arise at this point, for why is this equation not to be doubted along with everything else? But therapeutic considerations demand only that the equation be prima facie plausible to Everyman: not an unreasonable assumption.

(2) René also tells us that accepting the commitment to search for

something "entirely certain and indubitable" evidently requires that we adopt the *methodological rule* which governs the skeptical arguments that are to follow: *Withhold assent from things that are not entirely certain no less than from those plainly false*; "reason persuades" him of it, he says. On my interpretation, "reason" here needs only to be reasoning, and no argument is required to excuse its use; while if we fail to distinguish reasoning from Reason, or, again, if we insist that René has already opted for antecedent doubt, we let ourselves in for a bad time. My only question is whether Everyman will find much to offend his reason in adopting this rule, given that he has agreed to come this far; and I cannot see that he should.

Still, there may be some confusion about what the rule means. Kenny says that:

Descartes distinguishes between two stages of doubt. His skeptical arguments [which occupy the remainder of Meditation I] convince him that none of his former ideas are beyond legitimate doubt: his opinions are no more than probable.

This Kenny identifies with what Descartes elsewhere calls "calling a belief into question." But:

To correct his natural bias toward regarding his beliefs as certain, he . . . "pretends" that all his beliefs are wholly false and imaginary. . . . it is clear that he meant the distinction between "calling into question" and "rejecting as false" to be the distinction between hesitant belief and suspension of judgment.[22]

This is wrong. As is plain from his procedure, by "calling into question" or "withholding assent from things not entirely certain and indubitable" Descartes means withholding one's assent on a matter tendered for belief in the light of reasons which are not themselves taken to be certain and indubitable—it is only required that the reasons not be taken to be completely false. By "rejecting as false" or "withholding assent from things plainly false" Descartes means withholding one's assent on a given matter on conclusive grounds; the reasons given are taken to be certain and indubitable.

Understanding the rule thus explains the procedure exploited in the skeptical arguments: to "doubt" a belief, or "call it into question," we must find grounds for doing so. But these grounds do not have to be things which we consider true; they have only to be considered possible. They may even be considered very far-fetched and improbable—then the doubt is said to be "hyperbolical" or "metaphysical." So the rule Descartes is adopting is: to suspend judgment on any matter where there are *any* grounds for doing so, no matter how improbable, *just* as one would do in the face of *conclusive* grounds for doing so. To "pretend that something is false" is, *here,* to pretend that one has conclusive grounds for doubting it (even when the doubt is in fact metaphysical).[23]

(3) The final point of importance that René makes in the passage quoted above is that, in general, the approach to be followed is to show that a given belief is dubitable by showing that it rests on, or originates from, a fallible principle. How this works is explained below.

VIII

After adopting the rule which gives shape to his procedure, Descartes enters immediately into the skeptical arguments of Meditation I. The first argument is an attack on "sense." It is said that the senses sometimes deceive us, "and it is wiser not to trust entirely to any thing by which we have once been deceived" (HR 1:145). But, importantly, it is immediately seen that this argument fails to give even probable grounds for suspending our judgment about the bulk of what the senses tell us; for as Polyander immediately rejoins to the same argument in the *Search after Truth*:

I am well aware that the senses sometimes deceive us when they are ill affected. . . . But all their errors are easily known, and do not prevent my now being perfectly persuaded that . . . in a word, that all that my senses usually offer to me is true. [HR 1:113]

This is an important move, and is repeated more than once. The move is, to distinguish between those beliefs of similar provenance that may reasonably be regarded as subjects to correction or rejection, and those that may reasonably be considered true. In order to discredit all beliefs resting on a given principle, say sensory beliefs, it is not enough to show that the principle upon which they are based produces some dubious beliefs. The principle is not discredited unless it is also the case that there is no recognizable characteristic of the dubious products of the principle by which they can be distinguished from the other products of the principle. *Seeing this is essential to understanding the procedure*—it is not quite as easy as many critics have claimed to discredit a principle on the Cartesian methodology.

Since there is evidently a way to distinguish dubious products of sense from other ones, the attempt to discredit sense must enter a second stage. Actually, as Frankfurt emphasizes, we find a series of skeptical arguments directed at the senses in Meditation I. Each is unsuccessful until René presents the dream argument, which, it seems to him, thoroughly discredits the principle of sense; this is precisely because, it is claimed, we cannot distinguish sensory experiences in dreams from waking experiences.[24]

IX

For simplicity, I shall ignore here the bulk of the difficult skeptical argument against knowledge of simple natures, and shall look only at the latter part of it, which is directed against the knowledge supposedly given by "arithmetic, geometry, and so on, which treat only of the simplest and most general subject-matter, and are indifferent [*parum curant*] whether it exists in nature or not": "Whether I am awake or asleep [René says], two and three add up to five, and a square has only four sides; and it seems impossible for such obvious truths to fall under a suspicion of being false" (HR 1:147; AG 63). In spite of this optimism, René finds grounds for doubting even such "obvious truths":

just as I judge from time to time that others err about such things as they think themselves to know most perfectly, do I likewise add two and three, or count the sides of a square, or do something easier, if that can be thought up, in such a way that I always go wrong? [HR 1:147; AT 7:2]

What René is doubting here seems clearly the reliability of the calculation (cf. Section II above) used to derive certain simple and general truths. It is not entirely obvious from this passage alone that such calculation is a form of reasoning, that is, reason *as he knows it*. But comparison with corresponding passages in the *Discourse* and in the *Principles* (which bracket the *Meditations* chronologically) makes this clear.

In the Discourse, the corresponding argument is:

because there are men who *deceive themselves in their reasoning and fall into paralogisms, even concerning the simplest matters* of geometry, and judging that I was as subject to error as was any other, I rejected as false all the reasons formerly accepted by me as demonstrations. [HR 1:101; emphasis added]

In this passage, indeed, it is specifically the reasoning which is put into question—geometry is just mentioned as providing the simplest (and presumably, therefore, most dependable) *examples* of reasoning.

Similarly, in *Principles* I. 5, we find Descartes saying that *in addition* to doubting of sensible things:

We shall also doubt of the *other* things [*reliquis*] which we formerly took to be quite certain; both mathematical demonstrations, and of the principles which until now we supposed to be self-evident: for in the past we have seen people erring in such things, and admitting as very certain and self-evident what seemed false to us. [HR 1:220; AT 8:6; emphasis added][25]

Notice particularly that what is here subjected to doubt is said explicitly to be something other than what is given in sense; and it is hard not to imagine that this passage is supposed to make virtually the same point that we saw being made in the *Meditations*.

Given the corroboration of these three texts by one another, it seems clear that Descartes means René to be putting reasoning into some kind of doubt.

Now, I agree with Frankfurt's well-argued view that René cannot be raising doubts about what is clearly and distinctly perceived, or about Reason, as we called it. Such doubts can only come when René becomes *aware* of the Natural Light in Meditation III.[26] But, because Frankfurt maintains no consistent distinction between reasoning and Reason, he thinks that he must deny that René can be arguing skeptically against *reason* in Meditation I—the skeptical argument *must*, Frankfurt thinks, be somehow directed at the senses. However, although René cannot, *we* must surely distinguish reasoning from Reason, and be clear about the fact that a Cartesian doubter *needs* reason in the form of reasoning from the beginning, else his enterprise cannot be carried out. Moreover, it ought to be quite clear to *him* that this is so (except that he will not understand the limitations in his understanding of reason). If we keep clear that there is a distinction between reasoning and Reason, *and* that René cannot yet make it, then we can see how reason *can* be doubted in Meditation I, and that it would be implausible if it were *not*. For otherwise there would be a lacuna in the therapy. In the state of prejudice, a man puts his faith first in "sense" and next in reasoning. Prejudice cannot be conquered unless his faith in both of these is defeated. After the dream argument, sense is discredited. This is a formidable defeat for prejudice, since sense was supposed to be the principle upon which rested knowledge of extramental things. Still, reasoning was also supposed to provide knowledge, and it is inevitable that, with the discrediting of "sense," the man of prejudice will turn to reasoning, which must, if prejudice is to be overcome, be attacked in its turn.

We can agree that Frankfurt is, after all, right in a way. Descartes *does* think, as we have remarked, that a prejudiced man cannot disentangle reason from the senses. Even so, reasoning is not purely sensation, and René would not identify it as such. Thus, in my judgment, Frankfurt's explanation obscures the important point that reason(ing) is available to be doubted in Meditation I, and is doubted. Moreover,

since the doubter cannot distinguish reasoning from Reason, he understands it to be reason that he doubts.

It is little wonder, then, that René is so gloomy at the end of
Meditation I. As a man of prejudice, he supposed that there were two
principles which produced ideas in which he could believe: "sense,"
and reason (which he identifies with reasoning). But, by skeptical argumentation, "sense" was discredited, and all the opinions which rested
upon it shown to be dubious. Now, reason has also been threatened,
and unless he can somehow prevent its being discredited, he will be
left with nothing to believe in, and no power in which he can place his
trust. As far as he can see, René has come very close to universal consequent doubt at the end of Meditation I, for he still has no inkling of
the Light of Nature.

X

In fact, the discrediting of reason in Meditation I is, as I understand things, *not complete*, and the consequent doubt, therefore, *not*
universal, even from René's still-restricted vantage point. If it were,
René would never have found the cogito, and through it, discovered
reason in the form of the Natural Light.

Those who wrongly think that René is questioning Reason in Meditation I are either forced to the conclusion that he must be defeated, or
forced to posit convoluted defences of his method.

But I look at the transition from the end of Meditation I to the
beginning of Meditation II as yet another case of the important move,
made more than once in the preceding skeptical arguments, to fend off
the discrediting of a principle. Some dubious thing is brought forward
which rests on the principle; then the question is whether there is anything that enables us to distinguish the dubious thing from the other
things resting on that principle. If not, then the principle, and all that
rests upon it, is found wanting. But if we *can* find a distinction, the
principle, and much of what rests upon it, is saved.

The skeptical arguments discussed in section IX above *are* attempts
to discredit reason; for, again, René draws no distinction between
reasoning and Reason. The senses have already been discredited, and a
significant portion of the habits of prejudice, therefore, weakened or
broken.[27] At this desperate point (for where will he turn for knowledge
if reason be discredited?), René is ripe for understanding—he is forced
to attend much more closely to reason than he has ever done in the
past, in order to see if a distinction can be drawn between cases of
reason which his skeptical arguments have thrown into doubt, and

other cases. He is, moreover, armed with the realization that whatever is to escape, the fate of "sense" has to be disentangled from it.

In the cogito,[28] he finds a product of reason which evidently resists the doubts he has raised, even the doubts involving the malignant spirit, which I have not discussed. But he must still discern what it is about this exceptional case that makes it exceptional; for, if he cannot do this, he cannot be confident that it is excepted from the doubt (e.g., if he cannot come to understand *sum* in another sense than "a man exists" or "a body exists" then the cogito *would* be subject to the doubts of Meditation I). To discern what it is that distinguishes the cogito from the dubitable products of reason, he is forced to clarify it, and, in the course of this intensely introspective clarification, to look at his own intellect and its products *in abstracto*. He has always had the *capacity*, but not until now the *ability*, to do this. This ability begins to develop here because (1) the distraction of the senses is diminished, and because (2) trying to fend off the doubt forces the exercise of the ability. As Aristotle pointed out, this is how abilities grow.

When his second Meditation is over, René is ready to characterize the special features of the cogito that distinguish it from the dubitable truths of reason—its clarity and distinctness. Thus does René discover Reason within reason.

Now we can see why René makes no appeal to Reason, that is, to the Natural Light, until Meditation III. And there, having once discovered it, he immediately does what he promised himself he would do, namely, tries to discredit it. This is the final and most "hyperbolical" doubt, and, as we know, Reason triumphs over it. But the doubts of Meditation III constitute the *second* attempt to doubt reason.

We saw in the case of sense how the first stage in the skeptical argument, the observation that the senses sometimes deceive, does not discredit the sense as a principle because we can characterize the dubious products of the senses as products of "ill-affected" sense, and can distinguish these from other products of sense. New arguments are then needed to bring into question the productions of the senses when *not* ill-affected.

In a parallel way, the argument that reason often goes wrong, although surely a skeptical argument against reason, does not discredit the principle of reason once we can characterize its dubious products as confused, i.e., unclear or indistinct. This characterization is harder to come by than the one that (temporarily) saved sensation; in Descartes's view, this is because René is initially well-acquainted with his senses, but ill-acquainted with his intellect. Making the characterization saves reason which *is* clear and distinct from the original skeptical argument, but asks for a new one. It also shows René that all of his former opinions, which rested either on "sense" or "reasoning," really were dubious. For although he possessed all along a principle, reason, which has so far resisted (and ultimately will resist) attempts to discredit it, he has discovered that in previously arriving at opinions by means of principle, the principle was wrongly used, and the opinions dubious.

Incidentally, although I here eschew discussing the famous "Cartesian Circle," some clever (and perhaps malicious) devil will ask whether I don't perhaps introduce a *new* circle. "You say René is doubting reason in Meditation I, but does he not have to *use* reason, the very thing he is doubting, in order to escape the doubt? True, there may be, as you say, a distinction to draw between reasoning and Reason, but *he* cannot draw it; so how can he proceed, without begging the question?" This misunderstands the procedure René uses throughout, at least if my previous accounts of it were accurate. Noticing some dubious products of a given principle—here, *reason*—does not discredit the faculty unless there is no way of distinguishing those products from the other products of the principle. Descartes finds some grounds for doubting reason, but the principle is not discredited—and therefore can still be used without violating the procedure—unless and until he is convinced that the dubious products of reason are indistinguishable from the rest. It develops, though, that they *are* distinguishable. So there is no *new* "Cartesian Circle"; and we might even learn something from this about the old one.

NOTES

I am greatly indebted to Billy DeAngelis, Eyjolfur Emilsson, Richard Lee, and Jeffrey Tlumak for their detailed and helpful comments on earlier versions of this paper. In addition, I owe profuse thanks to Eyjolfur Emilsson and Thorsteinn Gylfason for their help in checking and preparing translations of Cartesian material. The original translations that appear in this paper are reworkings by myself of word-for-word translations made by them, with occasional—and much appreciated—advice from Sigurdur Petursson.

1. The implied comparison with Spinoza is deliberate.

2. Harry Frankfurt, *Demons, Dreamers, and Madmen* (Indianapolis, 1970).

3. I have used this translation unless otherwise noted, and have always cited HR page no. for any translation quoted. Where that translation is not by Haldane and Ross, I have also cited the source of the translation used. In some cases, translations were specifically prepared for this text—here, the reader will find a reference to AT, giving the locus of the material translated, as well as the HR reference.

4. In fact, Descartes does not have a unified or unambiguous account. The account that follows is constructed out of things Descartes says in many places, most especially the following: *Meditations* I (esp. HR 1:147–48) and III (esp. HR 1:160–61); *Principles* I. 70–74; "Replies to Objections VI," 9–10; *Search* (esp. HR 1:311–12).

5. Descartes very often seems to use the word "demonstration" to mean "demonstrandum" or "theorem."

6. Descartes evidently believes this because reasoning and Reason bring to mind ideas which do not evidently come from sense, imagination, or memory. Moreover, both reasoning and Reason are, at least in part, powers of inference.

This is a rather deep question which I am exploring in my "Reason in Descartes" (in preparation).

7. Thus I must disagree with Frankfurt's remark that the "lack of sophistication" of the unenlightened man concerns *doctrine* (Frankfurt, *Demons*, p. 5).

8. Frankfurt, *Demons*, pp. 10, 33. I agree with Frankfurt, however, that the worrisome issues center on the *use* of faculties, which is governed by what he calls "rules of evidence." It is the latter which Frankfurt takes Descartes's "principles" to be.

9. Hume, *Enquiry*, ed. by L. A. Selby-Bigge (Oxford: Clarendon Press, 1902), XII. i (pp. 149–50).

10. "Consequent" is also Hume's term: "There is another species of scepticism, *consequent* to science and inquiry, when men are supposed to have discovered either the absolute fallaciousness of their mental faculties, or their unfitness to reach any fixed determination in all those curious subjects of speculation, about which they are commonly employed." (Hume, *Enquiry*, XII. i).

11. Frankfurt, for example, wants to except reason from antecedent doubt.

12. Anthony Kenny, *Descartes: A Study of His Philosophy* (New York, 1968), pp. 18–20.

13. Frankfurt, *Demons*, p. 16, quoting Descartes from translation in *ibid.*, pp. 19–20; emphasis added.

14. Ibid., p. 20.

15. Ibid., p. 17.

16. 12 January 1646: HR 2:126; Frankfurt, *Demons*, pp. 19, 21.

17. Frankfurt, *Demons*, pp. 18, 22.

18. Hume, *Enquiry*, XII. i.

19. Kenny, *Descartes*, p. 20.

20. Frankfurt, *Demons*, p. 28.

21. Ibid., p. 29.

22. Kenny, *Descartes*, pp. 22–23.

23. Here J. Tlumak asks whether this does not mean that we are to "operate with the demon hypothesis as if it were a certainty;" if it does, he points out, the consequences (I will not here recount his very well-directed arguments), rather than helping with the therapy, are disastrous. But I do not mean to say here that Descartes thinks we should treat the particular ground for doubt as certainties. His "pretense" is more like standing in front of the mirror each morning and telling yourself "Every day I'm getting better and better" without necessarily having in mind any of your actual improvements. Having found even the slightest grounds for doubting x, we should, to combat prejudice, tell ourselves, over and over, "Now x has been proved dubious." Descartes seems to think that we are likely to backslide *anyway*.

24. Frankfurt, *Demons*, pp. 34–35.

25. *Principles* I. 4 is entitled "Why we may doubt of sensible things" and recapitulates in condensed form the skeptical arguments against the senses from Meditation I. *Principles* I. 5 is entitled "Why we may likewise doubt of the demonstrations of mathematics."

26. J. Tlumak has rightly criticized me for identifying, without argument, the exercise of Reason (or the Natural Light) with clear and distinct perception, and for claiming, again without argument, that the Natural Light is subjected to doubt in Meditation III. These are controversial issues, J. Tlumak points out, and there are substantial arguments, which I have done nothing to answer, directed against my stand on both of these points. I am prepared to argue for my position, but have not the space to do so here. Rather I shall acknowledge my obligation to do so at an appropriate hour.

27. The extent to which prejudiced habits are weakened by the skeptical arguments depends upon the assiduousness with which they have been studied and reviewed, as Descartes stresses repeatedly.

28. In fact, there is nothing simply identifiable as "the cogito." See both Frankfurt and Kenny on this subject.

Science and
Certainty in Descartes

DANIEL GARBER

DESCARTES'S PRINCIPAL project was to build a science of nature about which he could have absolute certainty. From his earliest writings he argues that unless we have absolute certainty about every element of science at every level, we have no genuine science at all. But while the very general sketches Descartes gave for his project were clear, the details of just how he was to build such a science and precisely what it was to look like when he finished were not. The traditional view is that what Descartes had in mind was a science structured somewhat like Euclid's *Elements*, starting with a priori first principles, and deriving "more geometrico" all there is to know about the world. On this view, it is fairly clear why Descartes might have thought that he was building a certain science. A science built more geometrico would seem to be as certain as geometry itself. But among most scholars the traditional view has given way to the realization that observation and experiment play an important role in Descartes's scientific method, both in theory and in practice.[1] There is no question in my own mind that this view of Descartes's science is correct. But this new realization of Descartes the experimenter raises a curious question. If the geometrical model of Cartesian science is not correct, then what of certainty? How could Descartes have thought that he could find certainty in an experimental science? Or for that matter, did Descartes, in the end, think that certainty is possible for science? It is my main goal in this paper to present an alternative to the traditional geometrical model of Cartesian science in which it will be evident why Descartes thought his science both experimental and certain.

But there is an historical dimension to this problem that is often ignored. Descartes's work in natural science falls roughly into two parts.

In his earlier works, for the most part those which precede the *Principia Philosophiae* (1644), including the *Regulae ad Directionem Ingenii* (1628?), *Le Monde* (1633), the *Discourse on the Method, Optics,* and *Meteorology* (1637), and the *Meditations* (1641), Descartes is formulating his views on nature and presenting them little by little.[2] In this period, Descartes's work is filled with many promises: programmatic sketches of the science he claims to have formulated, and claims about arguments and deductions he thinks he has found. It is only in his later work, his *Principia Philosophiae,* that he attempts to present his science with any completeness. It is here that we find Descartes's earlier promises kept, and, all too often, broken. If we examine Descartes in this way, we find a noticeable difference between these two periods. In the earlier period Descartes is quite confident that he has found the way to certain knowledge, and it is in this period that the insistence on certainty is strongest. But in the later period, Descartes must come face to face with the extreme difficulty of actually presenting such a science, and his commitment to certainty undergoes interesting changes.

My discussion of certainty in Descartes's science falls into three sections. In the first, I shall discuss the notion of certainty in Descartes's earlier writings and present some of the basic reasons for rejecting the more traditional view of Cartesian science as a deductive system on the model of Euclidean geometry. In the second, main section of this paper, I shall try to replace the geometrical model with a model of the inferential structure of Cartesian science that better reflects Descartes's thinking, at least in the earlier period. I shall present it in such a way that it will be evident how Descartes could think that his science is both experimental and certain. In this section I shall also discuss the status of hypotheses at this point in Descartes's thought. Having seen the outlines of Descartes's early, grand program for the sciences, I shall in section three examine how Descartes's earlier conception fares in the *Principles.* There we shall see strong suggestions that Descartes is moving to give up his earlier conception of certainty in science.

Before I begin this ambitious project, one remark is in order. I shall not offer any general account of Cartesian method, nor shall I offer any systematic interpretation of the early and problematic *Regulae,* as is common practice in methodological discussions of Descartes's science.[3] Rather, I shall concentrate on the many places in which Descartes talks specifically about the epistemic and inferential structure of his theory of the world. I shall bring in passages from the more general and abstract discussions of method when I feel that their interpretation is sufficiently obvious, and when they bear on the interpretation of some specific point Descartes is making about his conception of science. I make no general claim about the unity of Descartes's methodological thought over and above the specific continuities that I shall point out in the course of this paper.

One last caution before we begin. Though Descartes's goal was certainty, mine is not. In a paper as short as this, I cannot hope to present the case I would like to make in sufficient detail. My only hope is to clear away some of the obscurity surrounding some of the important questions about Descartes's science, and sketch, in broad strokes, one line for reinterpreting his scientific enterprise.

I

Preliminary Remarks on Certainty

Early on in his youthful *Regulae*, Descartes declares:

We should be concerned only with those objects regarding which our minds seem capable of obtaining certain and indubitable knowledge [cognitionem].

All science [*scientia*] is certain, evident knowledge [*cognitio*], and he who doubts many things is not more learned than he who has never thought about these things. . . . And so, in accordance with this rule, we reject all knowledge [*cognitiones*] which is merely probable [*probabiles*] and judge that only those things should be believed which are perfectly known [*perfecte cognitis*] and about which we can have no doubts. [Rule II: AT 10:362; HR 1:3]

Certainty was clearly of the greatest importance to Descartes. In this section I would like to explore briefly what he meant by certainty.

In the *Regulae*, Descartes gives us a straightforward account of what he means by certain knowledge, in terms of the cognitive operations that result in certainty, intuition and deduction, "From all these things we conclude . . . that there are no paths to the certain knowledge of truth open to man except evident *intuition* and necessary *deduction*" (Rule XII: AT 10:425; HR 1:45, emphasis added).[4] Certain knowledge, then, is that which can be presented as the product of intuition or deduction.

Descartes explains what he means by intuition in the following passage:

By intuition I understand . . . the conception of the pure and attentive mind which is so simple and distinct that we can have no further doubt as to what we understand; or, what amounts to the same thing, an indubitable conception of the unclouded and attentive mind which arises from the light of reason alone. [Rule III: AT 10:368; HR 1:7]

There is much over which one could pause in this account of intuition. For the moment, though, I would merely point out how open this definition is. In this passage of the *Regulae*, the only one in which he attempts a general characterization of intuition, Descartes sets no a priori limits to the domain of intuition. Precisely what knowledge it is that he thinks we can acquire through intuition can be settled only by examining the particular examples of intuition he presents, and cannot be derived from his definition alone. The examples he offers of intuited truths include our own existence, that we think, that a sphere has only one surface, and "other similar things" (AT 10:368; HR 1:7). More generally he associates the domain of intuition with what he calls "absolutes" and "simple natures."⁵

Descartes attempts to characterize deduction in the following passage:

Many things are known with certainty although they are not evident in themselves for the sole reason that they are *deduced* from true and known [*cognitis*] principles *by a continuous and uninterrupted process of thought, in which each part of the process is clearly intuited.* . . . We can therefore distinguish an intuition of the mind from a deduction which is certain by the fact that in the latter we perceive a movement or a certain [*quaedam*] succession of thought, while we do not in the former. [Rule III: AT 10:369–70; HR 1:8, emphasis added.]⁶

Deduction, then, can be defined in terms of intuition. A deduction is a succession of propositions, ordered in such a way that each one follows from the preceding through an act of intuition.⁷ While it is possible to start such a deduction from any premise, Descartes usually limits the applicability of the term "deduction" to those arguments and conclusions which begin with a premise that is derived from intuition, or is the conclusion of another deduction.

As we remarked with respect to intuition, Descartes's conception of deduction is quite loose. A deduction as defined seems to be any argument, whatever its form might be, all of whose steps can be connected by acts of intuition. In the *Regulae*, Descartes is quite clear in disassociating the kind of argument he has in mind from the more formal syllogism:

But perhaps some will be astonished that . . . we omit all the rules by which the logicians think they regulate human reason. . . . (We) reject those forms of theirs [*istas formas*] as opposed to our teaching, and seek rather all the aids by which our mind may remain alert. . . . And so that it will be more evident that the syllogistic art is of practically no assistance in the search for truth, we should notice that logicians can form no syllogism which reaches a true conclusion unless the heart of the matter is given, that is, unless they previously recognized the very truth which is thus deduced. [Rule X: AT 10:405–6; HR 1:32]

Obviously, Descartes conceived of deduction as a kind of argument much broader in scope than the syllogism. While nothing important will depend on my rather unorthodox reading, it looks as if he thought that deductive arguments (with intuitive premises, of course) could yield conclusions which are not merely contained in the premises, to criticize the "syllogistic art" the way he does. Precisely what arguments Descartes was willing to accept as deductive, though, cannot be determined by appeal to his definition. As was the case with intuition, to understand what he has in mind we must appeal to the examples of deductive reasoning Descartes gives, and note those arguments that he rejects as yielding uncertain conclusions.

Before I turn to later accounts of certainty in Descartes's writings, a short digression about the relation between certainty and method in the *Regulae* would be in order. The *Regulae* is intended to give us "directions" for finding certainties. Descartes gives a procedure that he thinks will put us in a position so that we can discover intuitive truths, and discover deductive connections. The certain knowledge that is the end product of the *Regulae* is certain, not because it was found using Descartes's method, but because it can be presented as the product of intuition and deduction. This plausible reading of the *Regulae* is supported by two features of that work. First of all, Descartes opens the work with a discussion of what certainty is (Rules I–III) and does not talk at all about the method for finding certainty until Rule IV. When he finally comes to discuss how we find certain truth, he uses a metaphor of finding the road that leads us to the "treasure" (Rule IV: AT 10:371; HR 1:9). This strongly suggests that the method is a way of finding something, like the treasure, whose worth and value lies in something other than the path we take to it. Also, Descartes admits that his method is not the only way of discovering certainty. He recognizes others, but argues that they are more difficult (Rule VI: AT 10:384–87; HR 1:17–19). Thus a given item of knowledge is certain not by virtue of the way we discover it (e.g., by using Cartesian method), but by the way in which we justify it (i.e., by presenting it as the product of intuition and deduction). Consequently, I see no problems in divorcing Descartes's notion of certainty in the *Regulae* from the details of the method offered there.

At the heart of the notion of certainty in the *Regulae* are the notions of intuition and deduction. Descartes's theory of certainty changes, however, in later works, where he adopts a new criterion for certainty, clearness and distinctness. Thus, in the *Discourse on the Method*, Descartes presents the rule that we quoted at the beginning of this section as follows:

The first rule was never to accept anything as true unless I recognize it to be evidently such: that is, carefully to avoid precipitation and prejudgment [*preuention*], and to include nothing in my conclusions unless it presented itself so clearly and distinctly to my mind that there was no occasion to doubt it. [AT 6:18; HR 1:92.]

There are a number of anticipations of this somewhat different conception of certainty in the *Regulae*. Descartes often talks about intuition and deduction in terms that involve the notion of distinctness and, occasionally, clearness as well.[8] But the clearness and distinctness account is substantially new in the *Discourse*.

With the introduction of this new vocabulary for discussing certainty come many problems for Descartes and the Cartesian scholar. For Descartes, with the new criterion of certainty comes a new enterprise, that of validating it. For the scholar comes the problem of explicating exactly what Descartes had in mind by clearness and distinctness, and exactly how he thought that his criterion of certainty could be validated (here is where the well-known Cartesian circle enters). In this paper I shall not discuss the criterion of clearness and distinctness or the difficulties raised by Descartes's attempt to validate that criterion. In fact, when discussing certainty I shall avoid the language of clearness and distinctness altogether, and return to the idiom of the *Regulae*, where certainty is characterized in terms of intuition and deduction. My avoidance of foundational problems with regard to certainty can be justified by noting that Descartes himself avoids such questions in his more narrowly scientific work, nor can I see any particularly good reason for raising the foundational problems in that context.[9]

My decision not to use the language of clearness and distinctness also derives from the texts. When talking about scientific questions and the structure of science, Descartes himself seems to avoid the terminology of clearness and distinctness, and falls more naturally into the terminology of intuition (sometimes) and deduction (quite often), as we shall see when we take up such passages in detail. There is thus a certain advantage to following Descartes in this, since it will be thereby easier for us to follow his discussions of certainty in science. The fact that the old way of talking about certainty persists throughout the later writings suggests strongly that Descartes thought that the earlier account could be translated into, or at least justified by, the later account. Just how such a justification, translation, or explication could be given is itself an interpretive problem of major proportions. I assume that everything I say (and Descartes said) about Cartesian science in terms of intuition and deduction can be given a reading *salva veritate* in terms of clearness and distinctness, though I shall not attempt to argue this. There are other problems raised by my choice of the earlier idiom. Most particularly, unlike clearness and distinctness, the characterization of certainty in terms of intuition and deduction gives us no real criteria that can be used for telling when something is certain and when it is not. Consequently we will have to appeal to what Descartes explicitly says is intuitive, deductive, or certain truth, as we noted earlier. But this is a small price to pay for what will turn out to be a major gain in simplicity and naturalness when we talk about Descartes's scientific reasoning.

So my criterion of certainty for Cartesian science will be the following: a body of scientific results will be certain for an individual if and only if that individual could present it as the product of intuition and deduction. The modal 'could' is important here. Descartes does not always have to present his science as derived from intuition and deduction for him to claim that it is certain. What makes it certain for him is that he could present it in that way.[10]

Having outlined Descartes's abstract notion of certainty and the relations it bears to intuition and deduction on the one hand, and clearness and distinctness on the other, I shall close this section with some remarks about the scope of certainty for Descartes.

I pointed out earlier that Descartes's notion of deduction is broader than the notion of deduction in syllogistic logic, and that it seems to allow for arguments that yield conclusions not "contained in" their premises. At this point it might be interesting to draw some consequences from this and bring in some related considerations. In the introduction I noted that the traditional conception of Cartesian science is that of a science more geometrico, conclusions derived logically from a priori first principles. What we noted and conjectured about deduction in Descartes already casts doubt on this picture, but there are other reasons for rejecting it. If that picture is correct, then Cartesian science is limited to a priori certain truth. But it is quite clear that Descartes was willing to admit certainties which can be classed only as a posteriori. For example, in the *Meditations* Descartes offers arguments which he claims meet his criteria for certainty. Yet at least one of these—the argument for the existence of material objects in Meditation VI—is quite definitely not an a priori argument. This argument depends upon a premise (itself apparently intuitive and certain) about the ideas we have of material objects that cannot be a priori on any conception of a priori truth I know of. Thus not everything certain is a priori, and the limitation of science to the certain does not commit Descartes to an a priori science. And furthermore, since the argument I have cited is itself part of Descartes's broadly scientific structure, it is clear that Cartesian science could not be a priori in any modern sense.

But if we are to reject the picture of Cartesian science in which truths of science are logically derived from a priori first principles, what are we to make of the passages in which Descartes compares his enterprise to that of the geometer? Consider the following such passage:

Those long chains of reasoning, so simple and easy, which enabled the geometricians to reach their most difficult demonstrations, had made me wonder whether all things knowable to men might not follow from one another in the same fashion [s' entresuiuent en mesme façon]. If so, we need only to refrain from accepting as true that which is not true, and carefully follow the order necessary to deduce each one from the others, and there cannot be any propositions so abstruse that we cannot prove them, or so recondite that we cannot discover them. [Discourse, pt. II: AT 6:19; HR 1:92]

From what I said earlier it should be clear that Descartes is *not* looking to build a science like geometry in the sense in which geometry derives theorems from first principles using deductive reasoning taken in the narrowest sense. When he talks about "refraining from accepting as true that which is not true" (intuition?) and carefully following "the order necessary to *deduce* each one from the others," (deduction?) he seems quite consciously to be referring back to his theory of certainty in the *Regulae*. There too he talked about mathematics as a model for natural science, but his explicit conclusion there was that, "In seeking the correct path to truth we should be concerned with nothing about which we cannot have a *certainty equal to that of the demonstrations of arithmetic and geometry*" (Rule II: AT 10:366; HR 1:5, emphasis added).[11] So, if Descartes is to be construed as building a science more geometrico, it is not because he seeks to build a science that is a priori, like geometry, but rather because for Descartes "more geometrico" means only *more certo*.

The rejection of the naive geometrical model of Cartesian science, and the realization that not everything that is certain is, strictly speaking, a priori constitute an important part of the way toward a proper understanding of the nature of Descartes's science. But even if we understand the true significance of the geometrical model, we must still explain how and why Descartes thought that the science of nature he found was certain. This will be the task of the following section of this paper.

Having noted something that Descartes does not seem to exclude from the possibility of being certain, we should also note briefly something that he does want to exclude from the domain of the certain: probability. While it is traditional to see Descartes's demand for certainty as a response to scepticism, it is no less correct to regard the demand for certainty as a response to those who are willing to make do with probability.

When Descartes says that we must "reject all knowledge which is merely probable," as he does in the passage from the *Regulae* with which this section opened, he meant something somewhat different than we currently do by "probability." The notion of probability he had in mind was largely a notion from dialectic and rhetoric—the theories of debate and public speaking. "Probable" was one way in which the premises and arguments used in such debate were characterized.[12] In that context, "probable" meant something close to "generally accepted."[13]

The rejection of probability is part of Descartes's rejection of the whole rhetorical-dialectical tradition of education so prevalent in the Renaissance university.[14] For the most part, though, Descartes gives little characterization of probability and particular probabilistic modes of argument, except negatively, as things which cannot be (or, maybe, are not) presented either intuitively or deductively. Only one kind of argument is singled out for Descartes's attention, the kind of argument that makes use of conjecture:

Let us also take heed never to confuse any conjectures [*conjecturas*] with our judgments about the true state of things. Attention to this matter is of no little importance, for there is no stronger reason why contemporary philosophy has found nothing so evident and so certain that it cannot be controverted, than because those eager for knowledge . . . venture to affirm even obscure and unknown things, about which we can make only plausible conjectures [*probabilibus conjecturis*] and then give their whole credence to these, confusing them indiscriminately with the true and evident. Thus they can finally reach no conclusion which does not seem to depend upon some proposition of this sort, and all of their conclusions are therefore doubtful. [*Regulae,* Rule III: AT 10:367–68; HR 1:6–7][15]

It is not entirely clear what Descartes means by "conjecture" in this passage. The notion of a conjecture comes up only once again in the *Regulae*. There Descartes gives the following example:

Persons compose their judgments by conjecture if, for example, considering the fact that water, which is farther from the center of the globe than earth, is also more tenuous, and that air, higher than water, is still more tenuous, they conjecture that above the air there is nothing but a certain very pure ether, and that it is much more tenuous than the air itself, and so on. [Rule XII: AT 10:424; HR 1:45]

This is something of an argument from analogy. But the earlier characterization of conjecture suggests that conjectures include more than such arguments from analogy. The formula that Descartes uses, talk-

ing of those who "venture to affirm even obscure and unknown things
. . . and then give their whole credence to these" suggests (though not
entirely clearly or unambiguously) that the modern hypothetico-
deductive method or method of hypothesis in which we frame hypotheses that best explain experience and hold them until they are falsified
would count as one such probabilistic argument by conjecture.[16]

II

Cartesian Science in Theory: The *Discourse*

In the previous section I outlined Descartes's conception of certainty
and made some comments about its scope. In the context of the latter
discussion, I argued that the picture of science as logically deduced
from a priori first principles is not correct. In this section I would like
to outline the grand plan for all of science that Descartes presents in
the period of the *Discourse*. In so doing, I hope to sketch something of
an alternative to the traditional geometrical model of Cartesian science.

In this section I shall organize my discussion around what seems to
be the clearest and most explicit statement of the inferential structure
of Descartes's science in the earlier writings. I have divided this single
passage up into four parts and labeled each. In the discussion that follows I shall refer to each by letter. The passage is the familiar and often
quoted one from the *Discourse*:

A. My own procedure has been the following: I tried to discover the general
principles or first causes of all that exists or could exist in the world,
without taking any causes into consideration but God as creator, and
without using anything save certain seeds of the truth which we find in
our own minds.

B.   After that I examined what were the first and commonest effects which
could be deduced from these causes; and it seems to me that by this procedure I discovered skies, stars, and earth, and even, on the earth, water,
air, fire, minerals, and several other things which are the commonest of
all and the most simple, and in consequence the easiest to understand.

C.   Then, when I wanted to descend to particulars, it seemed to me that
there were so many different kinds that I believed it impossible for the
human mind to distinguish the forms or species of objects found on earth
from an infinity of others which might have been there if God had so
willed. Nor, as a consequence, could we make use of things unless we discover causes by their effects, and make use of many experiments. After
this, reviewing in my mind all the objects which had ever been presented
to my senses, I believe I can say that I have never noticed anything which
I could not explain easily enough by the principles I had found. But I
must also admit that the powers of nature are so ample and vast, and that
these principles are so simple and so general, that I hardly ever observed

a particular effect without immediately recognizing several ways in which it could be deduced.

D.   My greatest difficulty usually is to to find which of these ways (of deducing the effect) is correct, and to do this I know no other way than to seek several experiments such that their outcomes would be different according to the choice of one or another ways of deducing the effect. [pt. VI: AT 6:63–65; HR 1:121]

In what follows I shall try to extract the inferential structure of Descartes's science from this and related passages. More precisely, I shall be looking to explicate how Descartes conceived the structure of his science and whether he thought that it could be presented as the product of intuition and deduction. Consequently, we shall appeal to Descartes's scientific practice only insofar as it clarifies his intentions with respect to his theory of science. (I shall point out in the course of this discussion a number of places where Descartes's practice misleads us with respect to his theory.) Because I am interested in eliciting the outline of the whole of Descartes's grand program for science, I shall only give cursory glances at the details behind sections A and B, where the conception seems clearest and seems closest to the Euclidean model. Rather, I shall concentrate on sections C and D where the intentions become foggy, and where he seems, by the introduction of experiment, to diverge most clearly from the Euclidean model.

In A, Descartes discusses his discovery of "general principles or first causes." It is clear that Descartes has in mind at very least the metaphysical first principles outlined in part IV of the *Discourse* and presented in detail in the *Meditations*. These writings include the proof of his own existence, the proof that God exists, the validation of the criterion of clearness and distinctness, the proof that mind and body are distinct substances, and that the essence of material substance is extension, and the proof that there are material things. The "general principles or first causes" mentioned in A include more than these metaphysical matters, though. Given that B begins with Descartes's cosmology, it is reasonable to suppose that Descartes meant to include in the matters mentioned in A the laws of motion; in the *Discourse* account, these are sandwiched between the metaphysical first principles of part IV and the cosmology taken up at the beginning of part V (AT 6:43; HR 1:107–8).

In section A of his outline of the structure of science, there is relatively little problem with certainty. Though he is not entirely explicit, there is every indication that at this point certainty is maintained, and at least Descartes thought that all arguments referred to in A could be presented in terms of intuition and deduction. In fact, Descartes seemed to regard the metaphysical arguments, at least, as paradigms of proper and certain argumentation. Before going on, though, we might remind ourselves that even at this beginning stage, we have left the a priori, strictly speaking. While all of the arguments Descartes offers for the conclusions cited in this section proceed "without using anything save certain seeds [*semences*] of the truth which we find in our minds," certain of the arguments, like the argument for the existence of material objects, are a posteriori, as we noted earlier in section I.

So much for A. In B, Descartes discusses the first effects "which could be deduced" (*deduire*) from the "general principles or first causes" of A. These effects include the cosmology (sky, stars), the earth, and at least some of the contents of the earth (water, air, fire, minerals, and "several other things").[17] Given that Descartes used the technical term "deduce" (of course, in its French translation) it seems evident that Descartes thought that the effects mentioned in B were, or could be, established with certainty. Though it is not clear just how such a deduction could be given, it seems as if the chain of intuition and deduction is not yet broken, at least in Descartes's own thinking.

One thing should be mentioned at this point. Though in B Descartes talks about "deducing" his cosmology, etc., from first principles, this is not exactly how the argument is presented in the passage of part V of the *Discourse*, where that argument is outlined as it was given in *Le Monde*. There he argues with respect to an imaginary world, not our own, "I therefore resolved to leave this world . . . and to speak only of what would happen in a new one, if God should now create somewhere in imaginary space enough matter to make one" (AT 6:42; HR 1:107). The "deduction" of cosmology that follows there is thus not for our world, but for this imaginary world, a world that Descartes builds on the basis of certain assumptions. Insofar as the phenomena so deduced resemble our world, Descartes takes his assumptions to be adequate and the explanations correct. Such an argument would not, it seems, particularly in the light of the passage of the *Regulae* about conjecture cited at the end of section I, tell us anything certain about our world. But, given the clear statement in B that cosmology is deduced from the first causes of A, we must suppose here, I think, that Descartes's practice does not reflect his *theory* of science. A number of explanations are possible. It is most likely that in this passage Descartes is describing the route he found he had to take in the early work, *Le Monde*, but in B he is describing a later version of his system, either actual or contemplated, presumably what he hoped would later become his *Principles*. In adopting this explanation, though, I do not mean to ignore the question of how Descartes argued in the part of his scientific practice corresponding to B. I intend only to put that discussion off to a more appropriate place.

In A we saw that the question of intuition, deduction, and the resulting certainty is relatively unproblematic. There can be little question but that certainty is preserved at this point. Section B is somewhat more problematic, since the outlined arguments in the *Discourse* that correspond to that section are given only hypothetically. But in this case it is not implausible to separate the practice of the earlier work (*Le Monde* in this case) from the program that Descartes outlines in B, as I have already suggested. Thus nothing we have seen so far would cause a radical revision of the traditional Euclidean model. While a careful examination of the arguments Descartes has in mind in sections A and B would show us that they are not strictly deductive in the modern sense, as I have argued, the Euclidean model is not a bad fit. But the Euclidean model breaks down completely when we progress to section C. There, where Descartes first explicitly introduces *experiment*, all hope of fitting his conception of science to the Euclidean model seems to end. For that matter, all hope of certainty in science seems to end as well. What, then, is to be made of C? What has happened to deduction and certainty?

Let us examine C carefully. The particulars he has in mind are not entirely obvious. Certainly he intended animals and human beings.[18] Though the text is hardly explicit on this, I would presume that he would include things like magnets (a favorite example in Cartesian science) and other reasonably complex terrestrial phenomena. However, it does not seem tremendously important to specify precisely what belongs under C and what under B. By "descending to particulars" he seems to mean the process of giving an account of what these particulars are, i.e., an account of their natures, their internal structures. Again, though, Descartes is not entirely clear about the kind of account that he has in mind in this passage. If this is what Descartes is talking about here, then what he seems to be claiming is that we cannot give an account of the nature of the particulars in the world without appeal to experiment and reasoning from effect to cause. Furthermore, he also claims that even when we introduce experiments, there are a number of ways in which we can explain any particular on our first principles.

But what precisely does Descartes have in mind when he suggests that we must discover causes through their effects? Though Descartes is not explicit about this here, his scientific practice in two of the three essays (in particular, the *Optics* and the *Meteorology*) for which the *Discourse* serves as an introduction, in the parts of the earlier *Le Monde* that survive, and in the later *Principles,* and his methodological remarks, suggest that Descartes may have in mind some sort of reasoning that makes essential use of hypotheses, perhaps something like the modern hypothetico-deductive method. If we adopt this interpretation of Descartes, then we would reason from effects to causes by making a number of experiments, gathering the results, and framing a hypothesis that would explain those results in terms of our basic principles. If it is the hypothetico-deductive method that Descartes has in mind, then the hypothesis would be supported by virtue of explaining the experiments.[19]

The evidence in favor of the claim that Descartes was seriously committed to hypothetical arguments in science and that this is what he had in mind when he wrote C is substantial. Although I shall later argue against this reading, I shall try to present what seems to be the best evidence for this view. Since we are concerned with Descartes's attitudes and theories before the *Principles*, I shall not consider at this point many of the passages from the later work often cited and discussed in connection with whether or not Descartes adopted a hypothetical mode of argument. Those passages will be discussed in the following section when I discuss deduction and certainty in the *Principles*. And finally, I shall put off the question of certainty until after we present the case for Descartes's endorsement of hypothetical modes of argument.

The evidence that Descartes had some sort of hypothetical mode of argument in mind in this early period comes from both his scientific practice and from his more theoretical writings. I have already pointed out one passage from the *Discourse* where Descartes seems to describe the use of a hypothetical mode of argument in his scientific practice. That passage describes how he argued in *Le Monde* from an imaginary model of our world which in all respects is claimed to agree with ours at the level of phenomena (AT 6:42–44; HR 1:107–9). The hypothetical mode of argument is used in a different but related way in the *Optics* and the *Meteorology*. At the very beginning of the *Optics* Descartes notes:

Thus, not having here any other occasion to speak of light than to explain how its rays enter the eye . . . . I need not undertake to explain its true nature. And I believe that it will suffice that I make use of two or three comparisons which help to conceive it in the manner which seems the most convenient to explain [*expliquer*] all of its properties that experience acquaints us with, and to deduce [*deduire*] afterwards all the others which cannot be so easily observed; imitating in this the Astronomers, who although their assumptions [*suppositions*] are almost all false or uncertain, nevertheless, because these assumptions refer [*rapportent*] to different observations which they have made, never cease to draw many very true and well assured conclusions from them. [AT 6:83; trans. Olscamp, 66–67]

And later, in the beginning of the *Meteorology*, Descartes notes:

> It is true that since the knowledge [*connoissance*] of these matters depends on general principles of nature which have not yet, to my knowledge, been accurately explained, I shall have to use certain assumptions [*suppositions*] at the outset, as I did in the *Optics*. But I shall try to render them so simple and easy that perhaps you will have no difficulty in accepting them, even though I have not demonstrated [*demonstrées*] them. [AT 6:233; trans. Olscamp, 364]

Though these passages seem to support the claim we are examining, a few comments are in order. First of all, the kinds of assumptions that Descartes has in mind here are quite general. In the *Optics* Descartes assumes that light is transmitted instantaneously, in straight paths, and so on, and in the *Meteorology* he assumes that things are made up of corpuscles, that there is no void, and so on.[20] These assumptions clearly correspond to the conclusions discussed in section B, and seem to have little to do with the particulars of C. Consequently, the appeal to these passages may establish little, if anything, about the sort of reasoning that Descartes had in mind in C. But leaving this aside, it is important to recognize that this method of proceeding, while hypothetical, is not strictly hypothetico-deductive. Descartes takes as his starting place certain assumptions, and claims to be able to explain a variety of phenomena on those assumptions. But he makes no claims that the ability to explain the phenomena and deduce new phenomena "which cannot be so easily observed" renders the assumptions in any way true, certain, or even confirmed. In fact, he compares his assumptions with those of astronomy, which he claims are all "false or uncertain." The conception of astronomy he is referring to is one according to which the problem of astronomy is to find hypotheses about the motion of heavenly bodies which will "save the phenomena," while making no claims about the true causes of any of the phenomena.[21] This kind of instrumentalistic conception of theories is often appropriate in astronomy, where for many practical purposes (the construction of calendars, navigation, etc.) it is more important to know when and where in the sky particular bodies will be observed, than why they are there. But such a procedure would seem much less valuable in physics, where we have a greater interest in understanding the phenomena than in saving them. In fact, by the 1630s the traditional instrumentalistic attitude toward astronomical theories had long been given up in favor of a more realistic attitude among the best astronomers, including Copernicus, Tycho Brahe, Kepler, and Galileo.[22] It seems curious that Descartes would recommend that physicists adopt the approach of the astronomers, long after astronomers had given up that approach in favor of the more realistic project of finding the true explanations of things, a project which they borrowed from physics.

Elsewhere, though, Descartes does argue in a more straightforwardly hypothetico-deductive fashion:

And in all of this, the explanation [*raison*] accords so perfectly with experience [*l' experience*] that I do not believe it possible, after one has studied both carefully, to doubt that the matter is as I have just explained it [*l' expliquer*]. [*Meteorology*, discourse VIII: AT 6:334; trans. Olscamp, 338]

Here Descartes is talking about his explanation of the rainbow, a matter much closer to the concerns of section C than is discussed in the earlier passages. Also here, unlike those earlier passages, it does seem as if the explanans gains significant credibility by virtue of its explanatory power. This claim is defended quite explicitly in another passage, one that looks like an unambiguous and theoretical endorsement of the hypothetico-deductive mode of argument, both when we are dealing with particulars, such as rainbows and their nature, and when we are dealing with the sort of general assumptions discussed earlier and compared with astronomical assumptions:

If some of the matters I deal with at the beginning of *Optics* and *Meteorology* should at first sight appear offensive, because I call them assumptions [*suppositions*] and do not try to prove [*prouuer*] them, let the reader have the patience to read all of it with attention, and I hope that he will be satisfied with the result. For it seems to me that the explanations [*raisons*] follow one another in such a way, that just as the last are demonstrated [*demonstrées*] by the first, which are their causes, so these first are demonstrated [*demonstrées*] by the last which are their effects. And one must not suppose that I have here committed the fallacy which logicians call circular reasoning; for as experience makes most of the effects very certain [*car l'experience rendant la plus part de ces effets tres certains*], the causes from which I deduce [*deduits*] them serve not so much to prove [*prouuer*] as to explain them [*expliquer*]; but, on the contrary, the causes are proved by their effects [*ce sont elles qui sont prouuées par eux*]. [*Discourse* VI: AT 6:76; HR 1: 128–29].[23]

This passage, which bears a striking resemblance to modern discussions of hypothetico-deductive method, is echoed in some of the correspondence following the publication of the *Discourse* and the accompanying essays.[24] This passage and the corresponding theoretical comments in the correspondence strike me as the best evidence there is for the claim that Descartes was genuinely committed to the use of hypothetical arguments in science, and that the hypothetico-deductive method is what he has in mind in section C.

Let us review the story up to now. There is considerable evidence that Descartes had in mind some kind of hypothetical mode of argument in the period of the *Discourse*. There are complications, however. For one, it looks as if there are two distinctly different kinds of hypothetical argument in the texts, an astronomical argument, and a hypothetico-deductive argument (it is not clear to me that Descartes distinguished between these two kinds of argument, though). There is a further complication, one that arises when we attempt to argue that this hypothetical argument is what Descartes has in mind in C. Many of the texts supporting Descartes's endorsement of hypothetical modes of argument involve general sorts of assumptions of the sort that arise in B and not in C. These complications hardly seem decisive. However, if this is what Descartes meant by reasoning from effects to causes in C, what of certainty? What of the grand picture of a science grounded in intuition and deduction, as indubitable as geometry?

At this point in the argument there seem to be only two directions in which we can go. We can argue either that Descartes thought (quite mistakenly) that the hypothetical mode of argument yielded certain knowledge, or that by this point, Descartes had abandoned his goal of a science that is certain, having realized that experimental reasoning from effect to cause and certainty are not compatible. One should be somewhat suspicious of both these alternatives. The former seems doubtful, given the remarks concerning assumptions I cited earlier in section I of this paper, and even more doubtful considering Descartes's apparent recognition in C of the multiplicity of causes all of which can explain the same effect. The latter account seems suspicious considering that in part II of the *Discourse* Descartes once again declares his intent to construct a science as certain as mathematics (AT 6:19; HR 1:92–93) and that he reasserts this at the very beginning of his outline of physics in part V: "I have always remained true to the resolution I made . . . not to admit anything as true which did not seem to me clearer and more certain than the demonstrations of the geometricians" (AT 6:40–41; HR 1:106). What then are we to do?

I would like to suggest that a serious mistake has been made in supposing that the hypothetical mode of argument is what Descartes really has in mind in C, and in believing that the hypothetical mode of argument plays a role in Descartes's considered views on reasoning in science, at this stage in his thinking. While we shall find a somewhat different situation when we examine the *Principles*, I shall maintain that in the works we are considering, those written before the *Principles*, Descartes has neither adopted any hypothetical mode of argument, nor has he given up his plan for a certain science, and that, furthermore, this certain science is one in which experiment plays an indispensable role. My argument will be in two parts. I shall first argue that Descartes considered the hypothetical mode of argument only a convenient way of presenting his scientific results without having to present his entire system, and he at least claimed to have in mind a truly deductive argument in cases where he appealed to hypothetical arguments. And secondly, I shall argue for an interpretation of C in which the reasoning Descartes has in mind is both experimental and certain. This will allow us to say that at least before the *Principles*, Descartes had retained the program of building a certain science founded on intuition and deduction.

The hypothetical reasoning that Descartes uses in the *Optics* and the *Meteorology* seems to have been one feature of those works that most disturbed his readers. One of the most revealing insights into Descartes's true intentions in presenting his work in that way comes in a letter to Vatier, where he explains why he chose to argue in a hypothetical mode:

I cannot prove *a priori* [i.e., from cause to effect] the assumptions I proposed at the beginning of the *Meteorology without expounding my whole physics*; but the phenomena which I have deduced necessarily from them, and which cannot be deduced in the same way from other principles, seem to me to prove them sufficiently *a posteriori* [i.e., from effect to cause]. I foresaw that this manner of writing would shock my readers at first, and I think I could easily have prevented this by refraining from calling these propositions 'assumptions' and by enunciating them only after I had given some reasons to prove them. However, I will tell you candidly that I chose this manner of expounding my thoughts for two reasons. First, *believing that I could deduce them in order from the first principles of my Metaphysics*, I wanted to pay attention to other kinds of proofs; secondly I wanted to try whether the simple exposition of truth would be sufficient to carry conviction without any disputation or refutations of contrary opinions. [AT 1:563; K 48, emphasis added.][25]

Descartes makes two important claims in this passage: that the use of a hypothetical mode of argument is a matter of convenience that allows him to present his findings in a convincing way without revealing the full foundations of his physics; and that for the conclusions presented in those works, he can give complete and certain deductions from first principles.

It is somewhat surprising that Descartes has to go into the question in such detail in the letter quoted and in the two others cited. Both of the points he raises in the letters were mentioned explicitly in the *Discourse*. On the first point, Descartes explicitly notes that in the essays that follow the *Discourse*, he does not intend to divulge fully the principles or the arguments on which his physics rests (pt. VI: AT 6:68–76; HR 1:123–28). In writing the essays he hoped only to:

choose some topics which would not be too controversial, which would not force me to divulge more of my principles than I wished to, and which would demonstrate clearly enough what I could or could not do in the sciences. [AT 6:75; HR 1:128]

Furthermore, even in the *Discourse*, the hypothetical mode of argument is defended not as a method of establishing conclusions, either with certainty or without, but as a convenient way of presenting material that is in no way intended to replace a proper deduction from first principles. Immediately following the lengthy and eloquent defense of the hypothetico-deductive mode of argument in the *Discourse* quoted above, Descartes declares:

And I have called them [i.e., the assumptions at the beginning of the *Optics* and *Meteorology*] assumptions only to let it be known that although *I think I can deduce them from first truths* . . . , I expressly desired not to make the deduction. [AT 6:76; HR 1:129, emphasis added.][26]

Though these remarks are directed largely at the very general assumptions that Descartes makes at the beginning of the *Optics* and *Meteorology*, some at least can be interpreted as indicating that the hypothetical mode of arguing with respect to assumptions about the nature and inner working of particular things was adopted for similar pragmatic reasons. Elsewhere, Descartes deals more specifically with those kinds of hypothetical arguments. In another letter written shortly after the *Discourse* and essays appeared, Descartes defends argument in the hypothetical mode with regard to the inner make-up of water, given without full demonstrative argument in the *Meteorology* as follows, "But if I had tried to derive all these conclusions like a dialectician, I would have worn out the printers' hands and the readers' eyes with an enormous volume" (AT 1:423–24; K 40).

Though Descartes talks here and elsewhere as if he has all of the deductions worked out, it is probably more accurate to say that he only thought that he could work them out given sufficient time, and in the case of particulars, given a sufficiently large body of experimental data. But even this position, somewhat weaker than the rather stronger claims that Descartes often makes, is quite sufficient for the argument I am making that the hypothetical arguments offered in Descartes's scientific works of this period do not represent a genuine commitment to that method of arguing in science. So, the hypothetical mode of presenting his science, at least in the essays, is intended only to save Descartes the trouble of presenting (or, perhaps, working out) his full system in complete detail, and does not represent a serious commitment to the use of hypothetical arguments in science. Similarly, his apparent defense of hypothetico-deductive method from a theoretical point of view is a defense of it as a method of presentation. In no way does Descartes intend the hypothetical mode of argument to replace strict Cartesian deduction as a way to insure the certainty of our scientific conclusions.[27]

But if the appeal to hypotheses is a matter of expository convenience, what, then, are we to make of section C? What kind of reasoning did Descartes have in mind there? What role does *experiment* play in that reasoning? What role does *certainty* play in that reasoning? In what follows I shall make a conjecture about the kind of argument Descartes may have had in mind in C when he talks about arguing from effects to causes.

Let us look back to C. It is interesting to note that while Descartes claims that when dealing with particulars, he found that he had to argue from effects to causes, and that when doing so, he could always envision a multiplicity of different causes for a given effect, he does not explicitly assert that it is impossible to argue from effects to causes either deductively or with certainty. In fact, after noting that there are often a number of ways of causally explaining a given effect, Descartes tells us just how it is that one can eliminate false causal explanations. The device he has in mind and mentions in D is that of *crucial experiment*. When we have an effect which can be explained by (deduced from) first principles in more than one way, Descartes tells us that we should "seek several experiments such that their outcomes will be different according to the choice" of causal hypothesis. Section D is not the only place in his writings where Descartes brings up crucial experiments in such an explicit way. In the *Description du Corps Humain* (1648), which is admittedly from a period later than the one we are dealing with, in the context of an argument against Harvey's theory of the heart, Descartes observes:

And all of this proves nothing but that experiments themselves can on occasion deceive us, when we don't examine well enough all of the causes they can have. . . . But in order to be able to note which of two causes is the true cause, it is necessary to consider other experiments which cannot agree with one another. [AT 11:242][28]

It is thus clear that Descartes was well aware of the utility of crucial experiments in scientific reasoning.

So, if there is a Cartesian deduction of the nature of particulars outlined in C, it appears that it makes use of crucial experiments. But crucial experiment, by itself, cannot lead to certainty. Even after we eliminate all but one cause using crucial experiments, we still don't know that it is the correct one, since there may be other possible causes that we just have not thought of yet. But, if we can enumerate all possible causes, then it seems as if we can use crucial experiments to eliminate all but one of those causes, and we will know for certain that the one that remains is the true cause. This, in essence, is what I suggest Descartes has in mind in sections C and D.

Before elaborating on this and defending it, let me return to those two sections. What I am claiming is not only that in these sections Descartes is *not* adopting a hypothetical mode of argument with respect to particulars, but that in those passages, Descartes is outlining what a certainty-preserving deduction with respect to particulars would look like. But if this is what is going on in those sections, why does it look so much as if Descartes is giving up deduction and certainty? Two things are in need of explanation. First of all, why, if Descartes claims to have found a way of deducing explanations about particulars, does he declare at the very beginning of C that "it seemed to me that there were so many different kinds [of particulars] that I believed it impossible for the human mind to distinguish the forms or species of objects found on earth from an infinity of others which might have been there if God had so willed"? It seems clear that though he believed that at one time, he later came to believe the contrary, and reports this later in C and D. In a semi-autobiographical account like the *Discourse* we must be careful to distinguish intermediary positions from those that Descartes later adopts. But there is a more serious problem here. If my claim is right, then sections C and D should be enthusiastic reports of a bold new way of reasoning to the nature of particulars with absolute certainty. Why, if certainty is preserved, is the passage so pessimistic? To explain this, we must put the passage into its proper context. Earlier I mentioned that it is more accurate to say that Descartes finds, in principle, no reason for thinking that certainty cannot be attained at every level than it is to say that he has actually found all of the necessary arguments. This is especially true with respect to particulars. Such arguments are especially difficult because they require great numbers of experiments. This seems to be the main point of C and D. Immediately following D in the *Discourse*, not even beginning a new paragraph, Descartes laments the fact that so many experiments are required and that he has so few:

As for the rest [i.e., those whose true explanation he has not yet been able to find (?)], I have reached the point, it seems to me, where I see clearly enough the direction in which we should go in this research; but I also see that the character and the number of experiments required is such that neither my time nor my resources, were they a thousand times greater than they are, would suffice to do them all. In proportion, therefore, to the opportunity I shall have in the future to do more or fewer of them, I will advance more or less in the understanding of nature. This I expected to convey in my treatise, and I hoped to show clearly how useful my project might be that I would oblige all those who desire human benefit, all those who are truly virtuous and not merely so in affectation or reputation, both to communicate to me the experiments that they have already made and to assist me in the prosecution of what remained to be done. [pt. VI: AT 6:65; HR 1:121-22]

So, the despair is not one of having to give up deduction and the certainty that comes with deductive argument when we "descend to particulars." The despair is clearly over the difficulty of providing such arguments.

Let me now set out the argument I have suggested more explicitly. My suggestion is that, for explaining the nature of particulars, Descartes imagined that we would begin with some general principles: metaphysics, the laws of motion, basic facts about the contents of the universe. This, presumably, is the conclusion of sections A and B. We also begin with immediate acquaintance with the phenomena to be explained, the particulars and their properties. This comes from observation and experiment. We then enumerate all of the possible causes that both explain the phenomena, and which are consistent with our general principles. Finally, we perform crucial experiments until we have eliminated all possible explanations except one. This is the true explanation.

There is another way of describing this mode of argument which is equivalent, even though it does not appeal to crucial experiments. On this way of proceeding, we would begin with the same first principles, but with a much wider variety of experimental data, perhaps, the data that we would have gotten if we had performed all of the crucial experiments. Examining the first principles, and the observational data, we would conclude (by intuition or deduction) that there is one and only one explanation of the phenomena consistent with both the phenomena and the first principles.

An example may make this clearer. Suppose that we are trying to find the nature of the magnet. We would begin with our first principles, and with common observations about how magnets behave. We would then, following the first version of this mode of argument, enumerate all possible explanations of the known phenomena that are consistent with our first principles, and eliminate all but one through crucial experiments. Following the second version, we would do the experiments first, and then intuit or deduce the single explanation that satisfies both the phenomena and our assumed first principles.

This form of argument is what I shall call an argument by complete enumeration of explanations, or more simply, argument by enumeration. It should be evident that the two versions of the argument (for convenience I shall call the first version A, and the second version B) are essentially equivalent, differing only in the temporal sequence of steps. In particular, in version B we do not frame any hypotheses until all of the experimental evidence is in, whereas in version A, we frame hypotheses before we have performed all of the experiments. It should be evident that the argument from enumeration is *not* a kind of hypothetico-deductive argument. While the two are very similar, in the argument by enumeration we have a complete enumeration of all possible explanations of phenomena. This is a step lacking in characteristic accounts of hypothetico-deductive argument. Because of this complete enumeration, the argument by enumeration can insure that a particular explanation is true, whereas in a hypothetico-deductive argument the most that can be established is that, since the explanation in question agrees with all observed phenomena, it is plausible to think that it may be true. Thus the argument by enumeration can make a prima facie claim to true and certain knowledge that cannot be made for the hypothetico-deductive argument. With this added power, though, come certain difficulties. It may not always be possible to produce a complete enumeration of possible explanations, nor may it always be possible to eliminate all but one by crucial experiments.[29] But we shall not consider these difficulties.

If the argument by enumeration is what Descartes has in mind, this casts a very interesting perspective on the notion of experiment in Cartesian science. Experiment is required, not as in Bacon or in more modern theories of experimental method to start possible lines of induction, but to close off possible lines of deduction. In the argument by enumeration, experiment eliminates incorrect deductive chains from first principles. It establishes what the facts of the world are that need to be explained, and does so with such finality that, at least in idealization, there is only one possible deductive path for us to follow. It seems curious to us to talk about experiment eliminating incorrect deductions. It would seem as if any deduction from first principles must be true. But in saying that experiment eliminates incorrect deductions, I don't mean to say that these other deductive paths are false, exactly. Rather, these other deductions simply lead to possible effects of our first principles not realized in the specific group of particulars with which we are dealing, which we are trying to explain. The problem experiment solves is the problem of distinguishing the "objects found on earth from the infinity of others which might have been there." Experiment does not eliminate incorrect deductions by showing them false, but by showing them inappropriate to the particular phenomena at hand. Consequently, there is an important sense in which an argument by enumeration is not strictly an argument from effect to cause. The argument is still from previously known causes to their effects, except that experiments tell us which are the "appropriate" effects.

This, then, is the argument that I think Descartes had in mind in sections C and D and in the numerous places where he claimed to be able to give deductive accounts of the nature of particulars. In what follows I shall argue that the argument by enumeration is a deductive argument for Descartes, and that it is the kind of argument that he had in mind in sections C and D.

The best argument for showing that the argument by enumeration is a deductive argument on Descartes's terms is that Descartes uses arguments of exactly the same form in circumstances where it is clear that he intended to give deductive and certain arguments. Most notable of these are the arguments for the existence of God and for the existence of material objects, the latter mentioned earlier as an example of an a posteriori deductive argument. These arguments can be represented schematically as follows:

GOD

1. First principles (assumed)
2. To be explained: I have an idea of God.
3. Possible explanations:
    (a) I caused that idea.
    (b) Nothing caused that idea.
    (c) God caused that idea.
4. Elimination: Further argument convinces me that only God could have caused that idea.
5. Conclusion: God exists.[30]

MATERIAL OBJECTS

1. First principles (assumed)
2. To be explained: I have ideas of sensible objects.
3. Possible explanations:
    (a) I caused those ideas.
    (b) God caused those ideas.
    (c) Bodies caused those ideas.
4. Elimination: Further argument convinces me that only bodies could have caused those ideas.
5. Conclusion: Material objects exist.[31]

Both of these arguments very clearly have the form of an argument by enumeration. If arguments like the arguments for the existence of God and material bodies lead us to true and certain knowledge of their conclusions, so should all arguments by enumeration.

There is one worry about this reasoning, though, a difference between the arguments I just outlined and arguments by enumeration that may be serious enough to warrant our withholding the certainty from the argument by enumeration that Descartes attributes to the other two arguments. In the two arguments from the *Meditations* that I just outlined, alternative hypotheses are eliminated by reasoning, whereas in the argument by enumeration, it is experience, in the form of crucial experiments, that eliminates alternative hypotheses. Given Descartes's well-known distrust of the senses, might this render the argument uncertain and probable, despite the strong parallels in form between that argument and those other clearly deductive arguments? While I cannot here give a complete defense of the use of experience in a deductive argument of the form of an argument by enumeration, a few remarks are in order. As has been pointed out before, Descartes's distrust of experience has been vastly overemphasized and misinterpreted.[32] Although Descartes does distrust experience *improperly used*, he is equally emphatic about the necessity of using experience *properly* in scientific reasoning.[33] An example of experience properly used is given in the wax example of Meditation II. There, as part of a digression on the utility of experience in gaining knowledge, Descartes discusses the "nature" of a piece of wax. He concludes that the wax is by nature an extended thing, using reasoning strongly suggesting an argument by enumeration. He considers a number of different candidates, color, shape, size, taste, odor, etc., and eliminates all but one by appealing to experience. Though Descartes concludes that "perception [*perceptio*] is not a vision, a touch, nor an imagination . . . but is solely an inspection by the mind [*inspectio mentis*]" (AT 7:31; HR 1:155), this seems too strong a conclusion. In the wax example, it seems as if experience does play a crucial role, that of eliminating incorrect hypotheses. It would be more accurate to say that for Descartes, experience is useless unless properly used by the understanding. And it looks from the wax example as if one of the proper uses of experience is in the context of an argument by enumeration. Thus, the particular use of experience in the argument by enumeration does not render its conclusions uncertain, and it is not a significant difference between the argument by enumeration and the arguments for the existence of God and material bodies that the one appeals to experience where the other appeals to reasoning.

So, the argument by enumeration is a deductive argument. But is it what Descartes had in mind in sections C and D? The evidence that it is is of two kinds. First of all, there is a very strong suggestion of a use of the argument by enumeration in one of the letters where Descartes is defending the claim that he made in the *Meteorology*, that water is made up of oblong, eel-like corpuscles. In the first discourse of the *Meteorology* (AT 6:237–38; trans. Olscamp, 267–68) this claim is presented as one of Descartes's assumptions, and given a hypothetico-deductive defense. But in the correspondence he outlines what he calls there a "proof" (*demonstratio*) (AT 1:422–24; K 39–40). The "proof" involves showing that the account of the make-up of water that Descartes favors is the only one consistent with all the phenomena. This argument closely resembles version B of the argument by enumeration, and thus supports my claim that this is what Descartes had in mind in sections C and D, where he is talking in general terms about such explanations of particulars, even though "water" is placed (misplaced, I think) among the elements in section B.

But there is another reason for thinking that the argument by enumeration is what Descartes had in mind, a reason that is derived more from Descartes's theoretical comments than from his scientific practice.

As I stressed earlier, Descartes does introduce the notion of a crucial experiment in D. Given the context, of course, the only thing that prevents us from saying with complete confidence that Descartes has in mind an argument by enumeration is the fact that Descartes does not explicitly say that we must make a complete enumeration of all possible causal hypotheses. But in the *Discourse*, while discussing the rules of method in science, Descartes adopts the following rule, "The last rule was always to make enumerations [*denombremens*] so complete and reviews so general that I would be certain that nothing was omitted" (pt. II: AT 6:19; HR 1:92). It seems reasonable to suppose that it is the violation of this rule that Descartes had in mind when, later, in the *Description du Corps Humain* he introduces the brief discussion of crucial experiment by noting that "experiments themselves can on occasion deceive us, when we don't examine well enough *all* of the causes they can have." It thus seems reasonable to suppose in C and D, where crucial experiment comes up as well, that Descartes has followed this rule and made an enumeration of possible explanations "so complete . . . that I would be certain that nothing was omitted," though Descartes did not mention this enumeration explicitly in that passage. So, while the interpretation that Descartes has the argument by enumeration in mind in C and D would involve reading something into that passage, all we have to assume is that Descartes means to follow the very rule that he earlier states, and later appeals to in a corresponding context.[34]

There is considerable further evidence in the *Regulae* that Descartes had an argument like the argument by enumeration in mind.[35] Moreover, I think that my conjectured argument by enumeration is supported by the simple fact that there seems to be no other way to explain how Descartes thought he could unite experiment, deduction, and certainty. But what is most important is that Descartes thought that an experimental argument could be given to establish facts about the nature of particulars with certainty; and that he thought that he could exhibit his entire science, or, at very least, the science presented in the *Optics* and *Meteorology*, as a deductive system. As we have found, this deductive system has a structure considerably different from that of Euclid's *Elements*. At the top are the first principles of metaphysics and the laws of nature, not established a priori in our sense, but established with certainty nevertheless (A). Next come the general principles of Cartesian cosmology, presented hypothetically in *Le Monde*, the *Optics*, and the *Meteorology*, but with deduction (and thus certainty) promised in B. And lastly comes the explanation of particulars. Here the argument gets complex, and we must appeal more and more to experimental arguments. But there is no indication that even at this stage Descartes was prepared to give up the claim to certainty, and much indication that he was not. This is what I propose to replace the traditional geometrical model of Cartesian science. If carried out, it would be a science both experimental and certain.

III

Cartesian Science in Practice: The *Principia*

I shall now turn to the *Principia Philosophiae*, the synoptic and systematic work of Descartes's last period, and examine the extent to which Descartes is able to carry out the program of the earlier period and provide a science based on intuition and deduction. In the earlier period, we found that in certain crucial respects Descartes's theory of science and his scientific practice bear only an indirect relation to one another. Though Descartes believes that his science *can* be presented as the product of intuition and deduction, he makes no serious attempt to do so in the scientific writings. Thus, as I argued, the hypothetical modes of argument used there do not represent an abandonment of the deductive picture of science. In the *Principles* there can be no such gap between theory and practice, insofar as the *Principles* is supposed to fulfill the program that Descartes earlier sketched. Descartes's principal excuse for using hypotheses in the earlier essays was that this mode of argument did not "force me to divulge more of my principles than I wish to" (*Discourse*, pt. VI: AT 6:75, HR 1:128). The fact that in the *Principles* Descartes starts from first principles leaves little doubt that it is there that he intended to fill in all the foundations and complete arguments lacking in the essays, mentioned in the *Discourse*, and promised in the correspondence.[36] But we shall find that, contrary to his earlier promises, Descartes finds that he is unable to present his science deductively, and that, as earlier, he has to appeal to hypotheses. But here he can no longer explain this appeal to hypotheses by claiming that it is not his intention to present the full system and all of the arguments. It is thus in the *Principles* that the necessities of scientific practice force some changes in the Cartesian program for science. I shall argue that in the *Principles*, Descartes makes some important moves away from the earlier program of a certain science founded in intuition and deduction.

Let us begin by examining Descartes's scientific practice in the *Principles*. There is little reason for us to pause over the first two of the four parts into which the *Principles* is divided. It is there that Descartes presents the first principles of metaphysics and the laws of nature described in section A of the programmatic outline in the *Discourse*. There is no question that Descartes was convinced both that the reasoning could be set out with intuitive and deductive certainty, and that he did set it out with certainty there. The arguments of *Principles* I correspond closely to those of the *Meditations* and part IV of the *Discourse*, and have been studied at great length. The arguments of *Principles* II, while less well known, are a direct continuation of the mode of argument of *Principles* I. At no point in these first two parts of the *Principles* is there any indication that Descartes is diverging from the master plan of the *Discourse*.

In *Principles* III Descartes begins the presentation of his cosmology and general theory of the universe. In this part, which corresponds to at least some of the material included in section B of the *Discourse* program, Descartes offers a general theory of matter (the three elements), a theory of the origin of the universe, and a theory of the nature and behavior of heavenly bodies. In the *Optics* and *Meteorology* he had discussed some of this material hypothetically, as we earlier saw. Descartes framed a certain number of plausible assumptions, and showed how all of the phenomena could be explained by (i.e., deduced from) these assumptions. But the material could be presented deductively, Descartes claimed, assuming nothing but first principles. The *Principles*, and more particularly, this part of the *Principles*, is where he was to have given this deduction. It is interesting to see just how well Descartes succeeds.

Descartes begins *Principles* III with the claim that we must first examine the phenomena, the effects, as a prelude to a proper deduction of effects from causes:

The principles we have discovered so far [in *Principles* I and II] are so vast and so fertile, that their consequences are far more numerous than the observable contents of the visible universe. . . . For an investigation of causes,

I here present a brief account (*historiam*) of the principal phenomena (*phaenomenωn*) of nature. *Not that we should use these as grounds (rationibus) for proving anything;* for *our aim is to deduce an account of the effects from the causes,* not to deduce an account of the causes from the effects. It is just a matter of turning our mind to consider some effects rather than others out of an innumerable multitude; all producible, on our view, by a single set of causes. [III 4: AT 8(1): 81–82; AG 223; emphasis added]

In this passage, highly reminiscent of section C from the *Discourse*, Descartes looks as if he is preparing for an argument by enumeration by setting out the body of data necessary for such an argument. Note at this point, Descartes explicitly says that he intends to give a deduction of effects from first principles.[37]

In the sections that follow, Descartes presents a body of data about the heavenly bodies, the heavens, and so on. The data are not exactly what we would call observational, but they are, by and large, presented in the spirit of facts in need of explanation, and appear to be in preparation for a deductive argument, perhaps an argument by enumeration. (Descartes also presents an astronomical hypothesis, which he compares with those of Copernicus and Tycho. But this seems something of a digression, an anticipation of material to be discussed in greater detail later.)

Having given some data, Descartes seemingly returns to the main thread of his deductive argument in III. 43:

And certainly, if the only principles we use are such as we see to be most evident, if we infer nothing from them except through mathematical deduction, and if these inferences agree accurately with *all* natural phenomena; then we should, I think, be wronging God if we were to suspect this discovery of the causes of things to be delusive. [AT 8(1):99; AG 223–24]

So, Descartes implies that a demonstratively certain argument to the causes of things is possible. (Note how this passage suggests the argument by enumeration.) But, though such an argument is implied, it is not the kind of argument that Descartes intends to give. Rather, in the section following, he declares his intention to argue *hypothetically*:

However, to avoid the apparent arrogance of asserting that the actual truth has been discovered in such an important subject of speculation, I prefer to waive this point; I will put forward everything I am going to write just as a hypothesis [*hypothesin*]. Even if this be thought to be false, I shall think my achievement is sufficiently worth while if all inferences from it agree with experience [*experimentis*]; for in that case we shall get as much practical benefit from it as we should from the knowledge of the truth. [AT 8(1):99; AG 224]

And at this point in the argument, Descartes follows the well-worn path he took in the *Optics* and *Meteorology*. He frames a number of hypotheses, some of which he claims to be outright false, and derives "explanations" of the phenomena from these (e.g. III. 45; AT 8(1):99–100; AG 224–25). Given that he has opted to argue hypothetically, the only restriction he places on these hypotheses is that their consequences agree with experience, "We are free to make any assumption we like . . . so long as all the consequences agree with experience" (III. 46: AT 8(1):101; AG 225).

It should be clear that by this point in the *Principles*, Descartes has broken the promise of section B. He has not given us a deduction of his cosmological principles from first principles. Rather, he has used the hypothetical mode of argument he used earlier. Why? He cannot argue, as he did in the *Discourse*, that he did not want to present his first principles and give an exposition of his whole system. The first principles are given in parts I and II, and the purpose of the *Principles* is just to give an exposition of the whole system. Perhaps one should take him at his word, and explain the hypothetical mode of inquiry by saying that Descartes was too modest to assert that he had found the truth about "such an important subject of speculation." But Descartes is hardly modest on other occasions, even earlier in the *Principles* where he doesn't hesitate to declare that he has found the truth about other matters. It is hardly less arrogant to imply that one has found the truth, as he does in III. 43. The natural explanation for the hypothetical mode of argument in this context is that, though he was earlier quite confident that he had a deductive argument for his cosmology, when he came to present it in the *Principles*, he discovered that it did not work. When it came to actually giving a deduction, he found that he had no deduction to give, even given his broad notion of deduction, and he was forced to return to his hypothetical mode of argument.

Before continuing with the argument, though, an alternative explanation for Descartes's use of hypotheses must be considered. There is a strong suggestion in these texts that Descartes may think he can deduce the hypotheses in question from first principles, but is reluctant to make that claim explicitly or display the deductions for religious reasons. The hypotheses that Descartes frames in *Principles* III. 46 relate to the original state of the universe. Might Descartes have suppressed his deduction and, in fact, even labeled the hypotheses false, in order to avoid a clash with the doctrine of creation in Genesis? This is suggested by considerations raised in *Principles* III. 45 and later in *Principles* IV. 1. But I find it implausible to suppose here that Descartes is purposely hiding a deduction. It is clear that he did not think that he could give a direct, nonexperiential deduction of the sort originally promised in section B, since he does admit with respect to the particles that made up the original state of the universe that "we cannot determine by reason how big these pieces of matter are, how quickly they move, or what circles they describe. God might have arranged these things in countless different ways" (AT 8(1):100–101; AG 225). This leaves open the possibility of a suppressed argument by enumeration, and Descartes suggests just this when he immediately comments that "which way he [God] in fact chose rather than the rest is a thing we must learn from experience." But in order to argue deductively from experience he would have to show that the hypothesis he adopts is the only one consistent with experience. The most he claims about these hypotheses is that he cannot imagine any principles that are "more simple or easier to understand, or indeed more credible [*probabiliora*]" (III. 47: AT 8(1):102; AG 225). Nowhere does he even suggest that the hypotheses in question are the only possible ones. In fact, in *Principles* III. 48 he suggests that a number of different hypotheses, including the assumption of initial chaos, would work just as well. So a suppressed argument by enumeration is also ruled out. The idea that Descartes has a deductive argument in mind will be made still more implausible when we later note the changes in the place of certainty in Descartes's theory of science, changes that he would hardly have made if he really had deduction in question. I would claim that Descartes is not presenting something he can deduce as a hypothesis for religious reasons, but rather, he seems to be appealing to religious considerations to hide the fact that he cannot make the deduction.[38]

Though, as it turns out, Descartes finds in practice that he has to appeal to hypotheses, there is evidence in the *Principles* that this is a move that Descartes strenuously resisted. In *Principles* III. 43, there is still the strong implication that a deduction is possible, even if, as it turned out, Descartes was not able to give one. And in *Principles* III. 4, as we have already seen, Descartes interrupts his deductions to consider some observed phenomena, with the promise that he will return to deduction. There is another notable instance of the earlier deductivism embedded in the account of the magnet given in *Principles* IV. There Descartes claims to have shown how the nature of the magnet follows (*sequentur*) from the principles of nature (*ex principiis Naturae*) (IV. 145; AT 8(1):284). Of course, if the principles of nature include the material of *Principles* II, then the hypothetical mode of reasoning introduced in *Principles* III. 44, makes such a claim obviously false. Another interesting passage is at the very end of *Principles* IV where Descartes is describing the way in which he claims to have found the nature of particulars:

Starting from the simplest and most familiar principles which are implanted in our understanding by nature, I have considered in general the chief possible differences in size, shape, and position between bodies whose mere minuteness makes them insensible, and the sensible effects of their various interactions. When I have observed similar effects among sensible things, I judged [*existimasse*] that they arose from similar interactions among such bodies, especially since this appeared to be the only possible way of explaining them. [IV. 203: AT 8(1):325–26; HR 1:299]

What is notable about this passage, besides the apparent reference to version B of the argument by enumeration, is the fact that, while Descartes was claiming to be describing his practice, there is no mention of any general hypotheses of the sort required in *Principles* III. My conjecture is that these last three passages, *Principles* III. 4, IV. 145, and IV. 203 were all written at an earlier stage in the composition of the *Principles,* when Descartes still thought that it would be possible to iron out the wrinkle in the argument of *Principles* III and before he realized that he would have to appeal to hypotheses. Their presence in the completed *Principles* suggests that it was not until the final stages in the composition of the *Principles* that Descartes finally realized that he had to argue hypothetically. This in turn supports my claim that Descartes attempted to give a wholly deductive argument in the *Principles,* but found in the end that he could not.

The deductive chain is broken in practice, and the argument offered is hypothetical. Starting in *Principles* III. 44, the only standard for correctness Descartes actually uses in practice is that theory should agree with experience. What is particularly interesting is that Descartes did not even have to get as far as section C of our outline from the *Discourse* before deduction failed. Deduction fails in the material that corresponds to B, where Descartes earlier seemed quite confident of being able to produce deductive arguments without having to appeal to experiment. Insofar as he argues hypothetically about his entire cosmology and his general theory of the world, his explanations of the nature of particulars must fail to have deductive certainty as well. Even if he *could* give deductive arguments with regard to the nature of particulars from his cosmology, they would not be true deductions, because they begin not with certainties, but with hypotheses.

So far we have been talking about Descartes's scientific practice. We have noted that there he makes do with hypothetical arguments. But what of the earlier goal of certainty? For this we must turn back to his program for science. In the earlier works, Descartes could tolerate a great deal of divergence between his theory of science and his scientific practice. But insofar as it was Descartes's seeming intention to realize his program in the *Principles,* such divergence should be an embarrassment. Thus we find that, although Descartes resisted the use of hypothetical reasoning as long as he could, once he finally adopted it his attitude seemed to change. Evidently, if the world will not bend to fit his conception of science, Descartes must bend his conception of science to fit the world. In the *Principles,* hypotheses and hypothetical reasoning seem no longer quite as objectionable as they earlier were in the *Regulae* and in the *Discourse.* Having come to them out of necessity (if my claim is correct) Descartes comes close to embracing them in his theory of science as acceptable modes of reasoning. The first hint of this is in *Principles* III. 44, where Descartes remarks:

Even if this the hypothesis be thought to be false, I shall think my achievement is sufficiently worth while if all inferences from it agree with observation; for in that case we shall get as much practical benefit from it as we should from the knowledge of the actual truth. [AT 8(1):99; AG 224]

Descartes here seems to indicate that it is sufficient for a science to agree with the data of experiment. Truth (not to mention certain truth) seems not to matter.

This position is the one Descartes seems to adopt at the very end of the *Principles.* Descartes admits that, at best, what he has provided is an account of things that agrees with experiment and observation, but which may not give us truth. But, he claims, this is his only goal:

I believe that *I have done all that is required of me* if the causes I have assigned are such that they *correspond to all the phenomena manifested by nature.* And it will be sufficient for the usages of life to know such causes, for medicine and mechanics and in general all these arts to which the knowledge of physics subserves, have for their end only those effects which are sensible and which are accordingly to be reckoned among the phenomena of nature. [IV. 204: AT 8(1):327; HR 1:300. Emphasis added.]

In the course of claiming that all he seeks is an explanation that agrees with the phenomena, Descartes admits that such an account is less than absolutely certain. To put it another way, Descartes admits that this way of proceeding, which he was forced to adopt, yields not true knowledge, or true certainty, but only *moral* certainty:

That nevertheless there is a moral certainty that everything is such as I have shown it to be.
In fairness to the truth, however, it must be borne in mind that some things are considered as morally certain—certain for all practical purposes—although they are uncertain if we take into account God's absolute power. . . . They who observe how many things regarding the magnet, fire, and the fabric of the whole world are deduced from so few principles *even*

if they thought my assumption of those principles haphazard and groundless, would admit that so many things could hardly cohere if they were false. [IV. 205: AT 8(1):327–28; HR 1:301. Emphasis added.]

So, Descartes claims, the results established in the *Principles*, at least as regards the sensible world, are established with moral certainty. But it should be quite evident that moral certainty is just a species of probability. And this, he argues, is quite sufficient and "all that is required" of him.[39]

The progression in Descartes's thought from the *Regulae*, through the *Discourse* and contemporary writings, ending up in the *Principles*, is quite remarkable. In the *Regulae*, Descartes is quite opposed to all use of probabilities in science, including the use of hypotheses or assumptions. All true scientific reasoning must be able to be formulated in terms of intuition and deduction. The attitude changes somewhat in the *Discourse* and other writings of the same period. There Descartes does make use of hypothetical and consequently nondeductive arguments. However, he consistently insists that such hypothetical arguments do not mean that he has abandoned the search for a deductive science. Rather, he claims to use such arguments as a matter of convenience, so as not to have to give the full argument in all of its deductive glory. He claims, at this point, to be able to give full deductive arguments for everything that he presents hypothetically. But in the *Principles*, it turns out not to be possible to give the full deductions, though he tries. Although he resists, he finds that he must make use of hypotheses, and in the end, seems finally to give up hope of a certain science grounded in intuition and deduction. In the end the practical difficulties of building a science from intuition and deduction force an important change in his very conception of science: scientific knowledge has become probable knowledge, it seems.

Although I say that in the end, Descartes gave up his earlier program and was willing to make do with moral certainty and probability, this is probably too strong a statement. Though in the passages I quoted from the end of the *Principles* Descartes does give this impression, it is also clear that he is not at all comfortable with this position. Before ending the *Principles*, in the penultimate section he says:

That we possess even more than a moral certainty.
Moreover there are certain things even among natural objects that we judge to be absolutely and mathematical demonstrations, the knowledge that material objects exist, and all evident reasonings about them. And with these my own assertions may perhaps find a place when it is considered how they have been deduced in an unbroken chain from the simplest primary principles of human knowledge. And the more so if it is sufficiently realized that we can have no sensation of external objects unless they excite some local

motion in our nerves, and that the fixed stars, being a vast distance from us, can excite no such motion unless there is also some motion taking place in them and in the whole of the intermediate heavens; for once these facts are admitted, then, at least as regards the general account I have given of the world and the Earth, an alternative to the rest of my explanation appears inconceivable. [IV. 206: AT 8(1):328–29; HR 1:301–2]

So, having admitted that probability is all we can have, Descartes makes one last attempt at saving his old program for certainty in science.

Descartes's extreme reluctance to give up his deductive program is also manifest in the introduction he wrote for Abbé Picot's French translation of the *Principles* in 1647, fully three years after the original Latin edition. There Descartes talks quite emphatically about how the proper method in science is to "seek out the first causes and the true principles from which reasons may be deduced for all that we are capable of knowing"[40] This apparent forgetfulness of the difficulties encountered in *Principles* III shows just how tentative Descartes's rejection of deductivism at the end of the *Principles* was, and how uncomfortable he was with that conclusion.

Although Descartes is forced to admit, however unwillingly and tentatively, that natural science cannot be deductive and certain, it is only later in the history of philosophy that deductivism is decisively rejected and natural science is unambiguously associated with the probable. This stop occurs in a philosopher usually counted among Descartes's contraries, but who is in some ways the direct successor to his enterprise, John Locke.[41] For Locke, knowledge is not the only product of the rational faculties. Unlike Descartes, he takes the notion of probability to be an important one for epistemology.[42] Knowledge for Locke is very close to Descartes's conception of certainty, in that the primary ways of attaining knowledge are intuition and deduction.[43] But Locke is aware of the narrow extent to which we have genuine scientific knowledge of material things in the world.[44] This conclusion has caused many to consider Locke a skeptic. But Locke's conclusion is not that we must despair with respect to scientific knowledge, but that where there is no certainty or true knowledge, we must make do with probability. In natural science this means that we must make do with experiment, and whatever can be inferred from experiment by a basically hypothetico-deductive reasoning.[45] It was, then, Locke who took the final step in the retreat from the certainty and deductivism of the *Regulae*. But it was a step that Descartes prepared in his *Principles*.

NOTES

I would like to thank David Kolb, Lesley Cohen Spear, and students and faculty in the Philosophy Department and the Committee on the Conceptual Foundations of Science at the University of Chicago for helpful comments on earlier drafts of this paper.

1. The traditional view is too widespread to require citation. On the latter view, see e.g., A. Gewirth, "Experience and the Non-Mathematical in the Cartesian Method," *Journal of the History of Ideas* 2 (1941):183–210; R. M. Blake, "The Role of Experience in Descartes' Theory of Method," in E. H. Madden, ed., *Theories of Scientific Method* (Seattle, 1960); L. J. Beck, *The Method of Descartes* (Oxford, 1952); G. Buchdahl, *Metaphysics and the Philosophy of Science* (Cambridge, Mass., 1969); A. C. Crombie, "Some Aspects of Descartes' Attitude to Hypothesis and Experiment," *Collection des Travaux de l'Academie International d'Histoire des Sciences* 11 (1960):192–201; and the introduction in *Discourse on Method, Optics, Geometry, and Meteorology* trans. P. J. Olscamp (Indianapolis, 1965).

2. Throughout I have given a reference to an English translation of the passage, when possible to HR. The translations used in the text, though, usually come from other sources, since there are many inaccuracies in HR, particularly in the *Regulae*. I have consulted: AG; CB; K; *Rules for the Direction of the Mind* (Indianapolis: 1961), and *Discourse on Method and Meditations* (Indianapolis: 1960) both translated by L. J. Lafleur; *Discourse*, trans. Olscamp. When no translation is available in HR, I will refer to the otherwise most available translation.

3. See Gewirth, "Experience in the Cartesian Method"; Blake, "Role of Experience"; Buchdahl, *Metaphysics*; and Beck, *Method of Descartes*.

4. Emphasis added. See also AT 10:366, 368 (the text here is disputed), 370, 400; HR 1:5, 7, 8, 28.

5. Cf. *Regulae*, Rule VI: AT 10:381–83; HR 1:15–16.

6. Emphasis added. See also AT 10:440; HR 1:55.

7. Alternatively, a deduction may be a proposition arrived at through such a succession of intuitively made inferential leaps. Descartes recognizes the ambiguity in his use. See *Regulae*, Rule XI: AT 10:407–8; HR 1:33.

8. See *Regulae*: AT 10:368, 401, 416, 418, 425, 427; HR 1:7, 28, 39, 41, 45, 46.

9. For a rare exception, see the letter to Regius, 24 May 1640: AT 3:64–65; K 73–74.

10. Presenting the criterion of certainty in this way leaves out the problems of validation and atheistic science discussed in the letter cited in note 9.

11. Emphasis added. Cf. AT 5:177; CB 48–49.

12. See, e.g., Aristotle, *Topics*, 100ᵃ18–21 and 100ᵇ21–23, and the various Latin translations in *Aristoteles Latinus*, ed. L. Minio-Paluello, 5:1–3 (Leiden, 1969) for the use of the word *probabilis*.

13. See I. Hacking, *The Emergence of Probability* (Cambridge: 1975), ch. 3. Hacking's account is not entirely accurate in that it emphasizes the use of this archaic notion of probability and ignores quite definite instances of distinctly modern probability concepts in antiquity and the Middle Ages.

14. Cf. *Regulae*: AT 10:367; HR 1:6; and *Discourse*: AT 6:6, 8, 16, 69, 71; HR 1:84, 85–86, 91, 124, 125. For studies of the rhetorical-dialectical tradition of education in the 16th century see W. S. Howell, *Logic and Rhetoric in England, 1500–1700* (Princeton, 1956); N. W. Gilbert, *Renaissance Concepts of Method* (New York, 1960); and W. J. Ong, *Ramus, Method, and the Decay of Dialectic* (Cambridge, Mass., 1958).

15. See also AT 10:424 and HR 1:44–45. There is some dispute about this last text.

16. There are at least two places in the *Regulae* where Descartes uses hypotheses. Cf. *Regulae*, Rule XII: AT 10:412, 417; HR 1:36, 40. Nothing Descartes says here throws light on the epistemic status of hypotheses.

17. Precisely what Descartes included here and what he meant to include among the "particulars" of C is not entirely clear. But this will not be an issue.

18. Cf. *Discourse*, part V: AT 6:45; HR 1:109.

19. Cf., e.g., introduction in *Discourse*, trans. Olscamp; Buchdahl, *Metaphysics*; and J. Morris, "Descartes and Probable Knowledge," *Journal of the History of Philosophy* 8 (1970):303–12.

20. Cf. *Optics*, discourse I: AT 6:83–88; trans. Olscamp, 67–70; and *Meteorology*, discourse I: AT 6:233–35; trans. Olscamp, 264–65.

21. Cf. P. Duhem, *To Save the Phenomena* (Chicago, 1969). Duhem has a definite philosophical ax to grind, but he has presented a very accurate and useful catalogue of historical citations on the question.

22. See ibid., pp. 61–65, 96–97, 100–104, 108–9.

23. *Discourse*, part VI: AT 6:76; HR 1:128–29. What precisely Descartes means by "prove" and "explain" in this text are interesting questions, but ones that I shall not enter into.

24. See AT 2:141–44, 197–99; K 55–56, 57–58.

25. Emphasis added. See also AT 2:196–200; K 57–59; and AT 3:39; K 70–71.

26. Emphasis added. Cf. AT 2:200; K 59; and AT 3:39; K 71.

27. The only passage I know of that is at all difficult to reconcile with this reading is from a letter to Mersenne, 17 May 1638: AT 2:141–44; K 55–56. Read in the context of the other passages cited, though, this letter does not raise any serious problems for my view.

28. This is a curious thing for Descartes to say, though, given that he thinks that Harvey's theory is inconsistent with the basic principles of his physics.

29. The difficulty of enumerating possible explanations may not be insuperable, since, given the first principles Descartes is working with, there may be a rather limited set of possible explanations for any given phenomenon. This was pointed out to me by David Kolb.

30. Cf. *Discourse*, part IV: AT 6:33–35; HR 1:102–3; and Meditation III: AT 7:40–45; HR 1:161–65. My schematic version is closer to the text of the *Discourse*.

31. Cf. Meditation VI: AT 2:79–80; HR 1:191.

32. Cf. Gewirth, "Experience in the Cartesian Method," part III.

33. Contrast *Regulae*, Rule II: AT 10:365; HR 1:4–5, with Rule V: AT 10:380; HR 1:14–15.

34. "Enumeration" in the *Regulae* seems to have a narrower meaning than later on. There, enumeration is characteristically the process of going through the steps of a deduction in order—cf. Rules VII and XI. However, elsewhere in the *Regulae* it seems to take on a broader meaning; see AT 10:390, 395, 404–5 and HR 1:21, 24, 31. Cf. also Gewirth, "Experience in the Cartesian Method," pp. 200–201, and Beck, *Method of Descartes*, pp. 126–33. In the *Discourse* it clearly has a broader meaning still.

35. Cf. *Regulae*: AT 10:410, 427, 430–31, 434–35, 439; HR 1:35, 46–47, 49–50, 52, 54–55. The argument suggested in these passages is close to version B of the argument by enumeration. In Gewirth, "Experience in the Cartesian Method," pp. 198–99, a similar interpretation of these passages is suggested.

36. See, e.g., AT 2:200; K 59.

37. The claim that he seeks arguments from cause to effect suggests that it is not an argument by enumeration, a kind of argument from effect to cause like that of section C, that Descartes has in mind here, but a more straightforward sort of deduction as described in B. On the other hand, as I noted in section II, above, the argument by enumeration can be considered as a kind of argument from cause to effect.

38. For Descartes's later remarks on this, see, e.g., AT 4:698; and AT 5:168–69; CB 36–37. In the latter passage, dating from 1648, Descartes tells Burman that he thinks that he *could* give an explanation (a *deductive* explanation?) consistent with Genesis and his first principles. However, he admits both that Genesis is difficult to interpret, and that he has not found a satisfactory account yet.

39. This is not, by the way, the first time that the notion of moral certainty comes up in Descartes' writings. It is mentioned a few times in the *Discourse*, and

in the correspondence—e.g., *Discourse*: AT 6:37, 56, 57; HR 1:104, 116. But it is not until the *Principles* that Descartes even suggests that moral certainty is sufficient in science.

40. AT 9(2):5; HR 1:206. Cf. AT 9(2):2, 9–11, 12–13; HR 1:204, 208–9, 210. Note that his account of the role and necessity of experiment in scientific deduction accords perfectly with my account in section II, above. Cf. AT 9(2):20; HR 1:214.

41. I do not want to suggest that Locke is the only such figure; he is the most influential of those to follow Descartes, and the one responsible for breaking the influence of Cartesian deductivism. Other 17th-century figures did reject deductivism as well; see, e.g., Pierre Gassendi, *Dissertations en forme de Paradoxes contre les Aristotéliciens (Exercitationes Paradoxicae Adversus Aristoteleos)* trans. and ed. Bernard Rochot (Paris, 1959), liber secundus, exercitatio V.

42. *Essay* IV, ch. 1, 14, 15. All references to Locke are from *An Essay Concerning Human Understanding*, ed. P. H. Nidditch (Oxford, 1975). The references are given in such a way as to be locatable in any currently used edition.

43. See *Essay* IV, ch. 2. Locke adds sensation to Descartes's account. But his conception of sensation makes it look like a species of Cartesian intuition. *Essay* IV, ch. 11.

44. See *Essay* IV, ch. 3 (sect. 9–17, 25–26), 4 (sect. 11–12), 6 (sect. 10–15).

45. Above, notes 42–44, *Essay* IV, ch. 16 (sect. 12).

Limitations of the Mechanical Model in the Cartesian Conception of the Organism

GENEVIÈVE RODIS-LEWIS

I

The Cartesian Use of "Models"

THE *Dioptrics*, first of the three scientific essays published by Descartes, begins with a series of comparisons designed merely to illustrate the properties of light, rather than "truly saying what it is in its nature" (AT 6:83). In a similar way, astronomers construct ideal complexes of concentric circles to explain the relations among phenomena, from "suppositions . . . almost entirely false or uncertain" (ibid.). The concrete details of the model matter little, as the real nature of the phenomenon escapes us. The scientist merely aims at articulating the model in order to understand how it works. While the parallel with a close-range observation obliges us to abstract from the diversity of appearances, it makes evident what the *Regulae* calls *imitatio* (Rule VIII, AT 10:395), or "analogy" in the geometrical sense of the word, that is, an equality of *relations* between different terms. Modern science exploits a similar notion: "The proper use of models is the basis of scientific thinking. . . . Our lack of knowledge of the real mechanisms at work in nature is supplemented by our imagining something analogous to mechanisms which we know, which could perhaps exist in nature and be responsible for the phenomena we observe."[1] The determination of the conditions of a phenomenon by analogical experiment has been likened to scientific practice by Ernst Cassirer. And, in her introduction to the German edition of the *Dioptrics*, Gertrud Leisegang refers to the *Denkmodell* developed by H. Hertz in *The Principles of Mechanics*.[2] She analyzes in this manner each of the four models in the *Discourse*, part I: the continuous and instantaneous transmission of movement from one end of a rod to the other; the vat of pressed grapes, the juice of which, like an "aether," fills in all of the gaps in its rectilinear tendency to move in all directions; the simple reflection of a bouncing tennis-ball, or its deviation, as in the phenomenon of refraction, when it encounters a resistant medium. The last example is surprising: the ball travels at a finite rate of speed, whereas the first example, the rod, denies this in the case of light. But Descartes himself indicates the *limits* of the projectile model. Even when hindered, the tennis-ball bounces back, though at a lesser angle than in simple reflections; and refraction directs the deviated light ray downward.[3] In the *Meteorology*, the phenomenon of the rainbow is explained on the basis of concrete, analogous observations: the prism, and the iridescences of fountains, as well as an experiment that varies the distance and location of a spherical glass filled with water with respect to the eye of the observer.[4] In *Le Monde*, the principle of inertia, which stipulates that a single movement of a portion of matter "always tends to continue . . . in a straight line" is associated with the fact that the combination of these movements, demanding their mutual substitution in a vacuumless universe, results in the tendency to turn, "in a circle." This is established by the model of the sling: the stone stretches the cord and "goes straight out as soon as it is shot."[5] Finally, in chapter VIII of *Le Monde*, there appears the description of bodies floating in a river and sometimes "turning with the water which carries them along" (AT 11:59). This is what the *Principles of Philosophy* describe as a "vortex" or "whirlpool" (*tourbillon*): "in the bends of rivers . . . the water turns back upon itself and thus makes circles" (III. 30 and 33: "each vortex . . . constitutes a firmament"). Descartes himself makes "the water turn round in a large vessel" by "throwing bits of wood into it" which "collect in the middle of the circle made by the water."[6]

The advantage, or the danger, of all these models is that of introducing elements that enrich a pure mechanism with properly dynamic effects. Though the subsidiary characteristics of the tennis-ball are consciously ignored, there is still the notion of pressure and "tendency" to act in the example of the fermenting grapes. This is even clearer in the cases of the sling and the vortex, which involve the notion of centrifugal force as a factor of discrimination among parcels of matter. Similarly, there is a temptation to see the laws of gases in the model of the swollen bladder, in which internal equilibrium results from the agitation of the various parts, and which explains how "the whole universe is maintained in equilibrium." Descartes adds here that, "We are not sufficiently accustomed to thinking of machines."[7] The question, then, becomes that of determining whether such a consideration goes beyond the limits of a strict mechanism. Leibniz denounced as paradoxical a physics which claims to deduce the whole diversity of effects from the sole introduction of local motion into a matter reduced to the inert, homogeneous and undifferentiated extension of the geometer. But the configurations of matter are to be distinguished by a movement which is entirely relative to the constant changes of these figures.[8] Without considering the introduction of a first movement into the compact mass by the "coup de force" of a transcendent God,[9] it appears that the laws of motion themselves imply a certain dynamics which explains, for example, the separation of elements composed of various associated particles. Also, the fundamental notion of "action, that is, the inclination . . . to move," is distinguished from actual motion (*Le Monde*, ch. VII: AT 11:44); Descartes says that this is a "consideration . . . of such importance" (*Principles* III. 39) that it dictates, in particular, the entire theory of light which is the starting-point of an understanding of *Le Monde*.

While the forces implied in the models of the sling and the hydraulic vortex represent a positive advantage to science, should they not be considered, with respect to Descartes's principles, as "contraband" (*merces adulteratae*), the "smuggled goods" which Descartes accuses Henry More of introducing in his interpretation of the "little boat" example?[10] It is again, in this case, a matter of depriving the notion of "effort" of any internal strength, and reducing that of transport to the simple separation of two contiguous bodies.

Is not the same sort of problem raised when the habit of considering "machines" leads Descartes to make them models of the autonomous functioning of so-called "living bodies," with no other principle than that of mechanism? According to G. Canguilhem, who expresses very well the question of an analogy between the "organism and mechanical models,"[11] a machine is "a configuration of solids in motion, such that the motion does not abolish the configuration." For "though the functioning of a machine is explained by purely causal relations, the construction of a machine is not to be understood independently either of finality or of man."

II

"Automata or moving machines"

The term "automaton" does not appear in the treatise on *Man* (*l'Homme*), but rather in the fifth part of the *Discourse on Method*

(AT 6:55); the latter presents us with a summary of the former, which is itself an (incomplete) extension of *Le Monde*. (Both remained unpublished during Descartes's lifetime.) In each case, he begins with the organic functions of the *human* body, those "which are present in us without our thinking of them" (AT 6:46), and which are common to both humans and "the animals lacking reason" (ibid.). Even the reactions to external stimuli take place without "animation":

> This will seem in no wise strange to those who know to what extent human industry can produce various automata or moving machines with the mere employment of a few parts; in comparison with the multitude of bone, muscle, nerves, arteries, veins and all the other parts contained in the body of each animal, they will consider such a body to be a machine . . . incomparably better organized . . . than any of human invention. [AT 6:55–56].[12]

Descartes then says that he has "particularly resolved" to show the impossibility of distinguishing our own animals from "such machines," having the same appearance and organs (AT 6:56). The extant text of *l'Homme* does not contain this development (either it is lost, or the writing of the treatise was interrupted at the time of this resolute intention). But the letter of April-May 1638 (to Reneri for Pollot), section 6, recounts a fable which recalls the legendary "naturalist" experiments (as that, in Herodotus, of the two children raised by a goat, who invent a new language). In this case, the child would only have known men who taught him to construct automata imitating as closely as possible the appearance and behavior of real animals. He would then be shown real animals when he grew up; knowing that "all of human industry" is inferior to "that which appears in nature, in the composition of plants," he would "firmly" believe that, "should God or nature fashion automata which imitate our actions, they . . . would be incomparably better made than any of those invented by men." And, as he has been saved from the childhood prejudice which makes us attribute thought and feelings to animals, he would easily take them for pure automata.[13] The *Discourse on Method* makes public the paradox of animal-machines with the comparison of a "clock . . . composed . . . of wheels and springs," which measures time more precisely than our subjective judgments. The superiority of certain animal behaviors "does not prove that they have a mind . . . , but rather that they have none at all, and that it is nature which acts in them, according to the disposition of their organs" (ibid., 58–59).

This "disposition" is not a simple juxtaposition of independent elements, but rather a coordinated arrangement which defines the organism. At the beginning of his remarks on *l'Homme* (in the 1664 ediiton, p. 173), Louis de La Forge declares that a machine is "a body composed of organic parts which, being united, concur to produce a movement of which they would not be capable if they were separated." The "organic parts" are in turn defined as "all sorts of simple or composite parts which, being united together, are able by their conformation, figure, motion, rest and location, to assist in producing the motions and functions of the machine of which they are parts." As G. Canguilhem remarks, the construction of such well-organized machines seems to imply an intentional finality. The *Discourse on Method* unreservedly affirms their superiority over those "invented by men," for the former are made "by the hands of God" (AT 6:56). The initial hypothesis of *l'Homme* is also recalled: "I was content to suppose that God should form the body of a man entirely like one of our own" (AT 6:45–46). In *l'Homme,* Descartes says that "the body is nothing other than a statue or an earthen machine that God expressly fashions to render it as like us as possible" (AT 11:120). According to this text, the construction of a mechanical model refers back to a living original, to ourselves. Canguilhem says that "the mechanical artifice is inscribed in life and, in order to conclude from one to the other, one requires a passage to the infinite, that is, God"; thanks to this initial action, "all possible teleology is contained in the technique of production."[14]

Clearly, the anthropomorphic expressions of *l'Homme* and the *Discourse* must not be taken literally. We are still in the context of a "story," though it is an inversion of the "fable" of *Le Monde* (ch. V: AT 11:31) with which *l'Homme* is directly linked. Descartes constructs his "new world" (the title of ch. VI: AT 11:31) little by little out of "chaos," in order to establish that the mere differentiation of extended matter by the configurations carved into it by motion recaptures all of the particularity of the "real world."[15] To avoid disputes with the theologians, he puts to one side the world "that God made five or six thousand years ago" (*Le Monde,* ch. VI: AT 11:32)—the then current time-lapse estimated from creation. On the other hand, the conception of "man" formed from the earth by the hand of God resumes the tradition of Genesis II. 7. But in the Biblical creation of man from the dust of the earth, God breathes into his nostrils the "spirit" essential to life. Confronted with the whole tradition of vitalism, Descartes first describes the composition of a *body;* the *Discourse* states that this occurs "without its being composed of any other matter" than that described in *Le Monde*—i.e., pure extension—and "without putting into it at the beginning any rational soul" (part V: AT 6:46). The soul "must be expressly created" (ibid., p. 59) independently. Descartes refers several times to its later insertion in the body (*l'Homme*: AT

11:131, 177, 180, 181, 183, 200, etc.), although, as in the case of the text on animals, we do not have the development referred to in the *Discourse*, concerning its nature and intimate union with the body. Paradoxically, while both mind and body are necessary in order to "compose a real man" (*Discourse*: AT 6:59), if one considers only the published text, "René Descartes's man"[16] is limited to a description of the movements of the "machine," which "imitate as closely as possible those of a real man" (AT 11:202).

At this point, man considered simply as a body is indistinguishable from an animal-machine; it is at this stage that the problem of finality in the various mechanical models must be considered. The sole purpose in assuming a particular formation by "the hands of God" is that of insuring a maximum of complexity and "artifice" (*l'Homme*, AT 11:120). But the functioning of the automaton is analogous to what "we see" in "clocks, artificial fountains, . . . mills and other similar machines which, though merely man-made, have nonetheless the power to move by themselves in several different ways" (ibid.). Counter to the Platonic tradition which makes the soul the unique antonomous principle of motion ("*automaton*"), the baroque seventeenth century, fascinated with the artful machinery that often animated "the gardens of our kings,"[17] succumbs to the "charm of the automaton"[18] constructed by the ingenuity of men and improved upon since antiquity. The "personal thoughts," collected by Leibniz from the young Descartes's notebook of early reflections, already mentions "Archytas' dove" which flies in a straight line (AT 10:232). Eager to master the secrets of everything that arouses admiration, Descartes had himself constructed a few automata—including "a little machine representing a rope-dancer"—most likely before he had developed the hypothesis of animals without souls.[19] The generalization was made on the basis of a practical mastery of mechanisms maintaining already complex systems of movements. According to the principle stated by Mersenne, "we only know the real reasons of things that we can make with our own hands or minds."[20]

The intellectual path actually taken by Descartes is developed at the end of the *Principles* (IV. 203). After reducing the clear and distinct notion of matter to the modifications of extension and the various respective rules that distinguish shapes, sizes and movements— i.e., "the principles of geometry and mechanics"—, he begins by inquiring how the "sensible effects" that we observe are to be explained solely by these modal combinations, inasmuch as "no other cause capable of producing them" is found in nature. "The example of several bodies constructed by human artifice has greatly served me in this. For I do not recognize any difference between the machines made by craftsmen and the various bodies that nature alone composes"—if only that the latter contain elements that are finer, indeed, imperceptible. And he concludes: "It is certain that all of the rules of mechanics apply to physics, and that everything artificial is also natural; it is no less natural, for example, that a clock keep time by means of its inner works than that a tree bear fruit." Descartes is "particularly proud and conceited" with respect to his wholly "mechanical" philosophy. For "nothing is more consistent with reason than to judge of what is too small to be perceived by the senses by the example and likeness [ad exemplum et similitudinem] of what can be seen" (letter to Plempius for Fromondus, 3 January 1637: AT 1:420–21).

The numerous examples retain only the analogy involved and do not dwell on the concrete details, which vary from one machine to another: the clock moves by "counterweights" (l'Homme: AT 11:202; Meditation VI: AT 9:67), the watch by "springs" (Principles IV. 203); the tableau enlivened with "fountains" is, like the associated "movements of a clock or a mill" (AT 11:130–131), a function of hydraulic forces. Farther on in the text (ibid., pp. 165–66) the harmonies produced by "our church organs" depend "solely upon three things, namely, the air which comes from the bellows, the pipes which give forth the sound, and the distribution of the air in the pipes." As the great mythological machinery is set off by the visitors in the cavern, who "themselves cause, without being aware of it, the movements that are made in their presence" (AT 11:131; my emphasis), so "external objects . . . are like the organists' fingers which, depending on the keys that are pressed, force the air from the bellows into certain pipes." The point here is not that a musical program requires artistic direction, but that the organist's role is purely occasional in that he merely sets off the mechanism (like an animal walking on the keys). The air in this example corresponds to the "animal spirits," the subtlest matter in the body; they are forced into the brain by the "bellows" of "the heart and the arteries" (AT 11:165–66). This description is as valid for the animal as it is for man, who is here considered in his most automatic reactions to sensory stimuli. Likewise, in the earlier example, the movements are caused by the "strangers" in the cavern, who are unaware of what they are causing. Here, however, the particular status of man is anticipated in the role of the turncock who manipulates the sluice-gates to "cause, hinder or change in some way" the mechanism's movements (AT 11:131–32). Such is the function of the rational soul in its union with a body which independently lives, breathes, is nourished, advances and retreats, but which can be directed by a generalized intention.[21]

But because of its internal organization, the machine is sufficient unto itself and does not require this external finality; this is expressed in the term "automaton." Descartes abolishes the distinction stressed by Aristotle at the beginning of the second book of the *Physics*: the artisan applies his own intentional finality to an external object, while nature is spontaneity of motion, animated by an immanent finality. For Aristotle, the craftsman takes nature as a model. Descartes reverses the formula: "As art imitates nature and men are capable of making various automata which move but have no thought, it seems consistent with reason that nature produce its own automata, though far superior to our artefacts" (letter to More, 5 February 1649, AT 5:277).

III

The Formation of the Organism by "Nature"

The *Discourse* presents the supposition that "God fashions the body of a man entirely like that of one of ours, in both the external shape of its members and the internal conformation of its organs" as a substitute for the ideal genetical description "in the same style as the rest" of *Le Monde*. The philosopher does not yet have "enough knowledge" to make the a priori deduction, "demonstrating the effects by their causes and showing from what seeds and in what manner nature must produce them."[22] He assures us that

The multitude and order of the nerves, veins, bones and other parts of an animal do not at all show that nature does not suffice in forming them, provided that one supposes that nature always acts according to the laws of mechanics, and that God has imposed these laws.[23]

Alluding to his numerous experiments in dissection during the past eleven years, he claims to have found nothing of which he is not "able to explain the formation by natural causes," as, for example, in the case of snow and salt in the *Meteorology*. He then says that, "if I were to rewrite my *World*, in which I supposed the body of an animal completely formed, and contented myself with describing its functions, I should undertake to add the causes of its formation and birth."[24] The continuity of organic and inorganic is perfect; even if the former generally seems better organized, is there not just as much harmony and symmetry in "a grain of salt or . . . the little star of a snowflake"?

Productive nature no longer contains the internal dynamism, acting from the interior like a soul, that is peculiar to Aristotelianism. "By Nature I do not mean . . . some . . . imaginary power; but . . . matter itself," with the modal diversity of its extension and the permanence of its laws, maintained by God as they were created (*Le Monde*, ch.

VII: AT 11:36–37). Thus, when Descartes subordinates the "laws of mechanics," capable of "forming" so-called living organisms, to God, all that is required is the constancy of the rules established in chapter VII of *Le Monde* and based upon the fact that "God is immutable" and acts "always in the same way" (AT 11:43)—i.e., the principles of inertia and the conservation of the same quantity of motion. It is not, then, necessary to have recourse to a preformational theory of germs which contain for all time and in "all organized bodies the end and wisdom of the Artisan," and which act in "the construction of the machine" with "a definite purpose and from particular intentions."[25] Counter to the Epicureanism that he was then renewing, Gassendi argues for the reintroduction of finality, when one considers "the perfect order, the use and economy of the parts . . . whether in plants or in animals"; he praises the admirable wisdom of God, his "singular providence in the perfection and order which he has given to each of their parts."[26] Descartes's reply formally excludes any speculation on the ends of God; one could not "guess for what end he has created all things." He appeals to the "efficient cause" to explain "that admirable use of each part" in organized bodies. Does the literal repetition of Gassendi's words imply that he does recognize at least an internal finality which subordinates the parts to the whole, and that he only rejects the hazardous speculations popularised by examples attributed to the Stoics?[27] One cannot be sure on the basis of this text, in which only the "efficient cause" is to account for the construction of the parts and their situation in the body as a whole.

Though he was perfectly aware of the insufficiency of his observations, Descartes undertook, early in the year 1648, a completely mechanical description "of the formation of the foetus," which he apparently abandoned shortly after.[28] We have seen that this mechanicism clearly contains the centrifugal dynamism of vortices. Another contribution is "smuggled in" with the fermentation model, which produces "natural heat" or a "physical principle of motion."[29] *Le Monde* states that fire, with or "without light," is "mere motion" (ch. II: AT 11:9). But the seed "of animals . . . [is] very fluid, . . . [and] seems to be only a confused mixture of two liquids which, acting mutually as leaven, are heated such that some of their particles become as agitated as those of fire, expand and press against the others, and thus gradually dispose them in the manner required to form the members" (AT 11:253). An analogous process of expansion by heating explains the circulation of the blood.[30] In fact, the entire organism is thought of as a vast circulatory system. But the innovation consists in the fact that everything—the formation of the various organs by the assembling of the thicker parts, including that of the "tubes" (not only blood vessels, but also nerves which conduct the "animal spirits"), as well as their "valvules," necessary in directing the different currents—is explained by vortices and the principle of inertia, which causes particles to "tend to continue their movement in a straight line."[31]

This, then, is Descartes's scientific intention: the natural laws of mechanics, such as they are drawn from the observation of relatively simple phenomena (and even though the real nature of fermentation lies beyond his analysis, and the example of the sling involves the notion of "tendency"), are sufficient to "form" the bodies of the most complex living things. The anthropomorphic terminology of the "hands of God" is an abbreviated way of suggesting that his freely decreed laws contain a fecundity that infinitely surpasses what can be apprehended by a finite understanding.

IV

The "Disposition" of the Parts, a Condition
of the Functioning of the Whole

The construction of automata does not, then, require the immanent finality spontaneously found in Aristotelian "nature"; nor does it, strictly speaking, require the transcendent intervention of the divine wisdom of the perfect "Artisan" (Malebranche's appellation is the same as, in Greek, Plato's *Demiurgos*) in the fabrication of each organism (or, at least, the initial model). The machine is an effect of efficient causes, a resultant of the laws of mechanicism. It remains that these laws have been freely conceived by God to suffice in producing "the order and disposition of created things" (Meditation VI: AT 9:64; Latin text, 7:80). Descartes does not go so far as to say, with Lucretius, that "the eyes are not made to see, but one thinks of seeing because one has eyes."[32] The scientific theory underlying the making of spectacles provides both an explanation of vision and the means of improving it: "experiment shows that . . . the crystalline humor causes nearly the same refraction as glass" (*Dioptrics* III: AT 6:106). There is perfect continuity between the making of the instrument and knowledge of the "organ" (*organon* meaning "instrument" in Greek).[33]

From the formation of the "image" at the back of the eye, this functioning implies a complex composition which Descartes's dissections show to be analogous, "taking the eye of a newly dead man or, for want of the latter, that of an ox or other large animal" (*Dioptrics* V: AT 6:115). Clearly, judgments of distance—combining various elements such as the apparent size of the object with the curvature of the crystalline and the binocular angle—imply, both in *l'Homme* and in the *Dioptrics*, the presence of an interpretive soul. But prior to this, the physical makeup of the eye, common to both man and animal, is "established by nature"[34] to provide a coordinated set of objective indications which make more or less prompt reactions possible, in order to adapt to what is useful and avoid what is harmful. In its broad outlines at least, animal behavior manifests such a capacity of adaptation that one cannot deny them either a first degree of "feeling,"[35] or a set of reactions externally similar to those of our own "passions." This relative continuity between man and animal acutely raises the problem of a certain internal finality as the condition of the functioning of every machine.

In addition to the rejection of "final causes" as an answer to speculations about external finality, commentators of Descartes generally grant that an internal finality[36] appears in man, and in man alone, because the union of mind and body constitutes "as it were, a single whole" (Meditation VI: AT 9:64; 7:81). Sensations and passions assure, then, a "sense" which aims at safeguarding the survival of the whole. Considered independently, the body is a portion of extended matter which "by its nature, is always divisible" (ibid., 9:68; 7:85), thus, "the human body is no longer the same, from the mere fact that the shape of some of its parts is changed. From this it follows that the human body can easily perish" (*Synopsis of the Six Meditations*: AT 9:10; 7:14). It is the "entirely indivisible" (AT 9:68; 7:85–86) soul which gives unity to the body by *informing* it,[37] and thus making it "in this sense . . . indivisible: for . . . we do not think that he who has only one arm or leg is less a man than another" (AT 4:167). Consequently, says M. Gueroult, "the indivisibility of the human body is in no way characterized by a reciprocal relation among the different parts which constitute the whole organic mechanism as such, but solely by the fact that this machine belongs to the soul with which it is associated. . . . This conception of the indivisibility of the organism, which is uniquely ascribed to an actually *animated* organism, conceals a psycho-physical finality and is hence ascribed to man alone"; as a result, the absence of man entails the disappearance of indivisibility: "is it not sufficient to cut off the leg of a horse for it to become *less a horse than another?*" But the author rejects this: "it is clear that the body of a given animal remains the same body and the same animal when it is amputated."[38]

While he emphasizes the "break between the order of the animal-machine and that of the human body-machine," M. Gueroult recognises that certain texts in Descartes imply for the animal, as well, that "interdependence of Parts" which conditions the mind-body union.[39]

It would seem that this is a necessary, but not a sufficient, condition in itself. Each machine has its own particular dispositions and, in order to give itself over to a body, the soul perhaps requires that it have a higher degree of organization than that of unthinking animals. It remains that the question of a finality said to be internal is indirectly raised by these texts. Formulated in the context of man, they are applicable, at least as a whole, to any living organism, "We believe that this body is a single whole so long as it contains all of the dispositions necessary to preserve this union" (letter to Mesland, 9 February 1645: AT 4:166). A one-armed man is no less a man, but I cannot conceive of him "without a head."[40] "Death never occurs through the fault (= deficiency) of the soul, but only because one of the *principal* parts of the body becomes corrupted" (*Passions*, sect. 6; my emphasis). The condition of the body's union with a soul is "the disposition of its organs which are so related to one another that, when it is deprived of one of them, the entire body becomes defective"; and the soul "leaves it altogether when the assemblage of its organs is dissolved" (ibid., sect. 30). This text extends the reflexions on "necessary dispositions," hinted at in the letter to Mesland, by giving a new meaning to the claim that the body "is one and in some way indivisible, in virtue of the disposition of its organs."

But the two viewpoints constitute two complementary steps, and they bring back to the forefront the analogous questions raised by a pure mechanicism applied to both man and animal. This seems to be clear in the successive answers to the problem of the derangement of the machine, advanced by Descartes in Meditation VI. The whole beginning of his development of the question would be otherwise, as M. Gueroult puts it, "another approach which, let us note, is not his own, but that of the materialists."[41] "I consider," says Descartes, "the human body to be a machine," comparable to a clock (Meditation VI: AT 9:67; 7:84). This is the thesis developed in *l'Homme*. While the metaphysical *Meditations* make no reference to animal-machines, everything that Descartes says here is equally applicable to them; the functions and movements of the body occur without the aid of the soul, "but merely by means of the disposition of its organs" (ibid.)— a recurring theme in all of these texts.

In this first perspective, it is a matter of indifference whether the machine as such functions perfectly or irregularly, or breaks down; the clock "observes no less exactly all the laws of nature when it is ill-made and does not keep proper time, as when it completely satisfies the design of the craftsman" (ibid.) The artificialist terminology, along with the intention that governs the making of the clock, refer to an "end" which is foreign to mechanism, and which is only apparent to the observer who expects a clock to keep proper time. "My thought . . . compares a sick man and an ill-made clock with my idea of a healthy man and a well-made clock," but with respect to the machine, this "is . . . only a simple denomination," entirely "external" (ibid., 9:67–68; 7:87). A composition such as the sculptor Tinguely's absurd cogworks corresponds to the concept of art as finality without an end; without envisaging any other *function* than that of sustaining the admiration and wonder of the spectator, it still *functions* according to the same laws that govern a useful machine. Nevertheless, in order to keep time, a clock must be composed of wheelworks and organized in a definite manner. In the case of animal-machines, Descartes takes them as simple matters of fact and refuses to consider *why* nature makes them this way; the artificialist model here reaches its limit.

Moreover, in a vacuumless matter subject to friction and, consequently, attrition, every machine, no less than any simpler body, tends progressively to wear out;[42] each assemblage of parts remains eminently precarious in a matter that is always divisible and itself an orderless mass, with no functional "dispositions." But, as nothing is *due* the machine, there is no producer's *fault*. The "derangement" is relative to external laws which are merely used, along with their necessity, by God. Descartes's first answer accounts for the fact that organisms are doomed to sickness and death, that the horse which breaks a leg is put away, as a watch is discarded when its works are sprung.[43] Ambivalence is a characteristic of matter because man alone judges of good and evil. This is also why animal instinct seems at times a marvel of regularity—"when the swallows return in the spring, they thus act like clocks"—while, at other times, their behavior seems absurd: "Dogs and . . . cats . . . scrape at the ground to bury their excrements, though they hardly ever actually bury them."[44] Habit is, then, a factor in either bondage or freedom; its blind mechanism equally registers noxious associations as well as those that successfully oppose them.

Here is where the finality peculiar to man enters in. Through his understanding of the mechanism, he masters it and is capable of enriching the programming of an animal-machine by training, as well as remedying certain deficiencies of his own body.[45] At this point, Descartes recognizes that his "nature," understood as "the whole composed unit . . . of the mind or the soul united with this body" is "faulty" (Meditation VI: AT 9:68; 7:85): a normally useful signal like that of thirst becomes, in the case of dropsy, a misleading indication. It is no longer a question of simply noting the irregularity of a worn-out machine; the mind is here incited to interpret a distorted meaning. This goes beyond both external and internal finality. The mind conceives of purposes on the craftsmanship model and thinks in this manner of the "assemblage" of "dispositions" necessary for the maintenance of an organism's relatively stable equilibrium in spite of the constant renewal of its parts. A body is never "the same"; the mind, which is always "the same," assigns its unity to the body with which it forms "a single whole." Adapted to the preservation of this whole, the finality of sensations and passions appears to be its "due." There is no longer, then, just an absence, the disappearance of some element which insures the regularity of a set of motions, but rather a positive "error" which is defined by "the lack of some knowledge that it seems I should possess" (Meditation IV: AT 9:44; 7:55): "I am *directly* deceived by my nature" (Meditation VI: AT 9:66). This second stage of the problem involves both the internal adaptation common to man and animal (for as long as the machine functions), and another, properly intentional, finality, that of the "sense" which man gives to these natural warning signals. They then appear as a "natural language,"[46] to the extent that man invents his own language by mastering mechanical associations between physical elements (auditory or visual signs) and mental meanings. The animal's status is that of "all or nothing"; it either continues to exist or perishes. Man sometimes envies its immediate reactions to the situation: an animal jumps into the water and swims because its machine automatically establishes equilibrium with the new environment. Man, on the contrary, "hesitates"[47] and debates the issue; only those movements that he makes "without thinking" are perfectly appropriate.

But his weakness is also his greatness. Because his knowledge is limited, it is capable of growing. For want of a perfect science, he trusts in nature[48] by exploiting the animal in him. But he is still able to know when the adaptive spontaneity begins to wear out. He then employs all his mental resources; he struggles and risks making mistakes. This is the ransom of his freedom.

NOTES

1. R. Harré, *The Philosophies of Science* (London, 1972), pp. 174–75, quoted in CB, pp. 111–12, whose commentary relates as well to P. H. J. Hoenen, *Descartes's Mechanicism*, in W. Doney, ed., *Descartes: A Collection of Critical Essays* (London, 1968), pp. 353–68. See also A. Kenny, *Descartes: A Study of his Philosophy* (New York, 1968), pp. 203ff.

2. G. Leisegang, *Descartes Dioptrik* (Meisenheim am Glan, 1954), p. 22; for an analysis of the four models, pp. 25–31. Cf. E. Cassirer, *Das Erkenntnisproblem in der Philosophie und Wissenschaft der neueren Zeit* (2nd ed., Berlin, 1911; Hamburg, 1958), p. 13: Cassirer comments that as early as the *Rules for the Direction of the Mind*, the determination of "order and measure" (Rule IV) establishes an "abstract structure" that today would be called "isomorphism"; also, p. 20; he notes that the

Cartesian theory of matter is, in modern terms, a "hydrodynamics." Cf. G. Rodis-Lewis, *L'Oeuvre de Descartes* (Paris, 1971), 1:182–84 and notes; 2:506, n. 78.

3. On the parallel between light and projectiles from the time of Alhazen, and the tennis-ball model in reflection, see J. Leurechon, *Récréation mathématique* (Paris, 1627); see also Rodis-Lewis, ibid., 1:191–94, 2:509, n. 93–94 (and ch. 2, in 2:470–471, n. 65, for the recurrence of one of Leurechon's examples in the *Regulae*).

4. N. Poisson, *Commentaire ou remarques sur la méthode de R. Descartes* (Vendôme, 1670), comments upon the ideal nature of this experiment, in which only the circularity of the ball, its refraction in water and the angle relating the eye and the source of light are considered, by calling it an "analogous or proportional manner" of explanation (p. 90).

5. *Le Monde* VII: AT 11:44. The text also refers to the example of a wheel turning on its spindle; if one of the parts comes off, "immediately . . . its motion ceases to be circular and continues in a straight line." The model of the sling is reconsidered in ibid., pp. 71, 75, 85–87 and *Principles* II. 39.

6. They "are supported as is the earth in the midst of the aether," in a letter to Mersenne, 30 July 1640: AT 3:134–35. An analogous experiment, using a mixture of granulated lead and larger but lighter bits of wood which are also driven to the centre, is described in the letter to Mersenne of 16 October 1639: AT 2:593–94.

7. CB no. 73, p. 44 (AT 5:174), and the commentary (cited above, n. 1), pp. 110–12.

8. Leibniz, *De ipsa natura*, section 13. There is a vicious circle, "because shape, the definition or distinction of different parts, cannot arise from a perfectly homogeneous, undifferentiated and solid mass, except by means of motion itself. Therefore, if motion has no distinguishing characteristic, it can give none to shape." On the complete relativity of motion and rest, see *Principles* II. 24–26.

9. *Principles* II. 36: "That God is the first cause of motion" by act which is inseparable not only from that of creation ("the Almighty has created matter in motion and rest"), but also from the conservation, or continuous recreation, of the same quantity of motion and rest.

10. In the letter to H. More of 15 April 1649 (AT 5:346), the "little boat" is pushed away from the shore by one man, while another, in the boat, pushes against the riverbank. More thinks that the state of rest as resistance or effort represents an "advantage" (*merces*; letter of 23 July, ibid., p. 380). For Descartes's criticism, see his letter of August 1649, ibid., p. 403.

11. "Organisme et modèles mécaniques" is the title of an article by G. Canguilhem in the *Revue philosophique* n° 165 (1955):281–99 (referring to vol. 2 of M. Gueroult's *Descartes selon l'ordre des raisons* [Paris, 1953]). Cf. G. Canguilhem, "Machine et organisme," *La Connaissance de la vie* (Paris, 1965), p. 114.

12. The words omitted here will be taken up later on: "a machine . . . made by the hands of God."

13. AT 2:39–41. It will be noted that the equivalency of expression—"God or nature"—indicates, without implying immanence, God's action by the sole laws of nature. Cf. Meditation VI (AT 9:64): "By nature considered in general, I now understand nothing other than God himself, or the order and arrangement that he has established in created things." Descartes alludes to Herodotus' example in the letter to Mersenne of 4 March 1630: AT 1:125–26.

14. Canguilhem, *Connaissance de la vie*, pp. 113–14.

15. AT 11:34. Shortly after announcing to Mersenne "the fable of my World," (letter of 25 November 1630, AT 1:178), Descartes writes: "I am now in the course of disentagling Chaos to extricate light, one of the most lofty and difficult subjects that I could ever undertake" (letter of 25 December 1630, ibid., p. 194). This rejoins the theme of the original creation: *Fiat lux.*

Descartes emphasizes the fact that he recovers "all of the particularity . . . observed . . . in the real world" (AT 11:63; cf. 72, 80, 83, 104, 108). The "fable" thus serves as an *hypothesis* which explains the ideal genesis "of everything in the world" by "a few . . . very intelligible . . . principles" (*Principles* III. 45), which imply no metaphysical "reduction" of our world to a mere object of physics.

16. The title of the text published by C. Clerselier in 1664, though independently of *Le Monde* which appeared the same year. A Latin edition (*De Homine*), published at Leyden in 1662, contains very beautiful drawings, the exactness of which was contested by Clerselier.

17. *L'Homme* (AT 11:130–32) describes at length a machinery which is set off by the entry of visitors whose weight on the paving-stones triggers a mechanism which causes a voluptuous Diana to flee and makes threatening Neptune appear in her place. This example is taken from models described, in particular, by Salomon de Caus, *Raisons des forces mouvantes* (Frankfurt a.M., 1615), problem 27, in which "a Neptune . . . prowls . . . about a cliff." Montaigne's *Journal de voyage* in Italy also mentions the hydraulic "movement of several statues" in the Pratolino gardens.

18. L. Mumford, *The Myth of the Machine* (2nd ed., London, 1971), p. 85. Mumford notes (p. 177) that the degree of perfection attained in clockmaking at the time made the clock a privileged model for other automatic machines.

19. Cf. the beginning of the *Meteorology*, AT 6:231; and the projected Quest for Truth by Natural Reason (*La Recherche de la vérité par la lumière naturelle*), AT 10:505, in which, after "causing the most powerful machines, the rarest automata, to be admired," Descartes will reveal their "secrets." On his interest, dating from youth, in mechanical and optical wonders, cf. my article, "Machineries et perspectives curieuses dans leurs rapports avec le cartésianisme," *XVIIe siècle* 32 (1956): 461–74; also, *L'Oeuvre de Descartes*, 1:86–88 and 2:469–72.

Archytas' dove is described (as well as "a mechanical partridge flushed by a spaniel") from early manuscripts, no longer extant, in Poisson's *Commentary . . . ,* p. 156; cf. AT 10:232.

I have discussed the dating of his interest in machines in *L'Oeuvre de Descartes*, 1:88–89; and 2:471–72, n. 70, disputing Baillet, who dates the thesis of animal-machines at "15 or 16 years" earlier than the *Meditations*. He seems to have been confused by a letter to Newcastle (October 1645), which refers to the undertaking of a treatise on animals, "fifteen years ago" (AT 4:326), i.e., during the winter of 1629–30. This corresponds with the time of the writing of *Le Monde* and the full possession of the principles of mechanicism.

20. M. Mersenne, *L'Harmonie universelle*, cited by R. Lenoble, *Mersenne ou la naissance du mécanisme* (Paris, 1943), pp. 383–84. This principle relates to that of F. Sanchez: no one can know what he has not created: T. Gregory, *Scetticismo ed empirismo* (Bari, 1961), pp. 70–77.

21. The soul is only aware of this "inclination of the will," and not of the physical details of movements: letter to Arnauld, 29 July 1648: AT 5:222; *Passions*, sect. 44–45. Cf. G. Lewis, *Le Problème de l'inconscient et le cartésianisme* (Paris, 1950), pp. 55–61.

22. Part V: AT 6:45 46. Cf. *Le Monde*, ch. VII: AT 11:47. On the basis of the "eternal verities . . . the knowledge of which is . . . naturally in the soul" (on innateness, cf. letter to Mersenne, 15 April 1630: AT 1:145), one can "know the effects by their causes" and "have a priori demonstrations." Also, *Principles* I. 24, which defines the "perfect science."

23. Letter to Mersenne, 20 February 1639: AT 2:525.

24. Ibid., 2:525. It will be noted that the description of the animal body is included in *Le Monde*. The extant text stops at chapter XV, though, in the preface to the independently published *l'Homme*, Clerselier refers to the latter as "chapter XVIII" (AT 11:119).

25. N. Malebranche, *Méditations chrétiennes*, VI. 7.

26. *Fifth Set of Objections*, on Meditation IV, sect. 1 (Latin text, AT 7:309). As Clerselier's translation was not published in the French edition of 1647, it is not included in AT, vol. 9 edition, but can be found, along with Descartes's replies to these objections, in the edition by F. Alquié, *Descartes, Oeuvres philosophiques*, vol. 2 (Paris, 1967), pp. 748–49, 821. M. Alquié notes: "One wonders whether Descartes's disagreement with Gassendi is as great as it seems. Though he rejects the search for final causes, does he not recognize the existence of what is generally

called "finality," by admitting the *use* of each part of a living body?" Ibid., n. 2. This is precisely the question that I am raising; but here, Descartes quotes Gassendi literally, and attributes the matter of fact "to the efficient cause."

27. E.g., Plutarch, *Contradictiones stoicorum* 21: quoting Chrysippus (*De Natura*, Book V), "bugs serve to rouse us and mice warn us not to put things just anywhere." Cf., on the extensive developments of finality by the Stoics, Cicero, *De Deorum natura* 2. 35–66.

28. The text, published just after *l'Homme* in Clerselier's edition, is entitled, *The Description of the Human Body* (*La Description du corps humain*), with the subtitle, *On the Formation of the Foetus* (*De la Formation du foetus*). The latter actually concerns only the end (AT 11:252ff., parts IV and V). The letter to Elisabeth of 31 January 1648 specifies that Descartes has just "reworked" the "description of the functions of the animal and man," the draft of which is "12 or 13 years old" (the time of the writing of the *Discourse on Method*); for the past week he has wanted "to explain the manner in which an animal is formed from the beginning of its origin" (AT 5:112). In CB no. 61, p. 39 (April 1648), he comments. "But these were all matters which he did not wish to go into at such length and so he gave up writing the treatise" (here called, *Treatise on the animal*; Latin text, AT 5:170–71).

29. *Passions*, sects. 5, 6; *l'Homme*: AT 11:121; *Discourse*, AT 6:46: "One of those fires without light that I had already explained, the nature of which I did not conceive to be other than that which causes hay to ferment when it has been stored before it was dry, or which makes new wine boil." Chemistry in Descartes's time was not yet distinguished from alchemy; of what he calls its "sophistications," he retains only the "generalities of nature"—the unity of material substance, and the "diverse figures or modes" which are a sole result of local motion (letter to Villebressieu, summer 1631, AT 1:216).

30. *Discourse*, part V: AT 6:46, 48–50; Descartes relies on the observation of "the heat that one feels with one's fingers" (ibid., p. 50); he believes that "there is always more heat in the heart than in any other place in the body" (ibid., p. 48).

31. AT 11:254, sect. 29. See also sect. 38, ibid., p. 260: the blood travels "first in a straight line," and its subtlest parts advance "to the place where later is formed the brain"; for the formation of "the skin and . . . other solid parts," sect. 61, ibid., p. 274; for the valvules, sect. 69, ibid., p. 279. J. Roger speaks of a "sort of living vortex" (*Les Sciences de la vie dans la pensée française du XVIIIᵉ siècle* [Paris, 1963], p. 148; on Descartes, see pp. 140–54).

32. These lines of Lucretius (*De rerum natura* 4. 322–23 and 332) are translated by Malebranche (*La Recherche de la vérité*, bk. II, part I, ch. IV, sect. 3), who finds the thesis "ridiculous."

33. Cf. D. Dubarle, "L'esprit de la physique cartésienne," *Revue des sciences philosophiques et théologiques* 26 (1937):221: "The artificiality of the relation between the instrument and the physical sphere of man is so little that Descartes develops the entire theory of visual improvement by considering eye and instrument as a *single* optical system."

34. *Dioptrics* VI:AT 6:134–35, 137 ("as though by a natural geometry"; the term is also found in *l'Homme*, AT 11:160). This anticipates the "natural judgments" that Malebranche attributes to "the author of nature" because they imply an infinite science (*Recherche de la vérité*, 17th Enlightenment, sect. 43, no. 8; etc.).

35. *Replies to the Sixth Set of Objections*, sect. 9: "what is immediately caused in the physical organ by external objects" (AT 9:236). The letter to H. More, 5 February 1649, no. 5: AT 5:278, grants them a *sensus*, to the extent that it depends upon a physical organ.

The training of certain animals to "speak" relies on "the movement of one of their passions . . . , movements of their fear, hope or joy . . . , that they can have without any thought" (letter to Newcastle, 23 November 1646: AT 4:574–5). Also *Passions*, sect. 50: they have "all of the movements . . . that arouse the passions in us," but which sustain and reinforce "not the passions, as in us, but the movements of nerves and muscles which customarily accompany them"; and sect. 138: "all reasonless animals lead their lives merely by physical movements, similar" to those of our own passions; they are also subject to their excesses.

36. J. Laporte develops this distinction derived from Kant, though the *Critique of Judgment*, sect. 65, distinguishes between the organism and the Cartesian example of a "watch," unable to reproduce and repair itself. "Internal finality," in which the organization of the whole determines the existence of the parts, is restricted to man (*Le Rationalisme de Descartes* (Paris, 1945), pp. 343–61 and pp. 355–56). My *L'Individualité chez Descartes* (Paris, 1950), pp. 80–81, takes up the issue again, but raises the question (pp. 60–66) of the organisation of living things, whose death represents a rupture, "for animals as well as for men" (p. 66). M. Gueroult, *Descartes selon l'ordre des raisons*, vol. 2 emphasizes the unity of the psycho-physical sphere as a condition of internal finality: ch. 16–18, passim, particularly p. 177. (This finality is proved by the union, and not the contrary: p. 194).

37. Letter to Mesland, 9 February 1645: AT 4:166–67; and another letter of 1645 or 1646, ibid., p. 346. F. Alquié recalls that the soul as "form of the body" is the Aristotelian-Thomistic thesis, and finds it difficult to reconcile with "Descartes's real doctrine" which is, for him, "an indivisibility deriving from the organic solidarity" of the parts of the body (*Passions*, sect. 30; cf., in his edition of *Descartes, Oeuvres philosophiques*, vol. 3 [Paris, 1973], notes, p. 976, and his comment on the letter to Mesland, p. 548). I am attempting to show that the two views are complementary. At first, the "dispositions" of the body are considered to be necessary (this is the case in the letter to Mesland). But the "reply" transmitted to Regius for Voëtius (January 1642: AT 3:503 and 505) specifies that man alone is truly *one*, in virtue of his soul, the unique "substantial form." Our inner experience of this accounts for its anthropomorphic projection on to the whole of Aristotelian "nature." *Replies to the Sixth Set of Objections*, sect. 10: AT 9:240–241, reiterates Aquinas's formula, describing the mind-body union; the mind is "wholly in the whole and wholly in each part" (*Summa contra Gentes* 2. 72). Thus, the comparisons between this union and the notion of gravity as an animistic projection: letter to "Hyperaspistes," August 1641, sects. 2, 14: AT 3:424–25, 434; letter to Elisabeth, 21 May 1643: ibid., pp. 667–68; letter to Arnauld, 29 July 1648, AT 5:222–23.

38. Gueroult, *Descartes selon l'ordre des raisons*, 2:180, 181, 184.

39. Ibid., 2:179; cf. pp. 178 and 194: "this incomprehensible break" relates back to the "inscrutable abyss of divine wisdom".

On p. 193: "Do not animal-machines . . . have the same characteristics of organization and interdependence of parts and whole which theoretically permit their union with a soul?" This passage is commented upon by G. Canguilhem, "Organisme et modèles mécaniques," p. 195, and in his *La Formation du concept de réflexe aux XVIIᵉ et XVIIIᵉ siècles* (Paris, 1955), p. 56.

40. Only at the *cogito* stage does Descartes say: "It was necessary . . . that I consider myself without arms, or legs, or head, in short, without a body" (*Recherche de la vérité*, Latin text, AT 10:520. Did Pascal know of this text, which was not published until 1701? Cf. *Pensées*, ed. Brunschvicg, no. 339).

41. *Descartes selon l'ordre des raisons*, 2:172; cf. p. 161: "my human body, like that of an animal, is, then, reduced to a pure machine, to the modes of extension and movement; this is the materialist reduction." However, "the principle of this argumentation is based upon the theory of animal-machines" (p. 173). But this is the personal theory that Descartes develops in *l'Homme*; hence, it is not false, but insufficient when man is thought of as a "whole" mind and body.

42. G. Canguilhem, *Connaissance de la vie*, p. 116: "Maintenance demands the care and constant vigilance of the machinist. . . . Regulation and repair assure, as well, the periodical intervention of human action." This is why "there is no such thing as mechanical pathology", nor is there a "normal" state (p. 118). In "Organisme et modèles mécaniques," p. 193: "In mechanism, accidents may occur, but never 'failings.' A machine is not 'accountable' for anything."

43. *Connaissance de la vie*, p. 111: "Descartes treats the animal as Aristotle treated the slave; he devalues it in order to justify its use as an instrument." Being the

"master and owner of nature" supposes that nature—apart from man, but including animals—is to be treated "as a means" (ibid.).

44. Letter to Newcastle, 23 November 1646:AT 4:575–6: this behavior would now be associated with the marking of territory.

45. Ibid.; also, *Passions*, sect. 50, on training, and the learning of "speech" by association with emotive movements, but without there ever being a properly human invention of signs. The difference between the creativity of human language and a fixed association of reactions (verbal or otherwise) to external simuli is stressed by N. Chomsky, *Cartesian Linguistics* (New York, 1966), ch. 1.

46. Cf. my contribution to the Geneva Congress of 1966, "Langage humain et signes naturels dans le cartěsianisme," in *Le Langage*, (Neuchâtel, 1966), pp. 132–36. On the extensions of this twofold problem by Descartes's successors, "Un théoricien du langage au XVIIe siècle," *Le Français moderne* 36ᵉ année, no. 1 (1968): pp. 19–50. On the more general development of the latter, "Le domaine propre de l'homme chez les cartesiens," *Journal of the History of Philosophy* 2 (1964):157–88.

47. *Dubitantes* is the word in the manuscript fragment (copied by Leibniz and entitled "Cartesius"). Along with the example of animals' swimming, the text contrasts the arts subject to rules with those in which spontaneity prevails: "We should act for the best, following the impetus of nature, if we did not hesitate" (AT 11:650). On the authenticity of this generally ignored text, cf. my note, "Cartesius," *Revue philosophique* 161, (1971):211–20.

48. CB no. 82, p. 50; AT 5:178: "It should not be doubted that human life could be prolonged, if we knew the appropriate art." But Descartes is conscious of the insufficiencies of the medicine of his time; for want of something better, "the best method of keeping to a healthy diet, is to live and eat like animals." The finality of the appetites remains valid in most cases, as the "errors" described in Meditation VI are rare. In the practical sphere, one must be satisfied with what is "most commonly" or "almost always" the best (Meditation VI: AT 9:71).

Descartes's Denial

of Mind-Body Identity

MICHAEL HOOKER

AFTER ESTABLISHING the certainty of his existence, Descartes proceeds to investigate the nature of the thing whose existence is certain. That investigation results in his issuing two claims: one, that his essence is thinking; the other, that he is not identical with his body. In what follows I shall discuss Descartes's argument for the latter conclusion.

I

The Argument from Doubt

We can begin by looking first at an argument often derided by Descartes's commentators and generally taken to be his primary argument for the distinctness of himself and his body. The argument is suggested in the following passage from part IV of the *Discourse*:

> I then considered attentively what I was; and I saw that while I could feign that I had no body, that there was no world, and no place existed for me to be in, I could not feign that I was not; on the contrary from the mere fact that I thought of doubting about other truths it evidently and certainly followed that I existed. . . . From this I recognized that I was a substance whose whole essence or nature is to be conscious and whose being requires no place and depends on no material thing. [AG 32][1]

The argument in question (let us label it the "argument from doubt") is expressed more clearly in *The Search After Truth* when Polyander concludes that he is not a body, since if he were then when he doubts of his body existing he would also doubt of himself, which he cannot do (HR 1.319). The argument from doubt is most commonly rendered as a two-premise argument:

(1) I can doubt that my body exists.
(2) I cannot doubt that I exist.
--
(3) I am not identical with my body.

So expressed, the argument appears specious, and commentators have sought to expose its faults. The most often tendered objection, one offered by Anthony Kenny, is that the inference of the conclusion from the premises requires a principle not applicable in the context of the argument.[2] The needed principle, commonly called the principle of the indiscernibility of identicals, states a condition necessary to the identity of two things: that they share all properties in common. We can formally state the principle as:

(4) For all things, x and y, if x is identical with y, then for all properties, p, x has p if, and only if, y has p.

The principle of the indiscernibility of identicals has been much discussed, and it is thought by many, Kenny among them, to have a restricted range of application. In particular, its use in modal and intentional contexts is enjoined by the existence of counterexamples. For instance, while the number nine is necessarily greater than seven, and while nine is identical with the number of planets, we cannot use the principle to conclude that the number of planets has the property of being necessarily greater than seven. And while Smith may wish to be the first commander of an orbiting space station, he does not wish to be the twentieth fatality of the space race, though we can assume for illustrative purposes that the two are identical. Thus, it is argued, contexts such as the above that employ modal or intentional notions are contexts in which the principle (also called Leibniz's Law) cannot be employed. What makes its use unavailable to Descartes, according to Kenny, is that (1) and (2) provide a context that is both modal and intentional. So, he says, the argument from doubt is to be rejected as needing a principle not applicable to its premises; or, as some would say, a false principle.

Many philosophers remain unconvinced that modal and intentional contexts yield counterexamples to Leibniz's Law. For them, Kenny's objection to the argument from doubt is neither welcome nor convincing. But we should find Kenny's objection unconvincing irrespective of our feeling about the range of applicability of Leibniz's Law. It is unconvincing, because in the argument from doubt the principle is not applied to contexts bound by so-called opacity-inducing operators. Filled out, the argument from doubt goes as follows:

(1) I can doubt that my body exists.
(2) I cannot doubt that I exist.

(5) My body has the property of being possibly doubted by me to exist.

(6) I do not have the property of being possibly doubted by me to exist.

(7) For all things, x and y, if x is identical with y, then for all properties, p, x has p if, and only if, y has p.

(8) If I am identical with my body, then my body has the property of being possibly doubted by me to exist if and only if I have that property.

(9) My body, but not me, has the property of being possibly doubted by me to exist.

$\overline{(10)}$ I am not identical with my body.

We can see that Leibniz's Law is applied not to (1) and (2), as Kenny's objection suggests, but rather to (5) and 6), contexts that are purely extensional. Kenny's objection does not hold; he has failed to show us what is wrong with the argument from doubt.

Fortunately, we need not look far to discover where the real fault lies. To see where the argument goes wrong, it is helpful to suppose for a moment that Descartes offered a truncated version of the argument from doubt, one like our version except with premises (1) and (2) omitted. How should we assess such an argument? It is valid, but we must question the truth of its first two premises, (5) and (6) in our version. What is Descartes's justification for offering them? If he is entertaining the possibility at this juncture that he is identical with his body, then he is not warranted in merely asserting, without proof, that something is true of the one but not the other. That claim requires argued support, and what Descartes has available is the fact, represented by (1) and (2), that he is able to conceive the truth of the proposition that his body does not exist but unable to conceive the truth of the proposition that he does not exist. That, however, is not sufficient. The fact that Descartes doubts that his body exists and the fact that he does not doubt that he exists do not yield the de re truth that his body has a property not had by him, that of being doubted to exist.

If I have correctly represented his reasoning, Descartes's error lies in the move from (1) and (2), his only stated premises, to (5) and (6), premises required to get the desired conclusion by application of Leibniz's Law. There is something wrong with the inference from (1) and (2) to (5) and (6), from de dicto propositions to their de re counterparts. To see that the inference is amiss, suppose that I am attempting to discover whether John is Tom's father. I reason as follows. I can doubt that John has ever fathered a son, so John has the property of being possibly doubted by me to have ever fathered a son. I cannot doubt that Tom's father has ever fathered a son, so Tom's father does not have the property of being possibly doubted by me to have ever fathered a son. Since John has a property not had by Tom's father, the two are distinct.

Obviously, the argument is invalid. Leibniz's Law is not suspect, so the fault must lie in the move from a de dicto proposition to a de re proposition. Descartes's procedure is similar to the one above. He infers from its being possible for him to doubt that his body exists and its not being possible for him to doubt that he exists that his body has a property he does not have, that of being possibly doubted to exist. But, as we have seen, that is not a warranted inference. The argument from doubt does not work. If Descartes actually intended the argument in the passages in question, he shouldn't have.[3]

There is a reason, however, to withhold imputation to Descartes of the argument from doubt. That reason stems from the context in which Descartes is purported to have offered the argument. The problem is this: if we are to export from (1) to (5), then "my body" must be referential; it must refer to something that exists. But when Descartes is investigating the nature of himself, he does not yet know whether he has a body, or even that there are any material objects at all. A fortiori, he does not know that "my body" refers to anything. The argument from doubt, expressed as it is, has as a consequence:

(11) $(\exists x) (x = \text{Descartes's body})$

But at the juncture at which he is thought to have offered the argument, Descartes would not recognize (11) as true. And so, we suppose, he would not have offered an argument with (11) as a consequence. This, I think, is a good reason for withholding ascription of the argument from doubt to Descartes. But then we must seek an alternative interpretation for the passages from which the argument is derived. We should look for an interpretation that has no consequences that go beyond what Descartes knew at the juncture at which the passages occur.

II

The Argument from Conceivability

It would seem best to give up the attempt to construct an argument that relies on Leibniz's Law. If we go to the texts, we can find evidence that Descartes had a different argument in mind. In the fourth set of "Objections," when Arnauld summarizes Descartes's argument from Meditation II, he expresses the first premise by saying that Descartes is able to doubt whether he has a body. There is an important difference between the statement "I can doubt that my body exists" and "I can doubt whether I have a body." The former tends to suggest that I do have a body; the latter is neutral on the question. Descartes most often expresses himself in the fashion of the latter. Moreover, he often grants that while he is sure that he exists, he finds no difficulty in supposing the world to be devoid of objects. From that he is led to conclude that he is not a body. The evidence suggests that Descartes has in mind an argument like the following:

(12) I can conceive of myself existing and no bodies existing.

(13) I am not a body.

As it stands, the argument is shamefully enthymematic; we should attempt to make it respectable by adding some premises. Descartes gives no hint as to how the argument is to be filled out, but if it is his argument, we should be careful to supply only premises that would be acceptable to him.

As an initial step toward lending respectability we can appeal to the Humean doctrine that what is not possible is not conceivable, that is:

(14) (p) (if p is conceivable, p is possible).[4]

Applied to our first premise, the principle allows us to conclude:

(15) It is possible that I exist and no bodies exist.

Now the problem is to get from its being possible that Descartes is not a body to the conclusion that he is in fact not one. Alvin Plantinga has proposed a solution.[5] He suggests that we employ the principle:

(16) (x) (if x is a body, x is essentially a body).

It is not clear whether Plantinga thinks that Descartes held (16), but it is clear that he thinks that it, in conjunction with (15), yields the conclusion that Descartes is not identical with his body. Obviously, though, (15) and (16) are not alone sufficient for the conclusion; the argument is still enthymematic. Plantinga fails to tell us how it is to be filled out, but I think we can see how to proceed. If we understand essential properties to be among those without which a thing cannot exist, as Descartes seems to do, then if Descartes were essentially a body it would not be possible for him to exist in a world devoid of bodies. But we already have established that it is possible that Descartes exists and no bodies exist (given the truth of the thesis that what is conceivable is possible). Hence, Descartes is not essentially a body. And, by Plantinga's principle, he is not a body at all.

Let us pause to examine the fruit of our labor. We have constructed the following argument:

(12) I can conceive of myself existing and no bodies existing.

(14) (p) (if p is conceivable, p is possible).

(15) It is possible that I exist and no bodies exist.

(16) (x) (if x is a body, x is essentially a body).

(17) If I am a body, I am essentially a body.

(18) If I am essentially a body, it is not possible that I exist and no bodies exist.

(19) I am not essentially a body.

$\overline{(20)}$ I am not a body.

We now have a valid argument (call it the "argument from conceivability") with the conclusion that Descartes desires. We ought, then, to consider whether Descartes might have offered the argument. If we can agree that the premises are ones that Descartes would accept, we ought to ask whether they compel our assent. The argument has four independent premises, (12), (14), (16), and (18). I have suggested that (12) is a plausible interpretation of part of Descartes's intent in Meditation II. The evidence is strong that Descartes accepted it. To justify introducing (14) I have appealed to Hume; however, Descartes committed himself to the principle in several different passages.[6] (16) is never explicitly stated by Descartes, but there is evidence that he would accept it. He seems to hold, for example, that if something has properties that are modes of thinking or extension, then that thing is essentially thinking or extended.[7] Since bodies have corporeal properties, Descartes would seem bound to conclude that they have them essentially, and so are essentially bodies. Finally, (18) is a straightforward consequence of Descartes's notion of an essential property as he explains it. So I think we are justified in attributing the premises of our argument to Descartes. Let us examine them more closely to see whether Descartes ought to have embraced them.

My strongest reservations have to do with the first premise, so let us deal with the others before tackling it. With respect to the second premise, the claim that what is conceivable is possible, the view is, I have suggested, a well-rooted tradition in modern philosophy. To quote Hume:

It is an established maxim in metaphysics, *that whatever the mind clearly conceives includes the idea of possible existence,* or in other words, *that nothing we imagine is absolutely impossible.* We can form the idea of a golden mountain, and from there conclude that such a mountain may actually exist. We can form no idea of a mountain without a valley, and therefore regard it as impossible.[8]

I am willing to give tentative acceptance to the principle on the basis of its historical patronage, but not without first discussing the possible existence of counterexamples to the principle and the problems raised by those examples.

One of the uses Hume made of (14) was in the attempted refutation of the view that laws of nature are necessary truths. He argues: "We can at least conceive a change in the course of nature; which sufficiently proves, that such a change is not absolutely impossible. To form a clear idea of anything, is an undeniable argument for its possibility, and is alone a refutation of any pretended demonstration against it."[9]

William Kneale, noting the dependence of Hume's putative refutation on (14), argues against the latter. He says:

In any sense of the word "conceive" which is relevant to the argument, an ability to conceive the contradictory of a supposed law of nature does not disprove the suggestion that the supposed law is a principle of necessitation. This can be seen from consideration of a mathematical analogy. In 1742 Goldbach, an otherwise unknown correspondent of the Swiss mathematician Euler, suggested that every even number greater than two is the sum of two primes. This conjecture has been confirmed for all the even numbers for which it has been tested, but during the past two centuries no one has succeeded in demonstrating its truth. The attitude of mathematicians towards it can, therefore, be expressed by the statement 'Goldbach's conjecture looks like a theorem, but it may conceivably be false.'[10]

Kneale's argument seems to be that unproved and unrefuted mathematical propositions are conceivably true (and, we suppose, conceivably false). But, of course, being mathematical propositions they are necessarily true, if true at all, and hence, not possibly false. Similarly, if they are false, they are necessarily so, and thus not possibly true. So we cannot argue from the conceivability of their truth or falsity to the possibility of their truth or falsity.

I am inclined to think that Kneale has not made his case strong enough, though I think it can be so made. As he states it, his view seems to allow us to assert the conceivability of any proposition not known to have been shown false. But I think that is to confuse conceivability with epistemic possibility.[11] Surely there are some constraints on the conceivability of a proposition beyond not knowing it to have been shown false. A person, on being told only that a mathematician named "Goldbach" once issued a conjecture that has not been shown false, would not be sufficiently informed to conceive its being true. He could perhaps conceive that the conjecture he had been told about was true, but that is different from conceiving Goldbach's conjecture to be true. At least some more acquaintance with the content of the conjecture seems required for the latter state of affairs.

However, I think that a sufficiently informed person *is* in a position to conceive the truth or falsity of the conjecture. I think that I, for example, can conceive of, or imagine, Goldbach's conjecture being false. Certainly I can imagine the discovery by computer of a counterexample to the conjecture, the attendant discussion of it, the subsequent revision of philosophical examples, etc. Similarly, I think that there was a time when I could quite clearly conceive of trisecting an angle with compass and straightedge. But, as Kneale has pointed out, it does not follow from my conceiving those states of affairs that they are possible. We do have what seem to be at least two counterexamples to the second premise of the argument from conceivability.

I want to allow, though, the possibility that an acceptable analysis of "*p* is conceivable" can be found under which the foregoing objection fails. Also, I do not deny that I still may be persuaded that I have not really met the conditions, whatever they are, for actually conceiving what I claim to have conceived. The importance of the principle we are examining as a philosophical bedrock cannot be overestimated. Virtually the whole history of metaphysics pivots on the principle, so we should allow the possibility of its salvage and proceed now with an examination of the other premises in the argument from conceivability.[12]

With respect to (18), it should be accepted for the purposes of our discussion. We may be inclined to reject the notion of essential properties altogether, but since we have provisionally accepted the notion, we must allow (18) to stand.

With regard to (16) I am in much the same position I am in with respect to (14). Plantinga seems to think its truth obvious, but I know of nothing that can be said about it sufficient to compel acceptance or rejection. A proponent might argue in its favor by asking us to try to imagine some material body's losing its corporeal attributes. I can imagine my desk, for example, without its actual color, but not without some color or other. Or possibly I can imagine it becoming colorless, but certainly I cannot imagine its losing the property of extension without ceasing to exist altogether. The argument has a persuasive ring, and I think it a decent argument for one claim, albeit not the one it purports to support. I think it is rather an argument to the effect that a material body cannot lose all its corporeal properties and continue to exist. But that is consistent with an object's never having had corporeal properties to begin with. Especially when we turn our attention to persons, the important objects for our purposes, the argument loses some of its appeal. It is difficult for me to imagine myself losing all of my corporeal properties and continuing to exist, but I can imagine myself to have been instantiated in a world devoid of material objects. It may well be that, being in fact a material object, I cannot lose my corporeal properties and continue to exist. But I might have existed without ever having had corporeal properties to begin with. While I don't mean to suggest that my intuitions are persuasive in the matter, they at least lead me to suspend judgment with respect to (16). It is an important principle and more needs to be said before the question of its truth is settled, but for the purposes of assessing the argument under examination, we can pass on to the first premise and a more glaring difficulty.

Some would think it odd to challenge the truth of the first premise. As we have constructed it, (12) seems to report a psychological fact about Descartes. Presumably he knows whether he can conceive of himself existing and no bodies existing. However, I think it can be shown that another premise, like the first in form, can be used in the argument from conceivability to yield a conclusion unacceptable to Descartes and incompatible with the claim that Descartes is not a body. Further, it is a premise the truth of which Descartes must grant. If that is so, then the use of the argument from conceivability is not available to Descartes.

Recall that at the juncture at which Descartes offers the argument from conceivability, he has established that he exists and that he thinks, but he does not yet know what he is. That question remains to be decided. He is able to doubt that he is a body, but he still allows that so far as he knows he is a body. He says:

I am not that set of limbs called the human body; I am not some rarefied gas infused into those limbs . . . all these things I am supposing to be nonentities. But I still have the assertion "nevertheless I am something." But perhaps it is the case that these very things which I suppose to be nonentities, and which are not properly known to me, are yet in reality not different from the "I" of which I am aware? [AG 69]

Now it may seem that this passage is incompatible with Descartes's remark in Meditation II to the effect that " 'I am' precisely taken refers only to a conscious being; that is a mind, a soul, an intellect, a reason" (AG 69). It may be objected that for Descartes it is analytic that a mind is a thing that thinks and that what thinks is a mind. But compatibility between Descartes's claims that he is a mind and that he does not know whether he is a body can be obtained if we allow that mind and body may not be distinct substances. There is evidence that Descartes was allowing this possibility in the second Meditation. He says to Hobbes:

It is very reasonable, and prescribed by usage, to use different names for substances that we recognize as the subjects of quite different acts or accidents; we may then examine later on whether these different names stand for different things, or for one and the same thing. [AG 131]

Descartes here seems willing to grant that, while he knows himself to be a mind, he may also be identical with his body. This attitude is expressed again in a passage from Meditation IV:

I not only know that I exist, inasmuch as I am a thinking thing, but a certain representation of corporeal nature is also presented to my mind; and it comes to pass that I doubt whether this thinking nature which is in me, or rather by which I am what I am, differs from this corporeal nature, or whether both are not simply the same thing; and I here suppose that I do not yet know any reason to persuade me to adopt the one belief rather than the other. [HR 1:176]

Here, however, lies a problem for Descartes. If he is entertaining the possibility that he is a mind that is identical with a body and since he does not know at this point in his inquiry that there are any disembodied minds, then he is bound to grant the truth of:

(21) I can conceive of myself existing and no minds not identical with a body existing.

(21) is consistent with Descartes's being a mind that is identical with a body, and it is not ruled out by any proposition known to Descartes. If Descartes could not conceive of himself as being a corporeal substance with mental attributes, then he would not have grown to doubt, as he tells us he did, whether he was noncorporeal. Surely if reflective consideration of the proposition leads one to doubt that p, then the truth of not-p is at least conceivable to one. So, Descartes should accept (21).

However, (21) has consequences unacceptable to Descartes. In conjunction with (14) it yields:

(22) Possibly I exist and no minds not identical with a body exist.

In turn, from (22) and Descartes's notion of an essential property we get:

(23) I am not essentially not a body.

So far there is no difficulty. But if we are going to attribute (16) to Descartes, then we should also attribute:

(24) (x) (if x is not a body, x is essentially not a body).

There is compelling reason to suppose that Descartes would have regarded (24) as true.

Given the semantics that explicates the logic of metaphysical possibility, (16) says that if something is a body in this world, then in no possible world relative to this one does it have the property of not being a body. Now there is no reason to suppose this world special among possible worlds in regard to the property of being a body. In general there is no reason to suppose that metaphysical principles (like (16)) true of things in this world are not true of things in other worlds possible relative to this one.[13] Holding the contrary would be to advocate another metaphysical principle, no defense for which I can see and certainly none for which Descartes provided.

So, if we think (16) true, we ought to allow that what is a body in any world is a body essentially. But if that is true, then so is (24). To see why, let us suppose (24) false. If (24) is false, then there is something, label it "Bruce," that has the property of not being a body in this world but does have the property of being a body in some world possible relative to this one. Now we agreed above that if something is a body in any possible world, then in no possible world relative to that one does it have the property of not being a body. But that conflicts with our assumption that Bruce has such a property in this world. By reductio, we see that (24) is true.[14]

Now we can see the difficulty to which Descartes is led by (21). It leads, via (22), to (23) which, conjoined with (24), entails that Descartes is a body. That is a consequence that Descartes would not accept and one that is the denial of the conclusion of the argument from conceivability.

Something has gone wrong. Let us recapitulate to see where. We have given provisional acceptance to all the premises of the argument from conceivability. The first premise seemed least suspect of all. But if we allow it, then given Descartes's own remarks, we ought to allow as a possible alternative first premise (21). The argument we get using (21), though, when we add a premise we seem bound to accept if we accept (16), yields the denial of the conclusion of the argument from conceivability. We seem to be at an impasse. Given that the argument is unacceptable to Descartes, he must reject one of its premises. It is open to him, of course, to reject the claim that what is a body is essentially a body. Indeed, he may never have held it; the evidence that he did is conjectural. But to reject it is to reject the present line of argumentation altogether. I am led to suspect the second premise, the principle that allows us to infer possibility from conceivability, especially in the present context where we are playing freely with the notion of essential properties. It is clear, however, that Descartes would not reject the principle. That leaves only the generating premise, the claim that Descartes can conceive himself to exist bodiless.

III

The Argument from Epistemic Possibility

There is a way of rereading the first premise that holds some promise of avoiding the difficulties of the argument from conceivability and, I think, has the virtue of better representing Descartes's intent in the second *Meditation*. It is tempting to say that Descartes there never intended an argument with the claim "Conceivably I exist and no bodies exist" as one of its premises. Instead, we might argue, his claim is rather what we would express by saying that it is epistemically possible for Descartes that he exists and no bodies exist. The text contains evidence that points in that direction. For example, in reply to the objection that in the *Discourse* he assumes without warrant that nothing corporeal pertains to him, Descartes said that he did not there claim that he had no corporeal properties, but rather his claim was that he did not, so far as he was aware, possess any (HR 1:137). In reply to critics of Meditation II, Descartes often drew attention to the passage quoted above to deny that he was asserting that he was not corporeal. Rather, he said, he was not known to be corporeal. When he says in Meditation II, "it might possibly be the case if I ceased entirely to think, that I should likewise cease altogether to exist" we can see him as saying that it is possible, for all he knows, that if he did not have the property of thinking, he would not exist. So, instead of (17), as a first premise, Descartes might have used:

(25) It is epistemically possible that I exist and no bodies exist.

Now the problem is to get from (25) to "Possibly I exist and no bodies exist" where the possibility in question is logical. It has been suggested that the epistemically possible is a subset of the logically possible. If that is so, then it appears that Descartes can omit the troublesome first and second premises of the argument from conceivability and still have the conclusion he desires.

Unfortunately, the epistemic possibility interpretation has two flaws, both fatal. In the first place, it is not true that the set of propositions that are epistemically possible for someone is a subset of the propositions that are logically possible. For me, it is epistemically possible that Goldbach's Conjecture is false. We agreed earlier, though, that if it is true, it is necessarily so, and hence, not possibly false. So, we cannot conclude from something's being epistemically possible for someone that it is also logically possible.

The other fatal difficulty for the epistemic possibility interpretation is that Descartes is here in the same position that he was in with respect to the argument from conceivability. Given the evidence available to him, it should be epistemically possible for him both that he exists without a body *and* that he exists and no mind not identical with a body exists. Descartes simply does not know what he is. The proposition that he is bodiless as well as the proposition that he is identical with a body are both epistemically possible for him. That being the case, Descartes is not warranted in asserting (25) to the exclusion of:

(26) It is epistemically possible that I exist and no mind not identical with a body exists.

But if we allow (26), then all of the difficulties of the argument from conceivability return. Like it, the argument from epistemic possibility must be rejected. It is akin to the argument from conceivability in being unavailable to Descartes, and worse still in being clearly unsound.

IV

Concluding Postscript

The failure of the argument from conceivability and the argument from epistemic possibility leaves frustrated our attempt to reconstruct Descartes's argument for person-body distinctness. It is too soon, though, to suggest that no such reconstruction can provide a respectable candidate for the argument Descartes intended. Further attempts need to be made.[15]

Neither has our attempt been without value. In exposing the faults of the argument from conceivability we have indirectly challenged a whole tradition of such arguments. In one guise or another the argument from conceivability has enjoyed much popularity in the philosophical literature. For example, versions of the argument have recently been presented not only by Plantinga but also by Saul Kripke, Jerome Shaffer, and Anthony Quinton.[16] While their premises are not all made explicit, I think that the arguments of each of these philosophers are committed to something like the premises of the argument from conceivability. We should expect that the fault that marred that argument would also taint theirs.

Our challenge is on several fronts. Any successful attempt to argue from the conceivability of person-body distinctness to its logical possibility will first have to answer our objections to Hume's principle (14). Further, any attempt to circumvent Hume's principle by establishing possible nonidentity without appeal to conceivability will first have to explain the nature of our epistemic access to the logically possible, since conceivability and imaginability are the only routes found in the tradition. Also, any attempt to argue from the possible non-identity of persons and their bodies to its actuality will have to give persuasive considerations in favor of the claim that what is a body is essentially a body.[17] And lastly, any successful version of the argument from conceivability will have to block my final objection to Descartes by showing that while person-body distinctness is conceivable (or possible), person-body identity is not.[18]

NOTES

I am indebted to Vere Chappell, Roderick Chisholm, Edmund Gettier, Fred Feldman, Gareth Matthews, and Hilary Putnam for valuable comments on an early version of this paper.

1. At least two arguments are suggested in this passage. I have quoted only what pertains to the one I intend to examine.

2. A. Kenny, *Descartes: A Study of His Philosophy* (New York, 1967), p. 79.

3. For an analysis of why exportation is illicit in Descartes's case, see my *"De Re Belief,"* *Dialogos* 31 (1978): 59–71. Much of the preceding discussion is from that paper.

4. David Hume, *A Treatise of Human Nature*, ed. L. A. Selby-Bigge (London, 1888), p. 32.

5. Alvin Plantinga, "World and Essence," *The Philosophical Review* 79 (Oct. 1970): 483–86. A similar strategy has also been advocated by Douglas Long in "Descartes' Argument for Mind-Body Dualism," *The Philosophical Forum* 1 (Spring, 1969): 259–73.

6. The principle seems presupposed, for example, in Principle VII (HR 1:221), Principle LIII (HR 1:240), and Descartes's second reply to the third set of "Objections" (HR 2:63). Descartes's most direct affirmation of the principle comes in *Notes Against a Program* (HR 1:437–38) and a letter to Gibieuf of 19 January 1642 (K 123–26).

7. See Principle LIII (HR 1:240).

8. Hume, *Treatise*, p. 32.

9. Ibid., p. 89.

10. William Kneale, *Probability and Induction* (New York, 1949), pp. 79–80.

11. Epistemic possibility, so called, was first discussed by Moore ("Certainty" in *Philosophical Papers* [New York: Collier, 1962], pp. 223–46) and more recently it has been discussed by Wilfrid Sellars ("Phenomenalism" in *Science, Perception, and Reality*) and Paul Teller ("Epistemic Possibility," *Philosophia* 2 (1972):303–20). Kneale's argument has been more fully examined by R. S. Woolhouse in "From Conceivability to Possibility," *Ratio* 14(1972):144–54.

12. I have discussed the analysis of conceivability and its relation to possibility in "A Mistake Concerning Conception," in Stephen Barker and Tom Beauchamp, eds., *Thomas Reid* (Philadelphia: Philosophical Monographs, 1977), pp. 86–93.

13. This claim should not be confused with an affirmation of the Barcan Formula, which it is not. (The Barcan Formula says that if everything has some particular property necessarily, then necessarily everything has that property.)

14. More direct evidence that Descartes would have held (21) is provided by his explicit affirmation of it in the preface to the *Meditations* (HR 1:141). The passage in question also gives evidence that Descartes held (16); however, for various scholarly reasons I prefer in interpreting the *Meditations* not to rely on their preface.

15. I have here ignored Descartes's disclaimer to the effect that he argued for nonidentity in the sixth Meditation, not in the second. I think he presented arguments in both places, and I think that the sixth Meditation argument, when re-

duced to its bare essentials, turns out to be the argument from conceivability. But obviously that claim requires argued support, which it is beyond the scope of this paper to provide. Also it is left to be shown that in Meditation VI Descartes is not in a position successfully to parry my objections to the argument as it appears in Meditation II.

16. Saul Kripke, "Naming and Necessity," in Donald Davidson and Gilbert Harman, ed., *Semantics of Natural Language* (Dordrecht: Reidel, 1972), pp. 334–35; Jerome Shaffer, "Persons and Their Bodies," *The Philosophical Review* 75 (1966): 59–77; Anthony Quinton, "The Soul," *The Journal of Philosophy* 59 (1962):393–409.

17. Kripke's argument for this claim from the notion of rigid designators seems to me unpersuasive, since an identity theorist might want to hold that while he is identical with his body, he is not necessarily identical with the body he in fact has. He might have had some other body. The question for Descartes is whether he is necessarily identical with *a* body, not whether he is necessarily identical with some particular body.

18. See in this regard Douglas Long's "The Bodies of Persons," *The Journal of Philosophy* 71 (1974):291–301.

Descartes's "Synthetic"
Treatment of the Real Distinction
between Mind and Body

ALAN DONAGAN

THE PROOF IN Descartes's *Meditations on First Philosophy* that there is a real distinction between mind and body does not make its appearance until Meditation VI. It is not anticipated in Meditation II, nor could it have been; for a premise crucial to it, that there is an omnipotent God who can bring about all that is clearly and distinctly conceivable, is not established until Meditation III. This fundamental fact, often passed over in recent criticisms of Descartes, has been forcibly insisted upon by Margaret D. Wilson in a recent article, in which she has also drawn attention to two subtler points of which Descartes made use in his replies to Caterus and to Arnauld: that merely conceiving something is not the same as clearly and distinctly conceiving it; and that conceiving something as a being (*ens*) is not the same as conceiving it as a complete being (*ens completum*).[1]

It is now seldom disputed that Descartes accounted only results accomplished by the "analytic" method of the *Meditations*, that is, by following the *ordo cognoscendi* or order of knowing, as philosophically decisive.[2] Because of its lucid and nonscholastic style, however, unprepared readers of the *Meditations* often fail to perceive the accuracy with which it is written, and overlook important distinctions that are drawn in it, but not emphasized by technical terminology. A corrective may be found in Descartes's later *Principia Philosophiae*, in which, along with much else, the principal conclusions of the *Meditations* are presented, not according to the ordo cognoscendi, but, as befits a textbook, in a "synthetic" manner according to the *ordo essendi*, or order of being. In a work written in the synthetic method,

Descartes had no reason to deny himself the use of the accepted, technical scholastic vocabulary, suitably purged; and the scholastic technicalities he allowed himself in the *Principles* are invaluable as guides to distinctions he drew, but without fanfare, in the authoritative *Meditations*.

In the *Principles* Descartes compressed much of what he explained in replying to Caterus and Arnauld into three articles, in which he discussed the various kinds of distinctions in a terminology that is both traditional and memorable (I. 28–30). There are, he maintained, only three fundamental kinds of distinction between things: real (*realis*), modal (*modalis*), and of reason (*rationis*). This is a considerable simplification of the various traditional scholastic doctrines of distinction,[3] despite his assertion in reply to Caterus that the Scotistic formal distinction, for example between God's justice and his mercy, "does not differ from a modal one"—an assertion which, incidentally, is false: the Scotists would have denied that God has modes. Here Spinoza, whose views on this subject are taken from Descartes with a single major alteration, derisively avowed a contempt which Descartes prudently concealed from Caterus: "As for the rest of the farrago of scholastic distinctions, we take no notice of it."[4]

Descartes's classification of the kinds of distinction is best given by translating his own words.

(1) *Real* [distinction] is properly only between two or more substances; and we perceive these to be really distinct each from each [*a se mutuo*] by this alone, that we can clearly and distinctly think of [*intelligere*] one without the other. For, acknowledging God, we are certain that he can bring about [*efficere*] whatever we distinctly think of [*Principles*, I. 60: HR 1:242; AT 8:28][5]

(2) *Modal distinction* is of two kinds: namely, one kind between a mode properly so called and the substance of which it is a mode; the other kind between two modes of the same substance. The former is known from this, that we can indeed clearly perceive a substance without a mode which we say differs from it, but we cannot, vice versa, think of that mode without it. So that a shape and a movement are modally distinct [*modaliter distinguuntur*] from the corporeal substance in which they are, as also an affirmation and a recollection from the mind [in which they are]. [*Principles* I. 61: HR 1:244; AT 8:29]

(3) Finally, a *distinctio rationis* is between a substance and any attribute of it without which it cannot be thought of, or between two attributes of the same substance. [*Principles* I. 62: HR 1:245; AT 8:30]

Several special Cartesian doctrines are presupposed in this classification. First, in saying that there is only a *distinctio rationis*—a distinction in one's way of thinking about a thing, but not in the thing itself—between a substance and "any attribute of it without which it cannot be thought of," or between any two such attributes, Descartes presupposed a doctrine which he had laid down in *Principles* I. 53, that for each substance there is one and only one principal attribute (*attributum praecipuum*) which "constitutes its nature and essence" and to which "all its other properties [that is, its modes] are referred." In a system in which the essence of a substance is constituted by one and only one principal attribute, different words and thoughts for substance and principal attribute in general, or for a given principal attribute, must all stand for the same thing.

Secondly, all the properties of a thing other than its principal attribute are (in scholastic parlance) "referred to" that attribute: that is, roughly, are definable in terms of it as its modifications or modes.

Thirdly, this distinction between substance and mode coincides with the distinction between "complete beings" and "incomplete beings" which in his reply to Caterus, as Wilson notes, Descartes claimed to have "accurately distinguished" in the *Meditations*.[6] A complete being is simply a substance, and an incomplete being a mode. It is true that in his analytic treatment in the *Meditations* Descartes did not expressly state the distinction between substance and mode which he later drew in the *Principles*, or develop a technical terminology for it; but he accurately *observed* in the earlier work the distinction he expressly drew in the technical terminology of the later one, and that sufficiently justifies his claim to Caterus.

We are now in a position to restate, in the terminology of the *Principles*, Descartes's demonstration that the real distinction between mind and body does not follow from the results of Meditation II, and especially not from the result that, even though I know that I am a thinking being, I can doubt whether corporeal substance exists at all.

In the first part of Meditation II (roughly, down to "nihil aliud est quam cogitare"—HR 1:153; AT 7:29) Descartes professed to establish not only that he exists, but that he is a substance (a complete thing) whose essence is constituted by the principal attribute *cogitatio*. The so-called "cogito" proof, even in the form in which it is given in Meditation II (HR 1:150; AT 7:25), begins with the occurrence of certain modes—denying, persuading myself, mentally conceiving, and so forth—and Descartes argued, first, that those modes can, like all modes (or incomplete beings) exist only in a substance (or complete being), and secondly, that being of the kind they are, namely, modes of thinking (*modi cogitandi*),[7] such modes can only exist in a substance whose principal attribute is cogitatio. And he went on to claim that all these results are clearly and distinctly perceived to be true (Meditation II, see HR 1:151–53; AT 7:27–29).

However, these results, even taken together with the result of Meditation I, that there is doubt whether corporeal substance exists, do not, on Descartes's principles, entail that the mind is not corporeal. For they exclude neither the possibility that cogitatio, which constitutes the nature or essence of mind, also constitutes the nature or essence of body, nor the possibility that body is not a substance at all, but a mode of thinking substance.[8] In the first case, the distinction between mind and body would be a mere *distinctio rationis*: a single substance, with a single principal attribute, would be thought of in two ways. In the second case, the distinction between mind and body would be a modal one: mind could exist without body, as a substance can exist without any given mode, but body could not exist without mind. In his cautious admission in Meditation II (HR 1:152; AT 7:27), to which he drew Arnauld's attention, Descartes did not distinguish these two possibilities: "Perhaps indeed it happens [he wrote], that these things themselves [i.e. the human body, thin air, wind, fire, vapor, breath, and so forth] which I suppose to be nothing because they are unknown to me, nevertheless in the truth of the matter (*in rei veritate*) may not differ from that me which I have known"—may, that is, be either the very same substance, or may be among its modes.

Neither of these possibilities can be excluded until the nature of the various things called "corporeal" is determined; and in particular, whether body (*corpus*) is a substance, as it was taken to be in Galilean science, although not in Aristotelian; or whether, as a Cartesian Leibniz or Berkeley would have maintained, it is merely a mode or set of modes.

In the second part of Meditation II (HR 1:153–55; AT 7:29–32), Descartes professed to establish that body is a substance, and to identify its principal attribute, but without establishing its existence. His treatment was modeled on his treatment of mind: corporeal things are imagined and perceived by the senses by their modes or "external forms," which are, of course, "incomplete" beings, such as their sweetness, fragrance, hardness, coldness, sonority, shape, size, color, temperature, fluidity, and so on, all of which can either vary or be lost, while the "complete" being in which they are remains. In Meditation II Descartes treated perfunctorily the modes corresponding to what Locke later called secondary qualities; in Meditation VI and *Principles* I. 66–70, he was to make clear how they are not strictly modes of corporeal things. But he did incidentally present his final doctrine of the modes corresponding to what Locke would have called primary qualities: they are all referred to the principal attribute *extensio*.

The core of the derivation of this conclusion is the celebrated passage in which, to the question of what remains when, from a piece of wax, all that does not belong to it is removed, Descartes gave the answer: "Certainly nothing but an extended somewhat, flexible, changeable" ("extensum quid, flexibile, mutabile") Meditation II: HR 1:154–56; AT 7:30–34). His immediate object in this passage was to establish that one's soul is, scientifically speaking, better known than one's body, by showing that, far from being directly known as the soul is, my body, like a piece of wax, can only be known indirectly through a clear and distinct idea of the understanding (*intellectus*), namely, the idea of extension (Meditation II: HR 1:155, 157; AT 7:31, 34).[9] What changes when the piece of wax remains does not belong to it. Not only can all its sensible qualities change, but whatever shape it has at any time, and even what size, may change also. What remains is the invariant ground of those changes; and Descartes held that no invariant ground for them can be clearly and distinctly conceived except a geometical one, namely, an "extended" somewhat, all the properties of which can be clearly and distinctly conceived in terms of its geometrical relations to spatial coordinates. Meditation II, in which the existence of any bodies at all remains in doubt to the end, was not the place for investigating the nature of the particular invariant extended somewhat that is this piece of wax, which does such things as expand when heated—that was left to the physical treatises, for example *Principles* IV. 31. It was enough to lay down that a body such as this piece of wax can only be clearly and distinctly conceived at all by conceiving it as an invariant extended somewhat.

In the terminology of the *Principles*, the primary qualities of any body—its shape, size, and motion relative to other bodies—are all modes; none of them can be clearly and distinctly conceived except as referred to something else. Extension, on the other hand, cannot be clearly and distinctly conceived as referred to something else. An extended somewhat is something in itself: a complete being, a substance. Extension is, therefore, a principal attribute.

A human body, in consequence, can only be a complete being or substance, the nature of which is constituted by the principal attribute "extensio." By establishing this, Descartes eliminated one of the possible alternatives to the real distinction between body and mind, namely that body is an incomplete being—a mode of mind. Even though bodies have not been shown to exist at all, Meditation II has shown that, if they exist, they must be substances. But in the earlier part of Meditation II, Descartes had already shown to his own satisfaction that minds, or thinking things (*res cogitantes*) are actual substances. It is, therefore, impossible that minds are modes of bodies. The distinction between mind and body cannot be a modal one.

Yet an alternative remains to the doctrine that the distinction between mind and body is real: namely, that it is a mere distinctio rationis—that in thinking of a thing as "cogitans" and in thinking of it as "extensa" we are thinking of the same substance in two ways, or in other words, that "cogitatio" and "extensio" are two names of one and the same principal attribute.

Does it not follow that they are not, simply from the fact, on which Descartes emphatically insists in the two concluding paragraphs of Meditation II (HR 1:155–57; AT 7:32–34) that it is easier to know one's mind than to know corporeal things? For if I clearly and distinctly perceive (1) that I exist, (2) that my nature and essence is to think, and (3) that the nature and essence of corporeal substance is to be extended, does not the very fact that I do not know that corporeal substance exists show that I can clearly and distinctly conceive of thinking substances without corporeal substance? No. For it might be the case that I clearly and distinctly perceive the truth of (1), (2), and (3), and remain in doubt of the existence of corporeal substance simply because I have neglected the question, "Are "cogitatio" and "extensio" in truth one and the same attribute, or not?" Well, suppose that I remedy this neglect, attend to the question, and as a result clearly and distinctly perceive that they *are* the same attribute? I should then possess a proof of the existence of corporeal substance.

In Meditation II Descartes did not raise this crucial question. And until he had raised it, he could not have demonstrated the real distinction between mind and body. The additional premise provided by Meditation III, that an omnipotent God exists, and can bring about any state of affairs that can be clearly and distinctly perceived, would not have sufficed.

Since Descartes recognized only two kinds of created substance, and hence only one real distinction between such substances arising from kind, it should not surprise us that there is no exact parallel in his writings to the question whether or not the distinction between mind and body is real. But there is a near parallel in what he says about the distinction between space and body. We can even imagine a bad epistemological argument on that topic like what Descartes took to be his good one about mind and body. Somebody who had read Kant not wisely but all too well might argue: "Space must exist, because I cannot think it away, although I can think away everything in it; space is extended, the things in space which I can think away are all bodies; therefore space is really distinct from body." Descartes's reply would be: "Between extension and body, and hence between space and bodies, there is only a distinctio rationis; you fail to perceive this because, although you clearly and distinctly understand the principal attribute of space, you confusedly think that that attribute can exist without the substance whose essence it constitutes, and hence confusedly fail to perceive that to be extended and to be corporeal are the same; if you had not fallen into those confusions, you would clearly and distinctly perceive that space is not really distinct from body." The parallel, however, is not exact, because the source of confusion is not in what is perceived of the two specific attributes, extension and corporeality, but in what is not perceived of attributes as such—that they exist only as constituting the essences of substances (cf. *Principles* II. 11–18).

When, in Meditation VI, Descartes finally faced the question whether cogitatio and extensio are the same attribute or not, his answer was disappointingly dogmatic. He first rehearsed the pertinent results of Meditation II:

from this only, that I know myself to exist, and that while I do [*interim*] I notice [*animadvertam*] absolutely nothing else to belong [*pertinere*] to my nature or essence than this alone, that I am a thinking thing, I rightly conclude that my nature consists in this one [thing], that I am a thinking thing. [HR 1:190; AT 7:78]

He then continued, "And although perhaps (or rather, as I shall hereafter say, for certain) I have a body, which is conjoined to me very tightly [*arcte*]," inevitably recalling his admission in Meditation II that he had not excluded the possibility that some body or bodies "which I suppose to be nothing because they are unknown to me, nevertheless . . . may not differ from that me which I have known" (HR 1:152; AT 7:27). But he briskly concluded:

nevertheless because on one hand I have a clear and distinct idea of myself, inasmuch as I am simply [*tantum*] a thinking thing, not an extended [one], and on the other hand, a distinct idea of body, inasmuch as it is simply an extended thing, and not a thinking [one], it is certain that I am really and truly [*revera*] distinct from my body, and can exist without it. [HR 1:190; AT 7:78]

Here Descartes simply declares that he has a clear and distinct idea of himself as thinking, and hence of the attribute "cogitatio," and a distinct idea of body as extended, and hence of the attribute "extensio," and that each can be distinctly conceived without the other. As Dr. Johnson might have said, "There's an end on't."

In maintaining that in Meditation VI Descartes for the first time asks a crucial question (Can I have a clear and distinct idea of myself simply as a thinking thing, and not an extended one, and of a thing simply as extended, and not a thinking one?) and answers it, I depart from Wilson's view that "What is primarily needed [to establish the real distinction between mind and body], besides the conclusions of the second Meditation, is the validation of clear and distinct perceptions as reliable guides to reality."[10] As I interpret Descartes's argument, it is possible to have a clear and distinct idea of the principal attribute F, and a clear and distinct idea of the principal attribute G, without asking the further question whether it is possible to have a clear and distinct idea of one without the other. What is primarily needed besides the conclusions of the second Meditation in order to establish a real distinction between mind and body is, in my view, that a question of this kind be asked and answered, as it is in Meditation VI.

Yet the dogmatic way in which Descartes answered it in Meditation VI is disappointing, and goes far to explain why so many of his critics have dismissed his asseverations that Meditation VI substantially adds to his argument in Meditation II.

How, in Descartes's view, is one to tell whether the clear and distinct idea of a principal attribute F, and the clear and distinct idea of a principal attribute G, are ideas of distinct attributes? It will not do to answer, "They are distinct if one can have a clear and distinct idea of F without G, and of G without F"; for that is what is *meant* by having ideas of them as distinct attributes. What one wants to know is how to tell whether, in clearly and distinctly conceiving an F, I am (perhaps unwittingly) conceiving a G: for example, whether, in clearly and distinctly conceiving something extended, I am (perhaps unwittingly) conceiving something corporeal. Descartes certainly held that anybody who clearly and distinctly conceives *both* F and G is in a position to answer this question, but how?

Many readers have assumed that the Cartesian answer to this question is "by direct inspection," as though questions about the real distinction of principal attributes are to be settled as are questions whether two hues, say two shades of yellow, are or are not the same. It is worth noticing that Descartes did not think that the question whether or not space is really distinct from body can be settled in such a way. And examination of his conception of what clarity and distinctness in ideas are confirms one's disappointment that he did not treat the real distinction between mind and body with the same thoroughness as he did the real identity between space and body.

The scope of the present discussion forbids attempting to elucidate in any detail the distinction between clear and distinct conception and mere conception. All I can do is to refer to the well-known treatment of it by Alan Gewirth, which is the only one I know on which Descartes's position is defensible.[11] I take it to be generally agreed that, for Descartes, all the modes of thinking involve having ideas; that ideas are all that a thinking being has as immediate objects of thought; and that, as immediate objects of thought, ideas have what Descartes calls "objective being" (*esse objectivum*), that is, they stand for or represent some other object to the being whose ideas they are.[12] Gewirth's fundamental contention is that an idea has objective being by virtue of a twofold character: it is both the presentation or thinking of what Gewirth calls a "direct content," and the *viewing* of that direct content *as* (*spectare . . . ut*) representing something else, what it is viewed as being called by Gewirth its "interpretive content." On this interpretation, Descartes's famous remark that "ideas in me are as it were certain images" (Fr. "pictures or images") (Meditation III: HR 1:163; AT 7:42; 9:33), must be taken to mean, not that ideas in me are mental equivalents of carved pieces of stone or daubs on canvas, but mental equivalents of those things viewed as representing other things. The clearness and distinctness of an idea, as Gewirth argues in the light of a careful examination of Descartes's discussion of examples, is a matter of the relation between what it presents, and what that presentation is viewed in it as representing (in Gewirth's terms, between direct and interpretive content)—a relation that is internal to it. Roughly, an idea is clear and distinct if what is presented in it, and what that presentation is viewed in it as representing, correspond exactly.

Descartes has assured us that the ideas of cogitatio and extensio are clear and distinct: that is, as I interpret him, that what they present, and what that presentation is viewed in them as representing, exactly correspond. They will be clearly and distinctly perceived as distinct from one another if the ideas of a thinking substance that is not extended, and of an extended substance that does not think, are also clear and distinct.

What does the idea of extensio present? Something geometrically three-dimensional, all the primary qualities of the parts of which can be clearly and distinctly conceived in terms of their geometrical relations to spatial coordinates. And what is so presented is viewed as representing exactly that, neither more nor less.

Is the idea of a substance having the attribute cogitatio without the attribute extensio clear and distinct? It is if that attribute can be thought of or presented, and then viewed as representing something that thinks but is not extended. Can it be so viewed? Descartes held that it can, because he held it to be possible to conceive something having objective being, something representing other things, without viewing it as extended. Nothing in the concept of objective being seems to presuppose the concept of being extended. That is why Aquinas could correctly describe angels as he did in *Summa Theo-*

logiae I. 50–64. And in the same way, Descartes held it to be possible that a substance having the attribute extensio be thought of or presented, and then viewed as representing something that lacks objective being. To hold otherwise would be to confound standing in projective relations (what is called in Wittgenstein's *Tractatus* "picturing") with having objective being. These considerations, I suggest, lie behind his dogmatic affirmation. Nor do I think that, in the Elysian Fields, either would resent my implication that Descartes anticipated Brentano, rather than those who take the essence of mind to be infallible awareness of its contents.[13]

Descartes's line of thought seems to me to be very strong, but not unchallengeable. But if it is to be challenged, it must be along lines parallel to his own criticism of those who assert a real distinction between space and body. For example, it might be argued that in stopping when he had "referred" the various modes of thinking to cogitatio, and recognizing cogitatio as a principal attribute, he was precipitate. Can cogitatio in turn be referred, as a mode, to some deeper principal attribute—perhaps even to extensio? David Armstrong's *A Materialist Theory of the Mind* can be read as answering this question affirmatively.[14]

NOTES

The original version of this paper was read on 30 April 1976 at a meeting of the American Philosophical Association (Western Division) at New Orleans, my fellow-symposiasts being Margaret D. Wilson and George Nakhnikian. Research on this revised version has been supported by the John Simon Guggenheim Memorial Foundation, by a grant from the National Science Foundation to the Center for Advanced Study in the Behavioral Sciences, Stanford, and by the University of Chicago. I am also indebted to Michael Hooker for advice.

1. Margaret Wilson, "Descartes: The Epistemological Argument for Mind-Body Distinctness," *Noûs* 10 (1976):3–15, esp. pp. 8, 9–10.

2. Cf. Martial Gueroult, *Descartes selon l'ordre des raisons* (2nd ed., Paris: Aubier, 1968), 1:22–23.

3. In an unpublished ms., "Descartes: the Real Distinction between Mind and Body," Mark Sagoff has pointed out that Descartes certainly owed a debt to Francisco Suarez, *Disputationes Metaphysicae*, Disp. 7, "De Variis Distinctionum Generibus," in Suarez, *Opera Omnia* (Paris: Vivès, 1861), vol. 25. Edward Mahoney has drawn my attention to three papers by Norman J. Wells on Descartes's scholastic sources: "Descartes and the Scholastics briefly Revisited," *New Scholasticism* 35 (1961):172–190; "Descartes and the Modal Distinction," *Modern Schoolman* 43 (1965–66):1–22; and "Objective Being: Descartes and his Sources," *Modern Schoolman* 45 (1967):49–61.

4. "Caeterum Peripateticorum distinctionum farraginem non curamus," *Spinoza Opera*, ed. Carl Gebhardt (Heidelberg: Carl Winter, 1925), 1:259, from *Cogitata Metaphysica* II.6.

5. All translations are my own. I have given HR location for the convenience of the reader who may wish to compare.

6. Wilson, "The Argument for Mind-Body Distinctness," pp. 9–10.

7. This use of *modus cogitandi* is exemplified in *Principles* I. 32: "omnes modi cogitandi, quos in nobis experimur" (AT 8:17; and cf. HR 1:232). For a different usage, contrast *Principles* I. 57: "tempus . . . dicimusque esse numerum motus, est tantum modus cogitandi" (AT 8:27; and cf. HR 1:242).

8. Here I have been much helped by Mark Sagoff (see n. 3), who draws particular attention to the possible modal distinction which Meditation II does not exclude: "It is not enough [he writes] that Descartes prove that his mind can exist without his body. He must also show that his body can exist without his mind" (typescript, p. 3). But Sagoff does not remark that Meditation II also leaves open the possibility of a mere distinctio rationis.

9. For a searching examination of this argument see Gueroult, *Descartes selon l'ordre des raisons*, 1:119–49.

10. Wilson, "The Argument for Mind-Body Distinctness," p. 13.

11. Gewirth, Alan, "Clearness and Distinctness in Descartes," *Philosophy* 18 (1943): 17–36. For a different view, cf. Anthony Kenny, *Descartes* (New York: Random House, 1968), ch. 5. By the principle of charity, Gewirth's interpretation is to be preferred.

12. This conception of thinking was not Descartes's alone: Ian Hacking plausibly suggests in "Port Royal's Ideas," ch. 3 of his *Why does Language Matter to Philosophy?* (Cambridge: Cambridge University Press, 1975), that "mental discourse [i.e. discourse consisting of operations with ideas], utterly central to the seventeenth century world view, played the same role then as public discourse now" (p. 33).

13. For an implicit acknowledgment of affinity, see Brentano's admirable "Descartes' Classification of Mental Phenomena," from the notes to *Vom Ursprung sittlicher Erkenntnis* (1889), translated in Franz Brentano, *The True and the Evident*, ed. R. M. Chisholm (New York: Humanities Press, 1966), pp. 28–32.

14. David Armstrong, *A Materialist Theory of the Mind* (New York: Humanities Press, 1968).

Cartesian Dualism

MARGARET D. WILSON

In recent discussions of "the mind-body problem," a position called "Cartesian dualism" is frequently mentioned as a principal alternative to the various forms of materialism. What seems to be most often intended in such references to "Cartesian dualism" is the view that mental events—the most discussed examples in these contexts being sensations—are not identical with events in the body (brain, CNS, or whatever). Careful scholars also note that within the Cartesian system proper this distinction of mental and physical events is understood as involving a distinction of *substances* or "logical types of subject."[1] That is, sensations (understood as conscious states) are to be construed as belonging to, as modes, of mental substances, while physical states or occurrences, such as neural discharges, are ascribed to, or modally depend on, corporeal substance. By contrast, a materialist might hold (for example) that the sensation of pain is nothing but the firing of certain neurons (under the proper circumstances); that there are no irreducibly mental occurrences, and a fortiori no special mental substances that have such occurrences as modes.

It is entirely compatible with the conception of "Cartesian dualism" reflected in these discussions to suppose that every type of mental occurrence—from twinges of pain to metaphysical reflection—has a corresponding or correlated type of physical occurrence, distinguished perhaps by the part of the brain involved, complexity of the patterns of neural activity, and so forth. Further, it seems to be an essential tenet of this dualism that everything commonly identified as an experience or a conscious occurrence is conceivable independently of any physical occurrence or state. To be this sort of "cartesian dualist" I must hold, for example, that I can introspect a pain, and form a clear conception of it, without being aware of or conceiving any physical state at all. More precisely, the "Cartesian dualist" is supposed to argue that just because there is no conceptual connection between physical states on the one hand, and experiences on the other, we must conclude that experiences are never the same thing as physical states (and that experiences and physical states are "had" by two different sorts of substances). The lack of conceptual connection is supposed to be necessary and sufficient for claiming that experiences and physical events are two different sorts of things. Nothing whatsoever is supposed to follow about the results of neurophysiology. In particular, this contemporary understanding of "Cartesian dualism" does not maintain that the search for a neurophysiological account of "pure thought" is in any sense more chimerical than the search for neurophysiological account of sensation.

This conception of "Cartesian dualism" seems to derive its inspiration from the famous "epistemological argument" for mind-body distinctness that Descartes presents in Meditation VI, and defends and elaborates in various other places. Here is the argument as Descartes states it in the *Meditations*:

Because I know that all that I clearly and distinctly understand can be brought about by God as I understand it, it is enough that I can clearly and distinctly understand one thing apart from another, for me to be certain that one is different from the other, since they can be placed apart from each other at least by God; and it does not matter by what power this is done, in order for us to judge them to be different; and thus, from this very fact, that I know I exist, and that meanwhile I notice nothing else to belong to my nature or essence, except this alone, that I am a thinking thing, I rightly conclude that my essence consists in this one [thing], that I am a thinking thing. And although probably (or rather, as I will say afterwards, certainly) I have a body, which is very closely conjoined to me, because nevertheless on the one hand I have a clear and distinct idea of myself, in so far as I am only a thinking thing, not extended, and on the other hand I have a distinct idea of body, in so far as it is only an extended thing, not thinking, it is certain I am really distinct from my body, and can exist apart from it. [AT 7:78; HR 1:190]

Here Descartes says that he can "clearly and distinctly understand" himself as a thinking thing apart from any body; he does not mention particular sorts of mental or physical occurrences. Still, passages from other parts of the *Meditations* do seem to indicate that when Descartes says he can conceive himself as a thinking thing apart from anything corporeal, part of what he means is that his conceptions of the various episodes of his mental life are independent of any commitment to physical existence. Thus, he does not need to know anything about the workings of his own body—or even that he has a body—in order to know that he thinks, or that he seems to feel heat, see light, hear sound (i.e., have the "sensations" of warmth, light, sound) (Cf. Meditation II: AT 7:29; HR 1:153). Therefore, one might conclude, the "Cartesian dualism" of contemporary philosophical discussion is nothing more or less than Cartesian dualism—with the quotation marks removed.

This conclusion would be erroneous. Descartes's own dualistic position has quite different implications and, I think, quite different motivation from the "Cartesian dualism" of recent discussions. For Descartes, identifying "the mind" with "the intellect" or "reason," believes there are corporeal correlates of mental acts only in certain cases. Thus, in imagining and in certain kinds of remembering the mind is said to "utilize" or "turn to" impressions existing in the brain, and in the experiences of sensations and passion the mind is affected by changes in the bodies' organs and may even become aware of itself as united or "intermingled" with the whole body. In these sorts of mental occurrences "some understanding is comprised"—this is a necessary condition of their *being* mental occurrences—but because of the dependence of the thoughts on physical states or occurrences they cannot be construed as "pure understanding." But a person doing metaphysics, or thinking about God, or reflecting on mind itself, is exercising pure understanding—assuming, at least, that he has the true, nonphysical notions of God, the mind, and so forth. Pure understanding is carried on independently of all physical processes; any physiological study will necessarily be irrelevant to it. There is hence a very fundamental contrast, from the scientific point of view, between the exercise of pure understanding on the one hand, and all other mental occurrences on the other. For Descartes, of course, was firmly committed to the possibility of providing physiological accounts of the various emotions, sensations, and patterns of reflex behavior, as well as of imagination and what he calls the corporeal memory. Much of his life's research was devoted to developing just such accounts. (These accounts are always contrasted in his writings with the operations of the "rational soul" per se.)

The aspect of Descartes's dualism I am concerned to stress is brought out well in the fifth set of "Replies to Objections," where Descartes responds to Gassendi's "materialist" criticisms. Gassendi, for example, had commented:

In order to prove that you are of a diverse nature [from the brutes], (that is as you contend, an incorporeal nature), you ought to put forth some operation in a way different than they do, if not outside the brain, at least independently of the brain: but this you do not do. For you yourself are perturbed when it is perturbed, and oppressed when it is oppressed, and if somthing destroys the forms of things in it, you yourself do not retain any trace. [AT 7:269; HR 2:145]

Descartes answers:

I have . . . often distinctly showed that the mind can operate independently of the brain; for certainly the brain can be of no use to pure understanding, but only to imagination or sensing. And although, when something strongly strikes imagination or senses (as is the case when the brain is perturbed), the mind does not easily free itself to understand other things, we nevertheless experience that when the imagination is less strong, we often understand something completely different from it: as, when while sleeping we notice that we dream, the imagination is indeed necessary for dreaming, but only the understanding is necessary to notice that we dream. [AT 7:358–59; HR 2:212]

In a similar vein, Descartes denies Gassendi's claim that the mind develops or deteriorates with the body, arguing that Gassendi cannot prove it:

[F]or, from the fact that it does not act as perfectly in the body of an adult, and its actions can often be impeded by wine and other bodily things, it only follows that as long as the mind is joined to the body, it uses the body as its instrument in those operations in which it is usually occupied, not that it is rendered more perfect or less perfect by the body. [AT 7:354; HR 2:208–9]

According to Descartes, the mind may be distracted, impeded, or limited in its operations by the condition of the body (cf. also AT 7:228; HR 2:103). But he seems to allow no connection at all between the mind's basic capacity for pure intellection or ratiocination and anything that does or could occur in the brain or other parts of the body. That is, alterations in the brain are not even correlated with alterations in these capacities.

The contrast between strictly intellectual acts and mental acts involving reference to physical states is found already in Descartes's early work, *The Rules for the Direction of the Mind (Regulae)*. In a rather well-known passage in Rule XII he writes:

That power by which we are properly said to know things is purely spiritual, and not less distinct from the whole body than blood from bone, or hand from eye. . . . It is one and the same power which, if it applies itself along with imagination to the common sense is said to see, touch, etc.; if to imagination alone as [the latter] is clothed in different forms, it is said to remember; if to the imagination as fashioning new forms there, it is said to imagine or conceive; *finally if it acts alone it is said to understand.* [AT 10:415; HR 1:38–39; emphasis added]

And the contrast is still present, although perhaps somewhat muted, in Descartes's last published work, *The Passions of the Soul*. (Cf., e.g.,

Part I. 47; AT 11:364 ff.; HR 1:352 ff.) Similarly, in letters of the late thirties and early forties we find other aspects of the contrast spelled out. In a letter to Mersenne of 1639 Descartes contrasts the knowledge the soul gains "by reflection on itself" in the case of intellectual matters, with that it derives from reflection "on the various dispositions of the brain to which it is joined, which may result from the action of the senses or from other causes" (AT 2:589; K 66). And in letters of 1640 he also espouses a contrast between corporeal and spiritual memory:

[Concerning the folds of memory,] I do not think that there has to be a very large number of these folds to serve for all our memories, in that a single fold will do for all the things which resemble each other, and that besides the corporeal memory, whose impressions can be explained by the folds of the brain, I judge that there is also in our understanding another sort of memory, which is altogether spiritual and is not found in animals, and it is this that we mainly use. [AT 2:143; K 76][2]

One could go on, but I hope this will be sufficient to bring home the point that Descartes himself was committed to a much more robust and, in a sense, much more significant version of dualism than the position that often passes for "Cartesian dualism" in present-day seminars and colloquia.[3] We must further conclude, I think, that the true full-blooded (or perhaps one should say full-spirited) dualism of the historical Descartes is a dead philosophy. I expect there are few well-informed people today who would accept or even suspend judgment on the proposition that "the brain is not at all involved in pure understanding," or, say, the view that we must distinguish between corporeal memory, which involves the "use" of traces in the brain, and the purely intellectual memory, which does not.

In the rest of this essay I want to consider two questions that are suggested by the foregoing considerations. First, what motives and/or arguments did Descartes—a very dedicated scientific investigator—have for accepting and indeed insisting upon what seems like a most "unscientific" conception of the nature and workings of the human mind? Of particular interest in this connection is whether or not Descartes thought that any argument developed in the *Meditations* could support such a strong form of dualism. (As I have already said, the principal argument for mind-body distinctness does not seem to.) Second, did Descartes in the last analysis mean to hold that there is no conceptual connection between *any* "thought" or mental occurrence and *any* physical occurrence, as the contemporary interpretation of the epistemological argument would seem to imply? Or was his position rather that certain mental occurrences—such as acts of pure understanding—could be clearly and distinctly conceived without reference to the body?

In response to the first question it is natural to point out that "the cerebral basis of human intelligence" is little enough understood in the twentieth century; it seems no wonder that a seventeenth-century figure should refuse to credit such a notion at all. Further, Descartes did not have the opportunity we have had to observe the development of computer technology, and even in our own times this development has been met with various forms of self-serving resistance and denial: "Machines will never be able to ——— the way human beings do, etc." True, but we must notice (and I don't think this is usually sufficiently recognized) that Descartes stands alone among the major philosophical thinkers of the seventeenth century in denying both the possibility that thought inheres in material substance, and the possibility of any form of mind-body parallelism. Hobbes, Spinoza, and Leibniz all accepted some form of either materialism or parallelism— for reasons, partly, of scientific seriousness. Locke appears to embrace Descartes's dualistic interactionism in some passages, but elsewhere maintains emphatically that we simply cannot know whether the "substance of [our] thought" is immaterial or bodily.[4] As we have seen even a less bold and creative thinker such as Gassendi was defending a version of materialism against Descartes; in fact, even Descartes's minor critics objected that for all he had really shown, thought could still be a property of matter.

For somewhat similar reasons, theological considerations cannot be regarded as fully explanatory either. If we may judge by their published works, Spinoza and Leibniz were far more deeply concerned with the problem of immortality than was Descartes, yet both of these men accepted a more or less parallelistic position concerning the relation of mental states to states of the brain or body. It is true that Descartes seems to have been more shamelessly concerned even than Leibniz to gain acceptance for his views among the established political powers of the age. Yet it is impossible to believe that the enormous range and variety of Cartesian pronouncements concerning the independence of intellect from body, including all those we have already cited, could have been dictated by this type of prudence or hypocrisy.

Descartes's position as a scientist provides a much more plausible explanation for his insistence on the complete immateriality of the operations of the understanding. A motive for his dualism may perhaps be found in the universalist pretensions of his physics, which are unmistakable in several works. For example, he claims, or boasts, at the end of the *Principles* that "there is no phenomenon of nature that has been omitted from this treatise" (IV. 199; AT 8(1):323; HR 1:296).

Yet he must have perceived that the accounts of human behavior he was able to provide did not go beyond the level, roughly, of reflex action. To deny that reason has any corporeal basis would be a necessary condition of reconciling his ambitions with his limitations. A reason for his dualism may be found in his commitment to mechanistic explanation in physics, together with the perfectly creditable belief that human intelligence could never be accounted for on the available mechanistic models.

The latter view is only briefly indicated in the *Meditations*, when Descartes stresses (in the "piece of wax" passage in Meditation II) that the limited representations of the imagination are not sufficient for a distinct conception of a body. It is much more fully developed in a now-famous passage in the *Discourse on Method*. Here Descartes indicates that two aspects of human behavior tend to show that our actions must be governed by some nonmechanistic principle. The first of these, relating to our use of language, has been particularly stressed by Noam Chomsky, who is largely responsible for the celebrity of the passage in our time.[5] Descartes writes:

[Machines] could never use words or other signs in composing them as we do to declare our thoughts to others. For we can easily conceive a machine's being constituted so that it utters words, and even that it utters some à propos of corporeal actions, which cause some change in its organs; for instance, if it is touched in a certain place it will ask what we wish to say to it; if in another place it will exclaim that it is being hurt, and so on; but not that it arranges words differently to reply to the sense of all that is said in its presence, as even the most moronic man can do. [AT 6:51; HR 1:116]

Chomsky takes Descartes to be referring here to the "creative aspect of language use."[6] If Chomsky means, by "creative," *innovative* (e.g., the ability to invent and understand sentences different from any one has previously heard), it is not entirely clear that his reading of the passage is correct. What Descartes seems to be saying is that we could not imagine a machine sufficiently complex to have an appropriate verbal response to each of the enormous range and variety of occurrences to which we human beings do respond verbally. And I'm not sure whether or not this is the same as pointing to a peculiarly "innovative" feature. What is clear, in any case, is that Descartes is maintaining that an immaterial soul must be invoked to "explain" human language use, because a strictly mechanistic account is inconceivable.

The second consideration is, superficially, much less convincing:

And . . . although [machines] can do certain things as well as or perhaps better than any of us, they infallibly fall short in certain others, by which we may discover that they did not act from knowledge, but only from the disposition of their organs. For while reason is a universal instrument which can serve for all sorts of occasions, these organs have need of some particular disposition for each particular action. [AT 6:57; HR 1:116]

Or as Descartes elaborates the point with reference to animals:

It is . . . a very remarkable fact that although there are many animals which exhibit more skill than we do in some of their actions, we at the same time observe that they do not manifest any at all in many others. Hence the fact that they do better than we do, does not prove that they are endowed with mind, for in this case they would have more than any of us, and would do better in all other things. It rather shows that they have none at all, and that it is nature which acts in them according to the disposition of their organs. [AT 10:58–59; HR 1:117]

The underlying assumption here seems to be that if you do something, a, better than I do, and do it from reason or knowledge (and assuming perhaps that I also do a "from knowledge") then you will also excel me in every other activity (or at least in every other activity that I perform "from knowledge"). That is, if you excel me in bridge you will also excel me in chess—and in literary criticism, landscape architecture, in solving differential equations, and in the resolution of moral dilemmas or social predicaments. And this assumption is at best very implausible: even in those activities deemed most rational or reason-guided we exhibit varying degrees of specialization, knack, and skill.

But I think we must assume that Descartes is speaking hyperbolically in this passage. His point, surely, is only that if animals used something like human reason to accomplish their various remarkable feats, then they should show qualities of adaptability, and learning abilities, far beyond any they actually exhibit.[7] Conversely, the adaptability and educability of human beings, including their linguistic competence, cannot, according to Descartes's reasoning, be supposed capable of explanation on mechanical principles alone. Or rather, in Descartes's own words, "it is morally impossible that there should be sufficient diversity in any machine to allow it to act in all the occurrences of life in the same way as our reason causes us to act." This implies, at least, that it is morally impossible that we ourselves should turn out to be only very complex physical mechanisms.

The passage from the *Discourse* provides motivation for Descartes's dualism by suggesting he had reflected—perhaps more systematically than his contemporaries—on the possibility of a mechanistic account of human behavior. It suggests he had concluded that such an account was impossible, in view of the complexity and "diversity" that would be required in such a machine. If this was his reasoning he must be given credit for, at least, an admirable realism concerning the state of the art and the difficulty of the problem—in contrast, for example, with the unabashed mechanistic optimism of Hobbes (or, as Chomsky might point out, of latterday behaviorists).

One can make considerable sense, then, of Descartes's espousal of a quite "robust" form of dualism with reference to his understanding of the available forms of materialistic explanation. But it is still worth asking whether there is anything in the arguments of the *Meditations* themselves that is supposed to provide support for the true historical form of Cartesian dualism (as opposed to the relatively pallid if less discredited position that may go under that name today). I believe that there is.

We have noticed that Descartes answers Gassendi with the statement: "I have . . . often distinctly showed that the mind can operate independently of the brain; for certainly the brain can be of no use to pure understanding, but only to imagination or sensing" (AT 8: 358–59; HR 2:212). Now in the fifth set of "Replies" Descartes sometimes does make reference to the *Discourse* and other works, as well as the *Meditations*. However, this statement about the lack of a cerebral basis for "pure understanding" pretty clearly does not have reference to the arguments from the *Discourse* that we have just considered. Rather, Descartes seems to be referring to the discussion of understanding and imagination at the beginning of Meditation VI —a discussion foreshadowed, to some degree, by the passages we have already quoted from the *Regulae*, and from the letters to Mersenne. In the sixth Meditation Descartes remarks that when he imagines, for example, a triangle, he does not merely understand that it is a figure enclosed by three lines, but "at the same time I also view [*intueor*] these three lines as if present to the vision [*acie*] of the mind, and this is what I call imagining" (AT 7:72; HR 1:185). Imagination, that is, seems to be "nothing else . . . than a certain application of the faculty of cognition [*facultatis cognoscitivae*] to a body which is intimately present to it, and which therefore exists." In pure understanding, on the other hand, there is no such "application of the faculty of knowing," no such presence of a figure to the mind's eyesight:

If I want to think of a chiliagon, I of course equally well understand it to be a figure composed of a thousand sides, as I understand a triangle to be a figure composed of three sides; but I do not in the same way imagine those thousand sides, or view [*intueor*] them as if present. [AT 7:72; HR 1:185–86]

Descartes goes on to observe that the power of imagining differs from the power of understanding in that the former is not required "for the essence of myself, that is, of my mind"; whence, he says, "it seems to

follow that [imagination] depends on something different from me."
And, he continues:

I easily understand that if some body exists to which the mind is so conjoined that it can apply itself to inspect it at will, it could be that in this
way it imagines corporeal objects; hence that this mode of cognition differs
only in this from pure understanding: that the mind, when it understands,
in some way turns toward itself, and regards [respiciat] some of the ideas
which are in itself; when it imagines, however, it turns toward the body, and
views [intueatur] something conforming to the idea, either understood by
itself or perceived by the senses. [AT 7:73; HR 1:186]

Descartes stops short of saying that no other explanation of imagination is possible (than the supposition that corporeal figures are presented to the eyesight of the mind by a body joined to the mind). He
therefore concludes that this argument from the contrast between
imagination and understanding gives him a "merely probable" proof
of the existence of body. He then goes on to consider the nature of
sense perception, ultimately deciding that God "could not be defended from the accusation of deceit," unless it were the case that the
ideas of sense were caused in him by bodies; and further that he is
entitled to conclude from his bodily sensations that he in fact has a
body, to which he is more closely united "than a sailor to a ship."

Does Descartes really suppose these phenomenological considerations provide a reason for maintaining that "the brain is not at all
involved in pure understanding?" I do not see how we can avoid the
conclusion that he does. (What he hesitates about is not this "negative" conclusion, but rather the legitimacy of concluding that the body
is involved in our acts of imagination.) Pure understanding involves
neither the sensations or effects that are "caused" in the mind as a
result of its close union with all the bodily organs, nor "corporeal
images" that might be presented on a surface of the brain, as if on a
blackboard. Ergo the brain (or body) is not at all involved in pure
thought. For what task would there be left for it to perform?

Descartes's "epistemological" argument for the distinctness of mind
from body occurs more or less in the midst of the discussion of understanding, imagination, and sense, which we have just been considering. The next question I want to examine here is whether or not
Descartes considers it important to the success of his "epistemological"
argument that the pure understanding does not involve corporeal
images or other apparently physical presentations or occurrences. If
the distinction between pure understanding on the one hand, and
sense and imagination on the other hand, is important to this argument, then Descartes's position would differ from the contemporary

understanding of "Cartesian dualism" even more than has already been claimed. For, as I indicated at the beginning, contemporary discussions tend to represent "Cartesian dualism" as resting on the claim that *any and every* experience, or phenomenological state, is conceptually distinct from any and every physical occurrence or state.

We have already noted that earlier in the *Meditations* Descartes does indeed take the view that he can be certain about the existence and character of his own mental states ("thoughts"), including those we call sensations or perceptions, without any certainty about the existence or nature of any physical entity, including his own body. And this would seem to be all he needs to claim that his mind with all its contents is *conceptually* distinct from his body and hence (by the reasoning of Meditation VI) *really* distinct as well. However, these considerations are not conclusive. Descartes puts great emphasis on the distinction between mere conceivability and *clear and distinct* conceivability. He would not for example claim to know that a given mental occurrence could exist independently of any physical occurrence, unless he could claim clearly and distinctly to conceive that mental occurrence independently of anything physical. And it is perhaps not certain that this is the position he wants to take in Meditation II, with respect to his mental states generally.

Does Descartes want to hold that he can clearly and distinctly conceive sensations or acts of imagination independently of any physical events or states? The first thing to notice is that he does not need to make this claim in order for the epistemological argument to go through in the manner in which he expresses it. For he makes very clear in Meditation VI that he does *not* regard the "faculties" of sense and imagination as belonging to his essence as res cogitans. One relevant passage has already been cited:

I consider that this power of imagining which is in me, is different from the power of understanding, in that it is not required for the essence of myself, that is of my mind; for although it were separated from me, there is little doubt I would remain nevertheless the same thing I now am. [AT 7:73]

Still more significant is the fact that after Descartes states the epistemological argument—in the course of which he asserts, "I rightly conclude that my essence consists in this one [thing], that I am a thinking thing"—he continues:

Besides I find in me the faculties of certain special modes of thinking, that is the faculties of imagining and sensing, without which I can clearly and distinctly understand myself a whole, but not vice versa, them without me, that is without an intelligent substance in which they are. [AT 7:78; HR 1:190]

This is already sufficient to show, I think, that the epistemological argument of Meditation VI is not intended by Descartes to make any claim that he can clearly and distinctly conceive his *sensations,* for example, independently of anything physical. This argument is concerned only with the isolation of Descartes's essence as a thinking thing—and this, as we have seen, means *intellectus purus,* pure understanding.

For all that, Descartes might still be ready to agree (with contemporary understandings of "Cartesian dualism") that every one of his experiences or "cogitationes" is clearly and distinctly conceivable apart from any physical occurrence or bodily state. He could, in other words, be prepared to agree to this proposition, despite the fact that it is not strictly relevant to his demonstration that he is essentially only a thinking thing, and does not have any physical properties essentially. (In other words, is not relevant to the core of *his* form of "Cartesian dualism.") But is there even this much agreement?

We have seen that Descartes does not believe it possible conclusively to demonstrate the existence of body or brain from the experiences of imagination. The supposition of physical traces in the brain, which the mind "inspects," merely provides the "best explanation" of imagination that he is able to produce. It seems safe to conclude, then, that for Descartes there is no contradiction in supposing that my phenomenal states of imagination occur although no body exists. And this means (I take it) that the experiences of imagination can be clearly and distinctly conceived in separation from anything physical. But what about sensation?

Here the situation is less clear. We have noted that in Meditation VI Descartes finally derives the conclusion that his mind is closely conjoined with a body from considerations about sensations. Having remarked "that all things that nature teaches me have some truth," he continues:

However there is nothing that this nature more expressly teaches me than that I have a body, which is harmed when I feel pain, which needs food or drink when I feel hunger or thirst, and similar things. . . . Nature also teaches, through these sensations of pain, hunger, thirst, etc., that I am not merely present in my body as a sailor is present in a ship, but am very closely conjoined to it and as if intermingled with it, so that I compose one thing with it. For otherwise, when the body is hurt, I who am nothing but a thinking thing, would not on that account feel [*sentirem*] pain, but would perceive that injury by the pure understanding, as a sailor perceives by vision if something is broken in the ship; and when the body needed food or drink I would understand this expressly, not have confused sensations of hunger and thirst. For certainly these sensations of thirst, hunger, pain, and so forth are nothing but certain confused modes of thinking arising from the union and as it were intermixture of the mind with the body. [AT 7:80; HR 1:192]

Nature teaches me, through sensation, that I am so closely conjoined with my body as to form with it one thing. Is this, or is it not, consistent with the view that I can clearly and distinctly conceive my sensations in separation from anything physical?

One might suppose that sensations must be distinctly conceivable apart from physical occurrences, on the grounds that the latter are after all the causes of the former, and causes and effects must be distinct events. Descartes does say that sensations "arise from" the mind-body union. However, Descartes was no Humean: he notoriously subscribes to the view that one can make various inferences from the nature of the effect to the nature of the cause. In the passage just quoted, he is clearly making some kind of inference from the nature of his sensations to his own embodiment. I am not sure whether or not this shows that there is some kind of conceptual connection, for Descartes, between the notion of sensation and the notion of bodily cause: the argument from "what nature teaches me" is, I think, rather obscure and difficult to interpret precisely. Thus it is not clear whether the notion of sensations as standing in causal relations to physical occurrences provides evidence for or against the view that the two are conceptually distinct.

There are, however, other passages that seem to suggest somewhat more definitely that Descartes did not think of sensations as distinctly conceivable apart from body, in the way that "pure thoughts" are. (The passages suggest at the same time that the union of mind with body, as discoverable in sensation, is something not fully explicable in terms of causal interaction between distinct physical and mental events.) Both in his correspondence with Princess Elizabeth, and in *The Passions of the Soul,* Descartes indicates that sensation shows the mind forms "one thing" with the body in such a strong sense that we can think of mind itself as extended or material. For example, he writes to Elizabeth:

I should [in reply to your Highness's earlier letter] have shown that even though one wish to conceive the soul as material (which is properly speaking to conceive its union with the body), one still knows by further [considerations] that it is separable from the body. [AT 3:691; K 141]

He continues: "Things pertaining to the union of the soul and the body can not be known except obscurely by the understanding alone, or even by the understanding aided by the imagination, but they are known very clearly by the senses" (AT 3:692; K 141). And later in the same letter he even tells her that it is impossible for the human mind to conceive distinctly at the same time both the "distinction between the soul and the body and their union; because to do that it is necessary to conceive them as one thing, and also [*ensemble*] conceive them as two, which is self-contradictory [*qui se contraire*]."

Like most of what Descartes says on the subject of embodiment all this is pretty obscure. I do not wish to rest very much on it. I only want to suggest that Descartes's claim that in sensation we experience (or "know") mind and body *as one single thing*, should lead to some caution about attributing to him the view that we can clearly and distinctly conceive our sensations apart from any physical state or occurrence.

In this paper I've been concerned to emphasize certain peculiar features of the original historical form of Cartesian dualism which distinguish it from the mere claim that mental states are conceptually and therefore really distinct from states of the body or brain. Descartes supposes that the brain has nothing to do with pure understanding (in contrast to sense and imagination)—except in so far as "phantoms of the brain" might distract the understanding from its appropriate activity. There is evidence that he was led to this position partly by overhasty conclusions about the limitations of physical science, buttressed perhaps by reluctance to admit the existence of any genuinely physical phenomenon not accounted for by his own science. In addition, Descartes seems rather surprisingly to have believed that we can reach conclusions about the physical basis or concomitants of the various modes of thought by phenomenological analysis of those modes of thought. The question whether or not the brain is involved in a given mode is connected in Descartes's mind with the question whether the mode of thought somehow involves "corporeal" *imagery*. I have also raised the question whether or not Descartes would agree to the proposition of contemporary "Cartesian dualism," that all mental occurrences, including sensations, can be conceived in some valid manner independently of the conception of any physical occurrence. And I have argued that *whether or not* he would agree to this proposition, it is not entailed by or otherwise implicated in his argument for the distinctness of himself from his body in Meditation VI. In other words, the proposition is not required by the argument for mind-body dualism to which Descartes accords most importance. Finally, I have tentatively suggested that there is some reason for doubting that Descartes would accept this proposition at all.

NOTES

1. See J. Fodor, *Psychological Explanation* (New York: Random House, 1968), pp. 55–56.

2. Cf. AT 3:48; K 72.

3. For example, at a symposium on the Mind-Body Problem held at Princeton University on 9 January 1975, the term "Cartesian (or cartesian?) dualism" was repeatedly used as a label for the position that merely denies the *identity* (not necessarily the correlation) of physical and mental states. (Participants in the symposium were four major contributors to the literature on the subject.) However, the peculiarities of the historical Cartesian position have been accurately and concisely formulated by Wilfrid Sellars in "Philosophy and the Scientific Image of Man." For instance, Sellars writes: "As for conceptual thinking, Descartes not only refused to identify it with neurophysiological processes, he did not see this as a live option, because it seemed obvious to him that no complex neurophysiological process could be sufficiently analogous to conceptual thinking to be a serious candidate for being what conceptual thinking 'really is.' It is not as though Descartes granted that there might well be neurophysiological processes which are strikingly analogous to conceptual thinking, but which it would be philosophically incorrect to *identify* with conceptual thinking. . . . He did not take seriously the idea that there *are* such neurophysiological processes." (*Science, Perception, and Reality* [New York: The Humanities Press, 1963], p. 30.) Sellars goes on to remark that even if Descartes had taken the latter idea seriously, he still "would have rejected" the identification "on the grounds that we had a 'clear and distinct,' well-defined idea of what conceptual thinking is before we even suspected that the brain had anything to do with thinking." And this, I believe, is questionable. I agree that Descartes *could* have maintained his dualism even in the face of increased appreciation of the complexities of neurophysiology: as indicated in the text, his main argument for mind-body distinctness seems (overtly at least) logically independent of this issue. But it is entirely possible that the *motivation* for his dualism was quite bound up with false preconceptions about the limitations of physical explanation.

4. J. Locke, *An Essay Concerning Human Understanding*, ed. by Peter H. Nidditch (Oxford: Clarendon Press, 1975), pp. 539–43 (IV, ch. iii, sect. 6). Compare ibid., p. 313, 1. 16—one of the places where Locke seems to be tacitly adopting the Cartesian view. In "Locke on the Substance of the Mind" (Princeton University, 1977; so far unpublished) Milton M. Wachsberg has argued persuasively that Locke has no good philosophical reason for keeping alive the Cartesian notion of an immaterial soul in human beings. I am inclined to think—although this is only a hunch—that Locke himself came to realise this, but avoided acknowledging the point because of some of his contemporaries' vehement opposition to materialism.

5. Noam Chomsky, *Cartesian Linguistics* (New York: Harper & Row, 1966), ch. 1. For a more detailed discussion see K. Gunderson, *Mentality and Machines* (Garden City, New York: Doubleday (Anchor), 1971). (Gunderson also examines the historical sequel of Descartes's arguments in the work of La Mettrie.)

6. Chomsky, *Cartesian Linguistics*, p. 4.

7. Cf. Gunderson, *Mentality and Machines*, pp. 10–11: "[A]ll Descartes needs in order to show that S has not passed the . . . action test is that there is some (broad) range of actions where S (machine or beast, for example) fails to perform in ways comparable to the ways in which human beings perform."

Descartes's Correspondence with Elizabeth: Concerning Both the Union and Distinction of Mind and Body

RUTH MATTERN

PRINCESS ELIZABETH of Bohemia wrote to Descartes in the spring of 1643, begging him to clarify his conception of the relation of mind and body. In his two replies, he tried to elucidate the nature of this relation, and to diagnose her difficulty in understanding it. But what he says here is often unclear and enigmatic. An especially puzzling comment occurs in his second letter, of 28 June 1643:

ne me semblant pas que l'esprit humain soit capable de concevoir bien distinctement, et en mesme temps, la distinction d'entre l'ame et le corps, et leur union; à cause qu'il faut, pour cela, les concevoir comme une seule chose, et ensemble les concevoir comme deux, ce qui se contrarie. [AT 3:693]

[It does not seem to me that the human mind is capable of conceiving very distinctly, and at the same time, both the distinction between mind and body, and their union. To do that, it is necessary to conceive them as a single thing and at the same time consider them as two things, which is self-contradictory.][1]

It is not obvious what problem Descartes sees here. In Meditation VI, he had claimed that body and mind are both distinct and united (HR 1:190–92). He had also defended the compatibility of these claims in his "Reply to Objections IV," without suggesting that the conception of union interferes with the conception of mind-body distinctness: "substantial union," he wrote, "does not prevent the formation of a clear and distinct concept of the mind alone as of a complete thing"

(HR 2:102–3).[2] It seems that two things may have the *capacity* to exist apart, and be *distinct* things by virtue of this capacity, while presently forming a compound thing. What then is the difficulty expressed in the "incompatibility statement" above?

In the first section of this essay, I have argued against some interpretations of the incompatibility statement which are too weak or too strong. Descartes does not, I contend, mean to say that there is merely a psychological difficulty in conceiving both union and distinctness at the same time. Nor does he think that there is a logical conflict between union and distinctness per se. In the second section, I have elaborated his view of mind-body union in this correspondence, as it is expressed in his analogy with the "real quality" conception of heaviness. Section three explores a rather interesting shift in Descartes's conception of mind-body union, while the last section applies this account of his diverging views to the problem of interpreting the incompatibility statement.

I

Unsatisfactory Accounts

One might try to interpret the problem of conceiving both the union and the distinction of mind and body as merely a *psychological* difficulty in conceiving both at once. A possible version of this interpretation might refer to Descartes's belief that it is difficult to concentrate on intellectual matters and to have vivid sensory experience at the same time.[3] Elsewhere in this letter, Descartes attributes Elizabeth's inability to understand mind-body union to her excessively intellectual approach to the problem. "The notions which apply to the union of soul and body," Descartes writes, "can be known very clearly by the senses" but "only obscurely by the understanding alone" (Wilson 378; AT 2:69–92). However, the general interference of reason and the senses does not provide an interpretation of the incompatibility statement. Obviously Descartes has in mind a much more specific difficulty when he writes that conceiving the mind-body union and distinction together is problematic "because for this it is necessary to conceive them as a single thing and at the same time to conceive them as two things."

Another version of the psychological interpretation of the incompatibility appeals to the impossibility of having simultaneously the state of mind necessary for establishing mind-body distinctness, and the state of mind necessary for establishing their union.[4] Descartes writes that Elizabeth's overattention to the *Meditations* is the source of her difficulty in conceiving the union of mind and body. Perhaps he is thinking of the fact that the epistemological argument for mind-body distinctness in Meditation VI requires conceiving mind as though it were actually separate from body; it may not be possible to conceive this distinctly while also thinking of the mind as actually joined to the body. However, this interpretation does not fit well with the context of the incompatibility statement. Immediately after that statement, Descartes indicates that he does not wish to ask Elizabeth to put out of mind the *arguments* for mind-body distinctness:

> In explaining this matter I assumed that your Highness had reasons which prove the distinction of the mind and body still very much in mind, and I did not at all intend to furnish you with reasons to put them aside, to represent to yourself the notion of the union which everyone experiences in himself without philosophizing. [Wilson 379; AT 3:693–94]

To view the incompatibility which Descartes has in mind as merely psychological is to weaken his statement beyond recognition; his formulation indicates that he views the psychological incompatibility as deriving from a logical conflict. But if logical conflict is involved here, what is it that generates the absurdity? As noted at the beginning of this paper, for Descartes the mere fact that one thing is distinct from another does not appear incompatible with the fact that they are united, that they presently form a compound thing. Not only does he indicate elsewhere the compatibility of being two things and being united;[5] the letter itself gives evidence of his belief in this compatibility. "I should have made clear," the introduction states, that even in conceiving the union of soul and body "we do not thereby cease to know that it is separable from the body" (Wilson 378; AT 3:691). Descartes also writes that "your Highness will be able to recover easily the knowledge of the distinction of the soul and body, even though she has considered their union" (Wilson 380; AT 3:695). These comments, plus his remark that he did not intend to ask Elizabeth to put the arguments for the mind-body distinction out of mind in order to conceive the union (Wilson 379; AT 3:693–94), make very suspect the claim that Descartes finds a logical incompatibility between being united and having the capacity to exist apart.

II

Mind-Body Union and the Analogy with Heaviness

In his first reply to Elizabeth, Descartes had suggested that the concept properly applied to the mind-body relation has been incorrectly applied to gravity in the "real quality" view of that feature of bodies:

In supposing that gravity is a real quality, of which we have no other knowledge than that it has the power to move the body in which it is toward the center of the earth, we have no difficulty in conceiving how it moves this body nor how it is joined to it. . . . Yet I hold that we misuse this notion in applying it to gravity. [Wilson 376; AT 3:667–68]

Earlier in this letter, Descartes refers back to his discussion of the concept of the union of mind and body presented at the end of "Reply to Objections VI" (Wilson 375; AT 3:666). In that reply, he had elaborated his own earlier conception of gravity, a conception which he also attributes to the Scholastics elsewhere.[6] What intrigues him about this conception of gravity is that it relates to body in the following ways (HR 2:254–55):

(i) The gravity of the body causes it to move, but not mechanically.

(ii) The gravity of the body is a *"real* quality" of it: it is distinct from the body, capable of existing apart.[7]

(iii) The gravity of the body is "conjoined" with body in a special way: it is "coextensive" with the body, "diffused throughout the whole of the body possessing weight."

Though Descartes no longer endorses this view of gravity himself, he does take it to provide an illuminating analogy with the mind-body relation properly conceived. For all three of these points, Descartes feels, have analogs in the relation of mind to body; in the "Reply to Objections VI," and in the correspondence with Elizabeth, he portrays mind as capable of nonmechanically causing body to move, as distinct from body, and as "coextensive with body." That is why he uses the analogy in explaining his conception of mind to Elizabeth.

The third feature of the analogy, the conception of heaviness and of mind as "diffused throughout" body, is crucial for our purposes. In the "Reply to Objections VI," Descartes states that this conception of heaviness does provide a proper model for understanding the mind-body union: "it is in no other way that I now understand mind to be coextensive with the body, the whole in the whole, and the whole in any of its parts" (HR 2:255). Descartes also advances the same view of the relation between mind and body in his letter to Hyperaspistes: "The mind is coextensive with an extended body" (K 119). Even where he utilizes the analogy with heaviness to show that Scholastic philosophers are not justified in objecting to his view of the mind-body relation (K 236), Descartes does not speak of this analogy as merely an ad hominem argument. What he writes in his second letter to Elizabeth expresses a belief that mind really is coextensive with body. He writes that the common conception of gravity supposes such qualities "to be united to bodies just as thought *is* united to ours" (Wilson 379; AT 3:694; emphasis added). Also, Descartes tells Elizabeth to "feel free in attributing this matter and extension to the soul, for this is nothing else than to conceive it united to the body" (Wilson 380; AT 3:694). I do not see how to interpret this claim except as a formulation of Descartes's belief that mind is "coextensive with body."

I have already indicated that Descartes does not think belief in mind-body union to be incompatible with belief in mind-body distinctness. This point is underlined by considering his purpose in introducing the analogy between mind and gravity in the correspondence with Elizabeth. In his letter of 28 June, clarification of the function of this analogy is the third of four goals outlined in the introduction (Wilson 377–78; AT 3:691). In the paragraph in which he tries to fulfill this promise, Descartes alludes to the fact that the analogy with heaviness provides a concept of a quality which is *both* distinct from body *and* united with body: the gravity analogy is supposed to help her realize the nature of the mind-body union without putting mind-body distinctness out of mind. This is the context in which he comments that:

> I assumed that your Highness had reasons which prove the distinction of the mind and body still very much in mind, and I did not at all intend to furnish you with reasons to put them aside, to represent to yourself the notion of the union which everyone experiences in himself without philosophizing. [Wilson 379; AT 3:693–94]

Descartes continues,

> Thus in an earlier letter when I used the comparison of gravity and other qualities which we imagine commonly to be united to bodies just as thought is united to ours, I did not bother much that the comparison was not quite apt, because these qualities are not real in the way that we suppose they are, because I thought that your Highness was already entirely persuaded that the soul is a substance distinct from the body. [Wilson 379; AT 3:694]

Descartes is defending himself here against Elizabeth's objection that the use of the gravity analogy was inappropriate, since he had discarded the real-quality interpretation of gravity on the grounds that it is "not really distinct from body."[8] Descartes dismisses this objection as irrelevant because the point of the analogy was not to convince Elizabeth that mind is distinct from body, but to give her a true conception of mind-body union that does not conflict with mind-body distinctness.

III

Mind as Coextensive with Body or as Wholly Unextended

Descartes's conception of mind as "coextensive" with body is surprising, given the view of the mind-body relation that he suggests elsewhere. For in some other contexts, he makes a point of avoiding commitment to the view that mind is extended through the body. In the "Reply to Objections V," he states that "though mind is united with the whole body, it does not follow that it itself is extended throughout the body" (HR 2:232). A more explicit rejection of the view that mind is spread throughout the body is found in the *Principles*, where he locates mind at a point in the brain and states that "pain in the hand is not felt by the mind inasmuch as it is in the hand, but as it is in the brain" (HR 1:294). The *Meditations*, too, certainly conveys the impression that mind is not really spread throughout the body but is located at a single point in the brain.

Opposite attitudes toward sensory experience are one facet of this conflict between two conceptions of the mind-body relation in Descartes. At the points where he treats the mind as located at a single point in the brain, he contends that internal sensations (such as the experience of pains in the hand) lead naturally to mistaken beliefs about the location of mental states. He writes in the *Principles*, for example, "that we frequently deceive ourselves in judging of pain" (HR 1:247), for we mistakenly think of the pains as actually located in various parts of the body:

For although we do not believe that these feelings exist outside of us, we are not wont to regard them as existing merely in our mind or our perception, but as being in our hands, feet, or some other part of our body. [HR 1:247]

In the *Principles*, the false belief that mental states are located in the limbs of the body stands in contrast with the true account of mind as merely interacting with body. On this account the mind, located in the brain, interacts with other parts of the body indirectly by means of a network of nerves whose activities are merely physical operations (HR 1:289). The same physiological account is presented in Meditation VI, and here, too, Descartes carefully avoids the contention that a pain "represented as existing in the foot" ever actually is in a limb of the body (HR 1:192). The view suggested here is like that expanded in the *Principles*: the mind is located deep in the brain, and is totally unextended.

In these places Descartes does speak of such sensory experience as evidence for the union of mind and body, and he does stress that mind is "very closely united to body" (HR 1:192) or that it "informs body"

(HR 1:289). But mind-body union as portrayed at these points is really nothing more than certain special capacities of mind-body interaction. Here, nothing more than particular *causal* connections (especially the capacity of mind to be affected by internal sensations) distinguishes the intimate relation of the mind to its body from the less intimate relation of a sailor to his ship. Descartes avoids the suggestion of any union stronger than interaction by intimating that a stronger relation is only apparent. For example, Meditation VI refers to "the union and *apparent* intermingling of mind and body" (HR 1:192).

In the correspondence with Elizabeth, Descartes also makes mention of sensory experience, sense experience which gives one the conviction "that the soul moves the body and that the body acts on the soul" (Wilson 378; AT 3:692). In fact, a central part of his advice to Elizabeth here is that she should be sure to "experience the events which happen to the body" (Wilson 379; AT 3:694). Presumably the sense experience to which he refers throughout this correspondence is the experience of internal sensations.[9] But these experiences are taken as veridical here, not inherently deceptive. What Elizabeth should learn from them is that mind is coextensive with the body to which it is united.

On this conception of union, to say that two things are united is not merely to say that they have certain capacities of interaction. In his letters to Elizabeth, Descartes does not suggest that union can be analyzed into any causal capacities. What he says presupposes that the concept of union is not the same as the concept of interaction. The assumption of a distinction between these two concepts is especially evident when Descartes writes that our concept of mind-body interaction depends on the concept of their union.[10]

The conception of mind-body union in the correspondence, then, does seem to be significantly different from the interpretation of this union in the *Meditations* and in the *Principles*. His view appears to vacillate in a peculiar way, since the letters to Elizabeth followed the *Meditations* but preceded the *Principles*. Though the motives for such a vacillation are not obvious, we can construct an explanation of it which has some plausibility. Descartes may have felt impelled to develop an interpretation of mind-body union which allows for the genuine "intermingling" of mind and body, in order to do justice to the substantial union of these two things. The weak conception of union in the *Meditations* was the focus of considerable controversy. It was the target of criticism as soon as the *Meditations* was published (in Arnauld's objections, in particular); it was also a central source of friction between Descartes and the Scholastics at Utrecht in the period leading up to the correspondence with Elizabeth (as his correspondence with Regius shows). Arnauld, for example, had criticized Descartes for offering a view which implies that man is merely "a spirit that makes use of a body" (HR 2:84). Though Descartes haughtily rejects this accusation in his reply (HR 2:102), he sounds a bit more defensive in a later letter counseling Regius about strategies for defending the *Meditations* against Scholastic attacks. He writes that he had emphasized mind-body distinctness rather than mind-body union because this, he had assumed, "would please the theologians more," and because

many more people make the mistake of thinking that the soul is not really distinct from the body than make the mistake of admitting their distinction and denying their substantial union, and in order to refute those who believe souls to be mortal it is more important to teach the distinction of parts in man than to teach their union. [K 130]

Perhaps Descartes was more worried than he admitted by accusations that he had unacceptably weakened the concept of mind-body union. The move to a stronger conception of mind as coextensive with body is not so surprising as it first appeared, in the context of these controversies.

It is also easy to hypothesize about Descartes's reasons for omitting the conception of mind as "diffused throughout body" in his later published work, the *Principles*. Descartes had not been able to say exactly what it means to deny that the mind is located at a single point and to affirm that it is intermingled with body in a manner irreducible to mere interaction. Also, he may have felt that his physiological account of mind-body interaction committed him to a "pineal gland" conception of the mind's location, and he was too fond of his physiological theory to surrender it.

IV

The Incompatibility Statement

Now we may return to the initial problem of this paper: what Descartes means when he writes to Elizabeth that

It does not seem to me that the human mind is capable of conceiving very distinctly, and at the same time, both the distinction between mind and body, and their union. To do that, it is necessary to conceive them as a single thing and at the same time consider them as two things, which is self-contradictory. [Wison 379; AT 3:695]

The claim that we cannot conceive very distinctly both the mind-body distinction and union could be read in either of two ways. "Distinction" in this context might be a reference either to (a) mind-body distinctness, the fact that a mind and a body are nonidentical and capable of existing apart, or (b) the mind-body distinction interpreted as the qualitative difference between mind and body. One's first inclination is to opt for the former account, because of Descartes's statement that there is a conflict between conceiving mind and body "*as a single thing*" and "*as two things.*" But that interpretation is unacceptable, in light of Descartes's clear commitments to the compatibility of mind-body distinctness and union in the rest of the letter. Interpretation (b) is preferable; the problem arises in conceiving the union of mind and body and the *difference* between mind and body, that is, in conceiving mind and body as united and as two *different sorts* of things.

Even this interpretation is not yet restricted enough to explain why Descartes refers to a conflict here. For clearly there is *some* conception of the distinction between mind and body which is compatible with the view of union that he adopts in this correspondence. He states that he wishes Elizabeth to retain belief in the *Meditations'* arguments proving the distinctness of mind and body, and those arguments do require that mind and body are different. The argument contrasting the indivisibility of mind with divisibility of body can be retained. Also, the epistemological argument for mind-body distinctness can be kept as part of the Cartesian position in the correspondence with Elizabeth. For that argument requires that "nothing necessarily pertains to my nature or essence, excepting that I am a thinking thing" (HR 1:190), and this claim is consistent with the claim that mind is actually coextensive with its body. Descartes stresses in his letter that the conception of mind as extended throughout body does not undermine the claim that mind and body are different in nature, for body is impenetrable by other bodies while mind is not. After experiencing the extension of mind, Descartes writes,

it will be easy for you to consider that the matter which you have attributed to thought is not thought itself, and that the extension of matter is of a different nature from the extension of thought. For the first is determined at a certain location and excludes from that location every other corporeal extension, which the second does not. Thus your Highness will be able to recover easily the knowledge of the distinction of the soul and body, even though she has considered their union. [Wilson 380; AT 3:695]

Descartes's intent in the incompatibility statement, then, is not to deny the compatibility of his present conception of union and all versions of the distinction between mind and body. It is much more likely that he intends to assert the incompatibility of this conception of union and the strong version of the mind-body distinction portrayed in the *Meditations*, the version implying that mind is located only in the brain and is wholly unextended. Immediately before the incompatibility statement, Descartes writes that overattention to his own writings is responsible for Elizabeth's failure to understand mind-body union, suggesting that *something* in the *Meditations* is the source of the difficulty:

I am of the opinion that it was these meditations, rather than the thoughts which require less attention, which cause you to find some obscurity in the notion that we have of their union. It does not seem to me that the human mind is capable of conceiving very distinctly, and at the same time, both the distinction between mind and body, and their union. [Wilson 379; AT 3: 695]

The interpretation sketched here is not a literal rendition of the incompatibility statement, but it does not read into the text more than the minimal amount necessary to get a coherent reading at all. It also makes the statement relate well to its context, both to his earlier diagnosis of Elizabeth's problem and to his later discussion of the analogy with heaviness. And it is an interpretation which brings to light an aspect of Descartes's philosophy that is often neglected in caricatures of that rationalist. The correspondence with Elizabeth includes an unusually strong appeal to the role of sensory experience in forming a proper conception of the nature of things. It also reveals the hastiness of superficial glosses of Descartes's conception of mind as a "ghost in machine" view. Given the oddity of the "pineal gland" theory, what he says to Elizabeth deserves some attention in a balanced account of Descartes.

NOTES

I am grateful to Professor Margaret D. Wilson for helpful comments on a much earlier version of this paper. I am also grateful to Felmon Davis for many valuable conversations on the topic.

1. Translation by Emmett Wilson, in *The Essential Descartes*, ed. Margaret D. Wilson (New York: The New American Library), p. 379. Hereafter, references from this volume will be labeled "Wilson" in the text.

2. So far as I know, Margaret Wilson was the first to pose the problem about interpreting the passage in the June 28 letter to Elizabeth, and she cited this passage from the reply to Arnauld in her formulation of the problem.

3. The formulation of this interpretation and the criticism of it are Margaret Wilson's.

4. Margaret Wilson suggested a version of this interpretation in November 1972, but I do not know whether she holds it now.

5. As in the "Reply to Objections IV," cited above.

6. For example, see Descartes's letter for Arnauld, K 236.

7. Descartes states in the "Reply to Objections VI" that he had thought of

gravity as a substance; he states in the letter for Arnauld (K 236) that the Scholastics did not explicitly admit that gravity was a substance, but that they did in effect admit this because "they think that it is real and that it is possible, even if only by Divine power, for it to exist without the stone."

8. Elizabeth's objection is found at Wilson 376–77; AT 3:683–85. Descartes's denial of the real-quality interpretation of gravity is found, for example, at Wilson 376; AT 3:668.

9. I would suppose that Descartes thinks we have knowledge of volitional control over parts of our bodies by having knowledge of the correlation between volitions and internal sensations; this would explain why he cites "sense experience" as relevant both to knowledge that mind is acted on by body *and* that it acts on body.

10. Wilson 374; AT 3:665. The concept of union in the correspondence with Elizabeth is different, I take it, from the concept of "extension of power" that Descartes adopts in a later letter to More (K 249). In this later passage Descartes seems to identify the concept of being coextensive with a body and the concept of having power to act on that body.

Dualism in Descartes:

The Logical Ground

FRED SOMMERS

I PROPOSE TO EXAMINE the logical grounds of the position that persons are ontologically dual in the sense of being psycho-physical composites. Because the investigation is to be logical, I will begin by avoiding the area of controversy over the ontological status of persons. Instead I shall examine the grounds for maintaining of any given entity that it is dual or not in the sense that Descartes affirms, and his opponents deny, that persons are dual.

In the course of this investigation it will be useful to take some less controversial instance of a dual entity—something other than a person —which exhibits the logical features that led Descartes to his position on persons.

According to Descartes, a person is an ontologically composite entity in the sense of being composed of entities of different types. The distinction between incomposite and heterotypical entities underlies this characterization, and we shall see that Descartes had the distinction clearly in mind when he characterized persons as heterotypical.

As I say, I shall presently discuss what I take to be a noncontroversial example of heterotypical duality. The example I will choose is closely analoguous to the Cartesian case, but this is incidental, and for purposes of exposition. Later, after we have in hand the general principle of heterotypicality, I shall consider heterotypical entities that are quite far removed from the case of Cartesian persons.

Before I give my example of a "noncontroversial" heterotypical entity, I will take some time to lay bare a certain assumption concerning the distinction between heterotypical and nonheterotypical entities (henceforth I shall use "individual" for "nonheterotypical," other synonyms being "incomposite," "nondual," and "homotypical").

I assume that anyone who characterizes an entity as an individual needs no proof. For example, Descartes thinks of a piece of wax—a candle, say—as an ontological individual, and so do I. If anyone believes that a candle is heterotypical, the burden of proof is on him. Quite generally we assume that any entity is incomposite unless proven composite.

I hope it is clear that what I have in mind throughout is ontological composition in the sense of entities of different types. A table is in this sense an individual although it is composed of a top, legs, and so forth. But a Cartesian person is a nonindividual, since it is composed of a mind and a body, and this sort of composition is an instance of heterotypicality.

In saying that an entity is (heterotypically) incomposite until proven composite, I am in agreement with all of Descartes's critics, and with Descartes himself. For all agree that the burden of proof is upon whoever maintains that persons are composite. Many of Descartes's critics found that Descartes failed to satisfy the demand for a proof of the heterotypical nature of persons. But no one, including Descartes, thought that one could, without proof, simply take a dualistic stand on persons, or, for that matter, on any other entity that we commonly discriminate. And it is precisely because a claim of heterotypicality requires proof that we can speak of logical grounds for dualism. But the other side of the coin is that a claim of individuality needs no proof.

The situation here is closely analogous to the question of the ambiguity of words. If we examine Quine's position on sameness and difference of meaning, we find that he maintains that different words mean different things until we prove them to mean the same thing. On the other hand, a simple, recurrent word is univocal until proven equivocal. Moreover, proof of equivocality is always formal proof. The word "light," for example, is univocal in "This feather is light and not light," and any logician will—in the absence of any mitigating considerations—take this sentence to be in violation of the principle of noncontradiction. It is, however, open to us to use the principle to prove "light" equivocal. For if the sentence is, for practical purposes, accepted as *true* then we must apply the principle prohibiting a univocal occurrence of ϕ in ⌜This is ϕ and not ϕ⌝, thus enforcing a judgment of equivocation on ϕ.[1]

In a language that was purged of ambiguity, we would never use logical principles to enforce ambiguity. Every sentence in such a language would either be logically correct or incorrect. But in natural languages we do accept sentences that are prima facie violations of logical laws, and we then use the laws to "interpret," i.e. to ambiguate, the words in a manner that removes the violation.

Analogously, in an ontologically perfect language we should have no terms that denote heterotypical entities; all (nonsyncategorematic) terms would then denote individuals, and there would be no need to distinguish between individuals and composite things. As the matter stands, however, we do make the distinction between composite and incomposite things, and we do apply certain logical principles in order to make it.

I hope that what I have said about univocality and individuality is reasonably clear. It can be made clearer, but I wish to get down to cases. What we want is a typical and noncontroversial instance of an ontologically dual entity, and only one or two brief remarks are needed before I present it.

Anyone who examines Descartes's assertions concerning the difference between minds and bodies must be struck by his insistence that minds are characterized by predicates that do not apply to bodies, and that bodies are characterized by predicates that do not apply to minds.

Thus, Descartes says: "there is nothing included in the concept of body that belongs to the mind; and nothing in that of mind that belongs to the body." (HR 1:100)

For Descartes the distinction is radical: minds and bodies are of ontologically different types. He compares someone who says that minds are extended to one who says "Bucephalus was music," and he characterizes his own denial that minds are extended to one who is correcting the assertion that Bucephalus is music. If a man asks how much the mind weighs, he needs to be corrected in a radical way, for his question is a category mistake. Similarly, if a man wonders whether a candle is thinking of Vienna, he is mistaken in a radical way; his mistake is a category mistake. It is not that minds are weightless or that candles are stupid; these things, respectively, do not have the ontological *features* of extension and thought, and the predicates are simply senseless.

If we generalize Descartes's criterion for saying that minds and bodies are of different ontological types, we may formulate it thus: If it makes sense to say of an entity a that it is P and of an entity b that it is Q, but no sense to say of a that it is Q or of b that it is P, then a and b are entities of different types.

Applying this generalized Cartesian criterion for being of different types we are able to say what we mean by a dualistic position on an entity c. An entity c is ontologically dual if c consists of entities that are of different types. This definition of heterotypical composition does not amount to a criterion that can be applied to determine whether or not some given entity is heterotypically composite. For that, we would need to know how to tell *whether* the entity consists of heterotypical parts. But at least we understand what Descartes's dualistic claim amounts to. For we know what a type difference is, and we understand that a dualistic position on an entity c is the claim that c is composed of entities of different types.

I propose now to look at an instance of a heterotypical entity that is not burdened by the history of secular controversy surrounding persons. By examining the noncontroversial case we will arrive at a formulation of a criterion for heterotypicality. And by subsequently examining the Cartesian case we shall be in a fine strategic position to see how and why the case for persons becomes an area of controversy.

Much of what follows relies on a clear understanding of the difference between *features* and *properties* as two kinds of attributes. To a property like *red*, which characterizes the class of red things, there corresponds the feature |red|, which characterizes the category of things that are either red or *fail* to be red. The category includes colorless things, but it excludes things like odors, moods, and numbers, since those things are neither red, nor do they fail to be red. Features differ from properties in important ways. To anticipate: an ontological individual, a candle, for example, is smooth and at rest. It has the features of Texture, since it is smooth or fails to be smooth, and Motion, since it is at rest or fails to be at rest. An individual can be smooth without being at rest, but it cannot be |smooth| without being |at rest|. And, generally, if "is $|P|$" and "is $|Q|$" are true of some individual, then *either* it is the case that whatever is $|P|$ is $|Q|$, *or* it is the case that whatever is $|Q|$ is $|P|$.[2]

It is easy to show that land masses and social institutions are entities of different types. The evidence for this might reasonably be something like the following. Land masses have the features of being colonized or uncolonized, being subject to drought, subject to surveyors' measurements and the archeologists' art, subject to earthquakes, to being traversed, and so forth. Social institutions do not possess these features. It is not that they lack them in the way, say, that Manhattan Island is free of earthquakes. The features I have listed are *ontological* features. A social institution, unlike a land mass, cannot *fail* to be colonized. On the other hand, social institutions—in radical contrast to land masses—are either democratic or undemocratic, solvent or insolvent, politically stable or politically unstable, and so forth.

Now this evidence that land masses and social institutions are of different ontological types is taken by us as evidence that such entities as Trinity College or, say, Connecticut, are heterotypical. For Connecticut has the feature of being democratic or undemocratic, solvent or insolvent; and it *also* has such typical land-mass features as being sunny or not, prone to earthquakes or not, mountainous or not. I believe that most of us are prepared to say that Connecticut is, in this sense, a composite. More portentously, our philosophical position with respect to Connecticut is sociotopographical dualism.

The case of Trinity College is essentially similar. We are reminded of Ryle's reaction to the question, "Where is the University?" asked by someone who has just been shown the university buildings. Trinity College is heterotypical; it is a sociotopographical entity. To have been shown its grounds is to have been shown the college. Sometimes we are piously told that a college is not a set of buildings and grounds, but this is a mistake. A college is not *just* a physical plant; it is that and more.

Let us now accept the heterotypicality of Connecticut and Trinity College and go on to formulate with some precision the grounds for our acceptance. They are these. If a has the feature F_1 but not F_2, while b has the feature F_2 but not F_1, then any entity c that has F_1 and F_2 is a heterotypical composite.

I have stated this criterion in the material mode. Formally, the criterion is this: If a and b are of different types with respect to predicates P and Q, while P and Q are both predicable of c, then c is a heterotypical entity.

These formulations are not mere definitions of heterotypicality. They are criteria that can be used to determine whether an entity E is heterotypical or not. To determine this we examine the features of E. If any pair of E's features defines a type difference of two other entities, then E is heterotypical; otherwise E is an ontological individual. We recall that E is an individual unless proven to be composite, and we now know what a proof of composition consists of.

Those who are acquainted with my writings on categories will not find this new. I shall now argue that Descartes himself all but formulated this criterion for heterotypicality. If I am right, then the criterion goes back to the seventeenth century, and not to some article in *Mind* or *Philosophia*.

For textual support I shall draw on passages from the *Objections and Replies* where Descartes confronted the critical attacks on his doctrine of psycho-physical dualism. The objection to the monk Caterus is thematic, and it is one that Descartes wrestles with over and over again. Caterus argues:

It appears that the distinction between soul and body, if real, is proved by the fact that they can be conceived as distinct and as isolated from each other. Here I leave my opponent to contend with (Duns) Scotus, who says that in so far as one thing can be conceived as distinct and separate from another, the adequate distinction to draw between them is what he calls a formal and objective one, which is intermediate between a real distinction and a distinction of reason. It is thus that he distinguishes between the Divine justice and the Divine pity. They have, he says, concepts formally diverse prior to any operation of the understanding, so that, even then, the one is not the other: yet it does not follow that, because God's justice can be conceived apart from his pity, they can also exist apart. [HR 2:8]

Descartes's reply deserves to be quoted in full:

In the matter of the formal distinction which the learned Theologian claims to draw from Scotus, my reply is briefly to the effect that this distinction in no way differs from a modal one, and applies only to incomplete entities, which I have accurately demarcated from complete beings. This is sufficient to cause one thing to be conceived separately and as distinct from another by the abstracting action of a mind when it conceives the thing inadequately, without sufficing to cause two things to be thought of so distinctly and separately that we understand each to be an entity in itself and diverse from every other; in order that we may do this a real distinction is absolutely necessary. Thus, for example, there is a formal distinction between the motion and the figure of the same body, and I can quite well think of the motion without the figure and of the figure apart from the motion and of either apart from the body; but nevertheless I cannot think of the motion in a complete manner apart from the thing in which the motion exists nor of the figure in isolation from the object which has the figure; nor finally can I feign that anything incapable of having figure can possess motion, or that what is incapable of movement has figure. So it is also that neither can I understand justice apart from a just being, or compassion apart from the compassionate; nor may I imagine that the same being as is just cannot be compassionate. But yet I understand in a complete manner what body is (that is to say I conceive of body as a complete thing), merely by thinking that it is extended, has figure, can move, etc., and by denying of it everything which belongs to the nature of mind. Conversely also I understand that mind is something complete which doubts, knows, wishes, etc., although I deny that anything belongs to it which is contained in the idea of body. But this could not be unless there were a real distinction between mind and body. [HR 2:22–23]

Descartes is attempting to distinguish between the fact that a person has thought and extension, and the fact that a body has motion and figure. The first fact is evidence of the heterotypicality of persons; the second is not evidence for the heterotypicality of bodies. Wherein lies the difference? Descartes's answer is that one cannot think of a thing that is *capable* of motion that has not got some shape or other. So while its motion can be thought of without thinking of its shape, this manner of abstraction is incomplete. For whatever has the ontological *feature* of motion (i.e., is in motion or at rest) necessarily has the ontological feature of figure or shape. But when I characterize a person as thinking of Vienna, or as being five feet tall, the features of thought and extension are distinct. For what has the feature of extension does not necessarily have the feature of thought, and what has the feature of thought does not necessarily have the feature of extension. Thus, thought and extension—*unlike* motion and figure— are mutually independent and distinct; and this independence is evidence of heterotypicality in anything that has both of these features.

Arnauld's objections also bear on the crucial question of the mind's distinctness:

M. Arnauld . . . urges that although a certain notion of myself can be obtained without a knowledge of the body, it yet does not thence result that this knowledge is complete and adequate, so as to make me sure that I am not in error in excluding the body from my essence. He elucidates his meaning by taking as an illustration the triangle inscribed in a semicircle, which we can clearly and distinctly know to be right-angled, though we do not know, or even deny, that the square on its base is equal to the squares on its sides; and nevertheless we cannot thence infer that we can have a [right-angled] triangle, the square on the base of which is not equal to the squares on the sides. [HR 2:100]

To this objection, Descartes responds:

although our concept of the triangle inscribed in the semicircle may be such as not to comprise the equality between the square on its base and those on its sides, it cannot be such that no ratio between the square on the base and those on the sides is held to prevail in the triangle in question; and hence, so long as we remain ignorant of what the ratio is, nothing can be denied of the triangle other than what we clearly know not to belong to it: but to know this in the case of the equality of the ratio is entirely impossible. Now, on the other hand, there is nothing included in the concept of body that belongs to the mind; and nothing in that of mind that belongs to the body. [HR 2:100–101]

And, replying to the objection "urged by divers Theologians and Philosophers" that:

when you say that you think and exist, someone will maintain that you deceive yourself, and that you do not think, but are only moved, and that you are nothing other than a corporeal motion, since no one meanwhile has been able to grasp the demonstration by means of which you think that you have proved that no corporeal motion can be what you call thought. [HR 2:234]

Descartes reiterates that there are:

two ways in which things of which we have diverse ideas can be taken to be one and the same thing: to wit, either in respect of unity and identity of nature, or merely by unity of composition. Thus, for example, our ideas of figure and motion are not the same, neither those of understanding and willing, nor of bones and flesh, nor of thought and of an extended thing. Nevertheless we clearly perceive that to the same substance to which the possibility of having figure belongs, the possibility of moving also belongs, so that what has figure and is mobile is one by unity of nature; similarly we see that a thing which is intelligent and wills is one and the same by unity of nature. But we do not perceive the same in the case of the thing which we regard under the form of bone, and of that which we view as flesh; hence we cannot take these to be one and the same thing by unity of nature, but only by unity of composition, viz., in so far as the animal possessing bone and flesh is one and the same. But now the question is, whether we perceive a thinking thing and an extended thing to be one and the same by unity of nature, a unity such that we find that between thought and extension there is the same affinity and connection as we notice to prevail between figure and motion, or between understanding and willing. Or whether shall we rather say that they are one and the same only by unity of composition, in so far as they are found in the same man, in the way in which bones and flesh exist in the same animal. Now this latter alternative is that which I affirm, because I find a total diversity between the nature of an extended and that of a thinking thing, a diversity not less than that between bones and flesh.

.   .   .   .

It is self-contradictory that those things which are clearly understood by us to be diverse and independent, cannot be sundered, at least by God. So that however often we find them in one and the same subject as, e.g., thought and corporeal motions in the same man, we ought not on that account to believe that they are one and the same thing by unity of nature but only in virtue of unity of composition. [HR 2:242–43]

The point again is that the feature of mind is ontologically independent of the feature of body, for we conceive of something as thinking or failing to think of Paris without conceiving it to be, or failing to be six feet tall. In contrast to this, we cannot conceive of a triangle that is or fails to be right-angled without conceiving of its sides as having some relation of length to one another. Thus, the question of the ratio of the sides is always pertinent to whatever is or fails to be right-angled, but the question of height may be categorially inappropriate with respect to a being that thinks or fails to think of Paris.

Having established the ontological independence of thought and extension, Descartes feels secure in his judgment that *persons*, i.e. those entities that have both of these ontological features, must be heterotypical.

In Meditation VI, Descartes remarks:

because I know that all things which I apprehend clearly and distinctly can be created by God as I apprehend them, it suffices that I am able to apprehend one thing apart from another clearly and distinctly in order to be certain that the one is different from the other, since they may be made to exist in separation at least by the omnipotence of God; and it does not signify by what power this separation is made in order to compel me to judge them to be different: and, therefore, just because I know certainly that I exist, and that meanwhile I do not remark that any other thing necessarily pertains to my nature or essence, excepting that I am a thinking thing, I rightly conclude that my essence consists solely in the fact that I am a thinking thing (or a substance whose whole essence or nature is to think). And although possibly (or rather certainly, as I shall say in a moment) I possess a body with which I am very intimately conjoined, yet because, on the one side, I have a clear and distinct idea of myself inasmuch as I am only a thinking and unextended thing, and as, on the other, I possess a distinct idea of body, inasmuch as it is only an extended and unthinking thing, it is certain that this I (that is to say, my soul by which I am what I am), is entirely and absolutely distinct from my body, and can exist without it. [HR 1:190]

Here he is urging that we cannot even meaningfully debate the question whether or not an entity is heterotypical unless we acknowledge that the conceptual distinctness of its features would constitute a mark of heterotypicality.

Thus, suppose we raise the question whether Trinity College is an ontological individual in the sense of not consisting of heterotypical parts. Descartes's point is that this question could be answered by isolating such features as solvency and climate. We speak of corporations as solvent or insolvent, but we cannot ask for the mean temperature of a corporation. We speak of land as having this or that mean temperature, but land is neither solvent nor insolvent. These facts bear immediately on the question of the ontological status of Trinity College, considered as consisting of a corporation and a campus; for we have just shown that corporations and campuses are of ontologically different types, and we have done so by proving the ontological independence of such features as solvency and climatic characteristics. In our acknowledgment that Trinity College has distinct and independent ontological features is an ipso facto acknowledgment that Trinity College is a heterotypical entity—a nonindividual consisting of entities of different types.

Anyone who would still insist that Trinity College is an ontological individual must meet Descartes's challenge to provide some other criterion for heterotypicality. Descartes does not believe that this challenge can be met, and his position seems eminently reasonable. His point is that the question of the monistic or dualistic character of an entity—like a person, or a university—only makes sense on the assumption of a formal criterion for being an ontological individual. If we can show that the entity consists of heterotypical parts, we have done all we can, and all that needs to be done, to show that it is composite.

Reverting specifically to the matter of persons, we do talk of minds in a manner that categorially distinguishes them from bodies in the required way. We say of a man that his mind is coherent or incoherent, but we do not say this of his body; and we say of his body that it is overweight or underweight, but we do not say this of his mind. I think that one must agree with Descartes that these logical and ontological facts show that a man is a heterotypical entity, and that we need no more than this to settle the question of the heterotypical or autotypical character of persons. I, for one, can see no formal difference between the case of Trinity College, and the case of a person. Trinity College is heterotypical in the sense of having ontologically independent features, and so are persons. In passing, I remark that if this position is right, then Strawson's doctrine that persons are ontologically primitive individuals is incoherent.[3]

Having said this much, I must immediately enter a crucial caveat; for Descartes's dualism is not merely a dualism of discriminate *types*, but is also a dualism of *independent existence*. It is one thing to say that "mind in its nature is entirely independent of body," and another to add, "and in consequence it is not liable to die with it." It is one thing to maintain that mind is "an entity distinct from body," (Meditation VI), and another to go on to say, "and can exist without it."

Descartes moves, illegitimately in my opinion, from the correct judgment that persons are heterotypical composites to the judgment that persons are *substantially* dualistic. The illegitimacy of this move is easily made clear in the case of Trinity College. We talk of corporations, and admittedly cannot ask whether they are sunny or not, while we can ask this of a campus. But when we then acknowledge that the College consists of the corporation cum campus, we are far from saying that the Trinity College corporation could exist independently in disembodied form. Clearly, it could not; and just as clearly we cannot use the heterotypical distinction of minds and bodies to argue for their substantial independence.

It should be obvious that the question whether minds are existentially or substantially independent of bodies cannot be determined by category considerations. In accepting the categorial distinctness of a society and a peninsula, we commit ourselves to the recognition that a country like Italy is a categorial composite, but we in no way commit ourselves to the theory that societies are substances, and have an existence that is existentially independent of geographical location.

To be fair to Descartes, I must add that he does not rest his case for the substantial independence of mind solely on categorial grounds. The reasons he gives in Meditation II are quite independent of category considerations, and for an examination of some of these reasons, I refer you to Michael Hooker's "Descartes's Denial of Mind-Body Dualism" (Chapter 8, above); I shall not discuss them now.

It will suffice to say that Descartes believed that minds were distinct substances, and that he also thought their categorial distinctness tantamount to their substantial integrity. This I hold mistaken, and thus, although I am sympathetic to a dualistic position on persons, I must deny that Descartes proved anything like the substantial dualism that is often connoted by the phrase "psycho-physical dualism."

I am then, to sum up, a psycho-physical dualist in the category sense. I find Descartes wholly cogent and right in his insistence on the heterotypical character of persons. But I do not go along with Descartes's own radical brand of dualism of substance. I wish I could; for as Descartes points out, if minds are substances, then the death of the body would not mean the death of the mind. Unfortunately, the application of category theory cannot establish this heady conclusion.[4]

NOTES

1. For Quine's view of univocity see Willard Van Orman Quine, *Word and Object* (Cambridge, Mass.: MIT Press, 1960), pp. 129ff.

2. For a further discussion of these notions, the reader is referred to my "Types and Ontology," *Philosophical Review* 72 (1963):327–63 and "Predicability" in Max Black, ed., *Philosophy in America* (London: Allen & Unwin, 1965).

3. P. F. Strawson, *Individuals* (London: Methuen, 1959), ch. 3.

4. See Spinoza's Proposition X in Part I of his *Ethics*, where he argues that the independence of Thought and Extension does not establish their substantial dualism. Spinoza's *attributes* are *ontological features*. He says, "It is far from being absurd to ascribe to one substance a number of attributes. . . . but if anyone now asks by what sign, therefore, we may distinguish between substances, let him read the following propositions, which show that in Nature only one substance exists, and it is absolutely infinite. For this reason, that sign would be sought in vain."

Can I Know

That I Am Not Dreaming?

DAVID BLUMENFELD

JEAN BEER BLUMENFELD

IN MEDITATION I Descartes offers an argument to show that he cannot know that he is not dreaming. This argument has occupied a central place in the history of modern philosophy: it forcefully raises the problem of the external world, and, at the same time, leads to considerations that Descartes uses in his proof of dualism. Yet it has seemed to many philosophers that some more or less simple maneuver is all that is needed to refute the argument. It will be our contention that this is not so. Some of the criticisms miss the mark entirely; others show that the argument needs to be reformulated in certain ways. But none, in our view, disposes of the fundamental skeptical worry that lies at its heart. Our aim in this paper, however, is not to establish any form of skepticism about the senses. What we do hope to show is that Descartes's argument is a great deal more difficult to refute than has been commonly thought.

I

Descartes begins by considering the possibility that his senses deceive him. A line of argument which he finds compelling is contained in this well-known passage:

How often has it happened to me that in the night I dreamt that I found myself in this particular place, that I was dressed and seated near the fire, whilst in reality I was lying undressed in bed! At this moment it does indeed seem to me that it is with eyes awake that I am looking at this paper; that this head which I move is not asleep, that it is deliberately and of set purpose that I extend my hand and perceive it; what happens in sleep does not appear so clear nor so distinct as does all this. But in thinking this over I remind myself that on many occasions I have in sleep been deceived by similar illusions, and on dwelling carefully on this reflection I see so manifestly that there are no certain indications by which we may clearly distinguish wakefulness from sleep that I am lost in astonishment. And my astonishment is so great that it is almost capable of persuading me that I now dream. [HR 1:145–46]

As we shall see, the argument stated above is subject to some interesting variations. But as it stands its basic thrust is clear. Descartes thinks that the fact that his current experience has such and such perceptual features is never sufficient to show that he is awake. The fact that he has had dreams whose qualitative character was indistinguishable from that of waking experience convinces him that there can be no experiential criterion whereby he can determine that he is not dreaming. He does not pause to consider a long list of possible criteria, for he thinks that any qualitative feature of a waking experience could be a feature of a dream as well. Hence the presence of such a feature will never provide an answer to the question: Am I awake? One plausible way of setting out Descartes's argument is this:

Argument (D)
(1) I have had dreams which were qualitatively indistinguishable from waking experiences.
(2) Therefore, the qualitative character of my experience does not guarantee that I am not now dreaming.

It should be pointed out that the notion of the "qualitative character of my experience" which we use here to capture the intent of Descartes's argument is to be construed quite broadly. It includes, for example, my current recollections (memory impressions) of how things have been in the past. Given this broad sense of the phrase, one item that would count as an aspect of the qualitative character of my experience is its apparent coherence with my past. But it would be Descartes's (Meditation I) view that the satisfaction of this criterion is not sufficient to distinguish dreaming from waking. Since it could be that I am only dreaming that my present experience is coherent with my past experience, this criterion fails to provide a way of establishing that I am awake.

Descartes does not ultimately conclude from (2) that he cannot know that he is not dreaming. For although he thinks that he cannot know this simply on the basis of the qualitative character of his experience, he believes that he can go on to prove the existence of a veracious God, and that one who is in possession of this knowledge can know that he is not dreaming. Now, his strategy is notoriously dubious, and it has been criticized by so many others that we propose to ignore it. Clearly, Descartes's contribution to the topic of dreaming lies more in the skeptical considerations he raised than in the manner in which he proposed to combat them. (D) can be converted into a fully skeptical argument by the addition of the following (non-Cartesian) steps:

(3) If the qualitative character of my experience does not guarantee that I am not now dreaming, then I cannot know that I am not now dreaming.

(4) Therefore, I cannot know that I am not now dreaming.

(5) If I cannot know that I am not now dreaming, then I cannot know that I am not always dreaming.

(6) Therefore, I cannot know that I am not always dreaming.

(7) If I cannot know that I am not always dreaming, then I cannot know to be true any belief which is based on my experience.

(8) Therefore, I cannot know to be true any belief which is based on my experience.

Two qualifications with respect to (7) and (8) are necessary. Many skeptics would allow that there is a special sort of belief which might be said to be "based" on my experience, but whose certainty is unimpugned by the possibility that I am dreaming. These are beliefs which concern the character of my current experience itself, and which can be expressed by sentences of the form "It seems to me that . . .". Since we do not wish to discuss the issue of whether such beliefs do indeed have a special status, we want to stipulate that (7) and (8) are to be understood as excluding these beliefs. Secondly, a skeptic influenced by Descartes might hold that my belief that I exist is "based" on my experience of thinking, but that the certainty of this belief is unimpugned by the possibility that I am dreaming. Again, we do not wish to discuss the issues connected with the cogito, and so we want to stipulate that (7) and (8) are to be read as making an exception of my belief that I exist. Finally, since our primary concern is with the problems that Descartes left us, we shall direct our attention to the fully skeptical argument which includes steps (3) through (8); it is this that we shall refer to as argument (D).

II

Premise (1) of argument (D) is apparently denied by J. L. Austin in *Sense and Sensibilia*. In criticizing A. J. Ayer's claim that " 'there is no intrinsic difference in kind between those of our perceptions that are veridical in their presentation of material things and those that are delusive'," Austin says,

Is it the case that 'delusive and veridical experiences' are not 'qualitatively different'? Well, at least it seems perfectly extraordinary to say so in this sweeping way. Consider a few examples. I may have the experience (dubbed 'delusive' presumably) of dreaming that I am being presented to the Pope. Could it be seriously suggested that having this dream is 'qualitatively indistinguishable' from *actually being* presented to the Pope? Quite obviously not.[1]

But this is just the sort of thing Descartes *is* seriously suggesting. On his view, it is possible to have a dream which is qualitatively indistinguishable from actually being presented to the Pope. To refute such a suggestion, one would need an argument, and Austin does offer one in the passage that immediately follows. He says,

After all, we have the phrase 'a dream-like quality'; some waking experiences are said to have this dream-like quality. . . . But of course, if the fact here alleged *were* a fact, the phrase would be perfectly meaningless, because applicable to everything. If dreams were not 'qualitatively different' from waking experiences, then *every* waking experience would be like a dream.[2]

Austin clearly has Descartes (among others) in mind here, as he adds in a footnote, "This is part, no doubt *only* part, of the absurdity in Descartes' toying with the notion that the whole of our experience might be a dream."[3] Now, while it seems that the second passage cited from Austin contains an argument directed against something like our premise (1), it is not altogether clear what the conclusion of this argument is meant to be. Nevertheless, we believe that there are only three possibilities:

(A1) Every dream is qualitatively different from waking experience.
(A2) Most dreams are qualitatively different from waking experience.
(A3) Some dreams are qualitatively different from waking experience.

Each of these three interpretations of Austin's meaning renders his argument problematic, however. (A2) and (A3) may be plausible in themselves, but each of these is consistent with premise (1). Premise (1) says that some dreams are qualitatively indistinguishable from waking experience, and neither (A2) nor (A3) contradicts this. (A1), on the other hand, does contradict premise (1). But (A1), unlike (A2) and (A3), is dubious. If Austin meant to endorse (A1), then his argument for it is apparently this:

(A4) If it is not the case that every dream is qualitatively different from waking experience, then every waking experience is dreamlike, and hence the phrase "a dreamlike quality" is meaningless because applicable to everything.

But it seems perfectly possible that the following situation should obtain. Some dreams are vague and unclear, and in virtue of this fact are said to possess a dreamlike quality. Other dreams are clear and vivid, and thus do not possess a dreamlike quality. Most waking experiences are clear and vivid, although some few are vague and fuzzy. In such a situation, it might be that the clear and vivid dreams are qualitatively indistinguishable from the clear and vivid waking experiences, i.e., the antecedent of (A4) would be true. But it certainly would not follow that the clear and vivid waking experiences possess a dreamlike quality, nor that the phrase "a dreamlike quality" is meaningless. Hence (A4)—the support for (A1)—is false, and Austin has not succeeded in undermining argument (D).

III

Anthony Kenny attempts to show that premise (3) is false. According to (3) I can know that I am awake only if the qualitative character of my experience guarantees that this is so. In other words, I can know that I am not now dreaming only if there is some feature of my experience from which I can infer that I am awake. It is Kenny's view, on the other hand, that I can know that I am awake without appealing to the character of my experience. In fact, on Kenny's view I know that I am awake without appealing to any criterion at all. With respect to the question "Am I awake?" Kenny says, "there is a true answer to the question—namely, 'I am awake.' Moreover, I know this answer. . . . When I say 'I am awake,' I do so without grounds, but not without justification."[4] This justification is the alleged fact that in order to make a judgment or entertain a belief, one must be awake. Kenny agrees with Norman Malcolm that one cannot make judgments during dreams.[5] Hence, any time that I judge or believe that I am awake, it will be true that I am awake. For, any time that I make any judgment whatsoever, it will be true that I am awake. Kenny's claim is, "The judgment 'I am awake' cannot be mistaken. . . . The question 'Am I awake?' . . . is pointless . . . to the extent that if a man is in a position to ask the question, he is also in a position to answer it."[6] His argument to show that one can know that he is not dreaming can be summarized as follows:

(K1) If I judge that I am awake, I know that I am awake.
(K2) I now judge that I am awake.
(K3) Therefore, I now know that I am awake.

It might be objected that people do indeed make judgments during sleep, including some true ones. For example, during a dream one sometimes makes a correct mathematical judgment. And, it is quite common for a sleeping person to make the judgment that he is dreaming. So, it is not obvious that the support which Kenny gives for (K1) is satisfactory. But suppose that we grant (K1) for the sake of argument. It is nevertheless difficult to see what establishes that (K2) is true. One might be inclined to think that it is evident to me when I am judging. But in thinking this over I must remind myself that on many occasions in sleep it has seemed to me that I was judging. That is, it has seemed evident that I was judging when I was really only dreaming that I judged. So, the fact that I seem to judge is not sufficient to show that I do judge, nor to establish that (K2) is true. If we grant that judgments cannot occur in sleep, the question for Kenny is: How do you know that you are now *judging* that you are awake? Perhaps you are only dreaming and so it merely *seems* to you that you are judging.

Of course, many philosophers—Descartes included—have held that if it seems to me that I judge, then I do judge. To adhere to this thesis consistently, however, one must also hold that in dreams, when I seem to judge, I do judge. Kenny clearly cannot enjoy the benefits of this view, for according to (K1) judgments are not made during dreams. Thus, for Kenny, a necessary condition of making a judgment is that one be awake, and it is impossible to know that one is judging simply on the basis of the fact that it seems to one that he is judging. Kenny's claim that (K1) is true forces him to justify his claim that (K2) is true.

Unless he were to maintain that in dreams we do not seem to judge,[7] only one reply is available to Kenny. This is that one *can* know that he judges: he need only judge that he judges. To this, the Cartesian question will be: How does one know that he judges that he judges? Perhaps he is only dreaming that he judges that he judges. Kenny, of course, can make his move again, as can Descartes, ad infinitum. But the regress is clearly fatal to Kenny's position, not Descartes's. For Kenny has claimed to be able to dispose of the Cartesian question. In fact what he has done is only to push it back to another level. At each level the question reemerges, and, for this reason, Kenny cannot justifiably claim to have answered it.

IV

Another interesting critique of argument (D) is offered by G. E. Moore in his paper "Certainty." In trying to set out the reasoning which leads many philosophers to the view that one does not know that he is not dreaming, Moore says, "one premiss which they would certainly use is this: 'Some at least of the sensory experiences which you are having now are similar in important respects to dream-images which actually have occurred in dreams'."[8] Moore thinks that this premise is true (and indeed harmless), but he also thinks,

there is a very serious objection to the procedure of using it as a premiss in favour of the derived conclusion. For a philosopher who does use it as a premiss, is, I think, in fact *implying*, though he does not expressly say, that he himself knows it to be true. He is *implying* therefore that he himself knows that dreams have occurred. And, of course, I think he would be right. . . . But can he consistently combine this proposition that he knows that dreams have occurred, with his conclusion that he does not know that he is not dreaming? Can anybody possibly know that dreams have occurred, if, at the time, he does not himself know that he is not dreaming? If he *is* dreaming, it may be that he is only dreaming that dreams have occurred; and if he does not know that he is not dreaming, can he possibly know that he is *not* only dreaming that dreams have occurred? Can he possibly know therefore that dreams *have* occurred? I do not think that he can; and therefore I think that anyone who uses this premiss and also asserts the conclusion that nobody ever knows that he is not dreaming, is guilty of an inconsistency.[9]

Now it seems to us that Moore's point is correct, and further, that it is successful in refuting argument (D). For, if I cannot know that I am not now dreaming, then I cannot know that my belief that I have had dreams in the past is true. Therefore, if I can know that (1) is true, subconclusion (4) is false. But this shows that argument (D) is invalid. For it shows that the truth of (1), (2), and (3) does not guarantee the truth of (4): (4) is false if I can know (1) to be true.

It might be thought that the Cartesian could salvage his argument simply by denying that (1) can be known to be true. Moore, however, points out the difficulty with such a tactic: "a philosopher who uses it [(1)] as a premiss is, I think, in fact *implying*, though he does not expressly say, that he himself knows it to be true" (p. 249). If (1) cannot be known to be true, there is an oddity in using it as a premise in an argument. For if the truth value of one of the premises of an argument is unknowable, then the argument does not provide knowledge of the conclusion.

But while Moore's criticism of (D) is correct, we believe that the skeptical point about dreaming can be made without the claim that deceptive dreams have occurred. One who does not know whether he has actually had any dreams may still have the *concept* of a dream. That is, he may have the notion of a nonveridical experience which occurs during sleep[10]—even though he is in doubt whether he has undergone such an experience or, in fact, ever been asleep. Given this concept he is in a position to argue—quite apart from whether he has had any dreams—that it is logically possible that one should have a dream which is qualitatively indistinguishable from waking experience. The skeptic could then repair argument (D) by substituting the following in place of premise (1):

(1′) It is logically possible that my experience should have just the qualitative character that it does have, and yet that I be dreaming.

From (1′) he could legitimately move to (2) and from there the argument would proceed exactly as stated originally. Let us label the amended argument, consisting of (1′) and (2) through (8) of argument (D), argument (D′).

Moore very perceptively anticipates this move on the skeptic's part. Having (in effect) countered argument (D), he goes on to ask:

But what if our skeptical philosopher says . . . It is logically possible *both* that you should be having all the sensory experiences you are having, and also that you should be remembering what you do remember, and *yet* should be dreaming. If this *is* logically possible, then I don't see how to deny that I cannot possibly know for certain that I am not dreaming: I do not see that I possibly could.

Moore's reply is as follows:

But can any reason be given for saying that it *is* logically possible? So far as I know nobody ever has, and I don't know how anybody ever could. And so long as this is not done my argument, 'I know that I am standing up, and therefore I know that I am not dreaming', remains at least as good as his, 'You don't know that you are not dreaming, and therefore don't know that you are standing up'.[11]

Now Casimir Lewy, the editor of Moore's *Philosophical Papers*, tells us that Moore was particularly dissatisfied with the last four paragraphs of the paper "Certainty," in which this rebuttal to the skeptic occurs.[12] Lewy does not mention the source of Moore's dissatisfaction, but perhaps it was something like the following. Moore was interested in refuting skepticism. That is, he was interested in showing that one can assert firmly and without reservation that he knows that he is not dreaming. But Moore's argument does not show this. For even if we grant him everything that he claims, he still has not shown that premise (1′) is false, nor that his own argument is *better* than (D′). If Moore is right in claiming that his own argument is "at least as good" as (D′), this will at best achieve a stand-off. Barring further argument, the upshot of the stand-off is a slightly weaker form of skepticism, namely, that I do not know whether I can know that I am not dreaming.[13] Moore's strategy has placed him in a position that would have delighted the old Pyrrhonian skeptics. They argued, it will be remembered, that for every plausible argument, an equally plausible counterargument can be given. It was for this reason that they thought one must suspend judgment. It appears, then, that a version of skepticism remains untouched by Moore's attack. In order to avoid Pyrrhonism, one would have to refute argument (D′), and not simply offer an argument that is equally plausible.

V

An initially attractive attempt to refute (D′), which employs the notion of probability, runs as follows. Premise (3) says that if the qualitative character of my experience does not guarantee that I am not now dreaming, I cannot know that I am not now dreaming. But why suppose that a guarantee is needed? The fact that I can have no such guarantee only shows that I cannot be absolutely certain that I am not now dreaming; it does not show that my experience fails to provide me with grounds for asserting that it is extremely probable that I am awake. Unless the skeptic wishes to defend the implausible view that (for empirical propositions) "X knows that p" entails "X currently has experience whose qualitative character guarantees that p," there is no support for (3). For if my experience is sufficient to render it highly probable that I am not dreaming, then I can know that I am awake, even though my experience does not guarantee that this is true. It is quite possible, then, to concede the truth of (1′) and (2) while denying (3).

The criticism, however, is superficial. Once having conceded that he cannot rule out the possibility that he is dreaming, how can the critic of (3) go about supporting the claim that it is probable that he is awake? To justify it he must appeal to his past experience, citing, for example, the fact that his past beliefs of this kind (when grounded on experiences such as he has now) have been true more often than not. But if he allows that it is possible that he is dreaming, it appears that he is barred from relying on the data of the past. For he has conceded that all such data may be merely dream-data, and hence totally unreliable. If his memory impressions are merely states of a dream, then, for all he knows, they are no index at all of what has actually occurred. Thus, the possibility that one may be dreaming throws into question the reliability of memory, and with it, all of that material from the past on which a judgment of probability must ultimately depend. To find a basis for a probability judgment, it appears that one must first be able to rule out the possibility that he is dreaming.

It might be objected that it is not true that in order to be justified in relying on memory one must rule out the possibility that he is dreaming. For, all one needs to know is that his memory is *probably* reliable. If he knows this, then he can use memory in making empirical judgments. The difficulty with this suggestion, however, is that it is not clear how one can establish that his memory is probably reliable. It would seem that in order to do this he must again make use of memory, assuming that it has been generally reliable in the past. But this justification is obviously circular.[14]

The skeptic's reply to the probability argument does *not* commit him to holding that (for empirical propositions) "X knows that *p*" entails "X currently has experience whose qualitative character guarantees that *p*." His reply commits him only to the following: if X's claim to know that *p* is based on his view that *p* is probable, then he can support the former claim by means of the latter only if he can rule out the possibility that he is dreaming. The skeptic can allow that if one is justified in claiming that *p* is probable, it might very well be true that he knows that *p*—even though his experience does not guarantee that *p*. The skeptical difficulty is that unless one can rule out the possibility that he is dreaming, he cannot ever be justified in claiming that *p* is probably true (where *p* is an empirical proposition whose truth is not guaranteed by the character of his experience).[15]

VI

We have so far considered a number of attacks on the first four steps of argument (D′). Attempts to forestall its conclusion, however, have also consisted in attacks on (5). One such attempt is nicely stated by Bernard Williams in a recent discussion of the philosophy of Descartes. In criticizing Descartes's skepticism, Williams comments:

even if . . . considerations of past error were allowed to show that *any* occasion of supposed perception might be illusory (because, for instance, I might be dreaming), there would be no valid inference from this to the supposition that *every* supposed occasion of perception might be illusory.[16]

Williams's claim is that (6) does not follow from (4), that is, that premise (5) is false. According to Williams, even if I cannot know that I am not now dreaming, I can know that I am sometimes awake.

We want to argue, however, that the inference from (4) to (6) is actually legitimate. (4) says that at any time, for all I know, I may be dreaming at that time. But take any time, say now—if I am dreaming now, then my belief that not all my experiences have been dreams is itself a belief held in a dream, and hence it may be mistaken. If I am dreaming now, then my recollection of having been awake in the past is merely a dreamed recollection and may have no connection whatever with reality. The point we are making could be described as the mirror image of the one made so effectively by Moore against argument (D). Moore pointed out that if I cannot know that I am not now dreaming, then I cannot know that I have had dreams in the past. I might only be dreaming that I have had dreams. Thus Moore showed that the skeptic is not entitled to the claim that he has had dreams. Our point is this: if I cannot know that I am not now dreaming, then I cannot know that I have been awake in the past. I might only be dreaming that I have been awake. Thus the antiskeptic is not entitled to assert that he has been awake. The truth of (4) generates a special epistemic context: given (4), I am, for all I know, "inside a dream," and my belief that I have been awake may be mistaken.

It should be noted that our defense of (5) depends on the idea that if I believe that I have been awake in the past, this belief is to be justified by my apparent memories of having been awake. The argument is that if I am dreaming now, then my current memories are not to be trusted—they are not a reliable index of what has actually occurred, and hence cannot provide the required justification. It might be objected, however, that this argument still does not show that (6) follows from (4). What it shows is that, if (4) is true, there is no way that I can show on a posteriori grounds that I have ever been awake. To defend the claim that (6) follows from (4) it would have to be shown as well that (6) is not false a priori. For while the truth of (4) would undermine my beliefs whose justification depends on my past experience, it is not clear that it would undermine beliefs which are known a priori. Even Descartes held that a priori propositions (such as "2 + 2 = 4") can be known to be true in a dream (HR 1:147). It appears, then, that we still need to rule out the possibility that (6) can be known to be false a priori.

But how plausible is it to suppose that I can know on a priori grounds that I have not always been dreaming? The negation of (6), of course, could be established if there were some a priori incoherence in the very idea of a being who slept (and dreamt) all of his life. But clearly there is none. We can easily imagine a malevolent experiment in which an infant is drugged in utero so that it will sleep—and dream —all of its life. The child is born, artifically sustained for a period of years, and finally dies, having undergone nothing but dream experiences. But perhaps it will be said that while there is no incoherence in the idea of some being or other (e.g., a baby with only rudimentary sorts of experiences) dreaming throughout its entire life, this does not show that it is possible for a being with experiences such as I have to be dreaming all of its life. To show that (6) follows from (4), the case of the baby will not suffice. For perhaps I can know a priori that no one with experiences of a certain highly complex type could be continually dreaming. But this also seems very doubtful. To see this, let us imagine our evil experimenter equipped with a machine conceived by Keith Lehrer:

The machine operates by influencing the brain of a subject who wears a special cap, called a 'braino cap'. When the braino cap is placed on the head of a subject, then the operator of the braino can affect the brain of the subject in such a way as to produce any hallucination in the subject that the operator of the braino wishes. The braino is a superhallucination-producing machine. The hallucinations produced by it may be as complete, systematic, and coherent as the operator of the braino desires to make them.[17]

If (6) can be known to be false independently of experience, then I can know a priori that I have not been the victim of a uterine braino experiment. Since it is clear that I cannot know this a priori, we believe that the inference from (4) to (6) cannot be blocked on a priori grounds. And, since we have already argued that it cannot be blocked on a posteriori grounds, we take it that the inference is valid. Some philosophers, however, have offered independent argument to show that (6) is a priori false. We shall consider these arguments, along with some closely related variants, in the next section.

VII

Perhaps the most widespread criticism of (D′) is what might be called the contrast argument, (CA). There are various versions of (CA), but what they have in common is the idea that the skeptic's conclusions, (6) and/or (8), could not be true because it is not possible that one should always be mistaken. The idea of being mistaken, it is claimed, requires the existence of the contrasting state of being correct. The first version we want to discuss, (CA1), is mentioned by Anthony Kenny:

Critics have argued that sense deception is only possible against a background of veridical perception. There cannot be errors, it is reasoned, where there is no possibility of correction, for if it makes no sense to talk of something's being corrected, then it makes no sense to talk of its being wrong.[18]

J. L. Austin gives much the same argument in the following passage from *Sense and Sensibilia*:

Next, it is important to remember that talk of deception only *makes sense* against a background of general non-deception. (You can't fool all of the people all of the time.) It must be possible to *recognize* a case of deception by checking the odd cases against the more normal ones.[19]

Apparently, Austin is making two claims here. His first claim is that talk of deception only makes sense if it is possible to recognize cases of deception. If this is true, both (6) and (8) are senseless, since each implies that an undetectable deception is possible. His second claim is that it is possible to recognize cases of deception only if there is a background of general nondeception. We do not wish to discuss the second claim. But the first claim seems to us to depend on a principle which is highly suspect. The principle is: no fallibility without detectibility. A claim that a belief may be in error *makes sense* only if it is possible to determine whether it really is in error. In other words, unless it is possible to determine whether a statement is true, that statement is meaningless. This is, of course, (one form of) the verification principle. The objections to this principle, however, are well known and it would be pointless to try to review them here. But in view of the criticisms of verificationism which are available, (CA1) cannot be regarded as very powerful.

Gilbert Ryle, on the other hand, gives a version of the contrast argument which does not depend upon the verification principle. In *Dilemmas* he comments,

I must say a little about the quite general argument from the notorious limitations and fallibility of our senses to the impossibility of our getting to know anything at all by looking, listening and touching.

A country which had no coinage would offer no scope to counterfeiters. There would be nothing for them to manufacture or pass counterfeits of. They could, if they wished, manufacture and give away decorated discs of brass or lead, which the public might be pleased to get. But these would not be false coins. There can be false coins only where there are coins made of the proper materials by the proper authorities.

In a country where there is a coinage, false coins can be manufactured and passed; and the counterfeiting might be so efficient that an ordinary citizen, unable to tell which were false and which were genuine coins, might become suspicious of the genuineness of any particular coin that he received. But however general his suspicions might be, there remains one proposition which he cannot entertain, the proposition, namely, that it is possible that all coins are counterfeits. For there must be an answer to the question 'Counterfeits of what?'[20]

Ryle's claim is that in order for counterfeit coins to exist, real coins must exist as well. He does not explicitly apply his point to the case of dreaming, and there are several ways in which the analogy could be used. One interpretation of Ryle, (CA2), is that he wants to maintain that not all of my experiences could be dream experiences. In order for me to have dreams, I must have veridical experiences as well. If this is correct, then I know a priori that (6) is false.

(CA2) argues from an analogy with the case of currency to the conclusion that not all *my* experiences could be dream experiences. In order to derive this conclusion from the currency example, however, it would have to be claimed that not all my money could be counterfeit. But even if we grant that it is impossible that all coins should be counterfeit, this does not entail that it is impossible that all of my coins should be counterfeit. Surely we can imagine circumstances in which I possess nothing but counterfeit coin. So, the analogy provides no reason to deny that it may be the case that all my experiences are dreams. For all Ryle has shown, it is possible that I should have been asleep and dreaming since birth.

Perhaps (CA2) does not capture Ryle's intention, however. He says that not all coins of the realm (i.e., all the coins there are) could be counterfeit. So perhaps he means to claim only that it could not be the case that *everyone's* money should be counterfeit. In this case, all that is to be inferred from the analogy is that it is not possible that all the experiences there are should be dreams. If there are any dream experiences, then someone, at least, must have experience of real things. Let us dub this way of pushing the analogy (CA3). (CA3) makes a very weak claim against skepticism. Its success would not imply that any of my experiences are veridical, and so it does not place the truth of (6) in jeopardy. Nevertheless, (CA3) would guarantee that someone or other has veridical experience. So, if it succeeds then at least one of my beliefs based on my experience is true, namely, my belief that in addition to myself and my experiences, there exists an external world which is independent of any dream I may have. For, in order for anyone to have veridical experience, there must be an independent world which he experiences. Hence, if (CA3) is correct, it refutes premise (7) of argument (D′).

(CA3) rests on the claim that it is logically impossible that everyone's money should be counterfeit. But this claim is debatable. It is not evident that there are no conceivable circumstances under which we would say that all money is counterfeit. Consider the following possibility. Just as the first money is about to be printed, a band of criminals seizes the presses and issues its own currency, which is a facsimile of the original design. Later, when the shady origins of the currency are exposed, the community forever drops the institution of money. In such a situation, it would appear that all the money that has ever existed has been counterfeit.

Still, there is probably something to be learned from Ryle's analogy that has not been brought out by our discussion so far. We suspect that the intuitive idea behind (CA3) comes from imagining the following sort of situation. Suppose that the criminals described above are never caught, their plot never uncovered. The money they issue is accepted by the people as legitimate and is used by all. If we imagine this situation continuing indefinitely, then perhaps many philosophers would find it odd to describe such money as "counterfeit." They would be inclined to say that what functions systematically and continuously as money *is* money (real money), whatever its origins. Intuitions about this rather fanciful case may differ, and there is, if course, room for dispute.[21] But let us grant, for the sake of argument, that the money should be regarded as real. If so, then surely this would be for one fundamental reason: the currency is used by everyone as money in a systematic way. Similarly, the opponent of the skeptic may want to argue that if everyone were always "dreaming," and if everyone's experiences were systematically correlated, then it would be incorrect to describe such experiences as "dreams." Such a world would be quite like the one Berkeley thinks is the actual world (leaving theological considerations aside). In Berkeley's world, an object is real if it can be experienced intersubjectively: it is not required that it have material existence. In the currency example, the money is real if it is commonly used: it is not required that it be produced by the government. In both cases it is the *common* coin which is the real one.

Now, we agree that if the Berkeleyan situation did obtain, it would not be one in which all experiences are delusive. Given the Berkeleyan assumption that there are other minds which have experiences similar to mine, sense can be given to the idea that there are real objects. (CA3) can be resuscitated, then, if we can find some way of using the analogy with counterfeit money to show that we are justified in believing that this assumption is true. But it is precisely here that the analogy is weakest. For in the coin case there is no difficulty in principle in determining whether the coins are commonly used. In the dreaming case, however, there is a difficulty in determining whether the experiences I have are commonly shared. In fact, we cannot assume that there are other people without begging the question against the skeptic. Remember that (CA3) is a denial of premise (7); it does not purport to deny (6). But if I cannot know that I am not always dreaming, then I cannot know that other people's experiences are correlated with my own; nor can I even know that other people exist. Without this knowledge, however, I cannot know that the Berkeleyan situation obtains, and thus cannot use the idea of commonly shared experiences to resuscitate (CA3).

There is yet a fourth version of the contrast argument, (CA4). According to (CA4), a dream is, by definition, a merely subjective experience occurring during sleep. To call something a "dream" is to contrast it with a "real" or "nondream" state of affairs to which one might, conceivably at any rate, wake up. The skeptical supposition that there might exist nothing but the dreamer and his dream experiences is contradictory. For it is impossible that there should be dream experiences unless there is also an external world independent of the dreamer. So, if I am always dreaming, that in itself would imply that my belief that there is an external world is true.

Perhaps it is true that the word "dream" is normally used in such a way that it implies that the dreamer is asleep.[22] But this fact cannot seriously damage the skeptic's position. He uses the word because he thinks of dreaming as a purely subjective state in which one may be deceived about the existence of objects. When he denies that one can know that he is awake, the point he is making is that one cannot know that there is an external world. If he is told that the applicability of the words "dream" and "sleep" implies the existence of an independent world, then surely he is free to stipulate that he employs these words without any such connotation. This decision will involve no intellectual confusion as long as he makes clear how he uses the terms. Having done this, the skeptic need say no more to dispose of (CA4), which makes a purely verbal point.

VIII

A frequent charge against skepticism is that it shows that we cannot have knowledge only by adopting an implausibly strong definition of knowledge, viz., one that makes certainty a necessary condition. According to this view, although the certainty of empirical beliefs is unattainable, it is not required for knowledge. All that is required for knowledge is the justification of the belief and its truth.[23] In section V we argued that empirical propositions cannot be justified on the basis of probability, and, further, that this skeptical claim does not imply that in order to know that p, one must be certain that p. But, of course, there could be some other sort of epistemic justification for empirical beliefs, and in particular, for the belief that an external world exists. In this section we would like to pursue this suggestion. We will assume, along with the opponent of skepticism, that certainty is not a requirement for knowledge.

It should be noted, first, that the idea that my experiences are caused by an external world provides me with an explanation of the existence and character of my experiences, whereas the belief that these experiences are mere illusions or dreams does not. This fact might be used as a basis for the claim that the external-world hypothesis is epistemically preferable to the dreaming hypothesis. But, following Descartes's strategy in Meditation I, the skeptic could say that, for all one knows, there is an evil demon who, out of the desire to deceive him into believing there is an external world, causes his experiences (his dreams) to be as they are. In this case, the skeptic too will have a logically possible account of all of his sensory data. One would then have to show that the hypothesis of an external world of physical things is epistemically superior to that of a powerful and deceitful demon. One might think that this could be argued on grounds of the greater simplicity of the external-world hypothesis. But it is hard to see in what respect the external-world hypothesis is simpler than that of the demon. The latter is committed to the existence of the demon (a spirit) with the means of and a motive for producing sense experiences, to a mind in which these experiences are produced, and to the sense experiences themselves. The external-world hypothesis, on the other hand, is committed to all of the above, except the existence of the demon. But it is committed, in addition, to a physical world with the capability of producing sense experience. So, it is hard to see *how* the external-world hypothesis is simpler.

If a case for the greater epistemic reasonableness of the external-world hypothesis over that of the demon can be made out, it is surprising how little effort there has been to show this in detail. A notable exception, however, is an intriguing argument given by Michael Slote. Slote's aim is to establish that there is a valid principle of rational scientific inquiry which the hypothesis of a demon violates, but which the hypothesis of an external world does not.[24] He hopes to prove thereby that there is epistemic justification for accepting the latter hypothesis over the former. To prepare the way he introduces the notion of an "inquiry-limiting hypothesis." An hypothesis is inquiry-limiting as an explanation of certain phenomena just in case one who accepts it "ensures the impossibility of his coming to have rationally justified or warranted belief (consistent with his other beliefs) in more and more true explanations of various aspects of or facts about the phenomena in question." Slote argues that, other things equal, it will be unreasonable from the scientific point of view to accept an inquiry-limiting hypothesis over one which is not inquiry-limiting. Science, he says, is an enterprise which

seeks to give explanations of events, processes, etc., but also to give, as far as possible, explanations of all the various aspects of the very things it posits in its explanations. For it is a goal of scientific enterprise to gain deeper and deeper and more and more explanations of whatever things there are in the world, wherever possible.

With this conception of the goals and purposes of science in mind, Slote proposes the following two-part principle, which he refers to as the *Principle of Unlimited Inquiry*:

(a) that it is scientifically *unreasonable* for someone to *accept* what (he sees or has reason to believe) is for him at that time an inquiry-limiting explanation of a certain phenomenon, other things being equal; and (b) that there is *reason* for such a person to *reject* such an explanation in favour of an acceptable non-inquiry-limiting explanation of the phenomenon in question, if he can find one.

According to Slote, this principle provides the scientific and epistemic rationale for preferring the hypothesis of the external world over that of the demon. Clearly there is no reason to suppose that by believing in the external world one prevents himself from gaining more and more warranted beliefs in true explanations of various aspects of nature. So, there is no reason to suppose that this hypothesis is inquiry-limiting. But the hypothesis of a demon who causes one's experiences is inquiry-limiting. For the demon theory implies that all the data one wants to explain are supplied by a powerful deceiver. Hence, for any further explanation one conceives, he has no more reason to suppose that it is correct than he has to suppose that it is merely another product of the demon's deception. Even if there is a demon, a belief in his existence cuts one off from the possibility of gaining more and more warranted beliefs. As Slote puts it, "whatever in fact is the explanation of our sense experiences, if we accept the above sort of demon-hypothesis . . . we thereby frustrate our purposes as scientists." Consequently, we have rational scientific justification for rejecting the demon-hypothesis and believing in the external world.

Let us suppose, with Slote, that the demon-hypothesis is inquiry-limiting and that the external-world hypothesis is not. Allowing this, however, it is still a matter for debate how much of a threat this would pose to skepticism. For what Slote's argument purports to show is that there is *some* reason to reject the demon-hypothesis in favor of a belief in the external world. Even if certainty is not required for knowledge, it would have to be shown that the degree of justification conferred by his argument is adequate for knowledge. But we shall not pursue this issue, for we believe it can be shown that the argument does not provide *any* epistemic justification for a belief in the external world.

The situation is this. We have granted that the demon-hypothesis is inquiry-limiting. We are also willing to grant that this provides some sort of reason for rejecting the hypothesis. But it is absolutely essential for Slote to be able to show that the reason or justification in question really is epistemic justification, i.e., justification of the sort which could provide support for a truth claim. As he is well aware, to combat skepticism, it will not do to show that there are non-epistemic reasons for rejecting the demon-hypothesis. It is no part of argument (D′) (nor of most other forms of skepticism) to deny that there could be various sorts of nonepistemic reasons for believing a given proposition. The question, then, is: in what *sense* does the fact that the demon-hypothesis is inquiry-limiting make it reasonable to reject it? It seems to us that the sense in which it does this is a practical (or pragmatic) rather than a theoretical (or epistemic) one. Slote's argument shows that one who has as his goal the obtaining of more and more warranted beliefs, but who accepts the demon-hypothesis, does something which makes it impossible for him to achieve this purpose. As he puts it, "if we accept the . . . demon-hypothesis . . . *we thereby frustrate our purposes as scientists.*" But an argument of the form "You will frustrate your purposes unless you do such and such" is one that provides a practical reason for adopting a certain course of action. It is not normally one which provides an epistemic reason for belief (i.e., rational grounds that count in favor of the truth of the belief). It is an interesting feature of Slote's argument, however, that the "course of action" for which it gives support is the adoption of a belief. What he has produced is a practical justification for adopting a certain epistemic or theoretical attitude if one can (or, presumably, for trying to maintain the attitude if one already has it). Since the conclusion of his argument is that holding a certain belief would be reasonable, one may be misled into thinking that he has given epistemic support for this belief. But in fact he has only shown that holding the belief would be *practically* reasonable.

It may be objected, however, that although the argument is practical (indicates what is reasonable considering certain ends), the ends in this case are one's goals as a scientist or truth-seeker, and that this makes a crucial difference. If the argument shows that by accepting the demon-hypothesis one defeats his purposes as a truth-seeker, the support it provides is surely epistemic as well as practical. Now, we admit that if Slote's argument actually established that a belief in the external world is likelier to be *true*, it would provide the epistemic support which he desires. But it plainly does not do this. Recall that the demon-hypothesis was *not* ruled out because it is less likely to be true. It was ruled out because, even if it is true, its acceptance would cut one off from the possibility of having warranted beliefs about the nature of more and more phenomena. But an argument which gives no reason for supposing that its conclusion is true cannot provide epistemic support for that conclusion.

Slote does offer a direct argument to show that the considerations he has adduced are specifically epistemic. The argument is based on a definition of 'epistemic reasonableness' which he attributes to Chisholm. Slote says that Chisholm "defines 'p is epistemically reasonable in believing q' as 'if p were a rational being, and if his concerns were purely intellectual, it would be reasonable (i.e., a good thing) for him to believe q.' "[25] But Slote thinks this will suffice only if "one understands 'his concerns were purely intellectual' to mean 'his concerns were those of intellectual (or theoretical) understanding and knowledge in *general,* and included no other concerns or interests.' " So understood, however, he finds the definition plausible and conducive to his purposes. For the demon-hypothesis is an inquiry-limiting explanation; and, on the part of one whose concerns are purely intellectual, it is reasonable (a good thing) to reject such an explanation in favor of one that is not inquiry-limiting. Slote concludes that "it is *epistemically* reasonable to have tentative belief in an external world."

Note that this account of epistemic reasonableness is much broader than the one we have relied on. Slote defines the concept in terms of purely intellectual interests, but his definition does not imply that if one belief is epistemically more reasonable than another, then the former is likelier to be true. It is for this reason, we believe, that his definition is open to counterexamples. Consider the following case. I am a citizen in a totalitarian state in which it is a condition of my entering school, or of my doing any sort of serious research or study, that I accept a certain proposition, c. Let us suppose that I have no reason for believing c to be true or for believing it to be false except this: I will arrive at a much larger body of warranted true explanations of phenomena if I accept c than if I do not. From the point of view of my purely intellectual concerns it would be reasonable (a good thing) for me to accept c if I can. If I reject c, I will be allowed to learn nothing; if I accept c, I will almost certainly learn a great deal. Thus on Slote's definition I would have good epistemic or theoretical grounds for accepting c. But we submit that this is clearly not the case. Although I may have a very good practical reason to accept c if I can, I have no theoretical justification for doing so. For I have no indication that c is likelier to be true than it is to be false. Slote's argument, therefore, gives no epistemic reason for believing in the external world.

It appears, then, that (D') is capable of withstanding the criticisms brought against it by a number of contemporary philosophers. Although it has often been thought to be relatively weak, the dreaming argument is actually quite strong, and it continues to present a serious challenge to our supposed knowledge of the external world. Of course, it may be that this challenge can be met. But if so, we believe that this will have to involve means considerably different from those discussed here.

NOTES

We want to thank Laurence Bon Jour for helpful comments on an earlier version of this paper.

1. J. L. Austin, *Sense and Sensibilia* (Oxford: Oxford University Press, 1962), p. 48.

2. Ibid., pp. 48–49.

3. Ibid., p. 49n.

4. Anthony Kenny, *Descartes: A Study of His Philosophy* (New York: Random House, 1968), p. 30.

5. Norman Malcolm, *Dreaming* (London: Routledge & Kegan Paul, 1959), and "Dreaming and Skepticism," *Philosophical Review* 65 (1956):14–37.

6. Kenny, *Descartes*, p. 31.

7. Kenny appears not to hold this view, but Norman Malcolm clearly endorses it. He says, "to a person who is sound asleep, 'dead to the world', things cannot even *seem*" ("Dreaming and Skepticism," p. 26). On Malcolm's view, it is logically impossible that one may have any sensations, thoughts, or feelings during sound sleep. We acknowledge that Malcolm's position, if it were acceptable, would refute premises (1) and (3) of argument (D). Malcolm sees how far one would have to push the present line of attack to make it actually get at the dreaming argument. But his views have been widely discussed and criticized over the past twenty years, and space does not permit a review of the controversy here. A few of the many relevant articles to be consulted are: A. J. Ayer, "Professor Malcolm on Dreams," *Journal of Philosophy* 57 (1960):517–35; Donald Kalish, "Review: *Dreaming* by Norman Malcolm," ibid. 57 (1960):308–11; John V. Canfield, "Judgments in Sleep," *Philosophical Review* 70 (1961):224–30; D. F. Pears, "Professor Norman Malcolm: Dreaming," *Mind* 70 (1961):145–63; Hilary Putnam, "Dreaming and 'Depth Grammar'," in *Analytical Philosophy*, ed. by R. Butler (Oxford: Blackwell, 1962), pp. 211–35; Charles Chihara, "What dreams are made on," *Theoria* 31 (1965):145–58; E. M. Curley, "Dreaming and Conceptual Revision," *Australasian Journal of Philosophy* 53 (1975): 119–41.

8. G. E. Moore, *Philosophical Papers* (London: George Allen & Unwin, 1959), p. 248.

9. Ibid., p. 248–49.

10. This is not intended as a definition of "dream." See note 22.

11. Moore, *Philosophical Papers*, p. 250.

12. Ibid., editor's note, p. 251.

13. Of course, many philosophers would hold that knowing implies knowing that one knows. If this thesis is correct (and if Moore's argument is the best one can offer against skepticism), then it would follow that one cannot know that he is not dreaming. In this case the skepticism of (D') would be completely untouched by Moore's argument. But we cannot take up this complex and controversial thesis here.

14. Cf. James W. Cornman and Keith Lehrer, *Philosophical Problems and Arguments: An Introduction* (New York: Macmillan, 1974), pp. 114–18.

15. It should be pointed out that the problem raised here is distinct from one often noted in connection with the frequency interpretation of probability. According to this interpretation, a probability statement makes a factual claim concerning the frequency of a given property relative to a given reference class. But if a probability statement makes a factual claim, then it itself must be evaluated in terms of its probability, yielding another factual claim, which must in turn be evaluated for its probability, and so on. The upshot is that in order to know that a given statement is probably true, one would have to know to be probably true an infinite number of other statements. The problem concerning the reliability of memory is not peculiar to the frequency interpretation of probability statements: it is common to all theories which consider empirical data relevant to probability determinations. C. I. Lewis, in *An Analysis of Knowledge and Valuation*, distin-

guishes the two problems and discusses each of them (La Salle: Open Court, 1946), chs. 10 and 11. While we think Lewis's solution to the memory problem is unsuccessful, it is too complex to consider here. But certain essential elements of his position which are also endorsed by other authors are criticized in various sections of this paper.

16. Bernard Williams, "Descartes, René," in *The Encyclopedia of Philosophy* vol. 2 (New York: Macmillan and The Free Press, 1967), p. 346.

17. Lehrer, *Philosophical Problems and Arguments*, p. 81.

18. *Descartes: A Study of His Philosophy*, p. 25.

19. *Sense and Sensibilia*, p. 11.

20. Gilbert Ryle, *Dilemmas* (Cambridge: Cambridge University Press, 1960), pp. 94–95.

21. Perhaps this difference of intuition can be accounted for by the fact that there seem to be two parts of the concept of genuine money. One part is that it is money produced by a legitimate government, and the other is that it is universally and systematically used as money. Normally, of course, that money which fulfills one of these conditions fulfills the other as well. When we are asked to imagine money that meets one of these conditions and not the other, confusion arises. For while it is clear that these conditions are jointly sufficient, it is not clear that either one is by itself either necessary or sufficient.

22. But it should be pointed out that we also speak of daydreams, and the dreams of an opium eater (some of whose hallucinatory experiences occur while he is awake). So it is not clear that an experience must occur during sleep in order to count as a dream.

23. Further conditions for knowledge may be required in order to avoid Gettier-type counterexamples, but this issue is clearly not relevant to the present discussion.

24. Michael A. Slote, *Reason and Scepticism* (London: George Allen & Unwin, 1970), the quotations that follow are from pp. 66, 65, 67, 68–69; emphasis added. O. K. Bouwsma has also attacked the demon-hypothesis in "Descartes' Evil Genius," *Philosophical Review* 58 (1949):141–51. For criticism of Bouwsma's view, see *Reason and Scepticism*, p. 63; Cornman and Lehrer, *Philosophical Problems and Arguments*, pp. 87–92; and Kenny, *Descartes: A Study of His Philosophy*, pp. 36–37.

According to Slote, the idea that our experiences arise through chance also violates this principle. For the sake of a more manageable exposition, we do not describe the application of his argument to the hypothesis of chance, which will probably be obvious in any case. Also, we consider only what we regard as his most forceful argument against the demon. Our brief remarks on simplicity, which help set up the problem of this section, are derived from Slote.

25. Slote, *Reason and Scepticism*, pp. 85–86; Slote cites pp. 21f. of Roderick M. Chisholm, *Theory of Knowledge* (Englewood Cliffs, N.J.: Prentice-Hall, 1966). But it is not at all clear that Chisholm intends to *define* epistemic reasonableness. In the passage cited, he seems to be using this notion as a primitive in terms of which other notions are defined.

Descartes's

Dream Argument

GEORGE NAKHNIKIAN

IN DESCARTES'S METAPHYSICS there are five problems of transcendence: of the ego, of God, of universals, of the physical world, and of other minds. The dream argument concerns the last two only.

The transcendence of the ego is idiosyncratic. Typically, a problem of transcendence exists only if appearance and reality may not be the same. The transcendent is the real beyond the appearances. In Descartes's metaphysics nothing can count as the appearance to itself of any ego of any cogito. As conceived by Descartes, the ego of any cogito is "[a] thing which thinks. What is a thing which thinks? It is a thing which doubts, understands, conceives, affirms, denies, wills, refuses, which also imagines and feels" (HR 1:153). Note that every one of these items is conceived to be an action. The words are verbs. By "body," on the other hand, Descartes understands

all that which can be defined by a certain figure: something which can be confined in a certain place, and which can fill a given space in such a way that every other body will be excluded from it; which can be perceived either by touch, or by sight, or by hearing, or by taste, or by smell: which can be moved in many ways not, in truth, by itself, but by something which is foreign to it, by which it is touched [and from which it receives impressions]: for to have the power of self-movement, as also of feeling or of thinking, I did not consider to appertain to the nature of body: on the contrary, I was rather astonished to find that faculties similar to them existed in some bodies. [HR 1:151]

In contrast to the ego, the body is conceived as an inactive, a passive thing, that cannot act, that can only be acted upon, and is such that if it moves at all it moves only because something "foreign to itself" sets it in motion. This conception of body admittedly accords with "the thoughts which of themselves spring up in [Descartes's] mind, and which [are] not inspired by anything beyond [his] own nature alone when [he] applie[s himself] to the consideration of [his] being" (HR 1:150–51). Precisely this conception of body, however, survives critical scrutiny in the wax example, and emerges as official doctrine. According to it, body is inert. Body can be experienced and moved, but does not itself have experiences or move itself. Motion is imparted to it by mind. Mind alone is the active principle. At this stage of the *Meditations* all that Descartes knows is that the ego of any cogito is a mind, whatever else it may turn out to be. The ego of any cogito is conscious and active. Moreover, it is a self-identical unit that at one and the same time "doubts nearly everything, who nevertheless understands certain things, who affirms that one only is true, who denies all the others, who desires to know more, is averse to being deceived, who imagines many things, sometimes indeed despite his will, and who perceives many likewise, as by the intervention of the bodily organs" (HR 1:153). The *same* ego has all these *diverse cogitationes*, and it is in virtue of that fact that diverse modes of consciousness occurring at one time constitute a unity, the whole of that ego's present, conscious experience. These units are further constituted into a single mental history through the memory of the self-same ego who formed them in the first place. Because all modes of consciousness are mental acts, none of them can be an appearance of the ego of which they are the acts. The pain I feel is not, and cannot be, an appearance of me. Bodies, if they exist at all, can appear to us from various perspectives, but there can be no perspective from which the ego presents an appearance of itself to itself. For all we know (before we have proof that bodies are existentially independent of finite minds), "bodily" appearances may be nothing but the objective reality (the contents) of certain ideas, representing nothing real, in spite of our "natural" belief to the contrary. As such, "bodily" appearances could be products of the mind's activity alone.

In the exposition of Descartes's metaphysics, therefore, up to the end of Meditation II, it is conceivable that "bodily" appearances are not appearances of anything. But it is not conceivable that the acts we are aware of can be the acts of nothing. Although there is no appearance of the ego to set off against its reality, there is, nevertheless, its reality as discovered in the cogito itself. The ego has sufficient evidence to know with incorrigible certainty that it, itself, exists whenever it thinks, silently or out loud, that it, itself, is thinking. This knowledge is available to the self even at a time when the self has not yet formulated a clear and distinct idea of its own nature. The self knows its own transcendence, its own existence beyond any appearances, without the possibility of contrasting its own reality with appearances of itself, and independently of having formed a clear and distinct conception of its own essence. Even if it should turn out, as it will, that no one can know with *incorrigible* certainty at any time that at that time he, himself, is awake and not dreaming, the incorrigible certainty of the cogito remains intact. For the cogito reflection, Descartes holds, is no less cogent in a dream than it is in waking.[1]

There is no appearance of God any more than there is of the self. And there is nothing like the cogito argument for the existence of God. However, there is the idea of God. Descartes believes that when we conceive that idea clearly and distinctly we perceive clearly and distinctly that God exists. The structure of the ontological argument is radically different from that of the cogito argument. But like the cogito argument the ontological argument is known with incorrigible certainty even in a dream. Descartes's solution of the problem of the transcendence of God, like his solution of the problem of the transcendence of the ego, cannot be viewed skeptically in view of the dream argument because, Descartes believes, incorrigibly certain judgments can be made in dreams as well as in waking.

For Descartes there is a problem of transcendence regarding universals because Descartes is uncompromising, to the point of incoherence, on the meaning of divine omnipotence. According to Descartes, God's omnipotence is limited by nothing. If He so willed, He could make the circle to have unequal radii, or make it so that a proposition and its denial are both true. God's omnipotence means, for Descartes, that there is nothing other than God that is not dependent for its nature and existence on God's will. Thus, not only finite minds and the physical world, but also all abstract entities such as propositions and concepts (universals) are existentially and qualitatively dependent on God. Our ideas, all of which are innate, are not imprints of Platonic Forms. They are counterparts of concepts in God's mind. To secure the truth, reliability, authenticity (choose your own term) of our concepts Descartes must, accordingly, prove that the author of our being is not a malicious demon but a perfectly good, hence, undeceiving God.

This same proposition secures the "metaphysical" certainty of the cogito itself. For, according to Descartes, we have "perfect knowledge" of whatever we believe incorrigibly if, and only if, we have at sometime or other achieved a clear and distinct perception that our clear and distinct perceptions are reliable.

When we come to examine in detail Descartes's dream argument, we shall see that the cogency of the reasoning in the cogito argument, in the proofs for God's existence, and in the proof that our clear and distinct perceptions are reliable, is independent of whether or not the relevant inferences are being performed in waking or in a dream. From Descartes's point of view, then, the problem of the transcendence of the ego, and of universals is solved, if the problem of the transcendence of God is solved. And the solution of that problem can be worked out in a dream as well as in waking life.

The dream argument in Descartes is specific to the problem of the transcendence of the physical world and of other minds. Descartes accepts it as a datum that the human mind has the ineluctable propensity to conceive of physical objects as being existentially independent of the existence or the operations of finite minds. Moreover, for Descartes it is a datum of reason that mind and body have incompatible essences. Hence, nothing physical can formally be part of the essence, operations, or contents of a mind, be it man's or God's. However, God's mind, and His alone, is "eminently" physical; he means by this that although the formal reality of God is to be pure mind, God is eminently physical in having the power to create a physical world which, once it is created, exists as a category distinct from both finite minds and the infinite mind, namely, God. The physical world thus transcends the contents and operations of the human mind. Descartes must face the problem of whether or not, and how, he can have "perfect knowledge" that the perceptual contents of his mind that, according to him, are appearances representing to him a physical world distinct from those appearances, are, indeed, accurate representations of the properties inherent in physical objects. He must also deal with the problem of the independent existence of physical objects. Moreover, because of his methodological solipsism, Descartes has the parallel problem of securing "perfect knowledge" of his belief that there are finite minds like his inhabiting the many bodies like his that populate the physical world. Within the Cartesian metaphysical and methodological framework, the problem of other minds depends for its solution upon the solution of the problem of the real existence of the physical world.

By assuming that a demon, as clever and malicious as he is powerful, is deceiving me, I can find reason to doubt the articles of faith imbedded in my very nature about the reality and independent existence of a physical world. The demon can be deceiving me when I am awake by making me believe in the independent reality of the physical when there is nothing physical to be represented by the appearances parading before my mind. The demon can also cause me to believe that I am awake when, in fact, I am dreaming. He may have created me in such a way that I was born asleep, have never waked up since, and during that lifelong sleep I have a single continuous dream, or have periods of dreaming interrupted by total absence of dream contents; or I may be dreaming with no interruption, the continuous dream being made up of discontinuous segments such that the end of one segment coincides with the beginning of another that is continuous with an earlier interrupted segment. I may thus live as many different lives as you please. In order to know for certain that I am not dreaming, I need to know for certain that I am not the dupe of an evil demon. Any circumstance that prevents me from knowing incorrigibly that I am awake prevents me from knowing incorrigibly that I am perceiving physical reality. Consequently, as long as I do not know that an evil demon is not deceiving me, I do not know that I am perceiving physical reality.

Thus, the hypothesis of the evil demon has the same skeptical force against our belief in physical reality as the hypothesis that we might be dreaming. Nevertheless, the dream argument is not superfluous. Suppose that the demon hypothesis is clearly and distinctly perceived to be false. That is not enough to dispose of skepticism regarding the existence of physical objects. Knowing that I cannot possibly be a demon's dupe, or that I am the creature of an undeceiving God, is necessary but not sufficient for me to know that I am perceiving a physical world. It is also necessary for me to be in a position to know at any time that I am, at that time, awake and not dreaming. But, as we shall see, if we employ Descartes's own concept of knowing "with certainty," namely, knowing incorrigibly, and, as Descartes does, work with the everyday concept of dreaming, we can demonstrate that no one can know incorrigibly that he, himself, is awake and not dreaming here and now. I shall argue that Descartes provides no satisfactory solution for his own way of defining the problem of the transcendence of the physical world. The concept of incorrigible knowledge is a pervasive and dominant theme of Descartes's epistemology. This concept stands in the way of Descartes's completing his own metaphysical program. In the final analysis Descartes wants to be able to say that we can have "perfect," "metaphysically" certain knowledge that we, ourselves, are awake here and now, and also that we can with the same certainty know that we are perceiving physical objects. But Descartes's criteria for clearly and distinctly perceiving such things will not provide incorrigible knowledge of them.

Before we probe into the details of the dream argument and assess the argument's philosophical import, let us look at some recent attempts to discredit the assumptions on which Descartes premises his dream argument. If such attacks are successful, the dream argument is a congeries of egregious misconceptions. How successful are they? My answer is: not at all.

In *Sense and Sensibilia*, J. L. Austin attempts to show that there is "absurdity in Descartes' toying with the notion that the whole of experience might be a dream."[2] Austin is directly concerned with a couple of "Cartesians," A. J. Ayer and H. H. Price. Ayer says that "there is no intrinsic difference in kind between those of our perceptions that are veridical in their presentation of material things and those that are delusive." Price says that "there is no qualitative difference between normal sense-data as such and abnormal sense-data as such." Call the Ayer-Price assertion the "no-qualitative-difference hypothesis." Austin thinks that the hypothesis is absurd. He argues that the phrase "a dream-like quality" is in use. It applies correctly to some waking experiences. But if the no-qualitative-difference hypothesis were true, the phrase would be meaningless because it would be applicable to everything.

This way of putting it robs the remark of its point. An expression may be applicable to everything without being meaningless. Examples are "is self-identical," and "is red or not red." Austin's point, I take it, is that if the no-qualitative-difference hypothesis were true, then every experience would have a dreamlike quality, which, *as a matter of fact*, it does not have. What this shows is that Ayer and Price have spoken somewhat carelessly. What they say is not strictly true. Some waking experiences have a dreamlike quality, and some dream experiences have a vividness and a liveliness that is lifelike. Let us pass over what Ayer and Price might say about that. What Descartes would say is clear. From the fact that some dream experiences are lifelike and some waking experiences are dreamlike it follows that being lifelike is not a mark by which we can tell with incorrigible certainty at any time whether or not we ourselves are awake at that time. Descartes would make a further point. Even if we did not believe of any experience that we thought was a waking experience that it was ever dreamlike, we would be provided with no incorrigible clue for distinguishing our own states of waking from dreaming. Why could it not be that all of our conscious states are dream states, and that in these dream states some episodes are dreamlike and others are lifelike? There is no reason why not.

Austin makes another point. Dreams are narrated in the same terms as waking experiences. But, says Austin, it would be wrong to conclude from this that what is narrated in the two cases is exactly alike. Austin gives the example of "seeing stars" when one is knocked on the head. Narration is in terms of "seeing stars," both when one is knocked on the head and when one is looking at stars. But, Austin says, what is narrated in one case is not the same as in the other. Now, we might wonder. Is "seeing stars," when one is knocked on the head the same *term* as "seeing stars" when we look at stars? It is the same English locution, but it is not the same term, if a term is a locution with *meaning*. We do not mean the same thing by "seeing stars" when we use the phrase in the two narratives. However, when I report that in my dream I experienced terror I mean by "terror" the same as what I mean when I say that in waking life I experienced terror: extreme fear in the expectation of imminent disaster.

Norman Malcolm goes one better than Austin. Austin appears to agree with Descartes that the question: "How can I tell whether I am awake or dreaming?," is a sensible question. He offers a large number of criteria for the distinction. Malcolm sets out to demonstrate that the question itself is nonsensical.

The famous philosophical question 'How can I tell whether I am awake or dreaming?' turns out to be quite senseless since it implies that it is possible to judge that one is dreaming and this judgment is as unintelligible as the judgment that one is asleep. Furthermore, the question appears to presuppose that one might be able to tell that one is dreaming, which is double nonsense: for this would mean that one made an inherently unintelligible judgment while asleep.[3]

To show that the question, "How can I tell that I am awake?" is nonsensical, Malcolm sets out to prove that it is impossible to judge that one is dreaming, and this he argues for by trying to prove that judging in sleep is an unintelligible concept.

Malcolm has a battery of arguments. A point-by-point rebuttal would require a detailed study of each argument. That procedure, however, is unnecessary. Malcolm's central argument is in chapter 3, "Judging that One is Asleep." The argument is both central and typical of the way Malcolm thinks on the subject. If this central argument collapses, the rest of the structure goes down with it.

On pp. 9–10 there is an explicit argument and in it there is an implicit argument. The intended conclusion of the explicit argument is that "I am asleep" cannot be used to make an informative statement to others. The intended conclusion of the implicit argument is that "I am asleep" cannot be used to say something significant to oneself. That these are the intended conclusions is made clear on p. 35: "We saw that the sentence, 'I am asleep,' cannot be used to make an informative statement to others nor to say something significant to oneself."

Here is the explicit argument:

(1) If someone else is to verify [find out whether it is true or false] that you understand how to use "I am asleep" to describe your own state, then he would have to determine that you apply these words to yourself at the right time.

(2) If the other person determines that you apply these words to yourself at the right time, then, for the most part, and certainly at least sometimes, when you say "I am asleep" what you say is true.

Therefore,

(3) If the other person is to verify that you understand how to use "I am asleep" to describe your own state, then for the most part, and, at least sometimes, when you say "I am asleep" what you say is true.

But,

(4) If when you say "I am asleep" what you say is true, then you say "I am asleep" while asleep and also while aware of saying it.

(5) If you are aware of saying "I am asleep," then you are not asleep [i.e., the consequent of (4) is necessarily false].

Therefore,

(6) It is impossible for the other person to verify that you understand how to use "I am asleep" to describe your own state.

But,

(7) If it is impossible for a man to verify a certain indicative sentence, then that sentence is "without sense and necessarily so" (p. 35).

Therefore,

(8) There is no sense to another man's supposition that you understand how to use "I am asleep" to describe your own state.

The argument so far purports to prove that "I am asleep" "cannot be used to make an informative statement to others" (p. 35).

Implicit in the foregoing argument is another, purporting to prove that no one can understand how to use "I am asleep" to describe his own state, i.e., no one can use "I am asleep" "to say something significant about oneself" (p. 35).

Here is the implicit argument:

(1) If a man is to understand how to use "I am asleep" to describe his own state, then he would have to apply these words to himself at the right times.

(2) If a man applies the words "I am asleep" to himself at the right times, than at least sometimes when he says "I am asleep" what he says is true.

Therefore,

(3) If a man is to understand how to use "I am asleep" to describe his

own state, then for the most part, and certainly at least sometimes, when he says "I am asleep" what he says is true.

(4) But if a man says "I am asleep" and what he says is true, then he says "I am asleep" while asleep and also while aware of saying it (p. 10).

(5) But necessarily if a man is aware of saying "I am asleep" then he is not asleep, i.e., the consequent of (4) is self-contradictory.

Therefore,

(6) It is self-contradictory to suppose that a man understands how to use "I am asleep" to describe his own state.

Step (6) of the implicit argument and step (8) of the explicit argument together come to this: that it is impossible for anyone to understand his own or anyone else's use of the sentence "I am asleep," i.e., "I am asleep" is an unintelligible sentence.

A general principle seems to govern premise (1) and premise (2) of both the explicit and the implicit argument, namely, that no one can understand how to use a sentence unless for the most part, and certainly at least sometimes, when he "applies" that sentence what he says (or judges) is true. "Using a sentence *correctly* and using it to make a *true* statement are different concepts, but the former depends on the latter" in that using a sentence to make a true statement is a necessary condition for using that sentence correctly (p. 13). I am assuming that for Malcolm using a sentence correctly is the same as understanding it. But what is using a sentence correctly? Malcolm himself sees that it cannot be using it to make a true statement. Does Malcolm mean that in order that we may use a sentence correctly it must be *possible* for us to use it to make true statements? Surely he ought not to mean any such thing. If using a sentence correctly is the same thing as understanding it, then the possibility of using a sentence to make a true statement cannot be a necessary condition for its intelligibility. For we understand sentences that cannot be used to make a true statement. If it is true that snow is white, and we understand the sentence "Snow is white," then we understand the sentence "It is not the case that snow is white," but we cannot use it to make a true statement.

The general principle is, to say the least, unclear. Let us see if Malcolm's argument can be strengthened by restricting the principle as follows: no one can understand how to use a first-person, present-tense sentence to describe his own state unless he applies the sentence to himself at the right time. Now it is obviously true that no one can use a first-person, present-tense sentence to describe his own state unless he applies the sentence to himself at the right time, namely, when he is in that state. But it does not follow from this truism that no one can understand a first-person, present-tense sentence unless he is at times in a position to use it to describe his own state. A man born minus a right leg feels a pain in what he thinks is his right toe. This man is in no position ever to use the sentence "I have a pain in my right toe" to describe a state he is in. Yet surely he understands the sentence.

Consider another example: "I am immortal." When is it the "right time" to apply that sentence to oneself? It would seem that anytime is the right time, regardless of whether or not the corresponding judgment is true. A man who believes that he is immortal can say so or think it, even if it is false that he is.

The first two premises of both the explicit and the implicit argument boil down to the trivial truth that the sentence "I am asleep" can be used by me to judge truly that I am asleep only if I am in fact asleep when I judge that I am asleep. This in no way says or implies that I do not understand the sentence, "I am asleep," and that no one else can believe truly that I understand that sentence. This crucial defect in both the explicit and the implicit argument occurs by step (3). The other premises of Malcolm's arguments could not repair the breach, even if they were true. Step (7) of the explicit argument assumes a strong verifiability criterion of meaningfulness. Most philosophers, including Descartes, would reject it. Step (5) of both the explicit and the implicit argument is a dogma based on the unargued assumption that when someone is aware of something, he must be awake. Descartes assumes that a dreaming person is conscious while asleep. He assumes, following common sense, that there is a waking consciousness and a dream consciousness. Simply to assume, without argument, that there is only waking consciousness is to beg the question against Descartes.

Anthony Kenny agrees with Malcolm "that one cannot make judgments during dreams. It does not follow, however," Kenny continues, "that the judgment 'I am dreaming' is senseless. It can never be made truly, but it can be made falsely. To dream that one is dreaming is not to judge that one is dreaming, but a waking man might be persuaded that he is dreaming."[4] Kenny is right about two things. A waking man can indeed be persuaded that he is dreaming. And from "one cannot make judgments during dreams" it does not follow that the judgment "I am dreaming" is senseless. Kenny is wrong when he agrees with Malcolm that "one cannot make judgments during dreams." Malcolm's argument for this has been shown to be unconvincing. Kenny is simply taken in by it.

If we can make judgments during dreams, and if there are no incorrigible marks for distinguishing dreams from waking experiences, then the dream argument poses philosophical problems of great moment. Malcolm and Kenny, and Austin, of course, are in no position to take the dream argument with the seriousness it deserves, and with the seriousness with which it was, in fact, treated, for example, by Kant and Leibniz.[5]

Kenny makes another blunt assertion: "The question, 'Am I awake or dreaming?', is not senseless, if that means that it has a possible answer. For there is a true answer to the question—namely, 'I am awake.' Moreover, I know the answer. If I am asked *how* I know it, however, I can give no answer. I can give no grounds for the assertion. There is no fact better known to me than the fact that I am awake. When I say 'I am awake' I do so without grounds, but not without justification."[6] Kenny does not explain the difference between grounds and justification. But never mind. Kenny is arguing that I cannot give grounds for my belief that I am awake presumably because "there is no fact better known to me than the fact that I am awake." Well now, what is it to be better known? If it is to be believed with less risk of error, then there is something that I know better than that I am awake—namely, that I am conscious. But now the question is: am I waking-conscious or dream-conscious? The "better-known" belief that I am conscious cannot settle the matter unless it is assumed that being conscious entails being awake. But Descartes refuses to make that assumption, and rightly so. The assumption contradicts what we ordinarily mean by consciousness and its relation to dreaming. Neither Malcolm, nor Austin, nor Kenny has produced any convincing reasons for thinking that our everyday concepts of consciousness, of dreams, and their connection lead to contradiction or other troubles.

On p. 31 Kenny says that "I am dreaming" is a judgment one can never make truly. Descartes would deny this, and rightly so. In a dream I can judge that I am dreaming, and my judgment is then true. I regard this to be the expression of a fact, and no argument from our anti-Cartesian authors has the slightest tendency to show that this cannot be a fact.

Again on p. 31 Kenny writes: "The judgment 'I am awake' cannot be mistaken." Not so. I can in a dream judge that I am awake, and then the judgment is false. "To dream that I am awake is not to judge that I am awake," says Kenny. Again, there is no argument that proves the point.

I submit that the most determined critics in the recent literature, principally Austin and Malcolm, have failed to undermine the presuppositions and premises of Descartes's dream argument. Let us, then, begin our examination of the argument on its own merits. What are its premises, its conclusions? What is its import regarding the problem of the transcendence of the physical world, as Descartes defines that problem? How successful is Descartes's own solution to the problem? If Descartes's solution is unacceptable, what are the alternatives?

The dream argument as it appears in Meditation I is not articulated in a logically neat and explicit way. It is not presented as a formal argument. It is less like an argument and more like a cluster of comments. In the "Synopsis of the Six Meditations" Descartes announces that in Meditation I he will "set forth the reasons for which we may, generally speaking, doubt about all things and especially about material things" (HR 1:140). In Meditation I itself Descartes begins his doubts about the senses as follows: "All that up to the present time I have accepted as most true and certain I have learned either from the senses or through the senses; but it is sometimes proved to me that these senses are deceptive, and it is wiser not to trust entirely to anything by which we have once been deceived" (HR 1:145). But, he continues, "it may be that although the senses sometimes deceive us concerning things which are hardly perceptible, or very far away, there are yet many others to be met with as to which we cannot reasonably have any doubt, although we recognize them by their means." I should be mad, says Descartes, if I thought that this head of mine is made of glass or that I was dressed in royal finery when I am in fact covered with rags.

Having made this passing remark about the possibility that he might be mad, Descartes at once moves on to another point. However, "I remember that I am a man, and that consequently I am in the habit of sleeping, and in my dreams representing to myself the same things or sometimes even less probable things, than do those who are insane in their waking moments." The point of this remark has nothing to do with reliance on memory. Even if no one ever had memory impressions of having dreamt, anyone could, on reflection, conceive the possibility that at any time when he is firmly convinced that he is awake, he is in fact dreaming. This explains why Descartes does not pursue the skeptical hypothesis that he might be mad. More basic than that, as far as skepticism with respect to the senses is concerned, is the hypothesis that he might be dreaming. A madman could have veridical sense perceptions in waking life. But if no one can at any time be sure that he is at that time awake and not dreaming, then regardless of whether he is sane or mad, he is in no position to trust his perceptual judgments. For, according to Descartes, in every such judgment we take it for granted, because the propensity to do so is built into our nature, that an independently existing material object is present.

A recent commentator, Harry G. Frankfurt bases his interpretation of the skeptical arguments in Meditation I on two assumptions, both

of which, I think, are unjustified. The first is that in the first Meditation Descartes is speaking as would a philosophical tyro, one who has
no idea that reason and sense experience are distinct faculties and who
thinks "only within the confining limits of common sense."[7] Frankfurt's second assumption is that Descartes poses with respect to the
reliability of the senses the same question that he poses with respect
to the reliability of reason: "Do we have any reason to suppose that
the faculty in question may be leading us to hold incompatible
beliefs?" The first assumption implies the implausible proposition that
common sense would have the resources for conjuring up the dream
argument and the evil demon argument. The second assumption overlooks the fact that, given Descartes's theory that all ideas are innate
(congenital) capacities, it follows that even if no one ever dreamed,
had ever hallucinated, or had ever been led by the senses to believe
incompatible propositions about the perceptual world, a person might,
nevertheless, wonder if, after all, he could be certain that what he
naturally believed on the testimony of his senses was really true,
namely, that there existed a world independently of his experiencing
it. Suppose that the propositional contents of all his incorrigible
sensory awarenesses formed a coherent whole. He would not thereby
know with incorrigible certainty that his perceptual beliefs represented
aspects of a world that exists independently of his awareness of it. The
problem of the transcendence of the material world is, for Descartes,
the problem of its independent existence. The systematic coherence of
incorrigible sensory awarenesses is not sufficient for establishing independent existence. The coherence criteria at the end of Meditation VI
involve not only the coherence among themselves of incorrigible
sensory awarenesses from all sense modalities, but also the coherence
of these with memory and principles of reason. But, as we shall see,
even this more inclusive criterion is not enough to provide incorrigible
knowledge that there exists a material world that is existentially
independent of our ideas of it. Unless we are clear about these matters,
we cannot take Descartes's dream argument with the seriousness that
it deserves.

As I observed earlier, the fact that I can conceive of being the
creature of a demon who makes me believe that my dream life is a
waking life adds nothing to the dream argument. It does not matter
how I may have come to be nothing but a dreaming consciousness
which is under the delusion that it is a waking consciousness. The
points relevant to Descartes's formulation of the problem of the
transcendence of the physical world emerge from the supposition that
for all I know I may *be* just such a consciousness.

So much for Descartes's own remarks on dreaming. These, in conjunction with certain other characteristically Cartesian views, are richly suggestive. By following leads, clues, and hints·in the text we can, I think, come up with a philosophical translation (an interpretation) in which we render Descartes's discursive text in more rigorous fashion. What I shall henceforth call "the dream argument" is not to be found in so many words in the text. The argument will be rigorously formal. It has six premises. I shall produce textual evidence to support the contention that every one of them strictly accords with characteristically Cartesian views. The dream argument is a single, continuous inference. I shall break it up into three parts. The conclusion of the first part is that every perceptual proposition is corrigible for anyone. The second part establishes that no one knows incorrigibly at any time that at that time he, himself, is not dreaming. The third part establishes that no one knows incorrigibly any perceptual proposition.

We have two technical concepts here: that of a perceptual proposition and that of incorrigibility. In order to formulate the premises of the dream argument we need to define these concepts and to show, as best we can, that the proposed definitions are strictly in line with Descartes's commitments. "All that up to the present time [i.e., up to the time when Descartes is starting his philosophical investigations] I have accepted as most true and certain I have learned either from the senses or through the senses," says Descartes (HR 1:145). The dream argument questions the presumption that what I accept as true "from the senses," that is, from what my senses reveal to me, or "through the senses," that is, through what I have been told verbally or otherwise, is something that I am fully justified, and cannot be mistaken, in believing, solely on the basis of perceptual evidence that presents itself to me now. I seem to see a tree. I judge that I see a tree. "I seem to see (hear, taste, etc.)" propositions are not perceptual propositions. The "I seem . . ." forms of proposition are never put in doubt. "I see a tree," "That is a tree," are examples of propositions that are subject to skeptical scrutiny. They are examples of perceptual propositions. The "I seem . . ." forms are perceptual reports, recordings of the contents of consciousness here and now. A perceptual proposition, then, may be defined as being a proposition that ascribes to physical objects (e.g., sticks and stones), or to physical phenomena (e.g., thunderclaps, lightning flashes, rainbows, shadows, flames, after-images) visual, tactual, gustatory, auditory, or olfactory properties or relations. By these, in turn, let us mean properties or relations the presence of which in, or their absence from, the objects or phenomena to which they are ascribed, it is logically possible to ascertain, at any given time, by looking, touching, tasting, listening, or smelling. (These are the only sense modalities that Descartes lists. See, for example, HR 1:151.)

Everything that we believe "from the senses" is a perceptual proposition, but not everything that we believe "through the senses" is. "Methane is a hydrocarbon" is not a perceptual proposition, although I may come to believe it "through the senses" by having someone explain to me what it states and why what it states is true. But in this process I have to rely ultimately on what I apprehend "from the senses." In order for me to believe truly that I am hearing statements made to me by someone whom I understand, it has to be true that I am apprehending certain perceptual propositions, e.g., that I am hearing sounds that form intelligible speech patterns issuing from someone's mouth. Thus, if perceptual propositions are suspect, then so are all statements that are accessible to me "through the senses." The basic targets of the dream argument are perceptual propositions.

Next we come to incorrigibility. Descartes correctly thought that such contingent propositions as "I am in pain," "I seem to feel heat," "I exist," "I am conscious," and such necessarily true propositions as "All squares have four sides" are indubitably certain for me, in that I would be fully justified, and could not be mistaken, in believing them on the basis of evidence to which I am attending. The following definitions explicate, I believe, the sense in which Descartes conceived of indubitable certainty:

D1: It is incorrigible for S at t that $p = Df$. (i) It is logically possible that at t S believes attentively that p, and (ii) "At t S believes attentively that p" entails "At t S knows that p."

D2: At t S believes incorrigibly that $p = Df$. At t S believes attentively that p, and "At t S believes attentively that p" entails "At t S knows that p."

D3: At t S knows incorrigibly that $p = Df$. Either at t S believes incorrigibly that p, or at t S believes incorrigibly that q, and knows that necessarily if q then p.

D4: At t S believes attentively that $p = Df$. (i) At t S believes occurrently that p, (ii) at t S is paying attention to matters that would be his evidence for judging that p or for judging that not p, and (iii) among these matters stands revealed to S evidence that p, and no evidence that not p.

Note that according to D4, "S attentively believes at t that p" does not entail that S's belief is incorrigible. Attentive belief that p is incorrigibly true only if the evidence being attended to is sufficient to secure the truth of p.

I believe that definitions D1–D4 are accurate renditions of Descartes's thinking for two reasons. They accommodate Descartes's initial paradigms of indubitably certain propositions, "I think," and "I exist," and others that he subsequently adds to the list, e.g., "I am in pain," "I seem to feel heat," "A square is four-sided." Moreover, the definitions retain the central features of Descartes's theory of indubitable cognition. Descartes says of his paradigms that they are propositions that I "intuit in the most evident manner." In the *Rules for the Direction of Mind (Regulae)*, Descartes defines intuition as being "the undoubting conception of an *unclouded* and *attentive* mind, and springs from the light of reason alone" (HR 1:7, my italics). Descartes assumes that an unclouded and attentive mind cannot doubt its own intuitions. The metaphysical doubt is never intended to be about present intuitions. It is meant to raise only the second-order issue as to whether or not the intuitions that we cannot doubt while we have them may nevertheless be unreliable because perhaps "the state of being that I have reached [may be attributed] to fate or to accident, or . . . [to] a continual succession of causes, or [to] some other method" than divine creation; "since to err and deceive oneself is a defect, it is clear that the greater will be the probability of my being so imperfect as to deceive myself ever, as is the author to whom [I] assign my origin the less powerful" (HR 1:147). Perhaps "a God has endowed me with such a nature that I may be deceived even in respect of the things which seem to me the most manifest of all" (HR 1:158). Present intuitions are logically impossible to doubt because the structure of our minds is such that (a) whatever is present before our unclouded and attentive awareness is an indubitable datum. It is logically impossible for us simultaneously to be *aware* that p and to *doubt* that p. If my mind is unclouded and attentive, I can be aware of things clearly and distinctly, not hazily or confusedly, as happens in drunkenness. And (b) in an unclouded and attentive state the mind makes logical inferences from indubitable data, and it is logically impossible for such a mind to doubt the cogency of its own operations. It is logically impossible to believe with indubitable certainty both that p, and that p logically implies q, and to doubt that q. Such, for Descartes, is the structure of the mind. The question in the metaphysical doubt is whether or not this structure is isomorphic with a reality made by an undeceiving God.

Descartes does not elaborate on the notion of an *unclouded* mind. In the *Regulae* he contrasts "the fluctuating testimony of the senses" and "the misleading judgments that proceed from the blundering constructions of imagination" with "the conception which an unclouded and attentive mind gives us so readily and distinctly that we are wholly freed from doubt about that which we understand" (HR 1:7). Everyone would concede that our minds are clouded in psychosis, during periods of extreme agitation, in anxiety, in fear, under the influence of alcohol. Perhaps by "being clouded" Descartes means a condition of mind that interferes with the ability to be attentive. The attentive mind is in a position to discern that which might escape an inattentive mind. As I read Descartes, he relates his concept of in-dubitable certainty to intuition and to the impossibility of being wrong in some instances. Definitions D1–D4 incorporate these connec-tions. Given Descartes's definition of intuition, the connection with intuition suggests that incorrigibility (indubitable certainty) should be defined in terms of an *attentive* attitude of mind. The connection with the logical impossibility of being wrong is secured if the *definiens* includes reference to *knowledge* in the way that ours does. If "S attentively believes that *p*" entails that S knows that *p*, then it is logically impossible for S to believe attentively that *p* and to be wrong about it. The logical impossibility of being wrong can be secured another way, namely, by stipulating that: "S attentively believes that *p*" entails that *p*, and "S attentively believes that not *p*" entails that not *p*. But this is incompatible with some of Descartes's paradigms of incorrigible propositions, e.g., "I think," and "I exist." Besides, this and related alterations are, aside from Descartes, objectionable. It would be unfair to Descartes and textually indefensible, as well, to ascribe to him views when nothing in what he writes invites such attribution.[8]

The definitions D1–D4 are offered as part of a theory that renders Descartes's conception of indubitable cognition somewhat more pre-cisely and systematically than Descartes himself stated it.

We are now in a position to formulate the six premises of the dream argument.

(1) If a man dreams that he, himself, is attentively perceiving that *p* (*p* being a perceptual proposition), then he attentively believes that *p*.

(2) It is possible that a man is dreaming that he, himself, is attentively perceiving that *p* (where *p* is a perceptual proposition), when in fact it is false that *p*.

(3) If a contingent proposition entails that a certain man is not dreaming, then it is possible that in his dream that man attentively believes that that proposition is true.

(4) It is possible that *p* is false, and in a dream a man has a clear and distinct intuition that *q* (where *p* is a perceptual proposition and *q* is a proposition incorrigible for him.).

(5) If in a dream a man has a clear and distinct intuition that q (where q is a proposition incorrigible for him), then he attentively believes that q.

(6) A man knows incorrigibly a proposition that is corrigible for him, only if there is a proposition incorrigible for him that entails the proposition that is corrigible for him.

Taking these premises in the order (6), (2), (3), (1), (4), and (5), I shall explain why I believe that every one of them is faithful to Descartes's thinking.

According to D3, above, a man knows incorrigibly that p if, and only if, either he believes incorrigibly that p, or he believes incorrigibly that q, and knows that necessarily if q then p. This is my rendition of what I think is Descartes's criterion of incorrigible (indubitably certain) knowledge. The core idea here is that a man knows incorrigibly that p only if he believes that p on the basis of evidence to which he is attending and which is such that his reason cannot deny that p at a time when he is attending to that evidence. Moreover, the removal of the metaphysical doubt establishes that reason can find no grounds at all for mistrusting its own incorrigible beliefs. Hence, whatever we know incorrigibly we can know "perfectly." D3 entails (6). (6) is not the whole of Descartes's criterion of incorrigible knowledge. It is only a part of the criterion, a part that suffices for the dream argument.

Descartes is bound to accept premise (2) because it is an immediate consequence of his conception of dreaming. Descartes assumes what is commonly assumed, namely, that dreams are, or consist of, impressions, thoughts, feelings, sensations, images, or any other mental phenomena that occur during sleep. It is moreover, part of this conception of dreaming that it is possible to have a very vivid and lifelike dream that we are attentively perceiving that p, where p is a perceptual proposition, when in fact it is false that p. This is premise (2). Being an immediate consequence of the ordinary conception of dreaming, (2) is true, if the conception from which it follows is not self-contradictory or otherwise incoherent. And, as our examination of Austin and Malcolm indicates, we have no reason for supposing that it labors under such handicaps.

Premise (3) is what I take Descartes to be assuming when he says in Meditation I that "there are no certain indications by which we may clearly distinguish wakefulness from sleep." Could these "certain indications" be anything but premises that entail that we are awake, and that we know how to make the corresponding inference? Because "I am awake" is a contingent proposition, the required premises must be consistent, if they are to prove that I am awake. Now what would

have to be true in order for it to be true that no contingent proposition
that entails that I am awake is a "certain indication" of my not being
asleep? It would have to be true that it is possible at the same time to
believe attentively any such proposition, to infer from it that one is
not asleep, and yet to be dreaming. If so, then it is possible to believe
attentively any such proposition while one is dreaming. This last
possibility is what is assumed in premise (3), and it is a perfectly
reasonable assumption for anyone to make who subscribes to the
everyday conception of dreams. Like (2), (3) is an immediate consequence of that conception.

We have next to justify attributing premise (1) to Descartes. The
first part of the dream argument is to prove that all perceptual propositions are doubtful. Given our analysis of indubitability in terms of
incorrigibility, and given that premise (2) is already available, premise
(1) is the minimal assumption that, when added to premise (2) and
the definition of incorrigibility, will formally imply the intended conclusion that all perceptual propositions are doubtful. This in itself is
a strong reason for attributing (1) to Descartes. The case for making
the attribution becomes conclusive when we note that (1) is just what
one would expect Descartes to say when we add his theory of perception to his conception of dreaming.

According to the conception of dreaming, dreaming that one is
attentively perceiving that p, where p is a perceptual proposition,
involves the occurrence of certain mental phenomena. Descartes's
answer to what they are lies in his theory of perception. According to
Descartes, perception involves the making of judgments. When someone perceives that p, (a) he perceives that such and such is the case;
(b) perceiving that such and such is the case entails believing that such
and such is the case; (c) perceiving a thing or a collection of things
entails perceiving that such and such is the case. Furthermore, "S is
perceiving that p" entails three propositions: (i) p, (ii) S is having
certain visual, tactual, auditory, olfactory, or gustatory experiences,[9]
and (iii) on the basis of these experiences S believes that (judges that)
p. Exactly what is meant by "on the basis of these experiences" is not
altogether clear. For our purpose it is enough to note that the belief
instigated by the sensations need not involve the making of an inference on the part of the perceiver. On Descartes's view of dreaming
and of perceiving, the difference between S's perceiving that p and S's
dreaming that he himself is perceiving that p is that the latter entails
(ii) and (iii), and that S is asleep, but does not entail (i). "S is perceiving that p" entails (i), (ii), and (iii), but does not entail that S is asleep.
Rather, it entails that S is awake. Accordingly, the following two
entailments would seem to be axiomatic for Descartes: "S is attentively

perceiving that p" entails "S attentively believes that p," and "In a dream S is attentively perceiving that p" entails "S attentively believes that p." The latter entailment is our premise (1).

Told another way, the story is this. According to Descartes, perceiving is not a purely mental phenomenon. There is no perceiving unless there are physical objects or physical phenomena. But perceiving cannot occur unless two purely mental phenomena occur. He who is perceiving must be having certain experiences, and on their basis he must be believing that a certain perceptual proposition is true. Now according to Descartes the purely mental features of perceiving that p must occur whenever anyone dreams that he himself is perceiving that p. Else how can there be a difference between dreaming that one is perceiving a tree and dreaming that the weather has suddenly turned cold? Finally, according to Descartes, "S is dreaming at t that he himself is attentively perceiving that p" is the same proposition as "S is asleep at t, at t S is having certain experiences, and on their basis he attentively believes at t that p." From this it follows that "S is dreaming at t that he himself is attentively perceiving that p" entails "S attentively believes at t that p." The latter entailment is premise (1).

In Meditation III, and elsewhere, there are indications that Descartes means to affirm premise (4). He writes:

I have before received and admitted many things to be very certain and manifest which yet afterwards I recognized as being dubious. What then were these things? They were the earth, sky, stars and all other objects which I apprehended by means of the senses. But what did I clearly [and distinctly] perceive in them? Nothing more than that the ideas or thoughts of these things were present to my mind. And not even now do I deny that these ideas are met with in me. But there was yet another thing which I affirmed, and which owing to the habit I had formed of believing it, I thought I perceived very clearly, although I did not perceive it at all, to wit, that there were objects outside of me from which these ideas proceeded, and to which they were entirely similar. And it was in this that I erred, or, if perchance my judgment was correct, this was not due to any knowledge arising from my perception. . . . Of my thoughts some are, so to speak, images of the things, and to these alone is the title 'idea' properly applied. . . . Now as to what concerns ideas, if we consider them only in themselves and do not relate them to anything else beyond themselves, they cannot properly speaking be false; for whether I imagine a goat or a chimera, it is not less true that I imagine the one than the other. [HR 1:158–59]

Descartes is saying that purely phenomenal reports in the "I seem to see . . ." mode of speaking or thinking are "indubitable"; we have rendered this in terms of the concept of incorrigibility. About such judgments Descartes writes as follows: "everything which anyone clearly and distinctly perceives is true, although that person in the meantime may doubt whether he is dreaming or awake, nay if you want it so, even though he is really dreaming or is delirious" (in his reply to Bourdin, HR 2:267). In Meditation II he writes:

But it will be said these phenomena (that I hear noise, that I see light) are false and that I am dreaming. Let it be so. Still it is at least quite certain that it seems to me that I see light, that I hear noise and that I feel heat. That cannot be false; properly speaking it is what is in me called feeling; and used in this precise sense that is no other thing than thinking. [HR 1: 153]

Here again Descartes is distinguishing purely phenomenal reports from perceptual propositions. He is saying that phenomenal reports are incorrigible for me although every one of them is contingent; and that in the case of some contingent propositions that are incorrigible for me, it is possible that in my dream[10] I attentively believe them at a time when I am not perceiving that p, where p is a perceptual proposition. And if it is possible that in my dream I have a clear and distinct intuition that a certain phenomenal report is incorrigible for me even while I am not actually perceiving that p, then it is also possible that in my dream I have a clear and distinct intuition that a certain contingent proposition is incorrigible for me even while it is false that p. But if this is possible for some contingent propositions that are incorrigible for me, then it should be possible for all contingent propositions that are incorrigible for me. That takes us halfway to premise (4).

We go the rest of the way when we find Descartes leaving no doubt that in his opinion contingent propositions that are incorrigible for me are not necessarily the only propositions incorrigible for me that satisfy the condition in question. For it is possible that there are necessarily true propositions, q, that are incorrigible for me, and for any perceptual proposition, p, it is possible that, while p is false, in my dream I have a clear and distinct intuition that q. In the *Discourse on Method*, Descartes writes: "For even if in sleep we had some very distinct idea such as a geometrican might have who discovered some new demonstration, the fact of being asleep would not militate against its truth" (HR 1:105). As the class of propositions that are incorrigible for me is exhausted by all the contingent and all the necessarily true propositions that are incorrigible for me, (4) follows.

Premise (5) is analogous to premise (1). In connection with premise (1), the following two entailments appeared to be axiomatic for Descartes: "S is attentively perceiving that p" entails "S attentively believes that p," and "S is dreaming that he himself is attentively perceiving that p" entails "S attentively believes that p." The analogous entailments relevant to premise (5) are: "S clearly and distinctly intuits that q" entails "S attentively believes that q," and "In his dream S clearly and distinctly intuits that q" entails "S attentively believes that q." The latter entailment is premise (5), when q is any proposition incorrigible for S. Premise (5) entails that for any proposition, q, that is incorrigible for S, "In his dream S clearly and distinctly intuits that q" entails that S knows that q. This is as it should be. Descartes says, for example, that "I think" and "I exist" are incorrigible for me; whether I am awake or dreaming, each time that the thought that I am thinking or the thought that I exist occur to me clearly and distinctly I know that I am thinking and that I exist.

The conclusion of the first part of the dream argument is deducible from (1) and (2). The conclusion of the second part is deducible from (3) and (6); and (1), (2), (4), (5), and (6) entail the conclusion of the third part.

We are now in a position to formulate the three parts of the dream argument.[11]

The first part of the dream argument proceeds from two premises: (1) If a man is dreaming that he is attentively perceiving that p (where p is a perceptual proposition), then he attentively believes that p, and (2) It is possible that a man is dreaming that he himself is attentively perceiving that p (where p is a perceptual proposition), when in fact it is not the case that p. It follows from these two propositions that it is possible at one and the same time that a man believes attentively that p and that p is false. But if p is false, then no one knows that p. Therefore, it is possible at one and the same time that a man attentively believes that p and does not know that p. But this entails that it is false that a man's attentively believing that p entails his knowing that p. And, by our definition of "p is incorrigible for S," it follows that no perceptual proposition is incorrigible for anyone.

The second part of the dream argument begins with the assumption that, if a contingent proposition entails that a certain man is not dreaming, then it is possible that in his dream that man attentively believes that proposition to be true. Now let there be a contingent proposition that entails that a certain man is not dreaming. From this and our original premise it follows that it is possible at one and the same time that the man in question attentively believes that proposition and that the proposition is false. But if the proposition is false, the man in question does not know it. Therefore, it is possible at one and the same time that the man attentively believes that proposition but does not know it. That entails that his attentively believing it does not entail his knowing it. That in turn entails that the proposition is corrigible for that man. The result is true of any man and of any contingent proposition that entails that he is not dreaming.

In other words, we have deduced so far that (i) any contingent proposition that entails that a man is not dreaming is corrigible for that man. But because "S is not dreaming" is a contingent proposition, no necessarily true proposition entails it. It is true that every necessarily false proposition entails it, but no necessarily false proposition is incorrigible for anyone. Hence, there is no noncontingent, incorrigible proposition that entails it. But we have already deduced in (i) that no contingent, incorrigible proposition entails it. Therefore, no incorrigible proposition entails it. Moreover, the proposition that S is not dreaming is corrigible for S, and, like every proposition, entails itself. Hence, by (i), the proposition "S is not dreaming" is itself corrigible for S. Hence, there is no proposition incorrigible for S that entails that S is not dreaming. It follows, by the criterion of incorrigible knowledge, that no one knows incorrigibly that he himself is not dreaming.

The third part of the dream argument begins with the conclusion of the first part, namely, that a perceptual proposition is corrigible for anyone. Consequently, given the criterion of incorrigible knowledge (premise [6]), a man would know that a perceptual proposition was true only if he could deduce it from a proposition incorrigible for him. But according to premise (4), it is possible at the same time that in a dream a man has a clear and distinct intuition that q and that p is false (where p is a perceptual proposition and q is a proposition incorrigible for him). However, by premise (5), if in a dream a man has a clear and distinct intuition that q (where q is a proposition incorrigible for him), then he attentively believes that q. Now let there be a man, S, and a perceptual proposition, p, such that S knows incorrigibly that p. We know immediately that p is corrigible for S, because every perceptual proposition is corrigible for anyone. Also, from the assumption we have made, namely, that S knows incorrigibly that p, it follows that there is a proposition, q, that is incorrigible for S and entails p. And now from the assumptions we have made we deduce that, if a man knows incorrigibly that a perceptual proposition is true, then his attentively believing that q does and does not entail the perceptual proposition in question. But the consequent of this hypothetical is self-contradictory, and therefore its antecedent is necessarily false. Hence, it follows that no one ever knows incorrigibly that a perceptual proposition is true.

Let us now summarize our results. The conclusion of the first part of the dream argument asserts that every perceptual proposition is corrigible for anyone. The conclusion of the second part is that no one knows incorrigibly that he himself is not dreaming. The conclusion of the third part is that no one knows incorrigibly that any given perceptual proposition is true.

The second part of the dream argument is important for two reasons. First, it is interesting in its own right: it is an arresting fact that no one can know incorrigibly that he himself is not dreaming. Second, the second part of the dream argument provides an explanation of Descartes's affirmation that "there are no certain indications by which we may clearly distinguish wakefulness from sleep" (HR 1:146).

Descartes nowhere seems to be saying or implying that we have no conceptual distinction between dreaming and waking. We know very well that "S is dreaming" entails "S is asleep," whereas "S is awake" does not entail "S is asleep." On the contrary, it entails that S is not asleep. What Descartes seems to be saying is that at any given moment, no one can know incorrigibly that he himself is awake and not dreaming, by appeal to evidence that consists of propositions incorrigible for him. And this, I think, is necessarily true.

As to the conclusion of the third part of the dream argument, all its basic premises, except the criterion of incorrigible knowledge, are assumptions about dreaming. That is to say, the assumptions about dreaming and the criterion of incorrigible knowledge are enough to entail the conclusion that no person ever knows incorrigibly any perceptual proposition to be true. From this it follows that no one knows incorrigibly that he himself is perceiving a physical object.

We have deduced from premises we have attributed to Descartes three conclusions. A corollary of the third conclusion is that no one can prove, from phenomenal reports of sense-experience alone, that he himself is perceiving a material object. Are all these conclusions consistent with Descartes's metaphysical strategy?

Descartes ultimately wants to be able to say, among other things, it seems to me, that we know "with certainty" a perceptual fact, if we perceive it clearly and distinctly, and that we know "with certainty" that we ourselves are awake, if our senses, our memory, and our understanding together corroborate the proposition that we are awake. The conclusion of the first part of the dream argument, taken by itself, is not in conflict with either one of these assertions. The proposition that all perceptual propositions are corrigible does not, by itself alone, rule out the possibility of finding a suitable criterion of clarity and distinctness for perceptual propositions. And if such a criterion could be found, then clarity and distinctness would be a criterion of the truth of clear and distinct perceptual judgments. And eventually Descartes will claim to have proved that all clearly and distinctly perceived propositions are true. So far, then, we have no reason to suspect that Descartes did not mean to prove that all perceptual propositions are corrigible for everyone.

It is otherwise with the conclusion of the second part of the dream argument. The text gives no clear indication that Descartes meant to arrive at it. From premise (3), but without (6), the criterion of incorrigible knowledge, we deduce that no proposition that is incorrigible for anyone entails that he himself is not dreaming. This is the weaker conclusion, and it may be all that Descartes means to imply when he says that he sees "manifestly that there are no certain indications by which we may clearly distinguish wakefulness from sleep" (HR 1:146). But this quotation is also compatible with the stronger conclusion that no one knows incorrigibly that he himself is not dreaming. This we deduce from the conjunction of (3) with (6), the criterion of incorrigible knowledge. Now the stronger conclusion gives every appearance of being inconsistent with Descartes's assertion, at the end of Meditation VI, that it is possible to know "with certainty" that one is not dreaming. There appears to be a flat contradiction between the proposition that we can never know incorrigibly that we are not dreaming and the proposition that we can know with certainty that we are not dreaming.

Is this a genuine inconsistency? Strictly speaking, yes. But Descartes gives no indication of suspecting its existence. Descartes may be unmindful of the full force of his own dream argument because he did not pause to formulate rigorously its premises. He was, therefore, not in a position to infer its deductive consequences. I have argued that the first five premises are immediate consequences of the ordinary conception of dreaming, coupled with Descartes's judgmental theory of perception. If, as I believe, there is nothing wrong with the ordinary concept of dreams, then the conclusions of the dream argument can be faulted only if either premise (6), the (partial) criterion of incorrigible knowledge, or the judgmental theory of perception is defective. As I am inclined to find fault with neither of these, I accept the conclusions of the dream argument. If these conclusions are, indeed, acceptable, then Descartes's metaphysical defense of perceptual knowledge is unsuccessful. Hence, his solution of the problem of the transcendence of the physical world (and of other minds) is unsuccessful. He sets up the problem as follows: first, he introduces a very demanding criterion of knowledge, which I have explained as being the criterion of incorrigibility. The initial paradigms of "certain knowledge"—cogito and sum—conform to this criterion very nicely. He assumes, moreover, that we automatically and unavoidably believe that physical objects are realities represented to us by appearances of them. The solution of the problem of the transcendence of the physical world requires proof that when our perceptual judgments are clear and distinct they are known with exactly the same incorrigibility as cogito and sum, and, among the items so known is the proposition that the appearances are of physical objects that are distinct from the appearances and exist independently of them. Descartes thinks that he does have a criterion for the incorrigibility of perceptual knowledge, and, a fortiori, for knowing incorrigibly that we ourselves are awake. He proposes a single coherence criterion for both. Unfortunately for Descartes's program, the criterion is not adequate to the task.

The criterion for the clarity and distinctness of perceptual judgments is offered near the end of Meditation VI:

For knowing that all my senses more frequently indicate to me truth than falsehood respecting the things which concern that which is beneficial to the body, and being able almost always to avail myself of many of them in order to examine one particular thing, and, besides, being able to make use of my memory in order to connect the present with the past, and of my understanding which already has discovered all the causes of my errors, I ought no longer to fear that falsity may be found in matters every day presented to me by my senses. [HR 1:198]

A little farther on Descartes states this as a criterion for knowing incorrigibly that we ourselves are awake. Reason tells me that our

memory can never connect our dreams one with another, or with the whole course of our lives, as it unites events which happen to us while we are awake . . . when I perceive things as to which I know distinctly both the place from which they proceeded, and that in which they are, and the time at which they appeared to me; and when, without interruption, I connect the perceptions which I have of them with the whole course of my life. [HR 1:199]

then I can be perfectly certain that these are waking perceptions.

These quotations suggest strongly that Descartes thinks that reason provides certain principles, themselves known incorrigibly, from which, in conjunction with certain reports about presently occurring sense experiences and present memory impressions, we can deduce that we ourselves are awake and also that we are perceiving that p, where p is a perceptual proposition.

The first difficulty with the criterion for being awake is the contention that reason tells us that our "memory can never connect our dreams with one another, or with the whole course of our lives, as it unites events which happen to us while we are awake." That our dreams do not form a chain of connected episodes may be a matter of fact, but surely it is not a matter of necessity. It is possible for one dream to continue where an earlier one left off. The intervening experiences may have their own similar connections. Nothing in reason rules out the possibility of having two distinct chains of experiences. The whole of our life, moreover, might consist of these two distinct series. How could we tell which was the dream chain and which the waking chain? There is, as far as I can see, no principle of reason from which, in conjunction with presently coherent sense-experiences and presently cohering memory impressions, we can deduce that we are awake and not dreaming.

The second difficulty with what Descartes is saying in this passage is that he relies on memory. In order to tell that I am now having a waking experience, I must, according to the suggested criterion, be able to "connect [without interruption] the perceptions which I [now] have . . . with the whole course of my life." But in order to make such a connection, I must remember what my life has been up to now. But, in order to know that I am remembering correctly, I must know that my present memory impressions as to what my life has been up to now are correct memory impressions. And to be able to know that, I must be able to distinguish among my memory impressions the ones that are veridical from those that are not. Descartes is fully aware of the need to provide a reliable criterion for making the required distinction. At this point in Meditation VI, he would be assuming that he has already vindicated reliance on memory. The supposed vindication comes at the end of Meditation V, in the following argument (see HR 1:184).

(1) God exists. All things depend on Him. He is not a deceiver. (Supposedly proved in earlier Meditations.)

∴ (2) Whatever [at some time or other] I perceive clearly and distinctly cannot fail to be true.

But (3) If I recollect having clearly and distinctly perceived that p, and God exists, then no contrary reason can be brought forward that could ever cause me to doubt that p is true.

Assume that (4) I recollect having clearly and distinctly perceived that p.

∴ (5) No contrary reason can be brought forward that could ever cause me to doubt its truth.

∴ (6) I know that p is true.

The crucial assumption is (4). How can I know with certainty that something I recollect is true? Premise (2) applies only if I have a clear and distinct recollection of having clearly and distinctly perceived that p. But that calls for an independent criterion or test for distinguishing my clear and distinct recollections from their opposites.

Descartes sees that he must provide a criterion for this, and he does. At the end of Meditation VI, he says that the test is the corroborative testimony of the senses, memory, and reason. In short, Descartes proposes a coherence test for distinguishing clear and distinct recollections from the rest.

The theory under examination supposes that the coherence criterion will guarantee that we know with certainty any proposition that we clearly and distinctly remember having clearly and distinctly perceived. Now this certainty cannot be explained in terms of incorrigibility. The coherence criterion cannot provide the apodictic certainty that Descartes's epistemology requires. For, however much my present memory impressions "tie in" or "hang together" with my present perceptual experience, and however much the memory impressions among themselves "hang together" or "make a coherent story," it is possible that a part of what I seem to recall, or even the whole of it, is not true recollection, but a fabrication of my mind. The coherence test can, at best, secure high probability for what memory tells us. It cannot guarantee a particular memory impression as one that I am fully justified, and cannot be mistaken, in believing to be veridical on the basis of evidence present to my attentive apprehension here and now.

The coherence criterion is equally ineffectual as an explanation of how we can know perceptual propositions "with certainty." Its failure as an incorrigible criterion for distinguishing wakefulness from dreaming entails that it does not suffice to solve the problem of the transcendence of the physical world, and, a fortiori, of other minds, as Descartes construes them. But even apart from that point, the coherence criterion for clear and distinct perception of physical existence cannot work. In it there is a twofold reliance on coherence. The first is in the phrase, "and being able almost always to avail myself of many of [the senses] in order to examine one particular thing" (HR 1:198), where Descartes may plausibly be interpreted as saying that one necessary condition for discerning clarity and distinctness (the mark of truth) in a perceptual proposition is that all the relevant senses agree in its corroboration. Thus, I perceive a book only if my sight, smell, hearing, touch, and taste would all agree that the thing in front of me is a book.

The second reliance on coherence is in the phrase, "and being able to make use of my memory in order to connect the present with the past" (HR 1:198). Here Descartes appeals to memory again, and hence to the coherence test of its reliability, in order to provide a way of determining which of my perceptual judgments are clear and distinct. For example, in order to be perceiving clearly and distinctly that there is a book in front of me, I must be able to "connect the perceptions which I have of [it] with the whole course of my life" (HR 1:199). If I could not, then neither could I be certain that my present visual, tactual, auditory, olfactory, and gustatory experiences were not occurring in a dream. And if I could not be certain that they were not, I could not be certain that there was a book in front of me. And if I could not be certain of that, then I would not be perceiving clearly and distinctly that there is a book in front of me.

I have already argued that the coherence criterion for memory cannot provide for incorrigible knowledge by recollection. By similar reasoning, one could argue that the coherence of the relevant senses cannot provide for incorrigible perceptual knowledge. Let the testimony of all my senses converge on the proposition that there is a book in front of me. It is logically possible that I am having these experiences not because of the causal influence of an external object but under the influence of a drug, or because of an unusual quantum jump in my brain, or because of pure chance. The probabilities for these are very low indeed; very low probability is not the same, however, as logical impossibility.

Can Descartes persuade us that if coherence fails as a criterion for clear and distinct perception of wakefulness and of perceptual propositions, then God must be a deceiver? I think not. There is no reason to believe that the natural propensity to believe, without having to make any inferences, that we are experiencing an external physical reality, or that we ourselves are awake and not dreaming, is part of the structure of human reason. Suppose that, by exercising my God-given reason, I clearly and distinctly perceive that probable knowledge is different from certain knowledge. Moreover, probable knowledge seems to be enough for me to be able to conduct my daily life quite satisfactorily. Thus let perceptual propositions, the proposition that I am awake, and all my knowledge by recollection be knowable, not with certainty, but only to a high degree of probability. This would in no way conflict with the supposition that God is good and not a deceiver. If I have natural propensities to believe that I know with certainty propositions that reason tells me I can know only to a degree of probability, then I have to see to it that my natural propensities do not subvert my reason.

Or, if we should find it difficult to understand how the coherence of sense, memory, and understanding makes it even probable that physical objects are existentially independent of minds, we can at least entertain such metaphysical systems as that of Berkeley or of Leibniz.

The dream argument teaches us that every perceptual proposition is corrigible for anyone and not deducible from propositions that are incorrigible for that person. Hence, no one can know incorrigibly that any perceptual proposition is true. These conclusions are deduced from premises that appear to be characteristically Cartesian. Descartes is simply mistaken if he believes that his dream argument leads to limited skepticism with respect to perceptual knowledge and that coherence criteria can, in the final analysis, support the position that we can know, with incorrigible certainty, that we ourselves are awake and that we can also know incorrigibly perceptual propositions. The Cartesian requirement that knowledge be incorrigible would be fatuous were it the case that no proposition can be known incorrigibly. Descartes's own initial paradigms in the *Meditations*, "I think" and "I exist," and others he adds to the list, such as "A square has four sides," "I feel a pain," "I seem to see light," can be known incorrigibly. The concept of incorrigible knowledge is, thus, not empty. Descartes believes that such propositions as "I see a tree" and "I am awake" can also be known incorrigibly. But he is wrong about that. Because he is wrong, he has failed to solve the problem of the transcendence of physical objects and, a fortiori, the problem of other minds, as he himself defines them. Anyone who takes seriously Descartes's dream argument has to define these two problems differently, and he has to attempt to solve them within the boundaries set by the dream argument. Among these boundaries is the epistemological primacy of the immediacies of sense-experience as recorded in purely phenomenal reports, and of reason as a faculty of ordering principles. There is also the stringent requirement of incorrigibility as a condition for knowledge.

Those who do not take the dream argument seriously may be presumed to do so because they find flaws in it. The argument is valid. The only question is the truth of its premises. It is not an exaggeration to say that the principal discussions since Descartes about the nature of empirical knowledge may be regarded as reactions to Descartes, and, in particular, to the presuppositions of his dream argument.

NOTES

1. The certainty of the ego's existence coupled with its function as the unifier of "diverse cogitationes" implies, for Descartes, that the ego is a substance, a self-identical, existing, essence or principal attribute, the attribute of consciousness.

2. J. L. Austin, *Sense and Sensibilia* (Oxford: Clarendon, 1962), p. 49n.

3. Norman Malcolm, *Dreaming* (London: Routledge and Kegan Paul, 1959), p. 109.

4. Anthony Kenny, *Descartes: A Study of His Philosophy* (New York: Random House, 1968), p. 30.

5. See Hector-Neri Castaneda, "Leibniz's Meditation on April 15, 1976, About Existence, Dreams, and Space," *Studia Leibniziana*, in press.

6. Kenny, *Descartes*, p. 30.

7. H. G. Frankfurt, *Demons, Dreamers, and Madmen* (Indianapolis: Bobbs-Merrill, 1970), p. 15.

8. For more details see my "Incorrigibility," *The Philosophical Quarterly* 18 (1968):207–15.

9. Strictly speaking, Descartes views these as being purely mental occurrences. They are awarenesses reported by such locutions as "I seem to see a white rabbit." These devices are meant to be recording an immediate awareness. They are meant to leave out any implication that physical objects, sense organs, or the central nervous system including the brain are involved in the process.

10. In idiomatic English the two assertions, "In my dream I solved a problem" and "I dreamt that I solved a problem" are hardly distinguishable. Neither of them entails that I solved a problem. For a precise formulation of premises (4) and (5) of the dream argument, it is useful to stipulate that "In my dream I attentively believed that p" is to entail "I attentively believed that p" and that "In my dream I had a clear and distinct perception that q" is to entail that I had a clear and distinct perception that q. The locution "I dreamt that . . ." we shall continue to use in its idiomatic sense.

11. Their rigorous versions are given in Appendix I, pp. 289–92 of my *An Introduction to Philosophy* (New York: Knopf, 1967). The present essay is an amplified and, on one important point, revised version of my presentation of the dream argument in that book. Willis Doney's paper, "Descartes' Conception of Perfect Knowledge," *Journal of the History of Philosophy* 8 (1970):387–403, altered my understanding of Descartes's validation of reason. As a consequence I no longer believe that what in that book I called "the second interpretation of the dream argument" is relevant.

The Representational
Character of Ideas and the Problem
of the External World

ARTHUR DANTO

A false doctor is not a kind of doctor,
but a false god is a kind of god.
—Iris Murdoch, *Bruno's Dream*

I

DESCARTES CHARACTERIZED IDEAS as modes of thought and hence states of "res cogitans," but assigned two other sets of properties to them. These properties, which entitle us to treat ideas as semantical vehicles with marked analogies to other such species of these as pictures (ideas *sont comme les images des choses*) and sentences are: (1) they have representational properties, in that ideas are always *of* something—of chimerae, or bits of wax, or pieces of manuscript; and (2) they are subject to semantical evaluation in terms of truth-or-falsity, or values very like truth-or-falsity. Save in the altogether exceptional instance of the idea of God, representational properties normally underdetermine the semantical value of the ideas they characterize, in that ideas as such can either be true or false, all the while representing what they do represent. That is, except *par rapport à quelque chose*, no idea as such is true or false, where "quelque chose" is understood as something different from the idea itself (see Meditation III; the quotations that follow in this chapter all derive from that Meditation).

There is a standing ambiguity in the concept of falsehood, which connotes, in one of its senses, mere inauthenticity (e.g., false pregnancies or false friends), and, in the other, failure of descriptive fit with a purported denotation, or failure of denotation altogether (e.g., in false propositions). The best test for determining which of these senses is in issue is the following: a false friend is not a friend, but a false proposition is a proposition—or, if the first sense of *false* is used to form the expression "false proposition," the implication is that the thing so characterized is not really a proposition, not that it is a proposition which is really false. And indeed, it can really be false only if it really is a proposition, in contrast with a false pregnancy, which really isn't a pregnancy at all; there is no such thing as a real pregnancy which happens to be false.

It is essential to Cartesian epistemology that a false idea *is* an idea, which should mean that the idea remains characterized by just the same representational property, invariantly as to whether or not it is true: an idea-of-*x* is an idea-of-*x* no matter whether it is false or true. It is this which enables Descartes to suppose that I would have all the ideas which I in fact have, even should none of them be true, or at least that there should be no way of telling, merely from the fact that I have an idea and that the idea be of *x*, whether it is true or false (I am shelving the idea of God because of the complexities it would introduce at this point).

Since an idea is rendered true through some *rapport* with something other than and hence external to itself, the independence of ideas, as representationally characterized entities, from anything external to themselves gives rise to the Problem of the External World: how is one able to deduce, from what an idea is of, that there exists something, external to it, and in relationship to which it has the favored semantical value? And so it really is consistent with my having just the ideas I in fact have that none of them be true; and it is a problem for Descartes because, unless the blocked deduction can be made, there is no way to find out—there can be no question of comparing ideas with things.

In any case, it follows from these considerations that "of-*x*" designates a simple property of ideas: it is a one-place predicate true of the idea of *x*. Or, if it is not a simple property after all, whatever it is in virtue of which "of *x*" is true of the idea of *x*, it cannot at least be *x* itself, for then we could not know that it was an idea of *x* unless we could have independent access to *x* to see if the condition were satisfied—and then the Problem of the External World would not arise. It would not because the existence of *x* would be presupposed in the very characterization of some idea as "of *x*." So we may assume the individuation of ideas in terms of their representational properties can be carried out in complete independence of whatever it is in relationship to which they are true or false.

Their meanings, in brief, do not determine the truth-values of ideas, any more than they do (at least typically) in the case of sentences. And so we may conclude that it is a condition for Cartesian epistemology that we should always be able to say what an idea is of, without knowing or even caring whether it is true or false. It is an ultimate aim of this paper to discredit this condition, and hence Cartesian epistemology itself.

II

In addition to ideas, Descartes identifies a set of thoughts that have what he calls *quelques autres formes*, and these, because of their logical affinity to what came later to be designated "propositional attitudes," might here be designated "ideational attitudes"—mental operations over ideas whose linguistic representation might very well be sentence-forming operators over idea-descriptions. Let i stand for an idea, and let $R(\ )x$ symbolize the representational property "of x" so that the $R(i)x$ reads: "i is of x." The ideational operator is a mode of assigning truth-value to a suitably characterized idea. Letting (T) and (F) be truth-value names, and letting O stand for some ideational attitude, these operations have the form $O[\text{———}](T)$ or $O[\text{———}](F)$, where the blank is to be filled with the description of the idea, e.g., $O[R(i)x](T)$. Then to believe that there are goats is in effect to affirm that the idea of goats is true; and to believe that there are no chimerae is to affirm that the idea of chimerae is false. Descartes furnishes a presumably nonexhaustive list of these *pensées—Je veux, Je crains, J'affirme, Je nie*—which are in effect *action [s] de mon esprit*, while the ideas themselves are the (*sujets*) of such (mental) operations or actions.

It cannot be overstressed that these actions are on ideas and not on things or events in the ideationally external world, so that the fear of flying is not some sort of relationship between Erica and all episodes of aviation, but rather is something whose formal analysis runs roughly thus: "Erica fears that the idea-of-Erica-flying should be true," or, perhaps, "Erica believes that the conditional idea 'If Erica flies, Erica crashes' is true." Something like this representationalist theory of fear is required—however stilted our phrasing in consequence of it —by the fact that people fear things that don't exist as well as things that do; they fear chimerae as well as goats. Thus fear cannot generally be represented as a relationship between the timorous and concrete objects or events, any more than belief itself may be represented as a relationship between believers and the concrete objects of belief (facts, say)—for then we would be as hard put as Protagoras to account for false beliefs. By our semantical touchstone, a false belief is a belief, after all, one whose subject happens to be an idea which is false, where Protagoras's theory would require the inference that false beliefs are not beliefs (so mistakes are impossible). So a false fear is a fear, only a fear whose ideational subject itself is an idea which is false, as when Descartes fears demons which, if there are none, cannot then be *subjects* of Cartesian phobia.

It is crucial, I believe, for Cartesian philosophy that these ideational attitudes not be ideas in their own right, though of course there can be ideas of ideational actions. But the idea of an ideational action is itself no more an action than the idea of a goat is a goat. Thus I may have the idea of myself as fearing something, or wanting something, or even thinking something (is true)—but it no more follows from the fact that I have the idea of myself as thinking something that I really am thinking that, than it follows from the fact that I have the idea of myself seated in a cozy chamber in Germany writing meditations that I really am doing that. Perhaps it does follow from the fact that I have the idea of thinking that I really am thinking; but the latter follows only from the fact that it is an idea, together with the fact that the idea was thought: it does not follow from what the idea is of, for instance, myself as thinking something. Indeed, should I have the idea of myself as *not* thinking, e.g. as in deep, thoughtless sleep, naked between the sheets, it would equally follow from the fact that I am having this thought that I think.

Every idea, irrespective of content, is a thought, but nothing else follows from ideas so far as thought itself is concerned: the idea of fear is an instance of thought but not an instance of fear; the idea of belief an instance again of thought but not an instance of belief, and so on. So the knowledge I may have of my own mental actions is not mediated, as is my knowledge of external things, through ideas of these actions: it is direct in some way. And thus a man may have the idea that he is afraid of goats without it really following that he is afraid of goats, since ideas do not entail their own truth and *can*, just because they are ideas, be false. But he cannot be aware, in whatever way we are ever directly aware of our own actions, that he fears something and be wrong about that (even if the fear is "false," in the sense specified).

Berkeley drew much the same distinction when he argued that spirits have *notions* but not *ideas* of their own activities; it is a distinction which, moreover, would disqualify a Spinozistic conception of the mind as *idea ideae* if we took the latter literally. It would disqualify it simply because, once more, the idea of myself believing something is not an instance of believing something, at least not through its content, though it may, *as an idea,* be true *par rapport à quelque chose*

—in this case the very act of believing, which is not an idea but an operation on one.

Descartes takes the characterization of ideational attitudes as actions quite seriously, since he argues in Meditation IV that he has an absolute freedom so far as affirming or denying is concerned. By contrast, he regards himself as fairly passive as far as ideas themselves are concerned. His point, of course, is that, whatever their provenance and whatever ideas I may in fact happen to have, mistakes arise only through the affirmation or denial of ideas: I make a mistake when I affirm the truth of an idea $R(i)x$ when the latter is false, for example. But he evidently regards it as possible to "have" such an idea without operating upon it at all. (By contrast, ideational attitudes are logically transitive: they are *on* ideas, and cannot occur without a subject, there being no such thing as believing, for example, without believing something [to be the case]). I can, on the other hand, always describe an idea, say as an idea of x, without taking a posture regarding its semantical value. This, in effect, would be a kind of phenomenology: putting my ideas, as it were, in brackets, and scanning them for content without worrying whether they are false or true. It is a second aim of this paper to call this in question: to raise doubts as to whether, in a spirit of neutrality so far as ideational attitudinizing is concerned, I *can* merely describe my ideas in representationalistic terms, merely, that is, in Descartes' words, "comme de certain modes ou façons de ma pensée, sans les vouloir rapporter à quelque chose d'extérieure."

III

There must be specified two sorts of liaison between ideas and whatever it may be, external to themselves, upon which their truth depends when and if they are true: what we may term a *semantical liaison*, and a causal one.

(a) Consider an idea i suitably characterized in representational terms, an idea-of-x. Then $R(i)x$ is true just when there is some object, external to $R(i)x$, call it o, which $R(i)x$ denotes, and to which it is *semblable ou conforme*. Descartes was never very specific on this latter condition—let's just say that $R(i)x$ is true when its denotation satisfies its truth-conditions. When, for example, $R(i)x$ is an image, satisfaction consists more or less in satisfying some sort of resemblance function. Not all ideas are images in this sense, and Descartes himself sees no reason why ideas should resemble their denotations any more than words must. But, in any case—and however vague the matter may be— Descartes supposes that it is by an impulse of nature that he believes things outside himself resemble or conform to his ideas of them (these being symmetrical concepts)—a curious thought if it entails that representationalism is a matter of natural impulse as, say, the sexual appetite is.

(b) It seems to Descartes that the relevant ideas must come from the outside, inasmuch as they do not appear to him to depend upon his will, and so it seems reasonable for him to believe that "cette chose étrangère envoie et imprime en moi sa resemblance." This belief, however reasonable, is quickly disposed of by Descartes, inasmuch as there may, for all he knows, be hidden causes, within himself, quite capable of producing ideas it just seems to him must come from without. I shall not pursue here Descartes's fascinating thesis that the causes of ideas must bear some internal relationship to the latters' representational properties—that the idea of a substance must be caused by a substance, even if it be some substance other than the one represented by the idea itself—but merely indicate what I believe to be the causal theory required by him. One is justified in affirming an idea $R(i)x$ only when he is caused to have it by the object o which satisfies that idea's truth-conditions: "que ces choses-là etaient semblable aux idées qu'elles causaient." That is, not only must o satisfy the idea of its truth-conditions: it must be ultimately with reference to o that I explain the fact that I have the idea of it to begin with.

There are, then, three ways in which, for any such idea, I may be wrong in affirming truth: (a) when there is nothing ulterior to $R(i)x$ which the latter denotes, as in the case of ideas of chimerae; (b) when the idea has a denotation, but it fails to satisfy the further truth-conditions of the idea, as when I affirm that there are purple goats; and (c) when I am caused to have the idea by something other than anything which may satisfy its truth-conditions, as when I am caused to have an idea of goats in a dream by having eaten too much fondue (the case is only complicated, but not altered, if the fondue is made of goats' cheese). Anyone schooled in the devious sinuosities of post-Gettier epistemological analysis will appreciate that some constraints must be put on the manner of causation—for instance, my dog barking at night might cause me to dream that he is barking; so the fine animal which satisfies the truth-conditions of the idea also causes me to have it, yet the fact that I am dreaming is just the sort of condition which inhibits justified belief. Descartes would no doubt want to say something like this: the object must activate the right nerves in the right way. But let us merely acknowledge that these are sufficient conditions for error—without worrying about all the necessary ones—and that they imply necessary conditions for being right. The fact remains that it is consistent with my having all the ideas I in fact have, with just the representational properties phenomenology observes them to have, that they should be false or, if true, have devious causes of a sort which exposes me to mistake in affirming them. For, of the conditions of Cartesian certitude—namely (a) I have an idea which (b) is true and (c) I am caused to have it by what makes it true—(a) must be independent of (b) and (c); for otherwise the Problem of the External World could not arise.

Everyone is aware that in just one case Descartes denies this independence: it is inconsistent with my having the idea of God that it should be false or caused by anything less than God himself. So the question I want to pose in this paper finally is this: *Is* the idea of God an exception? Is it even *intelligible* to suppose of any of our ideas that, consistently with their having the representational properties they do have, they can be false, or their provenance can be accounted for save by reference to what satisfies their truth-conditions? It will be obvious that if this question is answered negatively, the Problem of the External World is solved. It is solved because it will have to be inconsistent with my having the ideas which I do have, representationally characterized as they are, that the idea be false or its occurrence deviously explicable. So the only intelligible position is that if the idea has the meaning it does have, that is, represents what I would describe it as representing, it must be true, and my having it must be explained by reference to what makes it true. So either the Problem of the External World is unintelligible, or it is solved. To the argument for this I now turn.

IV

Let us consider at this point some semantically interesting entities reasonably similar to ideas when the latter are considered as "prints," that is, on the most favorable (and, it will turn out, the only) assumption, as *envoyé* and *imprimé* by originals which they resemble or "conform to." Much the same connotations are evoked by the concept of "impressions." The natural metaphor of the perceiving subject of a wax tablet occurs as early as the *Theaetetus*, and the suggestion that the mind might be a kind of tablet or screen would have been natural enough in the seventeenth century when a systematic analogy was available to the camera obscura, with the eye box. The wax tablet had in favor of its metaphorical appropriateness the possibility that images could be fixed and modified, and it remained for the inventor Fox Talbot to interject a sensitized sheet into the camera obscura which would hold the image when its source disappeared. But though photography lay well beyond the technological horizon, the semantics of the simple snapshot will not be so violently different from the semantics of Cartesian ideas that we cannot exploit some projective analogies. So let us ponder snapshots for the moment.

Consider an aging snapshot of Ted and Alice at Big Sur in 1970. It is not difficult to state in a general way what are the conditions that must be satisfied in order that an object be described in this way. A snapshot of x must resemble x and be caused, via photochemical avenues, by x. The notion of resemblance opens some room for a certain amount of sophomore skepticism—a photograph of Ted and Alice taken from a passing helicopter at high speed, half a mile up, with a Baby Brownie will resemble them as much as it would any couple taken under those conditions. But the fact that it resembles others *they* resemble from that perspective does not entail that it does not resemble them, any more than that a photographic portrait of their identical twins will not resemble Ted and Alice, since they resemble their siblings and resemblance is transitive and (perhaps) symmetrical. Resemblance does not require *unique* resemblance; and anyway, what makes something a photograph of Ted and Alice, and not of their identical twins identically posed, is that the former is caused, while the latter is not, by Ted and Alice. And the notion of cause seems important in those cases in which one's photographs don't look all that much like oneself. Obviously, one won't expect a photograph of Charles Dickens to look like George Eliot, but still, it is possible for a photograph of Charles Dickens to look more like Charles Darwin than it looks like him. But let us block all such difficulties by considering a quite exact photograph of Ted and Alice, so that anyone who knew them and saw it would right away know it was of them. And now let us consider something that exactly resembles this photograph, but which is *not* of Ted and Alice because not caused by them: which is, say, caused by their identical twins, or merely by the chance fall of light on sensitized film. And the point I want to make is this: whatever it may look like, something is a photograph of x just if caused by x, and if caused by something other than x, it is not of x. In brief, the representational characterization of a snapshot, viz., as *of* x, always implies a causal condition which, if not satisfied, renders false the representational characterization.

I am of course thinking of simple photographs: the problem is considerably, but irrelevantly, complicated when photographers use models: e.g., let Eliot Gould and Dyan Cannon stand for Ted and Alice, so that something which is really a photograph of them is said to be "of" Ted and Alice, as a painting of a woman in a Phrygian cap on the Place Furstenberg is said to be a painting of *Liberté*. By a *simple* photograph I mean one of something which does not in turn stand for something ulterior.

I shall not press these matters further, but merely transfer them from photographs to ideas. There are, of course, special differences: one can always compare photographs with their objects and test for likeness, but as Descartes has set matters up, no such operations with ideas are possible; as Berkeley recognized, ideas can only be compared with ideas. Even so, I shall claim, as with photographs, that the representational characterization of something as an idea of x carries a causal implication which, if false, falsifies the representational characterization. But this directly entails the following: to the extent that I have doubts about the causal provenance of an idea, to just that extent must I have doubts as to what it is an idea of—or even if it is an idea at all, since if it lacks the proper causal credentials, it may in fact not be subject to representational characterization at all. For I can imagine ways in which a piece of photographic paper can be made to bear a pattern of lights and darks which makes it look exactly like a photograph of something would look, without being a photograph at all. So a putative idea may not be an idea at all—may merely resemble an idea—if it is analytical to the concept of ideas that ideas always are *of* something. And this finally entails that doubts about causal provenance contaminated the phenomenological description of ideas as ideas. To the degree that I have doubts as to whether I have ideas, the Problem of the External World itself is in doubt, since it arises only once the status of what I describe as ideas is presupposed. It arises, that is to say, only with regard to entities that can be about something, and stand susceptible to semantical evaluation. So it is as though that problem, if it arises, is solved: to describe something correctly as an idea of x conceptually entails the existence of something satisfying the truth-conditions of the idea and which causes me to have the idea in question. Once we know it is an idea and what it is an idea of, there can be no conceptual room for doubt. Every idea licenses an ontological argument.

V

It is a commonplace that truth presupposes meaning; that only once questions of meaning have been settled can we then go on to raise further questions of whether, meaning what it does, a proposition, for example, is true or false. With ideas we have a curious case in which the reverse of this seems true, where meaning oddly presupposes truth. From this it seems to follow that there are no false ideas, for roughly the same reason as there are no false snapshots, at least, not in the *semantical* sense of "false." There are only false ones in the sense of *inauthentic* ones: things which appear to be, but aren't, snapshots.

Of course, we speak of falsifying photographs, doctoring them in various ways; but then just to the extent that we intervene in this fashion does the photograph stop being *of* the thing we spontaneously believe it to have been (of course, a person can doctor something in this way so that it *becomes* a picture, but this just complicates the causal conditions without modifying the semantics of the case). The falsification of photographs has its counterpart in Cartesian epistemology in the persona of the *malin génie*, who may so intervene as to "falsify" our ideas. But to the extent that we suppose this a possible intervention, once more to that extent does the idea lose, or stand to lose, the meaning we would suppose it to have against standard assumptions about its provenance and history. So again it is as though the Problem of the External World, if it arises, presupposes the logical absence of the *malin génie*, since the very statement of the problem appears to require semantically fixed ideas—ideas whose meaning is, in terms of representationality, beyond question. But if *that* condition is satisfied, then, as I have sought to argue, there is nothing left to do in order to solve the Problem of the External World.

VI

The snapshot's semantics are fairly severe, given the causal presupposition of meaningfulness which snapshots, as well as ideas, carry. But this defines a negative analogy between these vehicles of meaning, on the one hand, and propositions or sentences on the other. For sentences may suffer alteration in truth-value without sustaining alteration in, or loss of, meaning. Or at least this is commonly the case. There may be sentences which play a central role in establishing the foundations of knowledge and which must be believed satisfied by what explains someone's believing them true—first-person reports, basic propositions, *Protokollsätze*, and the like. But I shall not explore these analyses here. For the most part, the semantics of ordinary propositions does not seem to require a causal explanation for meaning, though if someone were to insist upon it, for an important class of sentences at least, he might have made a fascinating beginning toward resolving a problem which has not been much discussed in recent philosophy of language: how, in coming to understand language, we simultaneously and as part of the same process come to understand the *world*. He would have the beginning of an answer to the question of why and how language *fits the world*.

Let us shun these visionary horizons, however, and return to the Cartesian context, from which I should like to draw now upon a feature which may help confirm the applicability of my argument, and which the applicability of my argument perhaps illuminates. I refer to the role which clarity and distinctness play in the evaluation of ideas. It is always, I think, puzzling to the reader of Descartes to come upon the abrupt criterion of truth he offers, which is that an idea is true if it is clear and distinct; that if it is clear and distinct, it *has* to be true. Clarity and distinctness have reference to the meaning or content of ideas; and it is the sudden shift from what appear after all to be characterizations of ideas at the phenomenological level, to their ulterior *rapports* which seems strange and illegitimate—as much so as the inference from meaning to truth upon which Descartes so heavily relies in the ontological argument. I think we now have some basis for understanding this shift if the sort of semantical apparatus I have sketched here has a structural basis in Descartes's thought. It is this: if the meaning of an idea is clear—if we clearly can say what it is an idea of—then it has to be true; and, contrapositively, if it is not after all true, neither is its meaning clear.

Descartes must have supposed that a mere phenomenological scanning of an idea would suffice to arbitrate over matters of clarity and distinctness, and hence settle the question of its truth. This is a natural supposition but a wrong one, I think, for an unclear idea in the required sense would not, after all, be one which, like a badly faded photograph, cannot be made out. For, in the case of two photographs we can imagine two items of equal clarity as far as aesthetic discrimination is concerned, only one of which is an authentic photograph and is of, say, Ted and Alice, the other merely looking like a photograph, but not really one, since caused by something which disqualifies it as such. The problem in any case is shifted from that of, "Which of my ideas, if any, correspond to ulterior objects?" to, "Which of the subjects of phenomenological scrutiny are ideas?" And it is difficult to believe that aesthetic discrimination can settle this.

The gulf, then between ideas and the world is replaced by a gulf between Descartes and the very contents of his mind; and the epistemological Problem of the External World replaced by the problem of understanding the contents of our minds, that is, of reading them for content. What I have argued is that if this problem is overcome, the epistemological problem falls as well. Of course, with Descartes, the entire apparatus of ideas might be corrupt from the start, and the Problem of the External World a misbegotten consequence of an initially bad theory. I have tried only to show that on Cartesian grounds alone, however theoretically shaky, there is a startlingly short way with that vexed and treacherous issue.

Some Recent Work

on Descartes: A Bibliography

WILLIS DONEY

In *Descartes; A Collection of Critical Essays* (Garden City, New York: Doubleday & Company, Inc., 1967), I published a bibliography of works in English relating to Descartes. This is a supplement to that bibliography and contains reference to works in English that have appeared since 1966 through 1975 or that inadvertently were not included in the original bibliography. The supplement is in three parts: (A) translations and reference works, (B) books, and (C) articles. For the sake of uniformity, I have used in (C) the not altogether satisfactory division of articles according to topics that I used in the original bibliography. I am sure that, despite fairly strenuous efforts on my part, I have not succeeded in locating and including every article in English published between 1966 and 1975, and I would be most grateful if omissions were called to my attention. In (C), I have also included chapters of books that can be read independently and that may be of interest to students of Descartes. There were of course borderline cases in which I had to decide whether an article contained enough material about Descartes to be included in the bibliography. On the whole, I believe I have followed a rather liberal policy in making these decision.

The standard critical bibliography is Gregor Sebba's *Bibliographia Cartesiana: A Critical Guide to the Descartes Literature 1800–1960* (The Hague: Martinus Nijhoff, 1964). In 1972 the first "Bulletin Cartésien" appeared. This is a critical bibliography prepared by *l'Équipe Descartes* (Centre National de la Recherche Scientifique) which lists and reviews works relating to Descartes that appeared in 1970 (*Archives de Philosophie* 35.2 (Apr.–June 1972):263–319). Three additional Bulletins have since been published: "Bulletin Cartésien" in 1973 for Cartesian studies in 1971, in ibid. 36.3 (July–Sept. 1973):431–95; "Bulletin Cartésien III" for 1972, in ibid. 37.3 (July–Sept. 1974):453–97); and "Bulletin Cartésien IV" for 1973, in ibid. 38.2 (Apr.–June 1975):253–309. A fifth Bulletin has been announced and is to appear in 1976.

A critical bibliography for the period 1960–69, which is not covered by the Sebba bibliography or by the Bulletins, has also been announced in *Archives de Philosophie* 35.2 (Apr.–June 1972):263, and is to be prepared under the supervision of Gregor Sebba and Wolfgang Röd. Some useful bibliographies of recent works are to be found in Edwin Curley's "Recent Work on 17th Century Philosophy," *American Philosophical Quarterly* 11.4 (Oct. 1974): 235–55, and in Hiram Caton's *The Origin of Subjectivity: An Essay on Descartes* (New Haven: Yale University Press, 1973), pp. 223–43, which lists works between 1960 and 1970.

A. TRANSLATIONS AND REFERENCE WORKS

Reprinting of the standard Adam and Tannery edition of Descartes's works has nearly been completed (Paris: J. Vrin, 1964——). Additions and corrections have been included at the end of each volume. This reprinting has been undertaken by Joseph Beaude and Pierre Costabel under the auspices of the Centre National de la Recherche Scientifique. Adrien Baillet's biography *La Vie de Monsieur Descartes* is also now available (Geneva: Slatkine Reprints, 1970).

Compendium of Music, translated by Walter Robert. Rome: American Institute of Musicology, 1961.

Descartes' Conversation with Burman, translated and edited by John Cottingham. Oxford: Clarendon Press, 1976.

Descartes Dictionary, translated and edited by John M. Morris. New York: Philosophical Library, 1971.

Descartes: Discourse on Method, translated by Arthur Wollaston. Baltimore: Penguin Books, 1960.

Descartes: Discourse on Method and Meditations, translated by F. E. Sutcliffe. Baltimore: Penguin Books, 1968.

Descartes: Philosophical Letters, translated and edited by Anthony Kenny. Oxford: Clarendon Press, 1970.

The Essential Descartes, edited by Margaret D. Wilson. This anthology contains new translations of parts of the correspondence with Princess Elizabeth. New York: New American Library, 1969.

René Descartes: A Biography, by Jack Rochford Vrooman. New York: G.P. Putnam's Sons, 1970.

Treatise of Man: René Descartes, French text with translation and commentary by Thomas Steele Hall. Cambridge, Mass.: Harvard University Press, 1972.

B. BOOKS

Aiton, E. J. *The Vortex Theory of Planetary Motion*. New York: Elsevier, 1972.

Broadie, Frederick. *An Approach to Descartes' 'Meditations.'* London: The Athlone Press, 1970.

Butler, R. J., ed. *Cartesian Studies.* New York: Barnes & Noble, 1972.

Caton, Hiram. *The Origin of Subjectivity: An Essay on Descartes.* New Haven: Yale University Press, 1973.

Collins, James. *Descartes' Philosophy of Nature.* Oxford: Basil Blackwell, 1971.

Cronin, Timothy J. *Objective Being in Descartes and in Suarez.* Rome: Gregorian U.P., 1966.

Doney, Willis, ed. *Descartes: A Collection of Critical Essays.* Garden City, N. Y.: Doubleday & Company, Inc., 1967. Notre Dame, Ind.: University of Notre Dame Press, 1968. London: Macmillan, 1970.

Fleming, Noel, and Alexander Sesonske, eds. *Meta-Meditations: Studies in Descartes.* Belmont, Cal: Wadsworth Publishing Company, Inc., 1965.

Frankfurt, Harry G. *Demons, Dreamers, and Madmen: The Defense of Reason in Descartes's Meditations.* Indianapolis: The Bobbs-Merrill Company, Inc., 1970.

Kenny, Anthony, *Descartes: A Study of his Philosophy.* New York: Random House, 1968.

Magnus, Bernd, and James B. Wilbur, eds. *Cartesian Essays: A Collection of Critical Studies.* The Hague: M. Nijhoff, 1969.

Mahoney, Michael Joseph, *Cartesianism.* New York: Fordham University Press, 1925.

Rée, Jonathan. *Descartes.* London: Allen Lane, 1974.

Ruestow, Edward G. *Physics at 17th and 18th Century Leiden: Philosophy and the New Science in the University.* The Hague: M. Nijhoff, 1973.

Sesonske, Alexander. *See* Noel Fleming.

Taliaferro, R. Catesby. *The Concept of Matter in Descartes and Leibniz.* Notre Dame, Ind.: University of Notre Dame Press, 1964.

Vartanian, Aram. *Diderot and Descartes: A Study of Scientific Naturalism in the Enlightenment.* Princeton, N. J.: Princeton University Press, 1953.

Watson, Richard A. *The Downfall of Cartesianism, 1673–1712.* The Hague: M. Nijhoff, 1966.

Wilbur, James B. *See* Bernd Magnus.

Williams, Bernard. *Descartes: The Project of Pure Enquiry.* London: Penguin Books, 1978.

C. ARTICLES

1. The Cogito

Articles from books cited in Section A are included, with an abbreviated reference to the book entry.

Abraham, William E. "Disentangling the 'Cogito.'" *Mind* 83.329 (Jan. 1974): 75–94.

Beck, Robert N. "Some Remarks on Logic and the *Cogito." In:* Magnus and Wilbur, pp. 57–64.

Booth, Curtis S. "Cogito: Performance or Existential Inconsistency?" *The Journal of Critical Analysis* 4.1 (Apr. 1972):1–8.

Bouwsma, O. K. "I think I am." *In*: Joseph Bobik, ed., *The Nature of Philosophical Inquiry* (Notre Dame, Ind.: University of Notre Dame Press, 1970), pp. 237–51.

Chopra, Y. N. "The *Cogito* and the Certainty of One's Own Existence." *Journal of the History of Philosophy* 12.2 (Apr. 1974):171–79.

Deutscher, Max. "I Exist." *Mind* 76.304 (Oct. 1967):583–86.

Erde, Edmund L. "Analyticity, the Cogito, and Self-Knowledge in Descartes' *Meditations*." *The Southwestern Journal of Philosophy* 6.1 (Winter 1975): 79–85.

Feldman, Fred. "On the Performatory Interpretation of the *Cogito*." *The Philosophical Review* 82.3 (July 1973):345–63.

Gombay, André. " '*Cogito Ergo Sum*' ": Inference or Argument?" *In*: Butler, pp. 71–88.

Johnson, Oliver A. "Descartes's Mistake" (abstract). *The Journal of Philosophy* 68.20 (Oct. 1970):833.

Kenny, Anthony. "Cartesian Privacy." *In*: George Pitcher, ed., *Wittgenstein: The Philosophical Investigations; A Collection of Critical Essays* (New York: Doubleday & Company, Inc., 1966), pp. 352–70.

Marc-Wogau, Konrad. "The Cartesian Doubt and the *Cogito ergo sum*." *Philosophical Essays* (Lund: CWK Gleerup, and Copenhagen: Ejnar Munksgaard, 1967), pp. 41–60.

Mitton, Roger. "Professor Hintikka on Descartes' 'Cogito.' " *Mind* 81.323 (July 1972):407–8.

Nakhnikian, George. "Incorrigibility." *The Philosophical Quarterly* 18.72 (July 1968):207–15.

———. "On the Logic of Cogito Propositions." *Nous* 3.2 (May 1969):197–209.

Prior, A. N. "The *Cogito* of Descartes and the Concept of Self-Confirmation." *In*: P. T. Geach and A. J. P. Kenny, eds., *Papers in Logic and Ethics* (London: Duckworth, 1976), pp. 165–75.

Sievert, Donald. "Descartes's Self-Doubt." *The Philosophical Review* 84.1 (Jan. 1975):51–69.

Suter, Ronald. "*Sum* is a Logical Consequence of *Cogito*." *Philosophy and Phenomenological Research* 32.2 (Dec. 1971):235–40.

Wilbur, James B. "The *Cogito*, An Ambiguous Performance." *In*: Magnus and Wilbur, pp. 65–76.

Yarvin, Herbert. "Language and the *Cogito*" (abstract). *The Journal of Philosophy* 71.17 (Oct. 1974):614.

2. *The Truth of Clear and Distinct Perceptions and the Charge of Circularity*

Alexander, Robert E. "The Problem of Metaphysical Doubt and its Removal." *In*: Butler, pp. 106–22.

Caton, Hiram. "Kennington on Descartes' Evil Genius." *Journal of the History of Ideas* 34.4 (Oct.–Dec. 1973):639–41.

———. "Rejoinder [to Kennington]: The Cunning of the Evil Demon." Ibid., 643–44.

———. "Will and Reason in Descartes's Theory of Error." *The Journal of Philosophy* 72.4 (Feb. 1975):87–104.

Dietl, Paul J. "The Feasibility of Hyperbolical Doubt." *Philosophical Studies* 20.5 (Oct. 1969):70–73.

Doney, Willis. "Descartes' Conception of Perfect Knowledge." *Journal of the History of Philosophy* 8.4 (Oct. 1970):387–403.

Evans, J. L. "Error and the Will." *Philosophy* 38.144 (Apr. 1963):136–48.

Feldman, Fred. "Epistemic Appraisal and the Cartesian Circle." *Philosophical Studies* 27.1 (Jan. 1975):37–55.

——— and Arnold Levison. "Anthony Kenny and the Cartesian Circle." *Journal of the History of Philosophy* 9.4 (Oct. 1971):491–96.

Frankfurt, Harry G. "A Reply to Mr. Nelson." *Dialogue* 4.1 (June 1965): 92–95.

Gewirth, Alan. "Descartes: Two Disputed Questions." *The Journal of Philosophy* 68.9 (May 1971):288–96.

———. "The Cartesian Circle Reconsidered." *The Journal of Philosophy* 67.19 (Oct. 1970):668–85.

Imlay, Robert A. "Intuition and the Cartesian Circle." *Journal of the History of Philosophy* 11.1 (Jan. 1973):19–27.

Kelly, Matthew J. "The Cartesian Circle: Descartes' Response to Scepticism." *Journal of Thought* 5.2 (Apr. 1970):64–71.

Kennington, Richard. "The Finitude of Descartes' Evil Genius." *Journal of the History of Ideas* 32.3 (July–Sept. 1971):441–46.

———. "Reply to Caton." *Journal of the History of Ideas* 34.4 (Oct.–Dec. 1973):641–43.

Kenny, Anthony. "The Cartesian Circle and the Eternal Truths." *The Journal of Philosophy* 67.19 (Oct. 1970):685–700.

———. "Descartes on the Will." *In*: Butler, pp. 1–31.

———. "A Reply by Anthony Kenny" [to Feldman and Levison]. *Journal of the History of Philosophy* 9.4 (Oct. 1971):497–98.

Levison, Arnold. *See* Fred Feldman.

Morris, John. "Cartesian Certainty." *Australasian Journal of Philosophy* 47.2 (Aug. 1969):161–68.

———. "Descartes' Natural Light." *Journal of the History of Philosophy* 11.2 (Apr. 1973):169–87.

———. "The Essential Incoherence of Descartes." *Australasian Journal of Philosophy* 50.1 (1972):20–29. Abstracted, *The Journal of Philosophy* 67.20 (Oct. 1970):833–34.

Nakhnikian, George. "The Cartesian Circle Revisited." *American Philosophical Quarterly* 4.3 (July 1967):251–55.

Nelson, John O. "In Defence of Descartes: Squaring a Reputed Circle." *Dialogue* 3.3 (Dec. 1964):262–72.

O'Hear, Anthony. "Belief and the Will." *Philosophy* 47.180 (Apr. 1972):95–112.

Rahman, M. Luftur. "Are Clear and Distinct Ideas True?" *The Pakistan Philosophical Journal* 10 (July 1971):100–111.

Ring, Merrill. "Descartes' Intentions." *Canadian Journal of Philosophy* 3.1 (Sept. 1973):27–49.

Rose, Mary Carman. "Descartes' Malevolent Demon." *Proceedings of the American Catholic Philosophical Association* 46 (1972):157–166.

Schouls, Peter A. "Cartesian Certainty and 'Natural Light.'" *Australasian Journal of Philosophy* 48.2 (May 1970):116–19.

————. "Descartes and the Autonomy of Reason." *Journal of the History of Philosophy* 10.3 (July 1972):307–22.

————. "The Extent of Doubt in Descartes' *Meditations.*" *Canadian Journal of Philosophy* 3.1 (Sep. 1973):51–58.

Tweyman, Stanley. "The Reliability of Reason." *In*: Butler, pp. 123–36.

3. Arguments for the Existence of God

Barnes, Jonathan. "The Arguments." *The Ontological Argument* (London: The Macmillan Press Ltd., 1972), ch. I, pp. 1–28.

Connelly, R. J. "The Ontological Argument: Descartes' Advice to Hartshorne." *New Scholasticism* 43.4 (Autumn 1969):530–54.

Cress, Donald. "Does Descartes' 'Ontological Argument' Really Stand On Its Own?" *Studi Internazionali di Filosofia* 5:127–40.

Dematteis, Philip B. "The Ontological Argument as Wishful Thinking." *Kinesis* 1.1 (Fall 1968):1–14.

Dilley, Frank B. "Descartes' Cosmological Argument." *The Monist* 54.3 (July 1970):427–40.

Forgie, J. William. "Existence Assertions and the Ontological Argument." *Mind* 83.330 (Apr. 1974):260–62.

Gracia, Jorge J. E. "'A Supremely Great Being.'" *The New Scholasticism* 48.3 (Summer 1974):371–77.

Hinton, J. M. "Quantification, Meinongism and the Ontological Argument." *The Philosophical Quarterly* 22.87 (Apr. 1972):97–109.

Humber, James M. "Descartes' Ontological Argument as Non-Causal." *The New Scholasticism* 44.3 (Summer 1970):449–59.

Imlay, Robert A. "Descartes' Ontological Argument." *The New Scholasticism* 43.3 (Summer 1969):440–48.

Kenny, Anthony. "Descartes' Ontological Argument" and "Reply." Joseph Margolis, ed., *Fact and Existence* (Oxford: Basil Blackwell, 1969), pp. 18–36, 58–62.

Magnus, Bernd. "The Modalities of Descartes' Proofs for the Existence of God." *In*: Magnus and Wilbur, pp. 77–87.

Malcolm, Norman. "Descartes' Ontological Proof." *In*: Joseph Margolis, ed., *Fact and Existence* (Oxford: Basil Blackwell, 1969), pp. 36–43.

Nakhnikian, George. "Descartes and the Problem of God: *Meditations on First Philosophy*, III–VI." *An Introduction to Philosophy* (New York: Alfred A. Knopf, 1967), Part III, pp. 165–241.

Penelhum, Terence. "Descartes' Ontological Argument." *In*: Joseph Margolis, ed., *Fact and Existence* (Oxford: Basil Blackwell, 1969), pp. 43–55.

Plantinga, Alvin. Review of *The Ontological Argument* by Jonathan Barnes. *The Philosophical Review* 84.4 (Oct. 1975):582–87.

Sosa, Ernest. "Comment" on Anthony Kenny's "Descartes' Ontological Argument." *In*: Joseph Margolis, ed., *Fact and Existence* (Oxford: Basil Blackwell, 1969), pp. 55–56.

Williams, Bernard. "Comment" on Anthony Kenny's "Descartes' Ontological Argument." *In*: ibid., pp. 55–56.

4. Substance, Mind and Body

Aldrich, Virgil C. "The Pineal Gland Up-Dated." *The Journal of Philosophy* 67.19 (Oct. 1970):700–710.

Bennett, Jonathan. "The Simplicity of the Soul." *The Journal of Philosophy* 64.20 (Oct. 1967):648–60.

Bertocci, Peter A. "Descartes and Marcel on the Person and his Body: A Critique." *Proceedings of the Aristotelian Society* N.S. 67 (1967–68):207–26.

––––––. "The Person and His Body: Critique of Existentialist Responses to Descartes." *In*: Magnus and Wilbur, pp. 116–44.

Brewster, Leonard E. "How to Know Enough About the Unknown Faculty." *Journal of the History of Philosophy* 12.3 (July 1974):366–71.

Cummins, Phillip D. "Vernon on Descartes' Three Substances." *The Southern Journal of Philosophy* 5.2 (Summer 1967):126–28.

Edie, James M. "Descartes and the Phenomenological Problem of the Embodiment of Consciousness." *In*: Magnus and Wilbur, pp. 89–115.

Götterbarn, Donald. "An Equivocation in Descartes' Proof for Knowledge of the External World." *Idealistic Studies* 1.2 (May 1971):142–48.

Hart, Alan. "Descartes on Re-identification." *Journal of the History of Philosophy* 13.1 (Jan. 1975):17–26.

Hartnack, Justus. "A Note on the Logic of One of Descartes' Arguments." *International Philosophical Quarterly* 15.2 (June 1975):181–84.

Henze, Donald F. "Descartes on Other Minds." *Studies in the Philosophy of Mind (American Philosophical Quarterly* Monograph Series, no. 6), pp. 41–56.

Hooker, Michael. "Descartes's Argument for the Claim that His Essence is to Think." *Grazer Philosophische Studien* 1 (1975):143–63.

Humphrey, Ted B. "How Descartes Avoids the Hidden Faculties Trap." *Journal of the History of Philosophy* 12.3 (July 1974):371–77.

Hussain, Shahid. "Descartes' Concept of a Person." *The Pakistan Philosophical Journal* 11 (Jan.–June 1973):108–18.

Kennington, Richard. "The 'Teaching of Nature' in Descartes' Soul Doctrine." *The Review of Metaphysics* 26.1 (Sep. 1972):86–117.

Kim, Chin-Tai. "Cartesian Dualism and the Unity of a Mind." *Mind* 80.319 (July 1971):337–53.

Lennon, Thomas A. "The Inherence Pattern and Descartes' Ideas." *Journal of the History of Philosophy* 22.1 (Jan. 1974):43–52.

Levin, M. E. "Descartes' Proof that He is Not His Body." *Australasian Journal of Philosophy* 51.2 (Aug. 1973):115–23.

Long, Douglas C. "Descartes' Argument for Mind-Body Dualism." *The Philosophical Forum* 1, N.S., 3 (Spring 1969):259–73.

Malcolm, Norman. "Mind and Body." *Problems of Mind: Descartes to Wittgenstein* (New York: Harper and Row, 1971), Ch. I, pp. 1–59.

―――. "Thoughtless Brutes." *Proceedings and Addresses of the American Philosophical Association* 46 (1972–73):5–20.

McRae, Robert. "Descartes' Definition of Thought." *In*: Butler, pp. 55–70.

Mijuskovic, Ben. "Descartes's Bridge to the External World: the Piece of Wax." *Studi Internazionali di Filosofia* 3 (Autumn 1971):65–81.

Norton, David Fate. "Descartes on Unknown Faculties: An Essential Inconsistency." *Journal of the History of Philosophy* 6.3 (July 1968):245–56.

―――. "Descartes' Inconsistency: A Reply." *Journal of the History of Philosophy* 12.4 (Oct. 1974):509–20.

Powell, Betty. "Descartes' Machines." *Proceedings of the Aristotelian Society,* N.S. 71 (1970–71):209–22.

Radner, Daisie. "Descartes' Notion of the Union of Mind and Body." *Journal of the History of Philosophy* 9.2 (Apr. 1971):159–70.

Riley, Gresham. "Self-Knowledge: A Tale of the Tortoise which Supports an Elephant." *The Philosophical Forum* 1, N.S., 3 (Spring 1969):274–92.

Roberts, George W. "Some Questions in Epistemology." *Proceedings of the Aristotelian Society* N.S. 70 (1969–70):37–60.

Scarrow, David S. "Descartes on His Substance and His Essence." *American Philosophical Quarterly* 9.1 (Jan. 1972):18–28.

Schiffer, Stephen. "Descartes on His Essence." *The Philosophical Review* 85.1 (Jan. 1976):21–43.

Tibbetts, Paul. "An Historical Note on Descartes' Psychophysical Dualism." *Journal of the History of the Behavioral Sciences* 9.2 (Apr. 1973):162–65.

Vendler, Zeno. "Descartes on Sensation." *Canadian Journal of Philosophy* 1.1 (Spring 1971):1–14.

―――. "Descartes' Res Cogitans." *Res Cogitans: An Essay in Rational Psychology* (Ithaca: Cornell University Press, 1972), ch. VII, pp. 144–205.

Vernon, Thomas S. "Descartes' Three Substances." *The Southern Journal of Philosophy* 3.3 (Fall 1965):122–26.

Wells, Norman J. "Descartes on Distinction." *Boston College Studies in Philosophy* 1 (1966):104–34.

Young, J. Z. "The Pineal Gland." *Philosophy* 48.183 (Jan. 1973):70–74.

5. Clear and Distinct Ideas and Method

Ashworth, E. J. "Descartes' Theory of Clear and Distinct Ideas," *In*: Butler, pp. 89–105.

Botkin, Robert. "Descartes First Meditation: A Point of Contact for Contemporary Philosophical Methods." *The Southern Journal of Philosophy* 10.3 (Fall 1972):353–58.

Buchdahl, Gerd. "Descartes's Anticipation of a 'Logic of Scientific Discovery.'" In A. C. Crombie, ed. *Scientific Change* (New York: Basic Books Inc., Publishers, 1963), pp. 399–417.

―――. "Descartes: Method and Metaphysics." *Metaphysics and the Philosophy of Science* (Cambridge, Mass.: MIT Press, 1969), ch. III, pp. 79–180.

Cook, Monte L. "The Alleged Ambiguity of 'Idea' in Descartes' Philosophy." *The Southwestern Journal of Philosophy* 6.1 (Winter 1975):87–94.

Crombie, Alistair C. "Some Aspects of Descartes' Attitudes to Hypothesis and Experiment." *Actes du Symposium International des sciences physiques et Mathématiques dans la première moitié du XVIIe siècle* (Florence: Bruschi, 1960), pp. 192–201.

Deutcher, M. "Descartes." *Early Seventeenth Century Scientists*, ed. by R. Harré (Oxford: Pergamon Press, 1965), ch. 7, pp. 159–88.

Edgley, R. "Innate Ideas." *Royal Institute of Philosophy Lectures* 3 (1968–69):1–33.

Hart, Alan, "Descartes' 'Notions.'" *Philosophy and Phenomenological Research* 31.1 (Sep. 1970):114–22.

Keaton, A. E. "Descartes' Method." *The Southwestern Journal of Philosophy* 5.1 (Spring 1974):89–95.

Lauden, Laurens. "The Clock Metaphor and Probabilism: The Impact of Descartes on English Methodological Thought, 1650–1665." *Annals of Science* 22.2 (June 1966):73–104.

McRae, Robert. "Descartes: The Project of a Universal Science." *The Problems of the Unity of the Sciences: Bacon to Kant* (Toronto: University of Toronto Press, 1961), ch. III, pp. 46–68.

———. "Innate Ideas." *In*: Butler, pp. 32–54.

Morris, John. "Descartes and Probable Knowledge." *Journal of the History of Philosophy* 8.3 (July 1970):303–12.

O'Neil, Brian E. "Cartesian Simple Natures." *Journal of the History of Philosophy* 10.2 (Apr. 1972):161–79.

Radner, Daisie. "Spinoza's Theory of Ideas." *The Philosophical Review* 80.3 (July 1971):338–59.

Rogers, G. A. J. "Descartes and the Method of English Science." *Annals of Science* 29.3 (Oct. 1973):237–55.

Rosen, Stanley. "A Central Ambiguity in Descartes." *In*: Magnus and Wilbur, pp. 17–35.

Salmon, Elizabeth G. "Mathematical Roots of Cartesian Metaphysics." *New Scholasticism* 39.2 (Apr. 1965):158–69.

Schouls, Peter A. "Reason, Method, and Science in the Philosophy of Descartes." *Australasian Journal of Philosophy* 50.1 (May 1972):30–39.

6. Extended Substance and Physics

Blackwell, Richard J. "Descartes' Laws of Motion." *Isis* 57.2 (June 1966): 220–34.

Blizman, James. "Models, Analogies, and Degrees of Certainty in Descartes." *The Modern Schoolman,* 50 (Nov. 1972):1–32.

Burke, John G. "Descartes on the Refraction and the Velocity of Light." *American Journal of Physics* 34.5 (May 1966):390–400.

Crombie, A. C. "The Mechanistic Hypothesis and the Scientific Study of Vision . . . ." S. Bradbury and G. L. E. Turner, eds., *Historical Aspects of Microscopy* (Cambridge, England: W. Heffer and Sons, 1967), pp. 3–112.

Dijksterhuis, E. J. "Descartes." *The Mechanization of the World Picture* (Oxford: Oxford University Press, 1961), pp. 403–18.

Doney, Willis. "Descartes' Theory of Vision" (abstract). *The Journal of Philosophy* 54.24 (Nov. 1957):775–76.

Ellis, Brian. "The Origin and Nature of Newton's Law of Motion." Robert Colodny, ed., *Beyond the Edge of Certainty* (Englewood Cliffs, N.J.: Prentice-Hall, 1965), pp. 29–68.

Haldane, J. S. "The Physiology of Descartes and Its Modern Developments." *Acta Biotheoretica* 1.1 (1935):5–16.

Hall, Thomas S. "Descartes' Physiological Method: Position, Principles, Examples." *Journal of the History of Biology* 3.1 (Spring 1970):53–79.

Harré, R. "Powers." *The British Journal for the Philosophy of Science* 21.1 (Feb. 1970):81–101.

Jaynes, Julian. "The Problem of Animate Motion in the Seventeenth Century." *Journal of the History of Ideas* 31.2 (Apr.–June):219–34.

Lennon, T. "Occasionalism and the Cartesian Metaphysic of Motion." *Canadian Journal of Philosophy* (1974), Suppl. Vol. no. 1, part 1.

Losee, John. "Descartes." *A Historical Introduction to the Philosophy of Science* (Oxford: Oxford University Press, 1972), ch. 7, pp. 70–79.

Prendergast, Thomas L. "Descartes and the Relativity of Motion." *The Modern Schoolman* 50 (Nov. 1972):64–72.

———. "Motion, Action, and Tendency in Descartes' Physics." *Journal of the History of Philosophy* 13.4 (Oct. 1975):453–62.

Reif, Patricia. "The Textbook Tradition in Natural Philosophy, 1600–1650." *Journal of the History of Ideas* 30.1 (Jan.–Mar. 1969):17–32.

Sabra, A. I. *Theories of Light: From Descartes to Newton* (London: Oldbourne, 1967), chs. I–IV.

Suppes, Patrick. "Aristotle's Concept of Matter and its Relation to Modern Concepts of Matter." *Synthese* 28.1 (Sep. 1974):27–50.

7. Comparisons

Allen, Harold J. "Doubt, Common Sense and Affirmation in Descartes and Hume." *In*: Magnus and Wilbur, pp. 36–54.

Aquila, Richard E. "Brentano, Descartes, and Hume on Awareness." *Philosophy and Phenomenological Research* 35.2 (Dec. 1974):223–39.

Bartley, W. W., III. "Approaches to Science and Scepticism." *The Philosophical Forum* 1, N.S., 3 (Spring 1969):318–31.

Bracken, Harry M. "Chomsky's Variations on a Theme by Descartes." *Journal of the History of Philosophy* 8.2 (Apr. 1970):181–92.

———. "Descartes-Orwell-Chomsky: Three Philosophers of the Demonic." *The Human Context* 4.3 (1972):523–51.

———. "Some Problems of Substance Among the Cartesians." *American Philosophical Quarterly* 1.2 (Apr. 1964):129–37.

Carr, David. "The 'Fifth Meditation' and Husserl's Cartesianism." *Philosophy and Phenomenological Research* 34.1 (Sep. 1973): 14–35.

Cooper, David E. "Innateness: Old and New." *The Philosophical Review* 81.4 (Oct. 1972):465–83.

Cronin, Timothy J. "Eternal Truths in the Thought of Suarez and of Descartes." *Modern Schoolman* 38.4 (May 1961):269–88; 39.1 (Nov. 1961): 23–38.

———. "Objective Reality of Ideas in Human Thought: Descartes and Suarez." *Wisdom in Depth: Essays in Honor of Henri Renard, S.J.* (Milwaukee: Bruce, 1966), pp. 68–79.

Curley, E. M. "Locke, Boyle, and the Distinction between Primary and Secondary Qualities." *The Philosophical Review* 81.4 (Oct. 1972):438–64.

Elzinga, Aant. "Huygen's Theory of Research and Descartes' Theory of Knowledge. I" *Zeitschrift für allgemeine Wissenschaftstheorie* 2.2 (1971): 174–94.

Furth, Montgomery. "Monadology." *The Philosophical Review* 76.2 (Apr. 1967):169–200.

Goodhue, William Walter. "Pascal's Theory of Knowledge: A Reaction to the Analytical Method of Descartes." *The Modern Schoolman* 47 (Nov. 1969):15–35.

Gutteridge, J. D. "Coleridge and Descartes's 'Meditations.'" *Notes and Queries* 20.2 (Feb. 1973):45–46.

Johanson, Arnold E. "Paper Doubt, Feigned Hesitancy, and Inquiry." *Transactions of the Charles S. Peirce Society* 8.4 (Fall 1972):214–30.

Koyré, Alexandre. "Newton and Descartes." *Newtonian Studies* (London: Chapman and Hall, 1965), ch. III, pp. 53–114.

Little, Ivan. "Freedom, Determination, and Reason." *Proceedings of the New Mexico–West Texas Philosophical Society* (Apr. 1974), pp. 21–27.

Meyers, Robert G. "Peirce on Cartesian Doubt." *Transactions of the Charles S. Peirce Society* 3.1 (Spring 1967):13–23.

Mout, Nicolette. "Comenius, Descartes and Dutch Cartesianism." *Acta Commeniana* 27 (1972):239–43.

Mouton, David L. "Hume and Descartes on Self-Acquaintance." *Dialogue*, 13.2 (June 1974):255–69.

O'Kelley, Thomas. "Locke's Doctrine of Intuition Was Not Borrowed from Descartes." *Philosophy* 46.176 (Apr. 1971):148–51.

Percival, Keith. "On the Non-Existence of Cartesian Linguistics." *In*: Butler, pp. 137–45.

Schouls, Peter A. "The Cartesian Method of Locke's." *Canadian Journal of Philosophy* 4 (June 1975):579–601.

———. "Reply to Professors Duchesneau and Yolton." *Canadian Journal of Philosophy* 4 (June 1975):617–21.

Sebba, Gregor. "Descartes and Pascal: a Retrospect." *Modern Language Notes* 87.6 (Nov. 1972):96–120.

Shugg, Wallace. "The Cartesian Beast-Machine in English Literature (1663–1750)." *Journal of the History of Ideas* 29.2 (Apr.–June 1968):279–92.

Turbayne, Colin. "Analysis and Synthesis." *The Myth of Metaphor* (Columbia, S.C.: University of South Carolina Press, 1970), ch. II, pp. 28–53.

Van de Pitte, Fred P. "Reservations on a Post-Wittgensteinian View of Descartes." *Philosophy and Phenomenological Research* 35.1 (Sep. 1974): 107–14.

Versfeld, Martinus. "The Moral Philosophy of Descartes and the Catholic Doctrine of Grace." *Dominican Studies* 1.2 (Apr. 1948):149–67.

Ware, Charlotte S. "The Influence of Descartes on John Locke: A Bibliographical Study." *Revue Internationale de Philosophie* 12 (Apr. 1950): 210–30.

Watson, Richard A. "Berkeley in a Cartesian Context." *Revue Internationale de Philosophie* 64.2 (1963):381–94.

———. "The Breakdown of Cartesian Metaphysics." *Journal of the History of Philosophy* 1.2 (Dec. 1963):177–97.

Wells, Norman J. "Objective Being: Descartes and His Sources." *The Modern Schoolman* 45 (Nov. 1967):49–61.

Wilson, M. D. "Leibniz and Materialism." *Canadian Journal of Philosophy* 3 (June 1974):495–513.

Yolton, John W. "Ideas and Knowledge in Seventeenth-Century Philosophy." *Journal of the History of Philosophy* 13.2 (Apr. 1975):145–65.

8. *General and Particular*

Aarsleff, Hans. "The History of Linguistics and Professor Chomsky." *Language* 46.3 (Sep. 1970):570–85.

Bell, E. T. "Gentleman, Soldier, and Mathematician: Descartes." *Men of Mathematics* (New York: Simon and Schuster, 1937), ch. 3, pp. 35–55.

Calvert, Brian. "Descartes and the Problem of Evil." *Canadian Journal of Philosophy* 2.1 (Sep. 1972):117–26.

Caton, Hiram P. "On the Interpretation of the 'Meditations.'" *Man and World* 3.3–4 (Sep.–Nov. 1970):224–45.

———. "The Problem of Descartes' Sincerity." *The Philosophical Forum* 2.3 (Spring 1971):355–70.

———. "The Theological Import of Cartesian Doubt." *International Journal for Philosophy of Religion* 1.4 (Winter 1970):220–32.

———. "The Status of Metaphysics in the 'Discourse on Method.'" *Man and World* 5 (Nov. 1972):468–74.

Chambers, Connor J. "The Progressive Norm of Cartesian Morality." *The New Scholasticism* 42.3 (Summer 1968):374–400.

Collins, James Daniel. "The Cartesian Theory of Wisdom." In *The Lure of Wisdom* (Milwaukee: Marquette University Press, 1962), pp. 40–122.

Crombie, A. C. "Descartes." *Scientific American* 201.4 (Oct. 1959):160–73.

Cropsey, Joseph. "On Descartes' Discourse on Method." *Interpretation: A Journal of Political Philosophy*, 1.2 (Winter 1970):130–43.

Curley, Edwin. "Recent Work on 17th Century Continental Philosophy." *American Philosophical Quarterly* 11.4 (Oct. 1974):235–55.

Dascal, Marcelo. "On the Role of Metaphysics in Descartes' Thought." *Man and World* 4 (Nov. 1971):460–70.

Dorter, Kenneth. "First Philosophy: Metaphysics or Epistemology?" *Dialogue*
11.1 (Mar. 1972):1–22.

———. "Science and Religion in Descartes' 'Meditations.'" *The Thomist*
37.2 (Apr. 1973):313–40.

France, Peter. "Descartes: la recherche de la vérité." *Rhetoric and Truth
in France: Descartes to Diderot* (Oxford: Oxford University Press, 1972),
ch. II, pp. 40–67.

Geach, P. T. "Omnipotence." *Philosophy* 48.183 (Jan. 1973):7–20.

Gokieli, L. P. "On the Logical Character of Descartes' Argument." *Soviet
Studies in Philosophy* 6.4 (Spring 1968):40–44.

Gueroult, Martial. "The History of Philosophy as a Philosophical Problem."
The Monist 53.4 (Oct. 1969):563–87.

Jaspers, K. "Descartes and Philosophy." *Three Essays: Leonardo, Descartes,
Max Weber*, translated by Ralph Manheim (New York: Harcourt, Brace
and World, 1964), pp. 59–185.

Keefe, T. "Descartes's 'Morale Définitive' and the Autonomy of Ethics." *Ro-
manic Review* 64.2 (Mar. 1973):85–98.

———. "Descartes's 'Morale Provisoire': a Reconsideration." *French Studies*
26.2 (Apr. 1972):129–42.

Koyré, Alexandre. "Descartes after Three Hundred Years." *The University
of Buffalo Studies* 19.1 (1951):1–37.

Lafleur, Laurence J. "Descartes' Place in History." *In*: Magnus and Wilbur,
pp. 3–13.

Lewin, Bertram D. "Psychoanalytic Comments on a Meditation of Descartes."
The Image and the Past (New York: International Universities Press, Inc.,
1968), ch. 7, pp. 81–102.

Morris, John. "A Computer-Assisted Study of a Philosophical Text." *Com-
puters and the Humanities* 3.3 (Jan. 1969):175–78.

———. "Pattern Recognition in Descartes' Automata." *Isis* 60.4 (Spring
1970):451–60.

———. "A Plea for the French Descartes." *Dialogue* 6.2 (Sep. 1967):236–39.

———. "Raison, Connaissance and Conception in Descartes' Méditations."
Sophia 36.3–4 (July–Dec. 1968):265–72.

Nakhnikian, George. "Discussion-Review of Frankfurt and Kenny." *Archiv
für Geschichte der Philosophie* 56.2 (1974):202–9.

O'Neill, William. "The Love of Wisdom." *Personalist* 52.3 (Summer 1971):
459–82.

Parkinson, G. H. R. "From Descartes to Collingwood: Recent Work on the
History of Philosophy." *Philosophy* 50.192 (Apr. 1975):205–20.

Saisselin, Rémy G. "Room at the Top of the Eighteenth Century: From Sin
to Aesthetic Pleasure." *Journal of Aesthetics and Art Criticism* 26.3
(Spring 1968):345–50.

Schall, James V. "Cartesianism and Political Theory." *Review of Politics*
24.2 (Apr. 1962):260–82.

Scharfstein, Ben-Ami. "Descartes' Dreams." *The Philosophical Forum* 1 N.S.,
3 (Spring 1969):293–317.

Sebba, Gregor. "Some Open Problems in Descartes Research." *Modern Language Notes* 75 (1960):222–29.

Weiss, Jonathan. "Descartes, Certainty, and the Future." *Iyyun* 19.2 (1968): 65–91.

Williams, Bernard. "René Descartes." *The Encyclopedia of Philosophy*, ed. by Paul Edwards (New York: The Macmillan Company and The Free Press, 1967) 2:344–54.

———. "Descartes." *The Concise Encyclopedia of Western Philosophy and Philosophers* ed. by J. O. Urmson (London: Hutchinson, 1960).

NOTE

I am very grateful to Mrs. Virginia Church for her great care and patience in typing this bibliography from cards that were in many places not easily legible, and I am also grateful to the Research Committee of Dartmouth College for financial assistance.

Contributors

DAVID BLUMENFELD teaches philosophy at the University of Illinois at Chicago Circle. He has published a number of influential papers on Descartes and Leibniz.

JEAN BEER BLUMENFELD teaches philosophy at the University of Texas.

ARTHUR DANTO is the author of many books on the history of philosophy, ethics, and metaphysics, among which is his *Analytical Philosophy of History*. He coedits the journal *Philosophy of Science* and teaches at Columbia University.

ALAN DONAGAN is the author of *The Later Philosophy of R. G. Collingwood* and *The Theory of Morality*. He teaches at the University of Chicago.

WILLIS DONEY is the editor of *Descartes: A Collection of Critical Essays*; he has recently completed a translation of Malebranche's *Recherche* with commentary and has authored several influential papers in the history of modern philosophy. He teaches at Dartmouth College.

HARRY FRANKFURT is chairman of the philosophy department at Yale University. He is the author of *Demons, Dreamers and Madmen: The Defense of Reason in Descartes' Meditations* and the editor of *Leibniz: A Collection of Critical Essays*.

DANIEL GARBER teaches philosophy at the University of Chicago and has published articles on Descartes and Leibniz.

JAAKKO HINTIKKA is a professor of philosophy at Stanford University and at the University of Helsinki. He has authored a large number of important books, including *Knowledge and Belief*, and he is the editor of the journal *Synthese*.

MICHAEL HOOKER teaches philosophy and serves as an academic dean at The Johns Hopkins University.

RUTH MATTERN teaches philosophy at the University of Pennsylvania. She has published articles on Locke and Descartes.

313

MIKE MARLIES, who teaches philosophy at the University of Iceland, served as the coordinator of a Descartes conference at Trinity College, where the papers by Danto, Hooker, Sommers, and Wilson were first presented.

GEORGE NAKHNIKIAN is the author of *Introduction to Philosophy* and the editor of several works in ethics and the history of philosophy. He teaches at the University of Indiana.

GENEVIÈVE RODIS-LEWIS is a professor of philosophy at the Université de Paris-Sorbonne. She has published three books on Descartes; this is her first publication by an American press.

FRED SOMMERS is Chairman of the Department of Philosophy at Brandeis University. He is the author of numerous papers, primarily in metaphysics.

JEFFREY TLUMAK teaches philosophy at Vanderbilt University. He has published articles on Descartes, Leibniz, and Kant.

MARGARET WILSON is the author of numerous papers in the history of modern philosophy. She teaches at Princeton University and is the author of the recently published *Descartes*.

Name Index

Abbé, Picot, 148
Allaire, Edwin, 71
Alexander, Robert, 50, 70, 71
Aquinas, Saint Thomas, 169, 194
Aristotle, 79–80, 82, 86, 111, 149, 159, 161, 169, 189
Armstrong, D. M., 195, 197
Arnauld, 58, 189
Austin, J. L., 236–38, 245–46, 254–55, 261–62, 285
Ayer, A. J., 71, 236, 254, 261

Barnes, Jonathan, 4, 22
Beck, L. J., 149, 150
Berkeley, Bishop George, 72, 189, 248, 290, 295
Blake, R. M., 149
Bowsma, O. K., 255
Brentano, F., 195, 196
Buchdahl, Gerd, 76, 83, 84, 88, 149, 150

Canfield, John V., 254
Canguilhem, G., 156, 166, 169
Cassirer, Ernst, 80, 152, 165
Castaneda, Hector-Neri, 286
Caterus, 6, 22, 188, 227
Caus, Salomonde, 167
Chihara, Charles, 254
Chisholm, Roderick, 253, 255
Chomsky, Noam, 203, 205, 211
Chryssipus, 168
Cicero, 168
Clerselier, 58, 100, 167
Cornman, James, 254, 255
Crombie, A. C., 149
Curley, E. M., 254

Doney, Willis, 56, 71, 72, 286
Dubarle, D., 168
Duhem, P., 150
Duns Scotus, John, 227

Elizabeth, Princess, 212–21
Euclid, 13–14, 81, 114, 124, 126, 140

Feldman, Fred, 46, 49, 54–55, 70, 71, 72
Firth, Roderick, 71
Fodor, J., 211
Frankfurt, Harry, 22, 45, 55–56, 60, 70, 72, 73, 88–90, 98–103, 105, 107, 109, 112, 113, 267, 286

Galileo, 75, 80, 189
Gassendi, Pierre,, 151, 160, 167, 168, 199, 200, 202, 205
Gettier, Edmund, 70
Gewirth, Alan, 56, 71, 73, 149, 150, 193, 194, 196
Gilbert, N. W., 149
Goodman, Nelson, 70
Gouhier, Henri, 5, 22, 25, 39
Gregory, T., 167
Grosseteste, R., 82
Gueroult, Martial, 4, 18, 22, 24, 25, 73, 162–63, 166, 169, 195
Gunderson, K., 211

Hacking, Ian, 149, 196
Harré, R., 165
Hartshorne, Charles, 7, 23
Herodotus, 155, 166
Hertz, H., 152
Hintikka, Jaakko, 57, 72
Hobbes, 202, 205
Hoenen, P. H. J., 165
Hooker, Michael, 184, 233
Howell, W. S., 149
Hume, David, 72, 99, 101, 113, 175–77, 184, 209
Husserl, Edmund, 72
Hyperaspistes, 215

Jardine, Nicholas, 88

Kalish, Donald, 254
Kenny, Anthony, 30–31, 39, 48–49, 56–57, 71–72, 90, 99–101, 103, 106, 113, 165, 172–73, 184, 196, 238–39, 245, 254–55, 265–66, 285, 286
Kneale, William, 177–78, 184
Kripke, Saul, 183, 185

Lafleur, L. J., 149
La Forge, Louis de, 156
Laporte, J., 169
Lehrer, Keith, 245, 254–55
Leibniz, 20, 79, 166, 170, 189, 202
Leisegang, Gertrud, 152, 165
Lenoble, 167
Leurechon, J., 166
Levison, Arnold, 71
Lewis, C. I., 254–55
Locke, John, 69, 148, 151, 189, 202, 211
Long, Douglas, 185–86
Lucretius, 161, 168

Mahoney, Edward, 195
Malcolm, Norman, 7, 23, 238, 254, 262–65, 285
Malebranche, 161, 167, 168
Marlies, Mike, 69
Mersenne, 69, 150, 157, 167
Miller, Leonard, 68–69
Montaigne, 167
Moore, G. E., 184, 239–42, 244, 254
Morris, John, 50, 57, 71–73, 150
Mumford, H., 167

Nakhnikian, George, 22
Newton, 75–76, 78, 81, 82, 86–87

Olscamp, P. J., 149, 150
Ong, W. J., 149

Pappus, 76, 78–79, 82–84, 88
Pascal, 169
Pears, D. F., 254
Plantinga, Alvin, 175, 178, 183, 184
Plato, 161
Plutarch, 168

Poisson, N., 166, 167
Price, H. H., 261
Prichard, H. A., 71
Putnam, Hilary, 254

Quine, W. V. O., 233
Quinton, Anthony, 183, 185

Randall, John H., 80
Regius, 58
Remes, Unto, 76, 88
Ring, Merrill, 69
Rodis-Lewis, G., 166, 167, 169, 170
Roger, J., 168
Rose, Lynn, 57, 72
Rubin, Ronald, 72
Russell, Bertrand, 70, 71
Ryle, Gilbert, 227, 246–48, 255

Sagoff, Mark, 195–96
Sanchez, 167
Scheffler, Israel, 70
Schouls, Peter, 57, 72
Sellers, Wilfred, 184, 211
Shaffer, Jerome, 183, 185
Shugar, Scott, 70
Slote, Michael, 250–53, 255
Spinoza, 112, 187, 195, 202, 233, 290
Stout, A. K., 56, 72
Strawson, P. F., 233
Suarez, 195
Swain, Marshall, 70

Teller, Paul, 184
Tlumak, Jeffrey, 113

Wachsberg, Milton M., 211
Wells, Norman, 195
Williams, Bernard, 50, 71, 243, 255
Wilson, Margaret, 186, 188, 192, 195–96, 221
Wolfson, Harry A., 24
Woolhouse, R. S., 184

Zabarella, Giacomo, 80

Subject Index

Analysis, 12–14, 48, 74–78, 186–87
  vs. synthesis, 8, 12
Analytic-synthetic distinction, 19–20,
  68–69
Animals. *See* Automata
Automata, 153–65
Axioms, 1, 60, 72–73

Body. *See* Extended substance

Cartesian circle, 26–27, 29, 67, 78, 119
Categories. *See* Ontological distinctions
Certainty, 34, 37–38, 41–43, 50–51, 58–59,
  60–62, 65–68, 105–6, 116–22, 124–26,
  130–42, 145–48, 249–53, 260. *See also*
  Clear and distinct perception;
  Indubitability; Necessity; Science
  and scientific knowledge
  definitions of, 45–46, 48–50, 116–19
  moral or practical, 44, 46–48, 146–47,
  251–53 (*See also* Probability)
Clear and distinct perception, 4, 8, 21–
  22, 28–32, 56–59, 67, 91, 118–19, 193–
  94, 279–84, 297. *See also* Compelled
  assent
Cogito argument, 78, 111, 188–89. *See also*
  Mind; Thought
Compelled assent, 30–32, 54–55, 57–58,
  60–63, 67, 271–72

Deceptive genius or demon. *See* Evil
  demon
Deduction, 116–18, 124–26, 136–48. *See
  also* Explanation
  vs. induction or experiment, 75 (*See
  also* Experiment; Science and
  scientific knowledge
Doubt, 98–112, 271. *See also* Dream
  argument; Evil demon; Scepticism
Dream argument, 234–53, 260–69, 272–
  80, 284–85

Evidence, 28, 33, 45–46, 48–50, 65–68.
  See also Indubitability
Evil demon, 34–36, 46–48, 64, 67, 70, 245,
  250, 259–60, 296. *See also* Doubt;
  Dream argument; Scepticism
Existence, types of, 3, 7, 9, 23, 172–84
Experiment, 75, 86–87, 126–27, 133–40,
  145
Explanation, 75, 127–29, 141–46
  nondemonstrative syllogisms as, 16–19,
  32–33
Extended substance, 91–94, 189–94,
  199–202, 205–6, 256. *See also*
  Materialism; Mind and body
External world, 91–95, 137–38, 143–47,
  246–47, 249–53, 259, 267, 288–97.
  See also Sense perception

Geometry, 5, 6, 95, 108–9
  as methodological model, 13–14, 78–82,
  84–87, 95, 114, 120–21, 157, 194
God, existence of, 1–3. *See also* Necessity
  perfection of, 3–4, 8–9
  role in knowledge of, 31, 62–64, 67–68
Goldbach's Conjecture, 177–78, 182

Hypothesis, 15–16, 122–33, 136, 140–47.
  See also Science and scientific
  knowledge

Ideas, types of, 6–8, 65, 193–95, 287–97
Imagination, 92–93, 97, 200, 205–8
Indubitability, 2, 45, 48–50, 270–72,
  275–77. *See also* Certainty
  vs. irrevisability, 51–53, 66–68
Intuition, 19, 25, 55–57, 64, 86, 116

Knowledge. *See* Science and scientific
  knowledge

Logic and logicians, 16–17, 95, 117. *See
  also* Explanation; Probability

Materialism, 163, 195, 199–203. *See also*
    Extended substance
Mathematics, 59, 63, 72–73, 121, 142.
    See also Geometry
Mechanism. *See* Automata
Memory, 58–59, 92–93, 281–82
Mind, 162–65, 179–84, 193–95, 199,
    203–4, 206–10, 256–57. *See also*
    Cogito argument; Reason; Thought
Mind and body, 162–65, 212–21
    independence of, 171–84, 187–95,
    197–210, 225–32 (*See also* Extended
    substance; Mind)

Natural light. *See* Intuition; Reason
Necessity, 41–43
    de re and *de dicto*, 172–73
    vs. possibility, 7, 179–84 (*See also*
    Certainty, moral or practical)
    and existence, 3, 7, 19

Ontological distinctions, 187–92, 227–33

Prejudice. *See* Scepticism; Sense percep-
    tion
Probability, 121, 146–48

Qualities, primary and secondary, 189–90

Reason, 94–97, 101–4, 109–12, 199–206.
    See also Cartesian circle; Clear and
    distinct perception; Mind; Sense
    perception

Scepticism, 35–36, 98–101, 235–53, 267–
    68, 278–80. *See also* Doubt; Dream
    argument
Science and scientific knowledge, 58–59,
    61–63, 66–68, 105, 116–18, 120–23,
    130–48. *See also* Certainty; Deduc-
    tion; Experiment; Geometry;
    Hypothesis
Sense perception, 28–29, 48, 91–95,
    107–8, 135, 138, 199–200, 208–10,
    217–18, 269–70, 274–77
Stoics, 168
Synonymy and logical equivalence, 14–16
Synthesis. *See* Analysis

Thought, 64–65, 95, 175–76, 188–89,
    193–95, 203–4, 206–10, 290. *See also*
    Cogito argument; Ideas, types of;
    Mind; Reason
Truth, 19–20, 36–37, 60, 65–68, 146–47
    and certainty, 48–49, 146–47 (*See also*
    Analytic-synthetic distinction; Clear
    and distinct perception)

Index of Citations
of Descartes's Works
in This Volume

HRi and HRii refer to the two volumes of *The Philosophical Works of Descartes,* translated by Elizabeth S. Haldane and G. R. T. Ross (1911–12; reprint, New York: Dover, 1955). HO refers to this volume.

Rules for the Direction of the Mind

	HRi		HO	
		3		116
		5		121, 149
		6		122, 149
		6–7		122
		7		41, 116, 271, 272
		7–8		116, 117
		9		118
		11		12, 118
		12		12, 74
		13		12
		14–15		150
		15–16		149
		17–19		118
		21		150
		24		150, 152
		28		149
		31		150
		32		117
		33		64, 149
		35–36		150
		38–39		149, 200
		40–42		64, 69, 149
		43		77
		45		116, 122, 149
		49–50		150
		52–55		149, 150

Discourse on Method

	HRi		HO	
Part I		84–86		149
Part II		91		149
		92, 93		4, 45, 119, 121, 130, 139

Discourse on Method (continued)

Part III		99–100	48, 225
Part IV		101	45, 47, 108
		103	4, 23
		104	3, 7, 22, 97, 150–51
		105	276
Part V		106	130
		107–9	124, 125, 127, 155, 156, 167, 168
		113	107, 168
		116–17	151, 155, 156, 203, 204
Part VI		121–22	124, 135
		123–25	131, 149
		128–29	78, 129, 131, 132, 140

Meditations

	HRi	134	HO	68
		135		44, 68
		137–38		43, 48, 182
Synopsis		140		267
		140–43		18, 68
		141		184
First Meditation		144–45		45, 98, 107, 267, 269
		146		235, 279
		147–48		44, 47, 55, 63, 105, 108, 112, 244, 271
Second Meditation		150		41, 43, 64, 68, 188
		151–53		42, 64, 192, 256, 270
		152–57		189–91, 257, 276
		154–57		41, 138, 189, 190, 191
Third Meditation		158–59		50, 58, 60, 65, 71–72, 271, 275
		160–61		6, 112, 150
		163–65		6, 150, 194
		167–70		62, 70
Fourth Meditation		170–72		50
		176		54, 72, 165
Fifth Meditation		180–82		3–6, 22, 63
		183–85		54, 58, 59, 63, 282
Sixth Meditation		185–86		205–7
		188		92
		190–91		150, 161, 192, 198, 207, 220
		192		162, 212, 217, 218
		198		164, 281, 283
		199		47, 281

Principles of Philosophy

Part I	HRi	204–14	HO	151
		219–20		47, 109
		221		184
		222		68
		224		58, 59, 64
		227		62
		228		42
		231		59
		232		196
		240		184
		242–45		73, 187, 196

		247		217
		250		92
Part II		254		91
		267		276
Part IV		289–94		217, 218
		296		202
		299–301		44, 145–48
		302		148

Search after Truth

	HRi	305–7	HO	91
		311–13		97, 104, 112
		314–15		45
		319		171
		325		69

Passions of the Soul

	HRi	352	HO	201

Notes against a Program

	HRi	437–38	HO	184

Objections and Replies

Objections and Replies I	HRii	6–7	HO	22, 24
		8		22, 228
		14–16		62, 63
		19–21		10, 16, 21–25
		22–23		1, 11, 24, 228
Objections and Replies II		26		113
		28		24
		31–32		97
		38–39		43–45, 58–59, 64
		41–43		37, 38, 45, 58, 60
		45		10, 16, 21
		48–51		13, 23, 24, 48, 74, 75
Arguments		52–59		78
		52		64
		53		9, 15, 69, 73
		55		9, 19, 22–23, 64
		56		62
		57		9, 23, 25
Objections and Replies III		63		184
Objections and Replies IV		84		219
		97		66
		100–1		229
		102–3		200, 213, 219
		105		65
		115		58, 65
Letter to Clersalier		126		100
		127		48, 60
		130–31		58
		133n		43
Objections and Replies V		145		43, 58
		206		44, 48, 50
		207		41
		208–9		200
		210		78

Objections and Replies (continued)

	212	78, 200, 205
	232	217
Objections and Replies VI	234	75, 229
	242–43	230
	245	44, 45
	248–51	12, 42
	254–55	215
	256–57	75, 97
Objections and Replies VII	266	43, 44, 47
	267	95
	267–77	41
	276–78	44, 47, 69
	282	41
	315	44, 60
	324	75
Letter to Dinet	352	75

THE JOHNS HOPKINS UNIVERSITY PRESS

This book was composed in Linotype Baskerville text and display type by Maryland Linotype Composition Co., Inc., from a design by Susan Bishop. It was printed on 50-lb. Publishers Eggshell wove paper and bound in Joanna Arrestox cloth by The Maple Press Company.

LIBRARY OF CONGRESS CATALOGING IN PUBLICATION DATA

Main entry under title:
Descartes.
  Bibliography: pp. 299–312
  Includes index.
  1. Descartes, René, 1596–1650—Addresses, essays, lectures, I. Hooker, Michael.
B1875.D38 194 78–8419

ISBN O–8018–2111–8   ISBN O–8018–2122–3 pbk.